AUG 1 7 2007

D0721975

New Mexico

A Biographical Dictionary
1540-1980
Volume I

New Mexico

A Biographical Dictionary
1540-1980
Volume I

Don Bullis

Rio Grande Books
Los Ranchos de Albuquerque, New Mexico

Published by Rio Grande Books
Printed in the United States of America

Book design by Paul Rhetts and Barbe Awalt

New Mexico: A Biographical Dictionary, 1540 - 1980 Volume I

ISBN   978-1-890689-60-5 (hardcover)
       978-1-890689-71-1(softcover)

Library of Congress Control Number: 2006928776

Rio Grande Books
Los Ranchos de Albuquerque, New Mexico

Table of Contents

Dedication

This book is dedicated to Gloria Bullis, my partner in life; the one person who can keep me focused on the task at hand.

It is also dedicated to Paul Rhetts and Barbe Awalt who took this effort to the next higher level.

Introduction

NEW MEXICO:
A BIOGRAPHICAL DICTIONARY

This is not a complete work. Not all historically significant New Mexicans are to be found on these pages. Hence, there will be a second edition, and perhaps, a third. Even then, *New Mexico: A Biographical Dictionary* will likely not be complete. These 600 or so entries do, however, represent a cross-section of people who have had an influence on life—and sometimes death—in the Land of Enchantment, from the time the first Europeans arrived around 1540, until, perhaps arbitrarily, 1980; the only exceptions being those who have died in the meantime.

People included in the *Dictionary* come from both sexes, all races and many cultures. They come from every corner of the colony/territory/state (plus a few that never set foot in New Mexico). The only basic qualification was they had to have left a mark on New Mexico, for good or ill. Entries do not fit neatly into any particular category such as politicians, artists, athletes, outlaws, lawmen, scientists or educators; although all of those groups, and others, are represented here. As one reader noted, "these entries are from all over the map." Quite so. My purpose was to include an eclectic mix of the people that I've found interesting, and significant, over nearly forty years of daily reading and research into New Mexico's past. These people seemed most obvious to me, but because someone is included here, and someone else is not, does not mean that one is more important than the other. Juan de Oñate, the first Spanish governor of New Mexico in 1598 is listed here but, Francisco Xavier Chávez, the first Mexican governor in 1821, is not (although Chávez is already included in a draft of Volume II).

A purpose of *New Mexico: A Biographical Dictionary* is to serve as a research tool and information pool for anyone interested in the history of the 47th state. Efforts have been made to provide readers with the dates and places of birth and death of as many entries as possible, simply to provide an historical context for their lives. Educational attainment is included where it seemed important, and when it was available. In some cases, numerous career highlights are provided; in others the entry may amount to the singular act that qualified the person for inclusion. Certainly, Dennis Chávez, who served for 27 years in the United States Senate, would have a larger entry than Doña Antonia Romero who is remembered for a single, but significant, act of heroism. And Lincoln and Doña Ana County Sheriff Pat Garrett, who has become larger than life in New Mexico territorial history, deserves more detail than does Chaves County Sheriff Charles Perry who served less than one term before he absconded with nearly $8,000 in county tax collections.

Each entry in *New Mexico: A Biographical Dictionary* concludes with a source citation in an abbreviated form that refers to entries listed in the bibliography. In some cases, the citation refers directly to the content of the entry; in others it may not. In every case, though, it offers readers at least one source for further information on the subject of the entry. In some cases, the entry for Governor Jerry Apodaca, for example, news accounts are too plentiful for inclusion here, so the notation is simply, "News accounts abundant."

This book also includes several specialized indices that are intended to facilitate the identification of individuals of interest to readers. Page references are not provided because all entries refer to the *Dictionary's* alphabetical arrangement. A comprehensive index is also provided that does include page references.

Finally, since this is an on-going project, I would like to have in-put from readers regarding the entries found here, or suggestions for future editions. On the last page of the book is a form designed for that purpose. Any comment will be appreciated.

Don Bullis
Rio Rancho, New Mexico
September 2006

Biographical Entries

-A-

Abeita, Pablo (1871-1940)
Isleta Pueblo Governor

A native of Isleta Pueblo, south of Albuquerque, Pablo Abeita was unique among his peers in territorial New Mexico; he received ten years of formal education. For several years in his youth he worked as a typesetter for both the Albuquerque *Journal* and *Tribune*. Beginning in 1905 he operated the family general store in Isleta. He served for many years as governor and tribal council member, as well as tribal judge. He also served on the All Pueblo Council. Historian Joe Sando (see entry) writes, "Abeita was an able spokesman for the Pueblo people and an avid writer to the newspapers, presenting his views on problems of the day." In 1927, Governor Abeita entered a contest to name a new theater in downtown Albuquerque. His entry won and the theater became the KiMo, which means, "king of its kind." He may be best remembered for a speech he made on the occasion of the Coronado Quattrocentennial on May 29, 1940, at what would become Coronado State Monument.

Pablo Abeita. Courtesy The Albuquerque Museum Photoarchives PC2003.009.001

He said to an audience that included the governor, a U.S. Senator and the Spanish Ambassador to the U.S., "I am afraid I will have to contradict some of the things you gentlemen have said. Coronado came by Isleta... was given food and royally received. He came up the valley, and what did he do? Well, we had better say no more about it, for his record isn't good and you know it." Abeita also used the occasion to state that about 90% of white man's history was wrong. He died seven months later.

Sando, *Pueblo Profiles*
Weigle & White, *Lore*

Abruzzo, Benjamin L. "Ben" (1930-1985)
Sandia Crest Tramway Builder, International Balloonist

Benjamin Abruzzo

Ben Abruzzo was born in Rockford, Illinois, and graduated from the University of Illinois in 1952. While serving in the U.S. Air Force he was assigned to Kirtland Air Force Base in Albuquerque and in 1954 he made New Mexico his home. Along with attorney Bob Nordhaus (see entry), he built the Sandia Peak Tramway between 1964 and 1966 at a cost of almost $2 million. It opened in May 1966. It is the longest jigback passenger tramway in the world. It rises to nearly 10,400 feet. Abruzzo, along with Maxie Anderson (see entry) and Larry Newman crossed the Atlantic Ocean, from Presque Isle, Maine to Miserey, France, in a gondola beneath the balloon, Double Eagle II, in August 1978. The flight took just over 137 hours and covered 3,100 miles. The team was awarded the Congressional Gold Medal for their exploit. Abruzzo was killed in an airplane crash near Albuquerque seven years later. The Anderson-Abruzzo International Ballooning Museum in Albuquerque is named for him and Maxie Anderson.

Salmon, *Sandia Peak*
News accounts abundant

Acosta, Oscar (1957-2006)
Major League Baseball Pitcher and Pitching Coach

Oscar Acosta was born in Portales, Roosevelt County, New Mexico, but moved 25 or so miles south, with his family, to the town of Elida at a young age. He excelled in rodeo, boxing, and baseball, but the latter became his primary interest. He attended Dallas Baptist College and Lubbock Christian College. He was the NAIA All-American pitcher for 1978 and he signed with the Philadelphia Phillies later the same year. He remained with the Phillies organization for three years and played a year in the Mexican League before he became a minor league coach and manager. He entered the major leagues when he signed with the Chicago Cubs in 2000, and then joined the Texas Rangers in 2002. At the time of his death in an automobile accident in the Dominican Republic he was the manager of the New York Yankees farm team in Tampa, Florida. He was interred at Portales.

Albuquerque *Journal*, April 21, 2006
Clovis *News Journal*, May 2, 2006

Acuff, Mark Douglas (1940-1994)
Newspaper Editor

Mark Acuff was born in Goodyear, and received a public education at Casa Grande, both in Arizona. He was national merit scholar and attended the University of New Mexico on a Navy ROTC scholarship. He gravitated to the student newspaper, *The Lobo*, and became its editor in the late 1950s. He moved it from a weekly to a daily before he moved on to other things. He was the first general secretary of the National Student Press Association. He worked on a union strike newspaper in Detroit, Michigan, and edited the Valencia County (New Mexico) *News*, served briefly as political editor for the Santa Fe *New Mexican*; worked on a paper in Omaha, Nebraska; and edited the Albuquerque *News*, all before he and his wife, Mary Beth Schaub Acuff (see entry), purchased the New Mexico *Independent* in 1970. The Independent Newspapers also included *El*

Mark Douglas Acuff

Independiente, and the Sandoval County *Times-Independent*. It was Acuff who coined the phrase, "Mama Lucy Gang" (see entry for Lucy Lopez) for a group of young, generally liberal, state legislators in the 1970s. Acuff was hard to pin down, politically; many liberals thought he was a conservative and many conservatives thought he was a liberal. Any and all public figures were fair game for his editorial barbs. Acuff died in Arizona.

Mary Beth Acuff, correspondence, April 7, 2006
Don Bullis, personal memories

Acuff, Mary Beth Schaub (1941-)
New Mexico Independent Newspapers, Publisher

Mary Beth Schaub Acuff was born in Baltimore, Maryland, and grew up in Ft. Wayne, Indiana. She graduated from Bryn Mawr College in 1964 and married Mark Acuff (see entry) the same year. She held a variety of positions while Mark pursued a newspaper career in various parts of the U.S., New York City to Omaha and Detroit along the way. In 1970 she and Mark bought the Independent Publishing Company in Albuquerque and Mary Beth became the publisher. By her own account, she was also personnel manager, bookkeeper, reporter, columnist, typesetter, proofreader, mailroom manager, and chief-cook-and-bottle-washer. The Independent Newspapers also included *El Independiente*, and the Sandoval County

Mary Beth Schaub Acuff

Times-Independent. It is no exaggeration to say the Mary Beth's business acumen, hard work, and faith in the project kept the Independent Newspapers afloat for the 13 years that it lasted. She left the *Independent* in 1983 and joined the staff of the Albuquerque Museum as Public Information officer. She and Mark were divorced in 1985. In 1990 she married Lee Bertram, an engineer from Sandia National Laboratories, and they moved to California in 1990. She became active in government in Dublin, CA, and took an interest in the town's heritage activities. In 1996 Mary Beth was diagnosed with multiple sclerosis and very soon became a leader in the local MS support group and served as facilitator newsletter editor. Lee died unexpectedly in 2002. Mary Beth continued to be active in the local Democratic Party.

Mary Beth Acuff, correspondence, April 10, 2006
Don Bullis, personal memories

Adams, Ansel Easton (1902-1984)
Master Photographer
A native of San Francisco, California, Ansel Adams is frequently identified with the many black and white photographs he took of the Yosemite Valley. As modern historian Ferenc Szasz writes, though, he had strong ties to New Mexico. He visited Taos a number of times beginning in the 1920s and took thousands of photographs. One of his early published works was *Taos Pueblo* (1930) which he did in collaboration with Mary Austin (see entry). He was also associated with Mabel Dodge Lujan (see entry) and the artists and writers that surrounded her. One of Adams' most famous photographs is *Moonrise, Hernandez, New Mexico*, which he shot in 1941. Szasz reports that Adams admitted in 1974 that the stark quality of the photograph was enhanced considerably by the work he did on it in the darkroom. "Reality was not that way at all. But it felt that way," he said. Adams published more than a dozen photographic books and four technical books. He was awarded the Presidential Medal of Freedom by President Jimmy Carter in 1980. Mt. Ansel Adams in California's Sierra Nevada was named for him in 1985.

Rudnick, *Mabel Dodge Luhan*
Szasz, *Larger Than Life*

Adamson, Carl (1856-1919)
Smuggler/Petty Criminal
Carl Adamson was present when former sheriff Patrick Floyd Garrett (see entry) was murdered on February 29, 1908 near Las Cruces, New Mexico. There were, and perhaps are, people who believe that he was in fact Garrett's killer. Some believe that Adamson and Jesse Wayne Brazel (see entry) both shot the old lawman. Adamson served prison time for smuggling Chinese people into the United States from Mexico. He was related by marriage to Jim Miller (see entry), who some also suspected of killing Garrett. Brazel confessed to the killing but was acquitted upon a plea of self-defense. Adamson was never charged and, as the only eyewitness to the crime, he was not even called upon to testify at Brazel's murder trial. Adamson died at Roswell of a fever. It is an interesting historical footnote that upon Adamson's release from prison, he worked for a Roswell sheep rancher named A. D. Garrett (1861-1913) who was not related in any direct way to Pat Garrett.

Curry, *Autobiography*
Metz, *Garrett*
Ross, Pete, "Western Lore," *Wild West*, December 2001
Tanner, John, correspondence, March 30, 2006
Thrapp, *Encyclopedia*
Other literature abundant

Agostini, Juan Maria
See Deagostini, Giovanni Maria (1801-1869)

Agreda, María de Jesús de (1602-1665)
"The Lady in Blue," a Miraculous Franciscan Nun

Fray Alonso de Benavides (see entry) told the tale of María de Jesús de Agreda in his 1630 *Memorial* to King Phillip IV. As the story goes, a nun, clad in blue, appeared before several New Mexico nomadic Indian groups, and spoke to each in its own language, telling them that they should summon the padres so that they, the Indians, could be taught and baptized. The Indians therefore eagerly received the priests. Fray Alonso himself confirmed that the miraculous nun, described by the Indians as young and beautiful, was Mary of Agreda, a Spanish Franciscan who wore a habit of gray beneath of mantle of blue. She never visited North American in her physical lifetime, but was reported to have made 500 bilocations.

María de Jesús de Agreda

Chávez, *New Mexico*
Weigle & White, *Lore*
Thrapp, *Encyclopedia*

Alberts, Dr. Don Edward (1935-)
New Mexico Civil War/Aviation Historian

Don Alberts was born in Shawnee, Oklahoma, and spent his early years in Seminole. He and his family moved to Albuquerque when he was 12. He was educated in Albuquerque and graduated from the University of New Mexico (UNM) in 1956 with a degree in aviation engineering. After working at Sandia Corporation for a time, he entered the U.S. Navy pilot program and earned his wings in 1960. He later served on the carrier Yorktown in Southeast Asia. He returned to Sandia Corp. and began work on an advanced degree in history at UNM. He earned a Ph.D. in 1975. After teaching stints at Texas Tech

Don Edward Alberts

and the University of Albuquerque, he became Chief Historian at Kirtland Air Force Base (1977-88). Books he has written over the years include *The History of Kirtland Air Force Base, Balloons to Bombers: Aviation in Albuquerque 1882-1945* (1987), *Rebels on the Rio Grande* (1984), *The Battle of Glorieta* (1998), and *General Wesley Merritt: Brandy Station to Manila Bay* (2001). Alberts is a frequent speaker on New Mexico historical subjects and is an active member of the Albuquerque Corral of Westerners International.

Alberts, correspondence, 2006
Rio Rancho *Observer*, "Westsider," October 31, 2004
Carol A. Myers, ed., "Biographical Sketches," Albuquerque Corral, Westerners International, *Newsletter*, 1995

Allison, Robert A. "Clay" (1840-1887)
Colfax County Gunman/Killer

(Note: Some sources cite his name as Robert A., others as Robert C. His 1862 Confederate Army discharge papers identify him as R. A. C. Allison. He gained fame as Clay Allison.) Born in Wayne County, Tennessee, Clay Allison served in the Confederate Army early in the Civil War (some report that he was discharged as mentally unstable). He arrived in Texas soon after the war in 1865 and spent time in New Mexico. His reputation reached almost mythical proportions during his lifetime. One Missouri newspaper alleged that he had killed 15 men by 1870, a number that Allison did not dispute, although it is probably not accurate. He was a participant in the Colfax County War (1875-76), during which he is known to have killed a couple of men. He died near Pecos, Texas, from injuries received when he fell off a freight wagon. One newspaper opined: "Certain it is that many of his stern deeds were for the right as he understood it to be." Damned by faint praise, some might say. Famed Texas historian and writer, J. Frank Dobie incorrectly states that Allison died in New Mexico in 1884.

Bullis, *99 New Mexicans*
Fitzpatrick, *New Mexico*
Metz, *Encyclopedia*
Metz, *Shooters*
Parsons, *Clay Allison*
Other literature abundant

Alvarado, Hernando de (c. 1517-post 1548)
Spanish Soldier/Explorer

Alvarado was a captain of artillery in the army of Spaniard Francisco Vásquez de Coronado who visited New Mexico in 1540-1542. According to historian Marc Simmons, Alvarado wrote the first description of the middle Rio Grande Valley: "This river flows through a broad valley planted with fields of maize. There are some cottonwood groves. The houses are of mud, two stories high. The people seem good, more given to farming than war...." The old Alvarado Hotel in downtown Albuquerque from 1902 to 1970 was named for him.

Simmons, *Albuquerque*
Thrapp, *Encyclopedia*

Alvarez, Manuel (1794-1856)
New Mexico Pioneer/Politician

Alvarez was born in Spain and reached Mexico in 1818 and Santa Fe by 1824. He engaged in the fur trade for a time before he became a successful Santa Fe merchant after 1834. In 1839 he became the American Consul and in 1846 he was appointed U.S. commercial agent. As such he frequently approached Mexican Governor Manuel Armijo (see entry) and urged him not to resist the coming American invasion. In 1850, more than three years after the American occupation, an effort was made to establish New Mexico as a state of the Union, and an election was held in May. Alvarez was elected lieutenant governor. That "state" government was abrogated by the death of President Zachary Taylor (July 9, 1850) and the Compromise of 1850 (September 9, 1850), but not before Alvarez entered into a controversy with Col. John Munroe, military governor of New Mexico, who forbade the civil government from taking office. The debate became moot with the establishment of territorial government in 1851. Marc Simmons (see entry) says Alvarez was erudite man with a "true philosophical bent."

Thomas Esteban Chávez, "The Trouble with Texans: Manuel Alvarez and the 1841 'Invasion,'" *New Mexico Historical Review*, April 1978
Chávez, *Manuel Alvarez*
Lamar, *Far Southwest*
Marc Simmons, "The Wit of Manuel Alvarez," *Prime Time*, January 2004
Tharpp, *Encyclopedia*
Twitchell, *Leading Facts*, Vol. II

Anaya, Rudolfo (1937-)
Writer, "The Dean of Southwest Ethnic Literature"

Rudolfo Anaya was born in Pastura, southwest of Santa Rosa in Guadalupe County, New Mexico, and lived in a Spanish-speaking world during his early years. "I grew up treasuring the few books I came across; I grew up believing my liberation was in books," he wrote in 1990. Anaya attended the University of New Mexico where he earned degrees in English and Guidance and Counseling. As a professor of English, he directed the creative writing program at UNM for many years. His first novel, *Bless Me, Ultima* (1971), caused a surge of interest in Chicano literature. While efforts have been made to ban the book in several places—in Texas, California and Colorado as well as variously in New Mexico where it was actually burned in one community—it has remained continually in print since it was first published, and it has been translated into Spanish, French, Italian, Russian and Japanese. Among his other books are *Heart of Aztlán* (1976), *Tortuga* (1979), *The Silence of the Llano* (1982), *Albuquerque* (1992), and *Zia Summer* (1996) and others. He has also written poetry, children's literature and plays. He has received numerous awards for his work over the years, and in 2002 was presented with the National Medal for the Arts by President George W. Bush.

Rudolfo A. Anaya, "Stand Up Against Censorship Anywhere it Occurs," *Book Talk*, New Mexico Book League, November 1990
Etulain, *Beyond the Missouri*
Garcia, *Albuquerque*
Montaño, *Tradiciones*
Szasz, *Larger Than Life*

Ancheta, Joseph A. (1865-1898)
Silver City Lawyer, Legislator

A native New Mexican, Ancheta was born in Mesilla, Doña Ana County, the son of a refugee who fled Mexico during the liberal/conservative struggle of the middle 1850s. He first attended St. Michael's College in Santa Fe, and then studied for four years at Notre Dame University, graduating in 1886. Ancheta entered the practice of law at Silver City, New Mexico. He was elected to the territorial legislature in 1890 and 1892. On February 5, 1891, he was the victim of one of New Mexico's most infamous attempted political assassinations. While he was attending a meeting with political boss Tom Catron (see entry) and legislator Elias Stover, shots were fired through an office window. Ancheta was hit in the neck with buckshot, but survived. Catron and Stover were not injured. No one was ever prosecuted for the crime.

Lamar, *Charlie Siringo's West*
Twitchell, *Leading Facts*, Vol. II
Other literature abundant

Anderson, Clinton Presba (1895-1975)
U.S. Congressman (1941-1945), U.S. Secretary of Agriculture (1945-1948), U.S. Senator (1949-1973)

Senator Clinton Presba
Anderson

A native of Centerville, Turner County, South Dakota, Anderson was educated at Dakota Wesleyan University and the University of Michigan at Ann Arbor. He arrived in New Mexico in 1917, seeking a cure for the tuberculosis from which he suffered. He was employed as a newspaper reporter and editor from 1918 to 1922; and engaged in the insurance business from 1922 until 1946. The Clinton P. Anderson Insurance Agency in Albuquerque is named for him. A Democrat, he was elected to the U.S. House of Representatives in 1941, a time when New Mexico had only one congressman in Washington, D.C. He was re-elected twice after the state acquired a second house seat in 1943, but resigned in 1945 to become Secretary of Agriculture under President Harry S Truman. He then served in the U.S. Senate from 1949 until 1973. His autobiography is titled *Outsider in the Senate, Senator Clinton Anderson's Memoirs* (published by the New World Publishing Co. in 1970).

Baker, *Conservation Politics*
Other literature abundant

Anderson, Max Leroy "Maxie" (1934-1983)
Albuquerque Businessman, International Balloonist

Anderson, who operated Ranchers Exploration and Development Corporation, a uranium mining company, and Ben Abruzzo (see entry) and Larry Newman, were aboard the gondola—called the *Spirit of Albuquerque*—beneath the Double Eagle II, a helium-filled balloon, that made the first successful balloon flight across the Atlantic Ocean in August 1978. The flight, from Presque Isle, Maine, to Miserey, France, took just over 137 hours and covered 3,100 miles. Anderson was killed in a ballooning accident in Bavaria, Germany, in June 1983. The Anderson-Abruzzo International Ballooning Museum in Albu-

Max Leroy Anderson

querque is named for him and Ben Abruzzo.

Garcia, *Three Centuries*
Salmon, *Sandia Peak*
Smithsonian, National Air and Space Museum

Anderson, Robert Orville (1917-)
New Mexico Oilman/Rancher

Robert Orville Anderson

A native of Chicago, Illinois, and a 1939 graduate of the University of Chicago, Robert O. Anderson purchased a one third interest in Malco Refineries, Inc. of Roswell, New Mexico, in 1941 and served as president. He bought out his partners in 1947. He increased the company's production and sold it to Atlantic Refining in 1962. As a major stockholder of Atlantic, he served as chairman and chief executive officer from 1965 to 1986, during which the company acquired the Richfield Oil Corporation. Atlantic Richfield became the 12th largest of U.S. Corporations. He created Hondo Oil & Gas in 1986 after leaving Atlantic Richfield. He is said to be one of the largest individual landowners in the United States with about 1,000,000 acres. He was the first recipient of the Dwight D. Eisenhower Medal of Excellence in 1989. He has been an active member of the New Mexico Republican Party and served as National Committeeman. The Robert O. Anderson Schools of Management at the University of New Mexico, founded in 1947, are named for him, and he sits on the National Advisory Board. He served on the Board of Regents of the New Mexico Institute of Mining and Technology at Socorro from 1987 to 1992. He maintains homes in Roswell and Picacho, New Mexico.

University of New Mexico
Patterson, *Hardhat and Stetson*
Other literature abundant

Angel, Frank Warner (1845-1906)
U.S. Government Investigator

Frank Warner Angel

President Rutherford B. Hayes dispatched Frank Angel to New Mexico in 1878 for the purpose of learning the facts surrounding the violent events in Lincoln and Colfax counties. The president did this in response to the murder of John Henry Tunstall (see entry) in February of that year. Angel took hundreds of pages of depositions that became first-person accounts used by a variety of historians in the years since. He was not particularly good at what he did. Historian Robert Utley wrote, "He turned out to be a young man of moderate ability, persistent though somewhat careless and imprecise in gathering evidence...." Historian Marc Simmons (see entry), though, credits Angel with exposing major government corruption in New Mexico, citing Angel, Simmons wrote "It is seldom that history states more corruption, fraud, plots and murder than New Mexico has seen under the administration of Gov. [Samuel] Axtell (see entry)." Angel spent four months in New Mexico, and never returned. He died at Jersey City, New Jersey. There is a bit of confusion about his names: one source spells his last name Angell, and another cites his middle name as Warren.

Keleher, *Violence*
Lamar, *Far Southwest*
Marc Simmons, "Trail Dust," Santa Fe *New Mexican*, June 10, 2006
Tuska, *Billy the Kid*
Utley, *High Noon*

Angel, Paula aka Pablita Martin (c. 1834-1861)
San Miguel County Murderess

Paula, or Pablita, is the only woman to legally hanged in New Mexico. That alone makes her stand out in a crowd of more than 60 men who were legally hanged between 1847 and 1923. Pablita was convicted of murdering her married lover by stabbing him in the back on March 23, 1861. Her trial was held only five days after the crime was committed. Sentenced to death by Judge Kirby Benedict (see entry), she was also obliged to pay the costs of all legal action against her, including her own hanging. The San Miguel County Sheriff, Antonio Abad Herrera, botched the hanging so badly that Paula had to be hanged a second time before the court's order of execution was carried out.

Ball, *Desert Lawmen*
Bryan, *Wildest of The Wild West*
Bullis, Rio Rancho *Observer*, July 21, 2005
Gilbreath, *Death on the Gallows*

Antrim, Henry (1859-1881)
See Bonney, William H.

Anza, Juan Bautista de (1736-1788)
Governor (Spanish) of New Mexico (1778-1788)

Juan Bautista de Anza arranged the most significant and enduring peace treaty between Spanish colonists in New Mexico and hostile, nomadic Comanche Indians during the 18th century. A third generation professional soldier, (his father was killed in an Apache ambush in 1740) Anza was born at Fronteras, Sonora, just south of present day Douglas, Arizona. He entered the army in 1751. The younger Anza also participated in action against the Apache in what is now southern Arizona, and he advanced through the ranks as he did so. In the early 1770s, he led expeditions into California and is credited with founding San Francisco. Anza was a Lieutenant Colonel when he was appointed Governor of New Mexico in 1778. His first priority was to halt nomadic Indian depredations and to that end he planned an assault on the Comanches, led by Cuerno Verde "Green Horn" (see entry), in their home territory in what is now southeastern Colorado. Anza first outmaneuvered the Indians and attacked them from the west and north capturing several camps and taking prisoners. In early September 1779, with his army of about 600 men, more than a third of whom were Indians from other tribes, he confronted Cuerno Verde and his main force of warriors near the present Walsenburg, Colorado. When the fighting was over, Cuerno Verde and his son were both dead, as were four sub-chiefs and a medicine man who claimed immortality, along with ten other warriors. One Spanish soldier was wounded and none were killed. This victory allowed Anza to negotiate a peace that lasted well into the 19th century. He resigned from the governor's office because of ill health in 1787 and returned home to Sonora where he died in December of the following year. Historian Marc Simmons writes of him, "His career as a frontiersman easily rivaled that of a Boone or a Crockett or a Carson. But unlike those national heroes whose names today are household words, Juan Bautista de Anza and his story remain unknown to most Americans."

Etulain, *Western Lives*
Chavez, *An Illustrated History*
Simmons, *New Mexico*
Tharpp, *Encyclopedia*

Apodaca, Jerry (1934-
Governor (State) of New Mexico (1975-1978)

A native of Las Cruces, Jerry Apodaca graduated from the University of New Mexico and engaged in several business enterprises before he was elected to the State Senate in 1965. He served until 1974 when he was elected governor by defeating Republican Joe Skeen by a narrow margin in the general election. He had previously defeated five other candidates in the Democratic primary election: Senator Tibo Chavez (see entry), Senator Odis Echols, State Representative Bobby Mayfield, Drew Cloud and former Attorney General Boston Witt (in that order). He was the first Hispanic to serve in that office after the election of Octaviano A. Larrazolo (see entry) in 1918. The cabinet system of state government was established during the Apodaca administration, and a number of boards and commissions were abolished. In the closing weeks of Apodaca's administration (November 7, 1978), he pardoned New Mexico land grant activist Reies Lopez Tijerina (see entry) for offenses committed during the famed Rio Arriba County courthouse raid of June 1967. President Jimmy Carter appointed Apodaca to the chairmanship of the President's Council on Physical Fitness in 1978. He was the founder of *Vista Magazine* and the first publisher of *Hispanic Magazine*. He served on the University of New Mexico Board of Regents from 1985 to 1991.

News accounts abundant

Apodaca, José María (1844-1924)
Master *Hojalatero* (Tinsmith)

José María Apodaca was born in Juarez, Chihuahua, but immigrated to Santa Fe County, New Mexico, as a teenager. He homesteaded at Ojo de la Vaca, southeast of the capital, and continued to live and work there for the rest of his life. He did his tinwork on the kitchen table and heated his soldering iron in the cast iron cook stove. He would pack his finished tinwork in canvas bags and, traveling by horseback, sell it in the villages along the Pecos River. His work is described as "sophisticated and imaginative combinations of wallpapers, cloth, printed materials, and colored portions of tin containers...." He produced tinwork for at least 40 years, until 1915 when failing eyesight obliged him to stop.

Coulter & Dixon, *New Mexican Tinwork*
Gavin, *Traditional Arts*
Montaño, *Tradiciones*

Aragón, José Rafael (1796-1862)
Artist, Altar Screen Maker, *Santero* **(A woodcarver of the images of holy people)**

José Rafael Aragón was born in Santa Fe and spent much of his life there, although he also lived in the village of Córdova near Española. He was a well-regarded community leader as well as a *santero* who produced many of his works on a commission basis. He is known to have used native woods such as ponderosa pine or cottonwood, and he painted with natural pigments. Author Mary Montaño writes that, "His work is characterized by clean, confident brush work, careful attention to facial expression and body proportions, bold use of color, and the influence of both the baroque and the Mexican rococo, particularly in terms of choice of colors, shading and expressiveness through body language." Altar screens by José Rafael Aragón can be seen at Córdova, Pojoaque, El Valle, Chimayó, Picurís, and Chama, among others.

Cobos, *A Dictionary of New Mexico & Colorado Spanish*
Esquibel & Carrillo, *A Tapestry of Kinship*
Gavin, *Traditional Arts*
Montaño, *Tradiciones*

Archuleta, Diego (1814-1884)
Mexican Military Officer/New Mexico Legislator

A native of New Mexico, Diego Archuleta engaged in military service in his early career. He was a part of the Mexican force that halted the Texan-Santa Fe Expedition in 1841, and by the time the U.S. Army of the West under General Stephen Watts Kearny (see entry) advanced on New Mexico during the summer of 1846, Archuleta was second in command to Governor Manuel Armijo (see entry). Several Americans, among them James Magoffin (see entry) and Captain Philip St. George Cooke (see entry), negotiated with the Mexican leadership to avoid a military confrontation. Archuleta was led to believe that the U.S. would only occupy New Mexico east of the Rio Grande, leaving the inference that Archuleta might become governor of the lands west of the river. Historian Sálaz Márquez writes that Archuleta accepted a bribe from the Americans. In any event, in December 1846, Archuleta organized a cabal with the intention of over-

Diego Archuleta. After Twitchell.

throwing the American Occupation. It quickly failed. He later swore allegiance to the U.S. and served as an Indian agent and representative to the Territorial Legislature from Rio Arriba County. He ran for the office of delegate to the U.S. Congress in 1859, but lost to John S. Watts. His funeral procession was said to have been one of the longest in the history of Santa Fe.

Crutchfield, *Tragedy*
Lamar, *Far Southwest*
Sálaz Márquez, *New Mexico*
Twitchell, *Leading Facts*, Vol. II

Archuleta, Felipe (1910-1991)
Folk Artist

Born in the Sangre de Cristo Mountains of northern New Mexico, Felipe Archuleta spent most of his life in the village of Tesuque. He was a carpenter by trade. In 1967 he asked God to help him find work and alleviate his poverty, after which he underwent a "religious awakening." Because he came from a tradition of *santo* makers, he began working in woodcarvings using elm and cottonwood and he developed his own style of animal carvings. He began with familiar beasts such as sheep, rabbits and burros but later did more exotic animals such as giraffes and cougars. According to one observer, his figures "are not literal renditions but are intended to embody the untamed qualities of the animal world." Some of his animals are life-sized, and his style emphasized the ferocious nature of animals.

"Hispanic-American Art," brochure, National Museum of American Art, Washington, DC

Armijo, Manuel (1790-1853)
Governor (Mexican) of New Mexico (1827-1829, 1837-1844 & 1845-1846)

A myth, probably created by Texan George Wilkins Kendall, circulated for years that Manuel Armijo was born of "low and disreputable" parentage; that he was illiterate and a thief and only luck at cards delivered him from such a scandalous life. Research by Fray Angélico Chávez revealed the truth of the matter. Manuel Armijo was born of two families, members of which were extensive land owners, and people of means. Nothing indicates that he was illiterate as a youth. Armijo served three terms as governor of New Mexico during the era of Mexican rule (1821-1846). He was controversial in a number of areas, but is best remembered for not resisting the 1846 invasion of New Mexico by the U.S. Army of the West under General Stephen Watts Kearny (see entry). He fled to Mexico where he

Gov. Manuel Armijo, August 1846. Courtesy The Albuquerque Museum Photoarchives PA1998.22.51.

was tried for treason, but acquitted. Rafael Chacón (see entry), who was present at Cañoncito, defended Armijo's action, "Had he [Armijo] rashly rushed to give battle, it would have been equivalent to offering his troops as victims to the invading army; the result would have been a useless effusion of blood, offering himself unnecessarily to death," he wrote. Armijo returned to Albuquerque after the American occupation, and ran for mayor, but lost. He wrote: "I am here as a Saint whose day has past." After his death, the Territorial Legislature memorialized him as a "Distinguished Citizen" and one of New Mexico's "greatest benefactors." Most modern historians believe Armijo was unjustly maligned, primarily by George Kendall, but also by Josiah Gregg and George Ruxton (see entry).

Bullis, *99 New Mexicans*
Fergusson, *New Mexico*
Janet Lecompte, "Manuel Armijo's Family History," *New Mexico Historical Review*, July 1973
Sálaz Márquez, *New Mexico*
Meketa, *Legacy of Honor*
Marc Simmons, "Trail Dust," Santa Fe *New Mexican*, February 4, 2006
Tórrez, *UFOs Over Galisteo*
Other literature abundant

Officer Richard Armijo

Armijo, Richard (1927-1958)
Albuquerque Police Officer

Officer Richard Armijo was killed in a motorcycle accident on September 30, 1958. Famed radio and television personality Arthur Godfrey was appearing at the New Mexico State Fair at the time and he paid Officer Armijo's doctor and hospital expenses. The motorcycle Armijo was riding when he was killed was reissued, and five months later Officer Max Oldham was killed while riding it.

Bullis, *New Mexico's Finest*

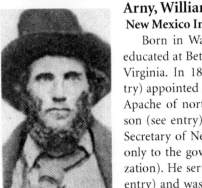

William F. M. Arny. After Twitchell.

Arny, William Frederick Milton (1813-1881)
New Mexico Indian Agent, Territorial Secretary

Born in Washington, D.C., William F. M. Arny was educated at Bethany College in what would become West Virginia. In 1861, President Abraham Lincoln (see entry) appointed him Indian Agent for the Ute and Jicarilla Apache of northern New Mexico. He replaced Kit Carson (see entry) in that position. Lincoln appointed him Secretary of New Mexico in 1862 (Secretary was second only to the governor in territorial governmental organization). He served under Governor Henry Connelly (see entry) and was interim governor in 1866. Arny opposed the relocation of the Navajo people to Bosque Redondo in 1863 and suffered political consequences for his stance. As "Special Agent for the Indians of New Mexico" he con-

ducted a census of New Mexico Indians in 1870; and later in the 1870s served another stint as territorial secretary. He also served as agent to the Navajos at mid-decade, but resigned in 1875 and returned to Santa Fe. He died virtually penniless. He is interred at the Santa Fe National Cemetery. Some of his recollections were published as *Indian Agent in New Mexico, Wm. Arny's Journal, 1870.*
Bullis, *New Mexico Historical Notebook,* July 27, 2005
Twitchell, *Leading Facts,* Vol. II

Arquette, Kaitlyn (1970-1989)
Albuquerque Murder Victim
Young Kaitlyn was killed, shot twice in the head, as she drove along Lomas Blvd. in Albuquerque on July 17, 1989. The police considered it a random shooting, and pursued the matter on that basis. Arquette's family disagreed and by means of a private investigator kept the investigation ongoing for years. Lois Duncan, Arquette's mother, wrote a book entitled, *Who Killed My Daughter?* published by Dell in 1992. At the end of 2005, the case remained unsolved.
Newspaper accounts abundant

Arviso, John B. (1906-1965)
Gallup Police Officer
John Arviso, captain and chief of detectives for the Gallup Police Department, was killed in a shootout with burglars in a Gallup automobile dealership. One of the thieves was killed in the battle, and a second captured and sentenced to a long prison term. The Gallup Department of Public Safety Building is named for Capt. Arviso.
Bullis, *New Mexico's Finest*

Plaque at Gallup Department of Public Safety Building honoring Captain John B. Arviso

Ashworth, Frederick L. "Dick" (1912-2005)
Los Alamos, Manhattan Project
U.S. Navy Vice Admiral
When the B-29 bomber called "Bockscar" flew over Japan carrying an atomic bomb called "Fat Man" on August 9, 1945, the man aboard who was in charge of arming the weapon was Dick Ashworth. Born in Beverly, Massachusetts, Ashworth graduated from the U.S. Naval Academy in 1933. In the early 1940s, during World War II, he was assigned to the Manhattan Project at Los Alamos, New Mexico, worked on development of the atomic bomb, and was subsequently directed to oversee the delivery of the weapon. His title was Director of Operations of Project A (Alberta) on Tinian Island where the bomb was prepared for delivery. As the story goes, the original target for the second bomb drop was Kokura (Hiroshima had been the target of the first atomic attack—the bomb was called "Little Boy"—on August 5), but bad weather required the Bockscar to seek a secondary target. That was Nagasaki. The Japanese surrendered less that a week later. Ashworth resided at Santa Fe after his retirement from the Navy.

Albuquerque *Journal*, Obituaries, December 7, 2005
The Manhattan Project Heritage Preservation Association, Inc.

Aubry, François Xavier (1824-1854)
Santa Fe Trail Merchant/Record Setter

Aubry (Twitchell spells it "Aubrey") was a Canadian by birth, but arrived in New Mexico in the mid 1840s and entered the Santa Fe Trail trade by 1847. His place in history is found in the record he set for his trips on horseback between Santa Fe and Independence, Missouri, some 800 miles. His first record was 14 days, and then he shortened it to eight days and 10 hours. His final record, which stands today, was five days and 16 hours. He came to be called the "Skimmer of the Plains." In August 1854, Aubry became engaged in an altercation with attorney and newspaperman Richard Hanson Weightman (see entry) who stabbed him to death in a saloon fight. Weightman was acquitted at trial upon a plea of self-defense.

Thrapp, *Encyclopedia*
Twitchell, *Leading Facts*, Vol. II
Other literature abundant

Austin, John Van "Tex" (1888-1938)
Pecos Rancher/Promoter

His real name was Clarence Van Norstrand and he was born in St. Louis, Missouri, but he reinvented himself as a cowboy named John Van Austin, of Victoria, Texas; known to one and all as "Tex." He did work on a few ranches and joined the Mexican Revolution (1910-1920) briefly but he came into his own as a rodeo producer in 1917. He did so well in the rodeo business that in 1925 he bought land along the Pecos River near Santa Fe, New Mexico, and called it the Forked Lightning Ranch, to which he invited paying guests. He is also said to have grazed several thousand head of cattle on about 100,000 acres. He went broke in seven years. He then operated Los Ranchos Restaurant near the plaza in Santa Fe. He committed suicide in 1938. Tex was inducted into the National Cowboy Hall of Fame in 1976. Texas rancher and oilman E. E. "Buddy" Fogelson (see entry) bought the Forked Lightning in 1941. Fogelson's widow, actress Greer Garson (see entry), donated the ranch to the Conservation Fund which then sold it to the National Park Service. It is now a part of the Pecos National Historical Park.

National Park Service

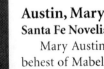

Mary Austin. Courtesy Frank Applegate family.

Austin, Mary (Hunter) (1868-1934)
Santa Fe Novelist, Playwright, Essayist, Poet

Mary Austin first visited New Mexico in 1918 at the behest of Mabel Dodge Sterne Luhan (see entry) of Taos, and she settled in Santa Fe in 1924. Austin collaborated with Ansel Adams (see entry) on *Taos Pueblo* in 1930. She only wrote one novel set in New Mexico, *Starry Adventure*, in 1931. Bibliophiles report that the book is quite scarce. In her writing career she produced 35 books and countless shorter works. She was preoccupied with "Amerindian" culture and Spanish arts. Erna Fergusson (see entry) wrote of her, "Crowned with queenly braids, wrapped in a Spanish shawl, and enthroned on the bootblack's stand in the Chamber of Commerce, she pushed for action. Her followers laughed at her, but they loved her...."

Fergusson, *New Mexico*
Hillerman, *The Spell of New Mexico*
Luther, *Collecting Santa Fe*
Rudnick, *Mabel Dodge Luhan*

Axtell, Samuel Beach "Sam" (1819-1891)
Governor (Territorial) of New Mexico (1875-1878)

Axtell was a man in motion; Will Keleher (see entry) called him a "political soldier of fortune." Born in Ohio, he'd resided in Michigan before he moved on to California where he was a prosecuting attorney before being elected to Congress in 1866. He was appointed Governor of Utah in 1875 but made himself so unpopular there that he was transferred to New Mexico within a matter of a few months. In New Mexico he aligned himself with Tom Catron (see entry) and the Santa Fe Ring. He was soon faced with the violence of the Lincoln County War. Montague R. Leverson, editor of the Mesilla Valley *Independent* wrote that Axtell was "...influenced more by weakness and want of intellect than by intentional criminality." Axtell served as chief justice of the New Mexico Supreme Court from 1882-1885, when he became counsel to the Southern Pacific Railroad Company, a position he held at the time of his death.

Gov. Samuel B. Axtell. After Twitchell.

Keleher, *Violence*
Lamar, *Far Southwest*

-B-

Baca, Don Domingo (fl. 1804)
Seboyetta Hero

In 1804, a large band of Navajos attacked the village of Seboyetta (then spelled "Ceboletta") in western New Mexico. "In the hand to hand combat, Domingo Baca had seven lances driven into him. One cut across his stomach so wide that his bowels fell out. Grabbing a pillow he tied it around his abdomen and was able to continue fighting until the attack subsided. Afterwards he replaced his entrails and sewed up his own wound." This story is told by Gary Tiejen in *Encounter with the Frontier* and cited by Peña.

Peña, *Memories of Cibola*

Baca, Elfego (1865-1945)
Socorro County Lawman, Bernalillo County Attorney

Elfego Baca. Courtesy The Albuquerque Museum Photoarchives PA1978.151.099.

Elfego Baca was born in Socorro, New Mexico, but spent his early years in Kansas. He returned to New Mexico when he was about 15 years old. Before he was 20 years old Elfego actually caused one of the most famous gunfights in the lore of the Old West, in which he single-handedly held off an attack by an estimated 80 Texas cowboys at Frisco Plaza in Western New Mexico (later called Reserve), on November 30, 1884. Baca was subsequently tried for murder as a result of the fight, but was acquitted. He later became an attorney, prosecutor, and sheriff, and involved himself in the Mexican Revolution after 1910. It is noteworthy that his life-span extended from the last year of the American Civil War—1865—to the first year of the Atomic Age—1945; from cap and ball pistols to atomic bombs. Quite a run.

Bryan, *Incredible Elfego Baca*
Bullis, *99 New Mexicans*
McLoughlin, *Encyclopedia*
Metz, *Shooters*

Baca, Santos (1933-2005)
New Mexico Peace Officer

Born in Veguita, in Socorro County, Santos Baca spent most of his life working in New Mexico law enforcement. He was a deputy chief for the Bernalillo County Sheriff's Department, chief investigator for the District Attorney in the 2nd Judicial District, Chief of Police at Acoma Pueblo, Undersheriff for Sandoval County and Chief of Police in the town of Bernalillo. He is interred in the Los Padillas Cemetery.

Obituary, Albuquerque *Journal*, October 27, 2005

Baker, Grafton (fl. 1851-1853)
Chief Justice, New Mexico Supreme Court

It is interesting that several leading New Mexico historians, including Paul Horgan (see entry), Marc Simmons (see entry), and R. E. Twitchell (see entry) mention Judge Baker and his quarrel with Bishop Lamy (see entry), but none of them indicate dates of birth and death. Simmons reports that he was a native of Mississippi who arrived in New Mexico, with a black slave, in the summer of 1851, having been appointed to the bench by President Millard Fillmore. Settled in Santa Fe, Baker adopted the old Spanish military chapel, called the *Castrense*, as his courtroom. When Bishop Lamy arrived in Santa Fe a short time later, he set about taking possession of all church property, including the *Castrense*. Baker objected. The judge, drinking in a Santa Fe watering hole, announced to everyone within earshot that he would not surrender his courtroom, and if Lamy and his vicar, Joseph Machebeuf, insisted, he, the judge, would see both of them hang. That intemperate remark was soon broadcast about the town and a mob quickly formed in front of the judge's house. It was Father Machebeuf who interceded with the irate crowd and saved the judge from harm. Baker quickly apologized to Lamy and on the following day formally surrendered the *Castrense* to the Bishop. Efforts to recall Baker were not successful, but it didn't matter too much. He was not reappointed in 1853.

Horgan, *Lamy*

Marc Simmons, "Baker, Brandy and the Bishop," Socorro *Defensor Chieftain*, January 1992

Twitchell, *Leading Facts*, Vol. I

Baker, John Willard "Upset John" (1944-1970)
Albuquerque Long Distance Runner

John Baker and his family arrived in Albuquerque in 1953, when John was nine years old. He attended Mark Twain Elementary and Monroe Junior High, before he went on to Manzano High School where his talent as a runner became obvious; he became New Mexico state champion in the mile. In spite of numerous athletic scholarship offers, he chose to stay at the University of New Mexico (UNM). While there, he won the Western Athletic Conference (WAC) cross-country championship twice, was the WAC champion in the mile, and ranked 8th among the world's milers. He graduated from UNM in 1967 and became a physical education teacher at Aspen Elementary School in Albuquerque. He began training for the 1972 Olympics by running 25 miles per day. In 1969, he was diagnosed with cancer.

Historian Marc Simmons wrote this: "John Baker's response to his plight lifted his tale far above the ordinary. With his Olympic dream in tatters and time running out, he resolved to devote all his failing energy to the school children in his charge. In a hundred ways and in a hundred little incidents, he pulled youngsters up, those with ability as well as those with emotional or physical handicaps.... His own worsening condition, he kept a carefully guarded secret." Baker also became founder and coach of the Duke City Dashers, an all-girl AAU track team that, the week of his death, went to the National Cross-Country Championships in St. Louis and won the national title. Aspen Elementary School was renamed in his honor, and many other tributes have been conferred upon his memory. Simmons went on to write: "It appears fairly safe to suggest that a thousand years hence if the name of only one Albuquerquean of the Twentieth century is still remembered, that name will be John Baker." The 1979 movie, *The Shining Season*, starring Timothy Bottoms, is about his all too short life.

Garcia, *Three Centuries*
Simmons, *Albuquerque*
UNM Archives

Ballard, Charles Littlepage "Charlie" (1866-1950)
Eastern New Mexico Peace Officer

Charles L. Ballard, 1898.
Courtesy Historical Society
of Southeast New Mexico,
No. 1512.

Charlie Ballard was born in Hays County, Texas, between Austin and San Antonio. He arrived, with his family, at Fort Sumner, New Mexico in 1878. He was variously employed, and married Mintie Corn in 1888. She was a member of the large, and still prominent, Corn family of southeastern New Mexico. Ballard served as a deputy sheriff at Roswell when it was still a part of Lincoln County, and as a cattle inspector and member, and president, of the New Mexico Cattle Sanitary Board. While serving as a deputy U.S. Marshal at Roswell, he was a member of the posse that pursued outlaw George Musgrave into southeastern Arizona in the late 1890s. Many years later he testified in Musgrave's favor at the latter's murder trial. Ballard served in the Rough Riders with George Curry (see entry), who would become New Mexico governor and congressman, during the Spanish-American War, and in the Philippines afterward. Ballard was elected to the New Mexico territorial legislature in 1905 and sheriff of Chaves County in 1906. He served until statehood in 1912. He was a rancher for many years and a mining speculator later in his life. He died at Duncan, in southeastern Arizona.

Bullis, *Observer*, June 16, 23, 30, 2005
Tanner, *Musgrave*
Other literature abundant

Bandelier, Adolphe Francis Alphonse (1840-1914)
Anthropologist

Adolphe Bandelier was born in Bern, Switzerland, to a Swiss army officer and a Russian aristocrat, but by the time he was eight, his family lived on a homestead near Highland, Illinois. He returned to Europe for his education, at the University of Bern, where he studied geology. Upon his return to the United States he became interested in the work of anthropologist Lewis Henry Morgan, author of *Systems of Consanguinity and Affinity of the Human Family* (1870) and *Ancient Society* (1877). Bandelier arrived at Santa Fe in 1880 and remained for about ten years (he never returned to New Mexico after 1892). During his time in New Mexico he worked diligently among the territory's many Indian groups, and wrote widely about them. One of his best-known works is a novel entitled *The Delight Makers*. Bandelier National Monument near Los Alamos is named for him. Most critics agree that Bandelier was responsible for discrediting the so-called Romantic School of American Indian history. He opened the door for critical and scientific research. Late in his life he settled in New York City where he lectured at Columbia University on Spanish-American literature. In 1911 he received an appointment to do archival research in Spain. He died at Seville and was originally buried there. His remains were later returned to New Mexico, cremated and the ashes scattered at the national monument in Los Alamos County that bears his name.

Albuquerque *Journal*, July 29, 1990
Keleher, *Fabulous Frontier*
Thrapp, *Encyclopedia*

Barber, Susan Hummer McSween (1845-1931)
See McSween, Susan

Barceló, Gertrudis, La Tules or Doña Tules (d. 1852)
Santa Fe Gambler/Philanthropist

La Tules operated the most successful gambling parlor in Santa Fe in the 1830s and 1840s. She accumulated great wealth with which she was quite generous. La Tules associated with the "best" people of her day including governors—both Mexican and American—military leaders, and businessmen. She even loaned money to the U.S. Army shortly after the American occupation of New Mexico in August 1846. Josiah Gregg in his *Commerce of the Prairies* besmirched her reputation, probably unjustly. Her funeral was largely attended and Bishop Jean Baptiste Lamy (see entry) led the procession.

Don Bullis, Rio Rancho *Observer*, April 3, 2005
Chávez y Chávez, *Wake*
Etulain, *Western Lives*
Other literature abundant

Barela, Patrocinio (c. 1900-1964)
Sculptor

Patrocinio Barela had a most unfortunate life while creating remarkable carvings. He was born at Bisbee, Arizona, to an impoverished family. His mother died when he was young, and when he was eight, he, his brother and father moved to Cañon near Taos. His father turned him out when he was 12 years old, and thereafter Patrocinio earned his way by day labor, migrant work, and mining. He left Taos for a time but returned in 1930 and married. It was about then that he began carving when a priest asked him to repair a *bulto*. His life of poverty continued and he was immoderate in his consumption of wine, sometimes trading his carvings for drink. He had a compulsion to carve, however, and when he could find work, he carved at night; and when there was no work, he carved all day. His wife did not understand, or appreciate, his lifestyle, and he was relegated to residence in a nearby shed. She also did not approve of his refusal to attend church. Historian Mary Montaño writes, "He loved the Bible but rejected organized religion." In 1935 he began working full time for the Federal Arts Project and in 1936, seven of his pieces were featured in "New Horizons of American Art" at the Museum of Modern Art in New York City. In spite of rave reviews for his work, not a single gallery show resulted. Barela's association with the Federal Arts Project was terminated in 1943, and he was obliged to go back to day labor for sustenance. He died when his workshop, in which he slept, burned to the ground in the middle of the night. Montaño writes, "The significance of Barela's work is that it redefined the traditional parameters of *santero* art." She added, "his work transcends place and time, yielding penetrating insight into human emotional and spiritual life."

Gonzales & Witt, *Spirit Ascendant*
Montaño, *Tradiciones*

Barker, Elliot Speer (1886-1988)
New Mexico Department of Game & Fish, Director (1931-1953)

Elliot Barker was born in Moran, Texas, and moved, with his family, to the Sangre de Cristo Mountains in New Mexico for his asthmatic mother's health. He attended school in Las Vegas, New Mexico, and graduated in 1905. Barker worked as a professional guide and hunter near Las Vegas before he joined the US Forest Service in April 1908. He worked in the Santa Fe National Forest near Cuba, New Mexico; the Pecos National Forest; and the Carson National Forest near Tres Piedras. He worked there under conservationist Aldo Leopold (see entry). In 1914 Barker was promoted to deputy forest supervisor and moved to Taos. He resigned in 1919 and ranched until 1930. In 1931 Barker was appointed state game warden and director of the New Mexico Department of Game and Fish. He held that position until 1953, when he retired to devote himself full-time to writing. His books included, *When the Dogs Bark "Treed": A Year on the Trail of the Longtails*, (1946); *Beatty's Cabin: Adventures in the Pecos High Country* (1953); *Western Life and Adventures, 1889-1970*, (1970); *Ramblings in the Field of Conservation* and *Eighty Years with Rod and Rifle* (both 1976); and *Smokey Bear and the Great Wilderness* (1982). Barker also published two books of poetry, *A Medley of Wilderness and Other Poems* (1962) and *Outdoors, Faith, Fun and Other Poems* (1968). Elliot Barker was responsible for the creation of Smokey Bear as the symbol of forest fire prevention (see entry). He was also an active supporter of the Girl Scouts. Elliot

was the older brother of writer and poet S. Omar Barker (see entry).
Handbook of Texas Online

Barker, Squire Omar "S.O.B." (1894-1985)
New Mexico's Cowboy's Poet
Barker was born in a log cabin in Sapello Canyon, east of the Sangre de Cristo Mountains. He spent his youth herding cattle and hunting in the mountains of northern New Mexico. He served in the military during World War I and he graduated from New Mexico Highlands University (then called New Mexico Normal College) in 1924. He became a full-time writer in 1925 and in his career he wrote more than 1,200 articles, 2,500 poems and 1,500 stories that appeared in more than 100 magazines. His most famous poem, "A Cowboy's Christmas Prayer" was recited on television by both Jimmy Dean and Tennessee Ernie Ford. Two collections of his works were published in 1998: *Ol S. O. B. Sez: Cowboy Limericks*, (TwoDot/Falcon Publishing, Helena, Montana) and *Cowboy Poetry Classic Rhymes* (Cowboy Miner Productions, Phoenix, Arizona). New Mexico newsman and history writer Ollie Reed, Jr., wrote this: "'A Cowboy's Christmas Prayer' will last because even though he never claimed to be a cowboy, S. Omar Barker had a cowboy's heart and a cowboy's soul." Omar was the younger brother of conservationist Elliot Barker (see entry).

Bullis, "A Cowboy's Christmas Prayer," Rio Rancho *Observer*, December 19, 2001
Ollie Reed, Jr. "Church on the Range" Albuquerque *Tribune*, December 23, 1998
David H. Townsend, "An English Teacher 'Plumb Off the Trail,'" *Book Talk*, New Mexico
　　　Book League, November 1996
Other literature abundant

Batton, George Washington (1864-1922)
Eddy County Sheriff
Batton was the Sheriff of Eddy County, New Mexico, when a Texas outlaw—wanted for escape and murder—who called himself the "Longhorn Will-O-Wisp" (Pedro Galindo) chose to go into hiding in the town of Hope, New Mexico. The sheriff, his deputies, and a posse of cowboys, surrounded the hideout and in the gunfight that followed, Sheriff Batton was shot and killed, as was the Longhorn Will-O-Wisp. Deputy Stone Wilburn was also wounded, but survived.
Bullis, *99 New Mexicans*

Beale, Edward Fitzgerald, Lt. (1822-1893)
U.S. Army Camel Corps Commander
A close friend of both Kit Carson (see entry) and John C. Fremont, Lt. Beale is often credited with the creation of the U.S. Army's Camel Corps, an experiment that was somewhat successful, but fell by the wayside as a result of the Civil War. Many of the animals were released into the wild, and the descendants of the first camels were still being spotted in remote areas of the American West well into the 20th century. Beale's camel train visited Albuquerque in 1857 en route to Ft. Defiance, which was then in New Mexico near where the Arizona territorial line would

be established in 1863. One observer said, "The U.S. Army Camel Corps, which had successfully carried military loads throughout the new West, finally died of mistreatment and neglect—because it was [just] too strange."

Bullis, *99 New Mexicans*
Thrapp, *Encyclopedia*

Beaubien, Charles Hipolyte "Carlos" (1800-1864)
Taos County Land Owner/Judge

Charles Hipolyte Beaubien.
After Twitchell.

Carlos Beaubien was born in Canada, probably in Quebec. He left Canada during the War of 1812 and arrived in Taos, by way of St. Louis, in about 1827. One source says he studied for the priesthood as a youth. He married Paula Lobato, daughter of a prominent New Mexico family, soon after his arrival at Taos. He also became associated with Guadalupe Miranda, and the two of them petitioned Governor Manuel Armijo (see entry) for a grant of land in northeastern New Mexico. Armijo made a grant amounting to about one million acres. Miranda sold his share to Beaubien, making Beaubien the largest landowner in New Mexico at the time. Beaubien's marriage produced nine children. One of them, Narciso, was killed by Mexican nationalists during the Taos Revolt of 1847. Another of his children, Luz, married Lucien B. Maxwell (see entry) and thus she became the mistress of the famed Maxwell Land Grant, previously known as the Beaubien-Miranda Land Grant. General Stephen Watts Kearny (see entry) appointed Beaubien to the superior court in 1846, a position he held until 1851. He sat in judgment of the rebels who murdered his son during the course of 1847 revolt. Fifteen of the insurgents were convicted of murder and hanged for their part in the slaughter.

Crutchfield, *Tragedy*
Keleher, *Maxwell Land Grant*
Thrapp, *Encyclopedia*
Twitchell, *Leading Facts*, Vol. II

Becknell, William (1788-1865)
"Father of the Santa Fe Trail"

Becknell was born in Virginia and migrated to St. Louis by 1810. He saw frontier service during the War of 1812 and moved to central Missouri after its close. In 1821 he set out from Arrow Rock, near Franklin, Missouri, with a pack train of goods he intended to trade with the Comanche Indians. As the story goes, in what is now northeastern New Mexico, he encountered a troop of Mexican soldiers who informed him that Mexico had become independent of Spain, and that Americans were welcome in Santa Fe. The soldiers escorted him there and he sold his goods at a good profit. He returned in 1822 with four wagonloads of trade goods, and that trip actually opened wagon traffic over the trade route known as the Santa Fe Trail.

As historian R. L. Duffus says, Becknell did not "discover" the trail, but he was the first to use wagons over the route, and it stayed open after he initiated trade over it. He migrated to the Red River County, Texas, in 1835 and remained there for the rest of his life amassing significant land-holdings. He is interred near Clarksville in northeast Texas.

Duffus, *The Santa Fe Trail*
Handbook of Texas Online
Simmons, *Along the Santa Fe Trail*
Other literature abundant

Bedford, Thomas C. Jr. "Tommy" (1949-1979)
Lincoln County Deputy Sheriff

A deputy for the Lincoln County sheriff, Bedford was shot to death by prison escapee Robert Elton Cox and his young companion, Louie Salandre, on October 8, 1979. During the manhunt for the two suspects, the killer left a note in an outhouse for officers that read, "Hee hee hee. You can't catch me, sheriff's office. I'm here and you're there." He was wrong about that. Officers arrested Cox without incident four days after the killing, at Corona, New Mexico. Cox was sentenced to life in prison.

Deputy Sherrif Thomas C. Bedford

Bullis, *New Mexico's Finest*

Begay, Harrison (1917-)
Navajo Painter

Begay was trained at the Santa Fe Indian School beginning in 1934. He was a student of Dorothy Dunn. He graduated in 1939 and the same year painted one of the murals on the façade of Maisel's Trading Post in Albuquerque. He served in World War II and afterwards became one of the first Navajo artists to earn his living by painting full time. According to the *Grove Dictionary of Art*, "Begay painted a timeless, peaceful and gentle world, recognizing only the beauty in the Navajo way of life."

www.groveart.com

Belcheff, George (1885-1980)
Sofia, New Mexico, Founder

Born in Bulgaria, Belcheff migrated to the United States in the early 20th century and, after working for a time as a laborer and miner, he filed on a quarter section (160 acres) in northeastern New Mexico. He believed that land ownership was the mark of success. He encouraged other Bulgarians to join him, and when they did he named the spot Sofia, after the capitol of his native country. By the time he died, he owned more than 3,600 acres. His descendants continue to reside in the region.

Julyan, *Place Names*

Bell, James W. aka Jim Long (1853-1881)
Lincoln County Deputy Sheriff

Jim Bell was a Texas Ranger with Company D of the Frontier Battalion before he moved on to New Mexico and participated in the later days of the Lincoln County War (1878-81). He became a deputy for Sheriff Pat Garrett (see entry) and, along with Bob Olinger (see entry), was assigned the duty of guarding William Bonney (Billy the Kid, see entry), who had been sentenced to hang in May 1881 for the murder of Sheriff William Brady (see entry). Bonney shot and killed Bell and Olinger when he made his final escape on April 28 of that year, from the Lincoln County Court House. Pat Garrett killed Bonney the following July at Fort Sumner, New Mexico.

Keleher, *Violence*
Metz, *Encyclopedia* & *Pat Garrett*
Utley, *High Noon*
Other literature abundant

Benavides, Fray Alonso de (fl. 1625-1635)
Custos (Custodian) of New Mexico's Franciscan Missions (1625-1629)

Fray Alonso is said to have constructed the first Santa Fe church *circa* 1626. It stood at what was then the eastern end of the Plaza. It was destroyed during the Pueblo Revolt of 1680. The church was replaced by *La Parroquia* early in the 18th century. Fray Alonso also conducted a rudimentary census, which was included in *The Memorial of Fray Alonso de Benavides* (see bibliography re: Ayer). Benavides estimated that the number of Apaches in the "Kingdom of New Mexico" numbered "400,000 souls." He returned to Spain in 1629 and became "New Mexico's seventeenth century promoter par excellence." His *Memorial* was presented to King Phillip IV in 1630 and to Pope Urban VIII in 1635. It included an account of the miraculous appearance of the Spanish nun, María de Jesús de Agreda, the Lady in Blue (see entry), before nomadic Indians.

Chávez y Chávez, *Wake*
Gutiérrez, *When Jesus Came*
Hammett, *Santa Fe*
Sálaz Márquez, *New Mexico*
Simmons, *New Mexico*

Benedict, Kirby (1811-1874)
New Mexico Territorial Judge

Kirby Benedict was born in Connecticut, and moved on to Illinois as a young man. There he became well acquainted with Abraham Lincoln and Stephen Douglas. President Franklin Pierce appointed him associate justice of the New Mexico Supreme Court in 1853. He was elevated to Chief Justice in 1858. Judge Benedict was involved in many major legal matters in territorial New Mexico, but not without controversy. He was a drinking man, and when complaints about his intemperate habits were reported to President Abraham Lincoln (see entry), the President is reported to have said, "I know Benedict. We have been friends for over thirty years. He may imbibe to excess, but Benedict drunk knows more law than all the others on the bench in New Mexico sober. I shall not disturb him." The judge was also a poker player, reportedly a poor one, who often resorted to cheating, and he was a poor cheater at that. He was often caught. Benedict is best remembered, in legend, for the oration he delivered while sentencing José Maria Martin to the gallows at Taos, but it is just a legend (complete text found in Gilbreath or Twitchell). Most historians concur that it never happened. Benedict left the bench in 1866 and was suspended from the practice of law in 1871;

Kirby Benedict. After Twitchell.

Twitchell says because "his personal habits were such that he had many difficulties with the presiding judges…." He petitioned for reinstatement several times, to no avail and died in February 1874.

Don Bullis, *Observer*, August 28, 2002
Gilbreath, *Death on the Gallows*
Remley, *Adios Nuevo Mexico*
Simmons, Santa Fe *New Mexican*, February 19, 2005
Twitchell, *Leading Facts*, Vol. II
Other literature abundant

Bent, Charles (1797-1847)
Governor (American Occupation) of New Mexico (1846-1847)

(Crutchfield reports the year of birth as 1799.) Bent, a native of Virginia and educated at West Point, left the army and arrived in New Mexico around 1829 and became a successful trader over the Santa Fe Trail. He entered into a business association with Cerán St. Vrain (see entry), which was likewise profitable. In 1833 and 1834, he and his brothers, William (1809-1869) (see entry) and George (1814-1847), along with St. Vrain, built Bent's Fort—originally called Fort William—in southern Colorado. Bent provided Col. Stephen Watts Kearny (see entry) with military and other information prior to the U.S. occupation of New Mexico. In turn, Kearny appointed Bent as the first civil governor of New Mexico after the

Gov. Charles Bent. After Twitchell.

occupation in 1846. Mexican nationalists and Taos Indians, in rebellion against the American Occupation, murdered him in January 1847. His wife, probably common-law, was Ignacia Jaramillo, the sister of Josefita Jaramillo, who was married to Kit Carson (see entry). Bent was initially interred at the Santa Fe Masonic Cemetery, but was moved to the Santa Fe National Cemetery in 1895.

James Abarr, "Frontier crossroads," Albuquerque *Journal*, March 18, 2001
Crutchfield, *Tragedy At Taos*
Gardner, *Bent's Old Fort*
Simmons, *Kit Carson & His Three Wives*
Other literature abundant

Bent, William (1809-1869)
Trader, Frontiersman

The younger brother of New Mexico's first American Governor, Charles Bent (see entry), William began his adventures on the Western Frontier at a young age. He became associated with his brother's trading venture and is generally credited with construction of Bent's Fort (originally called Fort William) on the Arkansas River in southeastern Colorado in 1833-34. This fort was a jumping off point for General Stephen Watts Kearny (see entry) and his Army of the West when Americans invaded New Mexico in the summer of 1846. Because William had rescued two Cheyenne warriors during a Comanche attack while on one of his early adventures, his warm relationship with the Cheyenne was of great benefit to his business ventures and to other Americans living in the area. William married a Cheyenne, Owl Woman, and some accused him of becoming an Indian. The couple had three sons, George, Charles and Robert, and while George and Charles were closely associated with the Cheyenne people, Robert was more closely aligned with the white world. At the Sand Creek Massacre (November 1864), Colonel John M. Chivington (see entry) forced Robert to serve as guide when Colorado volunteers attacked the Cheyenne village. Residing in the village were Robert's brothers, George and Charles. William was greatly disheartened by these events and traveled east during 1867-68 seeking compensation for the use of his fort by the U. S. Army. He was not successful. One source says he died at his ranch on the Purgatoire River in Colorado, while another indicates that he died in Westport, Kansas.

James Abarr, "Frontier crossroads," Albuquerque *Journal*, March 18, 2001

Crutchfield, *Tragedy At Taos*

Gardner, *Bent's Old Fort*

Thrapp, *Encyclopedia*

Other literature abundant

Berninghaus, Oscar Edmund (1874-1952)
Painter, Charter Member of The Taos Society of Artists

Oscar Berninghaus was born and educated in St. Louis, Missouri. He took up lithography in 1893 while he attended night classes at the St. Louis Society of Fine Arts. He first arrived in Taos in 1899 and observed, "I stayed … but a week, became infected with the Taos germ and promised myself a longer stay." He returned each summer until at last he settled there permanently in 1925. Berninghaus was one of the original six members of the Taos Society of Artists, which existed from 1915 to 1927. He was noted for his direct and objective approach to painting the Taos Pueblo people. One critic wrote, "The simple and clear part of Berninghaus' art…conceals a true psychological understanding of his major subject, the Pueblo Indians." Berninghaus died at Taos from a heart attack.

Meadowlark Gallery: The Artists Biographies

Nelson, *Legendary Artists of Taos*

Samuels, *The Illustrated Biographical Encyclopedia*

Schimmel & White, *Bert Geer Phillips*

Witt, *The Taos Artists*

Bibo, Nathan (1844-1927)
New Mexico Merchant

Nathan was the oldest of the several Bibo brothers and sisters who migrated from Westphalia, Germany, to New Mexico in the early territorial period. He arrived in 1867, a year after his younger brother, Simon. They were among the many young Jewish men who entered the mercantile trade of the day. Other family names were, and are, familiar yet today: Seligman, Ilfeld, Jaffa, Solomon, Spiegleberg. Nathan began his career as post trader at Fort Wingate in western New Mexico. Then he operated a trading post at Cubero and later a mercantile at Bernalillo. In 1884 he sold out to his brother and sister, Joseph and Lina, and moved on to California. He returned to New Mexico later in life.

Bullis, *99 New Mexicans*

Bibo, Solomon (1853-1934)
Acoma Tribal Governor, Merchant

Solomon Bibo left Germany in 1869 and by 1880 he was serving as the officially designated trader for the Pueblo of Acoma in west central New Mexico. He had a facility with languages and soon learned Keres, the tongue of the Acoma people. This was a great benefit to them because they had not previously had a representative who could speak their language, and Spanish and English as well. Solomon married an Acoma woman, Juana Valle, in 1885 and was elected governor of the Pueblo the same year. He was re-elected twice. In spite of his close ties to the Acoma people, he remained Jewish and wanted a Jewish education for his children. In the late 1880s, he and Juana and their children moved to San Francisco. He died there.

Bullis, *99 New Mexicans*

William J. Parish, "The German Jew and the Commercial Revolution in Territorial New Mexico, 1850-1900," *New Mexico Historical Review*, January 1960

Bingaman, Jesse Francis, Jr. "Jeff" (1943-)
U.S. Senator from New Mexico

Jeff Bingaman was born in El Paso, Texas, and educated at Silver City, New Mexico. He graduated from Harvard in 1965 and Stanford Law School in 1968. He was elected New Mexico Attorney General in 1979, unopposed in the general election, and to the U.S. Senate in 1982 when he defeated incumbent Republican Harrison "Jack" Schmitt (see entry). Bingaman was re-elected to the Senate in 1988 when he defeated Bill Valentine; in 1994 when he defeated Colin McMillan; and in 2000 when he defeated Bill Redmond. He served as Chairman of the Senate Impeachment Trial Committee from 1989 to 1991.

Senator Jesse Francis Bingaman

Congressional Biography
News accounts abundant

Blair, Francis Preston, Jr. (1821-1875)
U.S. Attorney for New Mexico (1846-1847)

A native of Kentucky and a graduate of Princeton, Blair began the practice of law in St. Louis in 1843. He joined the Army of the West under Stephen Watts Kearny (see entry) and arrived in Santa Fe in 1846. He assisted in the creation of the "Kearny Code" designed to establish civil rule in New Mexico. Kearny appointed him U.S. Attorney. He assisted in preparing indictments against those who participated it the 1847 Taos Revolt against American rule, and he prosecuted the accused. Later that year, he returned to his law practice in St. Louis after Col. Sterling Price (see entry), acting as military governor of New Mexico, abolished the office of U.S. Attorney. He was later something of a hero during the Civil War and well regarded by General William Tecumseh Sherman. He served in the U.S. Congress and was the Democratic candidate for Vice President of the U.S. in 1868. He died at St. Louis.

Congressional Biography
Crutchfield, *Tragedy*
Twitchell, *Leading Facts*, Vol. II

Blake, Ernie (1913-1989)
Taos Ski Valley Developer

The name he acquired at birth in Frankfurt, Germany, was Ernest Bloch. His mother was Swiss; his father German. His family moved to New York in 1938, and young Ernest worked in the retail trade for a time, selling ski clothing. He also had an opportunity to travel widely in the U.S. and thus became acquainted with the nation's ski areas. He met and married Rhoda in 1942. He served in U.S. Army Intelligence during World War II, and it was then that he changed his name to Blake. After the war, in 1949, Blake and his family moved to New Mexico and he became manager of the Santa Fe Ski Basin. Legend holds that he discovered the ski slope possibilities at Taos in 1954—some say by observing the area from the air and others that he was hiking in the mountains—and opened the ski area in 1955. Taos is today a world-class skiing facility that attracts a quarter-million skiers each year. Members of Blake's family continue to operate Taos Ski Valley.

Rick Richards, "Taos Turns 50, Ernie Blake's dream still going strong," *New Mexico Magazine*, January 2006
Nancy Salem, "Sheer Pluck," Albuquerque *Tribune*, December 5, 2005
Taos Ski Valley-Mountain History (webpage)

Bland, Richard Parks "Silver Dick" (1835-1899)
U.S. Congressman from Missouri

The Sandoval County, New Mexico, gold and silver mining town of Bland, which was active between 1894 and 1904, was named for the congressman because he was a great supporter of the silver monetary standard.

Bullis, *Rio Rancho Observer*, October 2, 2003

Blount, Helen (1923-2004)
Ghost Town of Bland Resident

Helen Blount was the last resident of the Sandoval County ghost town of Bland that flourished from 1894 to 1904. She lived there, in the Exchange Hotel, for the last 25 years of her life, and she is interred in the Bland Township Cemetery.
Bullis, *Rio Rancho Observer*, October 2, 2003

Blumenschein, Ernest Leonard (1874-1960)
Painter, Charter Member of The Taos Society of Artists

Born in Pittsburgh, Blumenschein was raised in Dayton, Ohio. His early training was at the Cincinnati College of Music, but while taking courses at the Art Academy, he came to believe that his true calling was in art. He moved on to New York City where he entered the Art Students League. He also studied at the Académie Julian in Paris. Tales he heard from Joseph Henry Sharp (see entry) sparked his interest in the American Southwest, and in 1898 he and fellow artist Bert Phillips (see entry) set out by wagon to travel from Denver to Mexico. Legend holds that as they were traveling near Taos, New Mexico, they broke a wheel. Blumenschein lost a coin toss and was obliged to haul the wheel into town for repair. He liked what he saw along the way and later wrote, "No artist had ever recorded the New Mexico I was now seeing. No writer had ever written down the smell of this air or the feel of that morning's sky. I was receiving ... the first great unforgettable inspiration of my life." He returned to the east and then on to Paris for a long sojourn. After his return to New York where he painted and taught at the Pratt Institute, he regularly returned to Taos. His work became widely recognized and by 1919 he was able to move himself and his family to Taos. He became one of the charter members of The Taos Society of Artists, which existed from 1915 to 1927. The number of awards Blumenschein won for his work in a long and active career are too many to list here. He remained in Taos for the rest of his life and died there.
Meadowlark Gallery: The Artists Biographies
Nelson, *Legendary Artists of Taos*
Samuels, *The Illustrated Biographical Encyclopedia*
Schimmel & White, *Bert Geer Phillips*
Witt, *The Taos Artists*

Boellner, Louis B. (1872-1951)
Roswell Pioneer Jeweler/Horticulturist

Louis Boellner was born at St. Charles, Missouri, but soon moved with his family to Butler County, Kansas, near the town of Leon. As a young man he apprenticed as a jeweler and later studied watch making and repairing. Back in Leon, he went into business for himself. He also studied optometry and added that skill to his business, which continued to grow. By 1904 he had married and moved his business to a larger Kansas town before he moved on to Roswell. He opened the community's first

Louis B. Boellner. Courtesy Historical Society of Southeast New Mexico, No. 3057.

31

jewelry store, and optometrist shop, on North Main Street. His business flourished and he and his family became important members of the town. All the while, Boellner was interested in horticulture and used the yard of his home as a place to experiment. He was particularly interested in walnuts and eventually produced the "Kwik-Krop Black Walnut, Boellner Strain." It was a large nut with a thin shell. It was patented and in 1951, after his death, and sold to Stark Brothers Nurseries. He was also interested in dahlias, and produced a new strain of the flower. Historian Elvis E. Fleming of Roswell calls him the "Luther Burbank of New Mexico," and he may well have deserved that title.

Elvis E. Fleming, "Luther Burbank of New Mexico: Dr. Louis B. Boellner, 1872-1951," *New Mexico Historical Review*, July 1983.

Bond, Franklin "Frank" (1863-1945)
Northern New Mexico Sheepman

Born in Quebec, Canada, Frank Bond followed his brother, George Washington Bond, to northern New Mexico in 1882. The two of them soon went into the mercantile business at Española, the venture bankrolled by their father to the tune of $25,000. Successful in business, they branched out into the sheep business. By the time the partnership was amicably dissolved in 1911, Frank had a net worth in excess of $500,000, a considerable sum at the time. After leasing the Baca Location No. 1 in Sandoval County, near modern Los Alamos, for a time, in 1918, Frank purchased it. Today it is known as the Valles Caldera National Preserve. It amounted to nearly 100,000 acres of grassy valleys, mountain streams and tall timber. Bond owned the Albuquerque Wool Warehouse and the Bond and Baker Co. at Roswell, also a wool warehouse. He owned other ranches in northern New Mexico and in 1930 he set a record by placing 30,000 sheep into 11 eastern markets in a single day. He reportedly grazed more than 140,000 sheep that same year. In 1925, Frank turned over operation of the family interests to his son, Franklin, and he moved to California where he died in 1945. It is noteworthy that the Bond family allowed access to the Baca Location by the Pueblo Indian people of the area for religious ceremonial purposes. They also allowed a limited amount of hunting. The Baca Location was sold to Texan James Patrick Dunigan (see entry) in 1963.

"Frank Bond Dies," Albuquerque *Journal*, June 22, 1945

Frank H. Grubbs, "Frank Bond: Gentleman Sheepherder of Northern New Mexico, 1883-1915," *New Mexico Historical Review*, July 1960.

Martin, *Valle Grande*

Bonney, William Henry "Billy the Kid" (1859-1881)
Lincoln County Outlaw/Killer

If New Mexico had a state outlaw as it has a state cookie—the bizcochito—he would certainly be William H. Bonney, "Billy the Kid." At various times he called himself Henry McCarty and Henry Antrim, among other aliases. He was a participant in the Lincoln County War, and dime-novel writers of the late 19th century made much more of his life and exploits than they deserved. He participated in several cold-blooded murders—he was convicted of killing Sheriff William

Brady (see entry)—and he was a thief of the first order. Little real doubt exists that Sheriff Pat Garrett (see entry) shot and killed Bonney on July 14, 1881 at Fort Sumner, New Mexico. Thirty years later, the *Ft. Sumner Republican* newspaper recalled Bonney as an "outlaw of unsavory memory."

Burns, *Billy the Kid*
Cline, *Alias Billy the Kid*
Fort Sumner *Republican*, July 6, 1911
Garrett, *The Authentic Life of Billy the Kid*
Tuska, *Billy the Kid*
Tatum, *Inventing Billy the Kid*
Utley, *High Noon*
Other literature abundant

Borman, Frank Frederick (1928-)
Astronaut

Borman was born in Gary, Indiana, but raised in Tucson, Arizona. He graduated from the U. S. Military Academy in 1950 and entered the U. S. Air Force (the Air Force Academy didn't graduate a class until 1959). He became a test pilot and was selected to be a NASA astronaut in 1962. His space flights include Gemini 7 and Apollo 8 during which he spent nearly 20 days in space. Borman retired in 1970 and became an executive with Eastern Air Lines, rising to chief executive officer in 1975. He left Eastern in 1986. Borman resides in Las Cruces, New Mexico, where he owns Borman Motors.

News accounts abundant

William Henry Bonney. After Twitchell.

Frank Frederick Borman

Botts, Charles Milton (1920-1945)
Albuquerque World War II Hero

A native of Albuquerque, Botts was a Harvard Law School student when he was inducted into the army in 1941. He served in major South Pacific campaigns at Guadalcanal, New Georgia, New Guinea and the Philippine Islands. A Lieutenant Colonel, Botts was awarded a Bronze Star with an oak leaf cluster during the Philippine campaign. He was killed east of Manila in May 1945. He was one of the more than 1,400 New Mexican causalities during World War II.

Albuquerque *Journal*, June 1, 1945

Bourke, John Gregory (1846-1896)
U.S. Army Officer, Western Folklorist

Bourke was born in Philadelphia. He joined the army at 16 and served as an enlisted man throughout the Civil War. He won the Medal of Honor at Stone River, Tennessee, in December 1862. He was appointed to West Point after the war and was assigned to Fort Craig, New Mexico, upon graduation. He became interested in the folklore and artifacts of the American West and wrote widely on the subject. He served as president of the American Folklore Society. During a brief stopover in Albuquerque in 1881, he observed: "At the moment of stepping upon the [railway] platform, two high-toned gentlemen of the town were blazing away with pistols at each other a little farther up the street. Unfortunately, neither were [sic] killed." Among his books are, *The Snake Dance of the Moquis of Arizona* (1884), *An Apache Campaign* (1886), *Mackenzie's Last Fight With the Cheyennes* (1890), *On the Border With Crook (1891)*, and *The Medicine Men of the Apache* (1892).

Simmons, *Albuquerque*
Marc Simmons, Santa Fe *New Mexican*, February 5, 2005
Thrapp, *Encyclopedia*
Other literature abundant

Bowdre, Charles (c.1848-1880)
Lincoln County War Figure/Billy the Kid Associate

Bowdre was born in either Mississippi or Tennessee. He arrived in New Mexico by 1876 and became acquainted with William H. Bonney (Billy the Kid, see entry). He is generally believed to have shot and killed Buckshot Roberts (see entry) during the battle at Blazer's Mill in April 1878, although Bonney claimed to have shot him, too. Bowdre was present in the McSween (see entry) house during the Five Days Battle at Lincoln in July of the same year. He was also present, along with Billy and others, when Tom O'Folliard (see entry) was killed in December 1880. He was himself killed a week later at Stinking Springs, near Taiban, by members of a posse led by Sheriff Pat Garrett (see entry). He is interred at Fort Sumner along with O'Folliard and Bonney. Describing the three of them, the tombstone is simply inscribed "PALS."

Burns, *Billy the Kid*
Garrett, *The Authentic Life of Billy the Kid*
Tuska, *Billy the Kid*
Tatum, *Inventing Billy the Kid*
Utley, *High Noon*
Wilson, *Merchants, Guns…*
Other literature abundant

Bowyer, Ralph Seymour (1914-2005)
Carlsbad Coach (1937-1967)
Highlands University Athletic Director (1967-1973)

A native of Albuquerque, Bowyer graduated from Albuquerque High School and the University of New Mexico (UNM), where he played on the 1932-35 football teams. He also played basketball and track and in all won nine letters. Bowyer coached high school athletic teams at Grants (1937-42), Belen (football in 1942), El Paso (basketball in 1943), and Carlsbad (1943-1967). He was athletic director

Ralph Seymour Bowyer

at New Mexico Highlands University from 1967 to 1973. He led his high school teams to eight football championships, three basketball championships and two track championships. Most notably, in the 1946-1947 school year, his Carlsbad teams won all three of those championships. Bowyer was inducted into seven halls of fame including the UNM Athletic Hall of Honor, Albuquerque Sports Hall of Fame, Carlsbad High School Hall of Fame, and the National High School Athletics Hall of Fame. At age 77 in 1991, Coach Bowyer was still athletic, and in the Senior Olympics of that year he threw the discus 98 feet six and one half inches.

Dottie (Bowyer) Hester, daughter, correspondence, December 2005
"Obituary," Albuquerque *Journal*, April 4, 2005
UNM Archives

Boyle, Andrew or Archibald "Andy" (fl. 1878)
Lincoln County War Figure, Newspaper Correspondent

Boyle, a former British soldier, arrived in Lincoln County, New Mexico in the 1870s. He was present in the town of Lincoln at the time of the Five Days Battle in July 1878, and he wrote about it from his personal point of view, contradicting the editor of the Mesilla *News*. Little is definitely known about him. Burns refers to him as, "…that harum-scarum old ruffian and blackguard…." Boyle may have been a heavy drinker. One source indicates that when he died, he may have been "pre-embalmed with alcohol."

Burns, *Billy the Kid*
Keleher, *Violence*
Thrapp, *Encyclopedia*

Bradbury, Norris Edwin (1909-1997)
Director, Los Alamos Scientific Laboratory (1945-1970)

Norris Bradbury was born in Santa Barbara, California. He earned an under-graduate degree from Pomona College in chemistry and a Ph. D. in physics from the University of California at Berkeley. He was a research fellow at the Massachusetts Institute of Technology before he joined the faculty at Stanford University. His area of expertise was conduction of electricity in gases, properties of ions, and atmospheric electricity. In 1941 he was called to active duty in the U. S. Navy and served for a time at a naval proving ground in Virginia before he was offered a position with the Manhattan Project at Los Alamos in 1944. Bradbury was responsible for the final assembly of the non-nuclear components of the world's first atomic bomb, often referred to as "the gadget." After two atomic bombs were successfully detonated over Japan in the summer of 1945, he prepared to return to teaching at Stanford. Lab Director, J. Robert Oppenheimer (see entry), however, asked Bradbury to remain at Los Alamos as Lab Director. Bradbury agreed to stay on for six months, and remained for 25 years. He is credited with moving the Laboratory from a single wartime project to a nuclear research facility. Bradbury was innovative and energetic in representing Los Alamos at a time when many thought it should be dismantled, or, in lieu of that, turned into a national park. One of his colleagues noted, "Oppenheimer was the founder of this Laboratory.

Bradbury was its savior." He died at his home in Los Alamos.
Los Alamos National Laboratory, Obituary, August 21, 1997
Szasz, *Larger than Life*
Other literature abundant

Braden, John (d. 1896)
Albuquerque Hero

A parade was held at the close of the October 1896 New Mexico Territorial Fair. Among the vehicles in the procession was one that carried fireworks that unexpectedly began exploding; the wagon soon engulfed in flame. The result was havoc, but the wagon's driver, John Braden, saved the day at the cost of his own life. At his funeral Albuquerque City Marshal Fred Fornoff (see entry) said, "No doubt that John Braden saved the young ladies on the Queen's float from death or serious injury. I never saw or heard of such heroism. He could have jumped from the wagon when the explosion occurred and saved himself, but he stayed at his post and prevented the frightened horses from trampling upon and doubtless killing a number of people."
Bryan, *Albuquerque*
Simmons, *Albuquerque*

Brady, William (1829-1878)
Lincoln County Sheriff

(Note that a second source gives the birth year as 1825.) Brady, a native of Ireland and a veteran of the U.S. Army where he attained the rank of Major, served as sheriff of Lincoln County in 1870 and 1871, and again in 1877 and 1878. He was generally considered a part of the Murphy (see entry) faction during the Lincoln County War (1878-81). He was murdered in cold blood—shot from ambush by William Bonney (Billy the Kid, see entry) and his friends—on the main street in the town of Lincoln on April 1, 1878. His deputy, George Hindman (see entry), was also killed. Brady's slaying is the only murder for which Bonney was ever convicted, although he is known to have been involved in several others. Brady was survived by a wife and eight children. A ninth, Primitivo, was born after the sheriff's death.

Lavish, *Sheriff William Brady*
Metz, *Pat Garrett*
Other literature abundant

Senator Sam Gilbert Bratton

Bratton, Sam Gilbert "Sam" (1888-1963)
U.S. Senator/Appeals Court Judge

A native of Limestone County, Texas, Bratton was educated there and became a schoolteacher as a young man. He studied law and was admitted to the bar in 1909. He practiced in Texas before he moved to Clovis and set up a practice there in 1915. He served as Judge in New Mexico's Fifth Judicial District from 1919 to 1922 and as Associate Justice of the New Mexico Supreme Court in 1923 and

1924. He was elected to the U.S. Senate in 1924 and re-elected in 1930, only to resign in 1933 to accept appointment to the U.S. Circuit Court of Appeals for the 10th District. He served on the court until 1961 when he assumed senior status. He died two years later.
Congressional Biography

Brazel, Jesse Wayne (1876-1915?)
Doña Ana County Cowboy, Goat Raiser, Confessed Killer

Wayne Brazel's claim to fame is that he confessed to shooting noted lawman Pat Garrett (see entry) in the back on February 29, 1908. He was tried for the murder and acquitted upon a plea of self-defense the following year. Many believe that he did not commit the crime, but was paid to take the blame because no one thought he could be convicted. Some believe that he shot Garrett through the body after the old lawman had already been shot in the head; perhaps by hired assassin Jim Miller (see entry) or local cowboy Billy McNew. Brazel ranched near Lordsburg, New Mexico, for a while after 1909 and lived in Arizona before he disappeared completely. One source reports that he may have been killed in Bolivia in 1915.
Hornung, Chuck, presentation, Historical Society of New Mexico, April 2006.
Metz, *Garrett*
Thrapp, *Encyclopedia*
Other literature abundant

Breen, Victor C. "Vic" (1916-1971)
Quay County District Attorney

Vic Breen had served as District Attorney for 20 years in Quay County, New Mexico, before he was murdered, shot down in front of his own home, by a mental patient. The killer was soon apprehended but ruled incompetent to stand trial. He spent three years in confinement for "safe keeping" but was then released. He was never tried for Breen's murder. Breen's daughter, Vicki, later became a significant part of the New Mexico arts community.
Bullis, *New Mexico's Finest*

Brett, Dorothy Eugenie "Brett" (1883-1977)
Artist

Dorothy Brett was born in London to the Second Viscount Esher and the daughter of the Belgian ambassador to the court of St. James. She was the product of a typical Victorian up bringing which meant that she and her siblings were generally ignored by their parents, although her mother did oversee her education. Her family had sufficient status that Brett took dancing lessons supervised by Queen Victoria herself. Brett was admitted to the Slate School of Art in 1910. She completed the four year program and, with her father's help, set up her own studio where she painted portraits of British personalities. She became acquainted with D. H. Lawrence (see entry) and his wife Frieda in 1915, and in 1924 traveled with them to Taos, New Mexico. Taos became her home and remained her residence until her death. She became a U. S. citizen in 1938. In Taos, she remained close to Frieda Lawrence and associated regularly with Mabel Dodge Luhan (see entry). One source reports that they were so close that they came to be called the "Three Fates." The relationship, however, seems to have been of the love/hate variety. A notable characteristic of Brett was her near deafness, which became a problem by the time she was 27. Her constant companion was an ear trumpet she called "Toby." She painted Native Americans in a primitive style that romanticized Indian life. She wrote a book about her early life called *Lawrence and Brett: A Friendship* (1974).

Hignett, *Brett*
Nelson, *Legendary Artists of Taos*
Rudnick, *Mabel Dodge Luhan*

Brewer, Richard "Dick" (1852-1878)
Lincoln County War Figure/Billy the Kid Associate

Dick Brewer was born in Vermont and moved to Wisconsin as a child. He went west as a young man and arrived in Lincoln County, New Mexico in 1870. He farmed for a time along the Rio Feliz and worked for Englishman John H. Tunstall (see entry) as ranch foreman until Tunstall was murdered in February 1878. Brewer was shot and killed in the fight at Blazer's Mill, by Andrew "Buckshot" Roberts (see entry), in early April of the same year. Roberts was also killed in the skirmish. The two of them were buried, side-by-side, on a hill near Blazer's Mill.

Keleher, *Violence*
O'Neal, *Encyclopedia*
Utley, *High Noon*
Wilson, *Merchants*

Bullis, John Lapham (1841-1911)
U.S. Army Officer

Born in New York, Bullis served in the 126th New York Volunteers during the Civil War, attaining the rank of Captain. He mustered out in 1866, but he returned to the army in 1867 with a permanent commission of 2nd Lieutenant. Bullis was initially assigned to command the Seminole-Negro Scouts in 1872, a position he held for nine years. During that time, the Scouts participated in 12 major engagements in Old Mexico, New Mexico and Texas and never suffered a single casualty; and yet Sgt. John Ward, trumpeter Isaac Payne and Private Pompey Factor won Congressional Medals of Honor. As a Captain, Bullis served as Indian Agent at the San Carlos Apache Reservation, in Arizona, from 1888 to 1891. Bullis Spring, Bullis Lake and Bullis Canyon, all in New Mexico, were named for him. So was Camp Bullis, near San Antonio, Texas. He retired to San Antonio, promoted to Brigadier General, from Major, by President Theodore Roosevelt. He died there.

John Lapham Bullis

Katz, *Black West*
Robinson, *Apache Voices*
Thrapp, *Encyclopedia*

Bunche, Ralph Johnson (1904-1971)
Scholar and Diplomat

While he was born in Detroit, Michigan, and received his early university education in California, Dr. Bunche spent a part of his youth in Albuquerque after his family moved to New Mexico in 1914. His father was a barber and both of his parents died in 1917. He was sent to Los Angeles to live with his grandparents. It is said that he credited one of his teachers at Fourth Ward School in Albuquerque (later Lew Wallace Elementary School), Miss Belle Sweet, with teaching him the basic concepts of peace. In 1962, she was summoned to New York City where Dr. Bunche recognized her as his most outstanding teacher. He said, "She treated me like everybody else and provided salve for the bruises inflicted earlier." Bunche was the only Black child in a class of 65 students. Bunche's grandmother is buried in Albuquerque. He received a Ph. D. from Harvard in 1934. Bunche served in the Office of Strategic Services during World War II and joined the State Department in 1944. He participated in the writing of the United Nations Charter and he was awarded the Nobel Peace Prize in 1950; the first African-American to win the prize (Martin Luther King won the award in 1964). He retired in 1969 as undersecretary general of the United Nations. He served on the board of the National Association for the Advancement of Colored People (NAACP) for 22 years, and in 1963 President John F. Kennedy awarded him the Medal of Freedom. He won some 40 other awards for his work.

Albuquerque *Journal*, "Former Albuquerquean," November 4, 1956

Bryan, *Albuquerque*

Encarta Reference Library

Dave Smoker, "Albuquerque's Belle Sweet Receives National Acclaim," Albuquerque Public School *Journal*, February 1962

Bunting, Bainbridge (1913-1981)
Art Educator/Architectural Historian

Bainbridge Bunting was born in Kansas City, Missouri, and received an undergraduate degree from the University of Illinois in 1937 in architectural engineering. He subsequently received a Ph.D. from Harvard University. His doctoral dissertation was titled, *The Architectural History of the Back Bay District in Boston.* Bunting was a conscientious objector during World War II. He joined the University of New Mexico in 1948 at a time when he was the only faculty member in the Art Department. He remained at UNM until 1980. He is most noted in New Mexico for the work he did on the state's architectural history. He wrote three books on the subject: *Taos Adobes* (1964), *Of Earth and Timbers Made* (1974) and *The Early Architecture of New Mexico* (1976). One reviewer wrote of *Of Earth and Timbers Made*, "[The book] must be credited with generating at least a portion of [the] heightened interest in New Mexican architecture and the impulse to preserve it." Bunting was also the co-editor of the journal, *New Mexico Architecture,* for a number of years. He did important studies on Zuñi Pueblo and the architecture of John Gaw Meem (see entry). Bunting received the Governor's Award in the Arts in 1978 from Governor Jerry Apodaca (see entry). Bunting served as a trustee of the

Albuquerque Museum and on the Old Town Architectural Review Board.

Albuquerque *Journal*, February 15, 1981
Susan Berry, *New Mexico Historical Review*, January 1992
Davis, *Miracle on the Mesa*

Burgen, William A. (d. 1882)
Colfax County Deputy Sheriff

Burgen had served only a few days as Colfax County deputy under Sheriff Allen Wallace when he came to an untimely demise in what is generally called "The Gus Mentzer Affair." Young Mentzer, called "The Kid," went on a drunken shooting spree in Raton, New Mexico, on June 26, 1882. Before it was over, four men were dead and Mentzer was hanged from a telegraph pole. Burgen was shot to death when he attempted to protect Mentzer from the lynch mob.

Bryan, *Robbers, Rogues*
Meketa, *From Martyrs*

Bursum, Holm (1867-1953)
Socorro County Rancher, U.S. Senator (1921-1925)

Senator Holm Bursum

A native of Fort Dodge, Iowa, and tubercular as a youth, he arrived in New Mexico at age 14 in 1881. He engaged in ranching near Socorro while he held several public offices including county sheriff from 1895 to 1898 and warden of the territorial penitentiary in the early 1900s. A Republican, he was a member of the state constitutional convention in 1910, and he ran for governor in 1911 and was defeated by a coalition of Democrats and "Progressive" Republicans led by former territorial governor Herbert J. Hagerman (see entry). In early 1921, when Albert B. Fall (see entry) resigned his seat in the U.S. Senate to accept appointment as Secretary of the Interior, Governor Merritt C. Mechem appointed Bursum to the seat. In a special election held the same year, Bursum was elected to the seat. Democrat Sam Bratton (see entry) defeated him when he ran for a full term in 1924. He died at Colorado Springs and was interred at the Protestant Cemetery at Socorro.

Ball, *Desert Lawmen*
Congressional Biography
Curry, *Autobiography*
Garcia, *Three Centuries*
Harrison, *Hell Holes and Hangings*

Bushnell, Samuel B. (1819-1887)
Mescalero Apache Indian Agent

A medical doctor, Sam Bushnell was appointed Mescalero Indian Agent in February 1873 and served until April 1874. A native of Indiana, his tenure in New Mexico was not a happy one: his son, Charles, died of an overdose of laudanum while serving as the town of Lincoln's postmaster. Many sources do not mention his service in New Mexico. Bushnell returned to Indiana and became a minister. He died there.

Nolan, *Bad Blood*

Bustamente, Pedro de (c. 1548-?)
Spanish Soldier/Explorer

Bustamente accompanied the 1581 expedition of Friar Agustín Rodriguez into New Mexico. He was under the command of Francisco Sánchez Chamuscado who died before the group returned to Mexico. Bustamente was able to read and write and his deposition, given in 1582, is one of the best sources on the Rodriguez expedition.

Thrapp, *Encyclopedia*

Butler, Edmund (1827-1895)
U.S. Army Officer

A native of Ireland, Butler immigrated to the United States and was promptly commissioned a 2nd Lieutenant in the 5th U.S. Infantry. By 1865 he was posted to Fort Wingate in western New Mexico where he commanded troops engaged against Navajo warriors who remained in the area after the relocation of the tribe to Bosque Redondo the year before. He accepted the surrender of several significant Navajo leaders. He was transferred in 1866, but spent the remainder of his life on the Western frontier. He won the Medal of Honor for his participation in action against the Sioux and Cheyenne at Wolf Mountain, Montana, in 1877. He retired in 1891.

Neil C. Mangum, "Old Fort Wingate in the Navajo War," *New Mexico Historical Review*,
    October 1991
Thrapp, *Encyclopedia*

Butterfield, John (1801-1869)
Stagecoach Line Operator

Born in Albany County, New York, Butterfield began his working life as a stagecoach driver and eventually owned not only the stage line, but an entire network of stage lines. In 1850 he worked out a merger of transportation companies into American Express. When the U.S. Congress established an overland mail route in 1857, and appropriated money to operate it, Butterfield was awarded a $600,000 contract to establish a southern route; about 2,800 miles from St. Louis to El Paso, then across southern New Mexico to California. (Note that Arizona did not exist at the time.) Travel time was 25 days, and the coaches were always on time. The Civil War put the southern route out of business in favor of a central route. Elected mayor of Utica, New York, in 1865, Butterfield died there, after suffering a stroke.

Columbia Encyclopedia, 6th Ed.
Clay Martin, "Butterfield Trail," *New Mexico Magazine*, November 2002
Thrapp, *Encyclopedia*
Other literature abundant

Bynner, Harold Witter "Hal" (1881-1968)
Santa Fe Poet

Bynner graduated from Harvard, *summa cum laude*, in 1902. He traveled widely before he settled in Santa Fe in 1922. Paul Horgan (see entry) wrote of him, "A man of commanding stature, splendid good looks, and infectious energy, he presided throughout five decades, by common consent, over the cultural and convivial life in Santa Fe." In addition to the many books of poetry he wrote over the years, 900 of his poems and 80 or so essays appeared in periodicals. He was ill during the last years of his life, and his final words are said to have been, "Other people die, why can't I?" That was on June 1, 1968. T. N. Luther wrote, "During his younger days, such poets as Yeats, Sara Teasdale, Lindsay, Robinson and Mary Austin (see entry) spoke favorably of his work. It is likely that his permanent position will be very high in the second rank of American poets." Through a bequest from him, The Witter Bynner Foundation for Poetry was established in Santa Fe in 1972.

Luther, T. N. "Collecting Santa Fe Authors," *Book Talk*, New Mexico Book League, March 1995.

Rudnick, *Mabel Dodge Luhan*

Witter Bynner Foundation for Poetry (Item by Horgan, Courtesy of the American Academy of Arts and Letters)

-C-

C de Baca, Ezequiel (1864-1917)
Governor (State) of New Mexico (1917)

A native of Las Vegas in San Miguel County, Ezequiel C de Baca was New Mexico's first Lieutenant Governor under Governor William C. McDonald, and second Governor, after statehood in 1912. That he was ill was well known when he received the Democratic nomination for Governor in the summer of 1916. He told the convention that he was well enough to conduct a campaign, and he was right; he won the election. He received treatment for a blood disorder in Los Angeles in December 1916. By January 1, 1917, though, when his term of office began, he was too ill to attend an elaborate inauguration ceremony and instead took the oath in his hospital room at St. Vincent's Sanitarium in Santa Fe. According to news reports of the day, Governor C de Baca never again left the sanitarium. He died on February 18 of the same year and was succeeded by Washington E. Lindsey, a Republican. A cold wind blowing on the day of his funeral did not deter the large number of mourners who formed a procession, "one of the longest and most notable ever seen in New Mexico." He was interred at Mount Calvary Cemetery in Las Vegas. De Baca County, created less than two weeks after the Governor's death, is named for him.

Albuquerque *Morning Journal*, January 1 & 4 1917; February 19 to 23, 1917.
New Mexico Blue Book, 2003-2004

C de Baca, Mackie (1913-1944)
New Mexico State Police Officer, World War II Hero

A native of Clayton, C de Baca joined the New Mexico State Police in 1937 and remained so employed until he was drafted into the army in 1941. He participated in the D-Day Invasion of France in June 1944 and was awarded the Bronze Star for gallantry in action near St. Barthelmy, France, in August. He was killed in action in December 1944. He was one of more than 1,400 New Mexicans killed during World War II.

Officer Mackie C de Baca

Bullis, *New Mexico's Finest*

Cabeza de Vaca, Álvar Núñez (c. 1490-1557)
Explorer

Cabeza de Vaca, or Baca, (cow's head) was not a surname, but rather a hereditary title in Núñez's mother's family dating back to 1212. He was called, simply enough, Álvar Núñez. Born near Seville, Spain, Núñez joined the New World expedition of Pánfilo de Narváez—a "grasping bungler" according to one historian—in 1528. The expedition to today's Florida fared badly, largely because of Narváez's poor leadership. He split his force into two elements, sending Núñez to what is now east Texas, where he and 80 men were shipwrecked and captured by local Indians. The number of survivors dwindled to 15, and finally only four of them escaped to the interior of Texas and points west: Núñez, Alonso del Castillo Maldonado, Andrés Dorantes and his Moorish slave, Estevánico (see entry). There is some dispute as to the route they took before they reached Culiacán, Mexico in 1536. Some believe that they traveled across what is now Texas, New Mexico, Arizona and even to California before they turned south. Others do not believe they were so far to the north, but crossed Texas and into northern Mexico. A map that accompanies Wake Forest University Professor Cyclone Covey's translation of Núñez's memoirs shows a route that reached the Gila River, near what is now west-central New Mexico, in late 1535. It was Núñez who first spoke of the Seven Cities of Cíbola—said to be constructed of gold—which gave rise to further exploration into that area called *la tierra incognita* (the unknown land).

Columbia Encyclopedia, Sixth Edition, 2001-05
Covey, *Cabeza de Vaca's Adventures*
Simmons, *New Mexico*
Thrapp, *Encyclopedia*
Other literature abundant

Cabot, Bruce (1904-1972)
Actor

Born in Carlsbad, New Mexico, as Jacques Etienne de Bujac, Cabot was the grandson of the French ambassador to the United States. He was educated at the University of the South in Tennessee and worked at various jobs before movie producer David O. Selznick offered him a screen test after the two men met at a Hollywood party. His first film was *Roadhouse Murder* in 1932, but his place in the history of movies was secured when he played the hero, Jack Driscoll, who rescued Fay Wray in *King Kong* (1933). Cabot played a variety of movie roles in a long career, and notably appeared in nearly a dozen films with John Wayne from 1947 to 1970. His last film was *Diamonds Are Forever* in 1971.

Bruce Cabot

Katz, *Film Encyclopedia*
Maltin, *Movie Encyclopedia*

Calhoun, James S. (1802-1852)
Governor (Territorial) of New Mexico (1851-1852)

Calhoun, born in Columbus, Georgia, served as mayor of Columbus and in the Georgia legislature. He also served as U.S. Consul to Cuba and rose to the rank of Colonel during the Mexican War. He was first appointed Indian Agent for New Mexico, then the first governor of the territory. He wrote this to Washington, D.C., "…[W]ithout a dollar in our territorial treasury, without munitions of war, without authority to call out our militia, without the cooperation of the military authorities of this territory, and with numberless complaints and calls for protection, do you not perceive I must be sadly embarrassed and disquieted?" He became ill with jaundice and scurvy, and left Santa Fe in late May of 1852 en route to Georgia. He died

Gov. James S. Calhoun. After Twitchell.

near Independence, Missouri, on June 30, 1852. Oddly enough, he was buried in a pauper's cemetery there, and the location of his remains has since been lost to history. Historian Calvin Horn wrote, "Governor Calhoun won the respect and confidence of the native New Mexican people and the Pueblo Indians for himself and thereby for the United States Government."

Fitzpatrick, *New Mexico*
Simmons, *Albuquerque*
Fritz Thompson, Albuquerque *Journal*, September 27, 1987
Twitchell, *Leading Facts*, Vol. II

Campbell, Glen (1937-)
Albuquerque Singer/Guitar Player

Glen Campbell was raised at Billstown, Arkansas, the son of a sharecropper who recognized Glen's musical talent. A five-dollar guitar got him started. His efforts to earn his way with music as a teenager in Wyoming didn't work out and he returned to Arkansas. In the late 1950s he began playing with his uncle's group in Albuquerque. Dick Bills and the K-Circle-B Boys performed widely in the area, but frequently at the Club Chesterfield on Central Avenue, west of the Rio Grande. They also performed live on local radio, notably station KOB (K-Circle-B). Campbell moved on to California in 1961, and the rest, as they say, is history.

Glen Campbell

Campbell, *Rhinestone Cowboy*
Garcia, *Albuquerque*
Other literature abundant

Campbell, John M. "Jack" (1916-1999)
Governor (State) of New Mexico (1963-1967)

A native of Hutchinson, Kansas, Jack Campbell practiced law in New Mexico before he was elected to state House of Representatives in 1956. He served as Speaker in 1961-1962 when he was elected Governor. The Rio Grande Gorge Bridge on U.S. Route 64 between Tres Piedras and Taos was constructed during his administration. At the time it was called "the bridge to nowhere."
King, *Cowboy in The Roundhouse*
Newspaper accounts abundant

Gov. John M. Campbell

Campos, Santiago E. (1926-2001)
New Mexico District Court Judge (1971-1978)
U.S. District Court Judge (1978-1992)

Born on Christmas Day in Santa Rosa, Guadalupe County, New Mexico, Campos served in the U.S. Navy during World War II. He served as a New Mexico District Court Judge from 1971 to 1978 and on the federal bench from 1978 to 1992. He died of cancer and is interred at the National Cemetery at Santa Fe.
Newspaper accounts abundant

Canby, Edward Richard Sprigg, Colonel (1817-1873)
U.S. Army Officer

In the early 1860s, while he was busy fighting the Navajos at Fort Defiance, Col. Canby was given command of the Department of New Mexico. When the Texas Confederates invaded New Mexico in early 1862, Canby is said to have understood that he did not have the military strength to withstand them—largely because many of his officers had gone over to the Confederate army—and he requested help from the Colorado Volunteers, and that strategy proved successful in halting the Rebels at the Battle of Glorieta. Later promoted to General, he was killed while attempting to negotiate a peace with the Modocs in the Pacific Northwest.

Col. Edward R.S. Canby.
After Twitchell.

Alberts, *Battle of Glorieta*
Thrapp, *Encyclopedia*

Candelaria, Emilio (1898-1930)
Bernalillo County Deputy Sheriff

A Bernalillo County deputy sheriff, Candelaria accompanied Federal Prohibition agents when they attempted to serve a warrant on suspected Tijeras Canyon

bootleggers in late January 1930. A gun battle came of the attempt, and Deputy Candelaria was killed by a shotgun blast to the face. A newspaper reporter wrote this: "When deputies approached the home of Candelaria's family...to notify them of his death, they saw a dim light burning within, despite the late hour. It was from the lamp that the young officer's mother always left burning whenever he was out late. She lit it as usual Wednesday night, but it burned in vain."
Bullis, *New Mexico's Finest*

Cannon, James Dean (d.1865)
U.S. Army Officer

A somewhat obscure player in events of the day, Cannon was a Lieutenant in the 1st New Mexico Infantry. He was assigned to Fort Lyon, Colorado and was a part of the Sand Creek Massacre (November 29, 1864). He apparently did not support Col. Chivington's (see entry) version of events and later testified to the atrocities committed against the Cheyenne Indians during the attack. His stated opinion was that two-thirds of those killed were women and children. Cannon returned to Las Vegas, New Mexico, and there he arrested a Colorado murder fugitive in 1865 and took the man to Denver. Three days later he was found dead in a Denver hotel room, perhaps a victim of poisoning, although the official cause of death was reported as "congestion of the brain."
Thrapp, *Encyclopedia*

Caravajál, Fernando de Argüello (fl. 1644-1647)
Spanish Governor of New Mexico (1644-1647)

Caravajál became the Spanish colonial governor of New Mexico a few years after the notorious Governor Luis de Rosas (see entry). A certain notoriety attended Caravajál's administration, too. During the first year of his administration, 40 Indians were executed—by hanging—or whipped for sedition. Jemez Pueblo historian Joe Sando writes, " Jemez Pueblo lost twenty-nine men when the governor [Caravajál] accused their leaders of working with the Apaches and Navajos and hanged them as traitors." It was that kind of arbitrary and summary punishment that ultimately spurred the Pueblos to unite for the purpose of expelling their Spanish conquerors, which they accomplished on the Feast Day of Saint Lawrence, August 10, 1680. The Spanish population at the time was estimated at 2,500; the Pueblo population at 17,000.
New Mexico Blue Book, 2003-2004
Sando, *Po'pay*

Cargo, David Francis "Lonesome Dave" (1929-)
Governor (State) of New Mexico (1967-70)

A native of Dowagiac, Cass County, Michigan, and a Republican, Dave Cargo served in the New Mexico House of Representatives from 1962 to 1967 and was the youngest man ever elected governor of New Mexico at age 37. He was called "Lonesome Dave" because he campaigned for governor in 1966 by driving around the state, alone, in a 1955 Chevrolet. The way in which he did things was something of a departure from his predecessors, and he was therefore often referred to as a maverick, a populist, and a carpetbagger. Popular with voters in both parties, one observer noted, "He's the only guy I know who could walk into a revolving door behind you and come out ahead of you." After he lost two bids for the U.S. Senate, in 1970 and 1972, he left New Mexico for Oregon in 1974. He returned in the 1980s and again ran for public office: U.S. Congress from the 3rd District in 1986 and Mayor of Albuquerque in 1993. He lost in each campaign. He did serve on the Governing Board of the Albuquerque Technical-Vocational Institute, and in 2006, Governor Bill Richardson appointed Cargo to the Cumbres & Toltec Scenic Railroad Commission, and he was soon elected chairman. (Note: Cargo was governor when the states of New Mexico and Colorado purchased the railroad in 1970.)

King, *Cowboy in The Roundhouse*
Dan Vukelich, "The Evolution of a Politician," Albuquerque *Tribune*, November 1, 1993
News sources abundant

Carleton, Gen. James Henry (1814-1873)
Military District of New Mexico, Commander (1862-1866)

A stern and inflexible military officer, he managed to keep New Mexico under Martial Law even after the Texas Confederates had been expelled in early 1862, although some say he was trying to end the arrangement. It was Carleton who ordered Kit Carson thus: "All Indian men of the Mescalero tribe are to be killed whenever and wherever you find them. The women and children will not be harmed, but you will take them prisoner and feed them until you receive other instructions." (Carson ignored the order regarding the slaughter of Indian men.) Carleton was the architect of the failed Bosque Redondo experiment that confined some 8,000 Navajo and Mescalero Apaches along the Pecos River in eastern New Mexico. His high-handed, arrogant, and domineering character finally caught up with him when New Mexico territorial officials complained loudly enough to Washington, D.C. that he was relieved of command and transferred to Texas in 1866. He died at San Antonio. (Note: Utley and Thrapp spell the name *Carleton*. Hutton spells it *Carlton*.)

James Abarr, "Tragedy at Fort Sumner," Albuquerque *Journal*, December 6, 1998
Allan Holmes, "Major General James H. Carleton: New Mexico's Controversial Civil War
        Commander," *Southern New Mexico Historical Review*, January 1994
Paul Hutton, "Why is the man forgotten," *True West*, March 2006
Thrapp, *Encyclopedia*
Utley, *Frontier Regulars*

Carlyle, James Bermuda (c. 1860-1880)
Lincoln County Deputy Sheriff

Young Jim Carlyle, born in Ohio, was working as a blacksmith in the New Mexico town of White Oaks when William H. Bonney (Billy the Kid, see entry) and some of his cohorts shot up the place. Carlyle joined the posse that pursued the outlaws to the Greathouse and Kuch ranch, near the present-day Corona, where a standoff developed. Carlyle was exchanged for Greathouse so that a cease-fire might be negotiated. Somewhat later, Carlyle crashed out of a window and was promptly shot to death. Each side claimed the other side killed the deputy, and the argument has never been satisfactorily resolved.

Bullis, *New Mexico's Finest*
Metz, *The Shooters*
Utley, *High Noon*
Other literature abundant

Carmichael, Mack R. (1897-1935)
McKinley County Sheriff

Mack Carmichael was sheriff of McKinley County, New Mexico, in the unhappy days of the Great Depression in 1935. There were labor-management troubles aplenty in the coal mines around Gallup at the time, and they grew into a violent confrontation between the McKinley County Sheriff and a mob one April morning. Shots were fired and Sheriff Carmichael fell dead with the first volley. Two of the rioters also died, one immediately and one eight days later. About 150 arrests were made, with nearly 50 charged with murder. Finally, three were tried and convicted of the crime.

Bullis, *New Mexico's Finest*
Fergusson, *Murder & Mystery*

Carson, Christopher "Kit" (1809-1868)
Taos Mountain Man/Soldier

Christopher Carson. After Twitchell.

Certainly one of New Mexico's most famous sons, Kit Carson's home in Taos remains a popular tourist attraction. Born in Kentucky and raised in Missouri, he arrived in New Mexico by 1826. From then until the early 1840s, he earned his way by trapping and was one of the last of the mountain men. He later served as a scout for John C. Fremont; as a courier during the Mexican War; and as an Indian Agent for the Apache and Ute tribes. He assumed the role of military officer during the Civil War, and he commanded the U.S. troops that defeated the Mescalero Apaches and Navajos in 1863. His first wife was an Arapaho woman, his second a Cheyenne, and his third was Josefa Jaramillo, by whom he fathered eight children. Kit and Josefa also adopted several Indian children. Carson died at Fort Lyon, Colorado, of an aneurysm of the trachea. Beginning in the early 1970s, a number of detractors emerged and began attacking his reputation, referring to him as a murderer of Indians who practiced genocide against the Navajos in 1863-64. Modern historians, among them Marc Simmons (see entry) and Paul Hutton, have worked to restore Carson's reputation. The late New Mexico writer Norman Zollinger (see entry) wrote: "I do not for one moment question the lofty goals of his [Carson's] detractors; but I also do not for one second believe that the deliberate dismantling of even *one solitary man's* [emphasis Zollinger's] reputation

is a justifiable means toward that end."
Dunlay, *Kit Carson*
Paul Hutton, "Why is this man forgotten?" *True West*, March 2006
Simmons, *Kit Carson*
Norman Zollinger, "Ambushed, The Late 20th Century Attack on Kit Carson," *Book Talk*,
        New Mexico Book League, July 1998
Other literature abundant

Carson, Joe (c. 1840-1880)
Las Vegas, New Mexico, Lawman

Carson was a deputy town marshal in Las Vegas, New Mexico, when he attempted to disarm four young toughs in January 1880. They shot and killed him on the spot. Within three weeks, all four were also dead. They were among the last to face a rope affixed to the so-called "hanging windmill" in the Las Vegas town square.
Bullis, *New Mexico's Finest*
Bryan, *Wildest*
Other literature abundant

Casey, Robert (c. 1828-1875)
Lincoln County Rancher

Born in Ireland, or Canada, or Massachusetts, he and his family arrived in New Mexico via Texas in 1868 and settled on a ranch at the confluence of the Rio Bonita and the Rio Hondo in Lincoln County. He sided with the Horrell Brothers (see entry) during the Horrell War (1873-74) and he opposed the Murphy-Dolan faction in 1875. He was murdered—shot to death—by William Wilson, who was in turn hanged for the crime in December 1875. Many believed that Murphy and Dolan paid Wilson $500 to kill Casey.
Gilbreath, *Death on the Gallows*
Klasner, *My Girlhood*
Nolan, *Bad Blood*

Cassidy, Butch (1866-1909?)
See Parker, Robert Leroy

Castañada, Pedro Francisco de (d.1565)
Spanish Soldier/Chronicler

Born at Najera (Náxera) in northern Spain, Castañada was a well-educated man and an experienced soldier when he joined Francisco Vásquez de Coronado's expedition (1540-1542) into what is now New Mexico. Thrapp says, "He set down his recollections of the expedition 20 years after it returned to Mexico, but the long period between event and chronicle did not dim his memory.... His testimony is the clearest inkling as to the causes of the Tiguex War, and is the most detailed account of the bloody Spanish treatment of Indians who had revolted at Arenal."
Thrapp, *Encyclopedia*

Cather, Willa Sibert (1873-1947)
Santa Fe Novelist

Cather was born in Virginia but moved west with her family at a young age. They settled in Nebraska, and she subsequently graduated from the University of Nebraska before she moved back east to Pennsylvania and then New York City in 1906. She became a full-time novelist in 1913 with her book, *O Pioneers!*. Of greatest significance to New Mexico is her novel *Death Comes for the Archbishop* (1927). Her protagonist, Archbishop Latour, is a thinly disguised Archbishop Jean Baptiste Lamy (see entry) who arrived in Santa Fe in 1851. Erna Ferguson reports that Cather resided with Mary Austin (see entry) in Santa Fe while she wrote the book; and that Amado Chávez (see entry) "told her the stories that lend such verisimilitude to her novel." While some critics consider it her greatest book, some modern historians take a dim view of her characterization of the "Mexican" clergy resident in New Mexico at the time, especially Padre Antonio José Martínez of Taos (see entry). Fray Angélico Chávez and his nephew, Dr. Thomas E. Chávez (see entries), have co-authored a book entitled *Wake for a Fat Vicar* (see bibliography) in which they debunk the Cather book as inaccurate in its history and racist in its treatment of Mexicans. Fray Angélico said, "Hers is a beautiful book, a masterpiece no less, but sadly taken as history by so many."

Chávez, Fray Angélico, "Truth Stalks the Archbishop," *Book Talk*, New Mexico Book
    League, February 1982
Chávez, *But Time and Change*
Chávez & Chávez, *Wake*
Rudnick, *Mabel Dodge Luhan*
Ferguson, *New Mexico*
Other literature abundant

Catron, Thomas Benton "Tom" (1840-1921)
New Mexico Land Baron, Santa Fe Ring Member, U.S. Senator (1912-17)

Born near Lexington, Missouri, Tom Catron attended the University of Missouri where he studied law. One of his classmates was Stephen B. Elkins (see entry). Catron served on the Confederate side in the Civil War and arrived in New Mexico in 1866. He briefly served as a clerk under noted Judge Kirby Benedict (see entry), but secured an appointment to Third Judicial District Attorney in Doña Ana County in January 1867, some five months before he was admitted to the New Mexico bar. In January 1869 he was appointed Territorial Attorney General, and he moved back to Santa Fe. He and his old friend, Stephen B. Elkins, also became law partners in 1869. In 1872, President U.S. Grant (see entry) appointed him U.S. Attorney for the Territory. A Republican, Catron, along with Elkins and several others, was a founding member of the Santa Fe Ring. (Henry Waldo represented the Democrats in the Ring.) Catron

Senator Thomas Benton Catron

was a significant New Mexico landowner by the end of the 19th century. In 1894, the Santa Fe *New Mexican* estimated that Catron owned about 2,000,000 acres and had an interest in another 4,000,000 acres, all in New Mexico. Much of it he had acquired from Spanish and Mexican land grants, in one way or another. He was one of New Mexico's first U.S. Senators after statehood. He and Albert Bacon Fall (see entry) were the only U.S. Senators from New Mexico to be elected by the state legislature (in 1911). After 1913, pursuant to the 17th Amendment, U.S. Senators were elected by popular vote. Catron County in western New Mexico is named for him. It is New Mexico's largest county in area. It is interesting that neither of the news accounts cited here, which appeared upon the occasion of his death, mention his land holdings.

"Thomas B. Catron Dies After Long Illness..." Albuquerque *Journal*, May 15, 1921
"Sketch of Long Life of Senator Thomas B. Catron..." Albuquerque *Journal*, May 17, 1921
Keleher, *The Fabulous Frontier*
Lamar, *Far Southwest*
Twitchell, *Leading Facts*, Vol. II
Other literature abundant

Chacón, Jose Medina Salazar y Villaseñor (fl. 1707-1712)
Governor (Spanish) of New Mexico (1707-12)

Governor Chacón authorized a proclamation in 1712 that authorized an annual fiesta honoring Don Diego de Vargas who had served as governor from 1691-1697, and who led the 1692 reconquest of New Mexico following the Pueblo Revolt of 1680. The annual Santa Fe Fiesta is the descendant of this fiesta.

elibrary, University of New Mexico
New Mexico Blue Book, 2003-2004

Chacón, Philip H. (1944-1980)
Albuquerque Police Officer

Officer Phil Chacón was shot and killed as he pursued armed robbers on September 10, 1980, near the corner of Wyoming and Central in northeast Albuquerque. Van Bering Robinson was arrested, tried and convicted of the crime, and sentenced to life in prison. The State Supreme Court, however, reversed the conviction and Robinson was acquitted at the end of a second trial. No one else was ever arrested or prosecuted for Chacón's murder.

Bullis, *New Mexico's Finest*

Officer Phillip H. Chacón

Chacón, Rafael (1833-1925)
New Mexico Soldier

Rafael was born to Albino Chacón and María Lopéz de Chacón in Santa Fe.

He was a member of two old and distinguished New Mexico families. As a child he was witness to the executions of the leaders in the Chimayó Rebellion of 1837. At age 13 he stood by an artillery piece at Cañoncito southeast of Santa Fe and awaited the advance of General Stephen Watts Kearny's (see entry) Army of the West before the Mexican defense of New Mexico was ordered abandoned by Governor Manuel Armijo (see entry) in August 1846. By the middle 1850s, he was a Sergeant serving under Kit Carson (see entry) in action against Utes and Apaches in northern New Mexico. In 1862, as a Captain, he fought with New Mexico Union troops against the Texas Confederates who had invaded the territory. After the Confederates were repelled in early 1862, Chacón was assigned to Fort Wingate in western New Mexico where he participated in the campaign against the Navajo that led to their five-year incarceration at Bosque Redondo. In 1864, as a Major, he was named commanding officer at Fort Stanton, near the present day town of Lincoln. As he was suffering greatly from rheumatism, he resigned from the Army effective in early September of the same year. He and his family moved to Colorado in 1870. His biographer writes of him, "Rafael Chacón was a *caballero* in the fullest sense of the Spanish word, with all its implications of honesty, decency, kindness, concern for others, gallantry, dedication and patriotism. His courage was truly impressive and was exhibited innumerable times with a valor sustained by his religious convictions...."

Meketa, *Legacy of Honor*
Marc Simmons, "Trail Dusts," Santa Fe *New Mexican*, February 4, 2006

Chambers, Marjorie Bell (1923-2006)
Historian, Educator, Congressional Candidate, Equal Rights Activist

Chambers, a cum laude graduate of Mount Holyoke College, who held an advanced degree from Cornell University, arrived in Los Alamos in 1950. She subsequently earned a Ph.D. from the University of New Mexico. Her dissertation was titled, *Technically Sweet Los Alamos: The Development of a Federally Sponsored Community* (1974). For many years she was active in the Girl Scouts of America, the League of Women Voters, the Los Alamos County Historical Society and the Santa Fe Opera Guild, among others. She served as national president of the American Association of University Women. Among her many educational endeavors, Chambers served on the University of New Mexico faculty and as President of Colorado Women's College. She worked at all levels in New Mexico Republican politics: from precinct captain to State Central Committee. She first ran for office in 1974 when she was elected to the Los Alamos County Council. She was re-elected in 1976. She won the Republican nomination for Congress in 1982 by beating Dwayne Jordan of Gallup. She was the first Republican woman in New Mexico to run for Congress. She lost to Democrat Bill Richardson. In 1986, she was also the first woman, in either party, to run for Lieutenant Governor of New Mexico. She lost to Jack Stahl in a very close Republican primary race. Chambers served in advisory capacities for several U. S. Presidents, both Republican and Democrat, including Gerald Ford, Jimmy Carter and Ronald Reagan. She also served in appointed positions under the administrations of several New Mexico governors.

The awards and recognition she received in a long career are too numerous to include here. As a politician, Marjorie Bell Chambers always followed her own conscience, and did what she believed best for the state and nation, never mind from whence came opposition. She offered a unique voice in New Mexico politics. She died at Los Alamos.

Albuquerque *Journal*, August 26, 2006
Albuquerque *Tribune*, August 26, 2006
Chambers for Congress Committee
Los Alamos County Republican Party
Sagamon State University, Interview, June 1985

Cháves, José Francisco (1833-1904)
New Mexico Soldier, Lawyer, District Attorney, Educator

José Francisco Cháves.
After Twitchell.

Col. J. Francisco Cháves, was the grandson of Francisco Xavier Cháves, who served as the first Mexican Governor of New Mexico in 1822. Well educated in St. Louis and New York, he returned to New Mexico in 1852. During that year and the next, he drove sheep to market in California. He participated in action against the Navajo in the years before the Civil War, and rose to the rank of Lt. Col. in the 1st New Mexico Infantry and served as commanding officer of Fort Wingate in western New Mexico. A Republican, he served in the New Mexico territorial legislature, representative to the U.S. Congress, District Attorney, Superintendent of Public Instruction and the territory's first official historian. Col. Cháves was assassinated at Pino's Wells in November 1904. His assassin was never identified.

Don Bullis, Rio Rancho *Observer* April 21, 2005
Sálaz-Márquez, *New Mexico*
A. Kenneth Stern and Dan D. Chávez, "New Mexico's Superintendency and the Superintendents of Public Instruction, 1891-1916," *New Mexico Historical Review*, Spring 2005
Tórrez, *UFOs*
Other literature abundant

Chávez, Amado (1851-1930)
New Mexico Educator

Chávez was born in Santa Fe and studied at St. Michaels College. He graduated from the National University Law School in Washington, D.C., in 1876. He was elected to the Territorial House of Representatives in 1884 and served as Speaker. He was New Mexico's first Territorial Superintendent of Public Education, appointed by Governor L. Bradford Prince (see entry) in 1891. He was reappointed twice by Governor William T. Thornton (see entry) in 1893 and again in 1895, serving until 1897. He also served as assistant superintendent and on the board of education. Governor Miguel Otero (see entry) appointed him to replace J. Francisco Cháves (see entry) after the latter's assassination in 1904. At Amado Chávez's death, the Santa Fe *New Mexican* described him this way: "…A consistent Republican; a gentleman in the true sense of the word; suave, obliging, courteous and polished and a hard worker; he is a finely educated man. He is a true, tried and trusted friend of the American public school system."

Mondragón & Stapleton, *Public Education*

A. Kenneth Stern & Dan D. Chávez, "New Mexico's Superintendency and the Superintendents of Public Instruction, 1891-1916," *New Mexico Historical Review*, Spring 2005

Chávez, Antonio José (d. 1843)
Santa Fe Trail Freighter

Antonio José Chávez left Santa Fe in February 1843 en route to Independence, Missouri, to purchase trade goods. He took five servants with him, along with two wagons, 55 mules, and a few furs. He carried $10,000 in bullion. What luck he had was all bad. He lost one of his wagons due to ill weather and 50 of his mules died. He was in dire straits by the time he reached Owl Creek, in what is now Lyons County in east central Kansas. There his luck turned much worse. A Texas brigand, who called himself "Captain" John McDaniel, had been commissioned by the Republic of Texas to organize a gang for the purpose of raiding Mexican caravans on the Santa Fe Trail. This was less than two years after Governor Manuel Armijo (see entry) had captured the Texas-Santa Fe Expedition in eastern New Mexico and sent its members off to prison in Mexico City. Historian Marc Simmons (see entry) writes that the gang of 15 men robbed Chávez, and while some of the thieves demurred, McDaniel murdered the merchant in cold blood. McDaniel and his brother, David, were subsequently arrested and hanged for their crime.

Duffus, *Santa Fe Trail*

Simons, *Murder*

Twitchell, *Leading Facts*, Vol. II

Chávez, Dennis (1888-1962)
U.S. Senator (1935-1962)

Dennis Chávez was born in Los Chávez, Valencia County, and attended the public schools. He graduated from law school at Georgetown University in Washington, D.C. and established a law practice in Albuquerque in 1920. He was first elected to the U.S. Congress in 1930 and served two terms. He ran for the U.S. Senate in 1934, but lost. Upon the death of Senator Bronson Cutting (see entry) in an airplane crash in May 1935, Governor Clyde Tingley (see entry) appointed Chávez to the U.S. Senate. He was then elected to the office in 1936, 1941, 1947, 1953, and 1959. A Democrat, he was generally a supporter of liberal causes and organized labor. Senator Chávez

Senator Dennis Chávez

developed a power base in Washington as chairman of the Public Works Committee and Defense Appropriations Subcommittee. Both allowed him to funnel federal money and projects to New Mexico. In the early 1950s, he was especially noted for his opposition to Senator Joseph McCarthy and the communist witch hunts. One newspaper columnist wrote: "Chávez knew thousands of his fellow New Mexicans by name, remembered details of their lives. He gave them the same advice he followed himself—get an education." Senator Chávez died of cancer in 1962. His statue was placed in Capitol Statuary Hall in Washington, D.C., in 1966. A stamp in his honor was issued in 1991.

Literature abundant

Chávez, Manuel Ezequiel "Fray Angélico" (1910-1996)
New Mexico Franciscan, Writer, Poet, Historian

The oldest of ten children, Fray Angélico was born in Wagon Mound, in north-eastern New Mexico. He was ordained as a Franciscan priest in Santa Fe in 1937 and assigned to the Parish at Peña Blanca where he ministered to the pueblos of Cochití, Santo Domingo and San Felipe. In 1939 his first book of poetry, *Clothed with the Sun*, was published in Santa Fe, and was well received by the literati of the day: Alice Corbin, Witter Byner (see entry), and John Gould Fletcher. He continued to publish poems in the late 1930s and early 1940s. He joined the U.S. Army as a chaplain in 1943 and participated in the World War II beachhead landings at both Guam and Leyte. He returned to Santa Fe after the war in 1946 and continued to publish short stories and poems. Around then, his interest changed to historical research. He became something of a protégé of France V. Scholes, noted University of New Mexico historian. He also continued to serve as parish priest at both Jémez Pueblo and Cerrillos before he became a full-time researcher and writer. Among the dozen or so books he wrote were biographies of three of New Mexico's most controversial clergymen: Padre Martínez of Taos (see entry), Padre Gallegos of Albuquerque, and Padre Juan Felipe Ortiz of Santa Fe (the latter with his nephew, Dr. Thomas E. Chávez, see entry). Professor Nasario García of New Mexico Highlands University wrote this upon the occasion of Fray Angélico's death: "In looking across time and space, Fray Angélico the poet, artist, historian, storyteller, archivist and Franciscan will always loom as the consummate humanist. His work, both within and outside the church, has left a legacy second to none and a memorable imprint for us and future generations to cherish and upon which to reflect for a long time to come."

McCracken, *Fray Angélico Chávez*
Nasario Garcia, "In Passing: Fray Angélico Chávez, 1910-1996," *New Mexico Historical Review*, July 1996

Chávez, Dr. Thomas E. (1948-)
Historian, Museum Administrator

Born in Las Vegas, New Mexico, Chávez received a Ph. D. from the University of New Mexico. He served as director of the Palace of the Governors in Santa Fe for 21 years and retired as Executive Director of the National Hispanic Cultural Center in Albuquerque. His published books include: *Conflict and Acculturation:*

Manuel Alvarez's 1841 Memorial (1989); *Manuel Alvarez, 1794-1856: A Southwestern Biography* (1990); *In Quest for Quivera: Spanish Exploration on the Plains, 1540-1821* (1992); *An Illustrated History of New Mexico* (1992); *Spain and the Independence of the United States: An Intrinsic Gift* (2002); also published in Spain as *España y la Independencia de Estados Unidos* (2006); and *Wake For A Fat Vicar: Padre Juan Felipe Ortiz, Archbishop Lamy and the New Mexican Catholic Church in the Middle of the Nineteenth Century,* with his uncle Fray Angélico Chávez (see entry) (2004). He is currently working on *New Mexico: Past and Future,* scheduled for publication in 2006, and *Benjamin Franklin in the Archives of Spain.* For his work

Thomas E. Chávez

over the years he has received the "Distinguished History Award Medal" from the Daughters of the American Revolution (1997), and the "Excellence in the Humanities Award" from the New Mexico Endowment for the Humanities. His work has also been recognized by the mayor of Santa Fe and the University of New Mexico Alumni Association.

Chávez, "Biography"

Chávez, Tibo J. (1912-1991)
New Mexico (State) Lieutenant Governor (1951-54), New Mexico State Senator (1948-1951 & 1954-1974), New Mexico District Court Judge, 13th District (1979-1991), New Mexico Author

Tibo Chávez was a native of Belen and a cousin to U.S. Senator Dennis Chávez (see entry). He attended Georgetown Law School, graduating in 1939. He spent most of his life in the practice of law and in public service, during the course of which he served in all three branches of government. A Democrat, he was elected to the state senate in 1948 and then served as Lieutenant Governor from 1951 to 1954. Chávez returned to the senate in 1954. He served for a total of 22 years in the senate, eight of them as Majority Leader. He was elected President of the Museum of New Mexico Board of Regents in 1975. Governor Bruce King (see entry) appointed him District Court Judge for the 13th Judicial District that included Valencia and Sandoval Counties in 1979. The district included Cibola County after it was created in 1981. He remained on the bench until his death. He also wrote, with Gilberto Espinosa, *El Rio Abajo,* a history of New Mexico's lower Rio Grande Valley, and *New Mexico Folklore of the Rio Abajo,* which offered numerous folk remedies and many *dichos.* He was an active member of the Historical Society of New Mexico and one of the founders of the Valencia County Historical Society. Tibo Chávez was well liked and a genuinely nice man.

Albuquerque *Journal,* June 19, 1975 & November 26, 1991 (*Other press accounts abundant*)
Espinosa & Chávez, *El Rio Abajo*
Jenkins, Myra Ellen, "Tibo J. Chávez 1912-1991, *La Crónica de Nuevo México,* April 1992
History of New Mexico: Family and Personal History

Chávez, Victoria "Vicky" (1953-1992)
Farmington Peace Officer

Working as a Community Services Officer for the Farmington, New Mexico, Police Department, Officer Vicky Chávez was shot and killed as she checked the residences of vacationing citizens. Her killer, Kevin Ogden, a fugitive, was quickly captured by State Police officers and subsequently sentenced to life in prison. Officer Chávez was the first female peace officer to be killed in the line of duty in New Mexico.

Bullis, *New Mexico's Finest*

Officer Victoria Chávez

Chino, Wendell (1924-1998)
President, Mescalero Apache Tribe

The fifth of eleven children, Wendell Chino was half Mescalero Apache and half Chiricahua Apache in heritage. He graduated from the Western Theological Seminary at Holland, Michigan, in 1951 and became an ordained minister of the Dutch Reformed Church and returned home to Mescalero. Not yet thirty years old, he became president of the tribe's Business Committee in the early 1950s. When the Mescalero tribal council was created in 1965, he was elected president. Except for four years, Chino held leadership positions in the tribal government until his death; a period of more than forty years. He is generally regarded as the leader who developed a viable economy for the Mescalero people. He fought and won the battles that resulted in the creation of the resort and gambling casino at The Inn of the Mountain Gods near Ruidoso. Chino was not, however, universally adored. Award-winning writer Eve Ball, who wrote extensively about the Mescalero people, visited Sam Chino one day during the winter of 1956. She wrote this: "I found him [Sam] living in a cave with a tarpaulin covering the south opening. His wife was dragging a dead log down the mountain to cut into wood. Wendell Chino, his son, was living in luxury in the best house in Mescalero."

Etulain, *New Mexican Lives*
Robinson, *Apache Voices*

Chisum, John Simpson (1824-1884)
"The Cattle King of New Mexico"

John Chisum was born in Madison County, Tennessee, and, at age 13, moved with his family to Lamar County in east Texas. As a young adult there he served a couple of terms as county clerk, but became engaged in the cattle business by 1854. After the Civil War, in 1865, he arrived in New Mexico with 600 head of cattle and settled at Bosque Grande, south of Fort Sumner. Ten years later,

John Simpson Chisum.
Courtesy Historical Society of Southeast New Mexico, No. 604-D.

when he moved his headquarters to Roswell, he claimed as his own a piece of land 150 miles long and 50 miles wide, which extended along the Rio Pecos. Called the "Cattle King of New Mexico," his herd varied in size from 80,000 to 100,000 head and his army of cowboys was up to 100 strong. He participated in the Lincoln County War to the extent that he entered into a partnership with John Henry Tunstall and Alexander McSween in a bank in the town of Lincoln, a venture strongly opposed by the power structure of the time. As a result, Chisum faced numerous lawsuits and even spent a few weeks in jail. By the late 1870s he realized that the days of free land and open range were coming to an end and he began selling off his stock. Chisum, never married, fathered two daughters by a slave woman named Jensie: Harriet and Meady. Harriet disappeared from history at a young age, but Meady is known to have married former slave Bob Jones—a very successful rancher—and to have had ten children by him. Many of their descendants live in the Fort Worth-Grapevine area of Texas. John Chisum died at Eureka Springs, Arkansas. Most sources agree that the cause was a large tumor on his neck, but one writer holds that it was stomach cancer. He left an estate of about $500,000. His body was returned to Lamar County for burial.

Curry, *Autobiography*
Elvis Fleming, "John Chisum's Negro Children," *Treasures of History II*, Chaves County
    Historical Society, 1991
Larson, *Forgotten Frontier*
Metz, *Shooters*
Thrapp, *Encyclopedia*
Other literature abundant

Chivington, John Milton (1821-1894)
Colorado Military Officer

Major John Chivington became something of a hero to New Mexicans when, in early 1862, as a part of the Colorado Volunteers, he led a flanking movement during the Battle of Glorieta that resulted in the destruction of vast amounts of Confederate supplies and ammunition at Johnson Ranch. This effort resulted in the defeat of the Texans and saved New Mexico from occupation by Confederate forces. The invaders soon retreated back from whence they came. Less than three years later, in November 1864, Chivington completely disgraced himself as the army commander who led the attack and massacre of at least 150 Cheyenne Indian men, women, and children at Sand Creek in eastern Colorado.

John Milton Chivington.
After Twitchell.

Alberts, *Battle of Glorieta*
Brown, *The American West*
Thrapp, *Encyclopedia*
Other literature abundant

Christian, Robert, aka Tom Anderson (1868-?)
Southwestern Outlaw

Bob was Will Christian's brother (see entry). He was a member of the High Fives outlaw gang. He disappeared into Mexico in the late 1890s and was not heard of again.

Simmons, *Ranchers*
Tanner, *Musgrave*

Christian, William T. "Will" "Black Jack" (1871-1897)
Southwestern Outlaw

Will Christian was one of two or three New Mexico outlaws who went by the name "Black Jack," the others being Tom Ketchum (see entry) and his brother Sam (see entry). A native of Texas, Will and his brother, Bob, got their introduction to crime in Oklahoma before they arrived in New Mexico and Arizona. Some writers consider him the leader of the High Fives gang, but other historians believe that leadership of the gang changed on an *ad hoc* basis. Will Christian was killed by a posse led by Deputy U.S. Marshal Fred Higgins (see entry) of Roswell, New Mexico, near Cole Creek, Arizona, on April 28, 1897.

Simmons, *Ranchers*
Tanner, *Musgrave*
Other literature abundant

Church, Peggy Pond (1903-1986)
Santa Fe Author/Poet

Peggy Church, a native of Mora County, lived at Los Alamos in the 1920s and 1930s. She is best remembered for *The House at Otowi Bridge; the Story of Edith Warner of Los Alamos* (1960). It is considered a classic of New Mexico literature. She also wrote *When Los Alamos was a Ranch School; Historical Profile of Fermor and Peggy Pond Church* (1974). She produced numerous books of poetry and a collection of her poems, called *This Dancing Ground of Sky*, was published six years after her death.

"Review," *Book Talk*, New Mexico Book League, Sept. 1993
Peggy Pond Church, "Writer's Editions 1933-1939: Some Distant Recollections," *Book Talk*, New Mexico Book League, February 1982
Mike Shearer, "Peggy Pond Church: an 'octogeranium' speaks," *New Mexico Magazine*, February 1985

Clark, Walter Van Tilburg (1909-1971)
Nevada Novelist

A native of Maine, Clark was educated at the University of Nevada. He resided in Taos for seven or so months in 1946. T. N. Luther reports that there is no evidence that he did much creatively during that time. He was in New Mexico because he had tuberculosis and because Mabel Dodge Luhan (see entry) invited him, as she had so many other writers and graphic artists. Clark's most famous books are *The Ox-Bow Incident* (1940) and *Track of the Cat* (1949), both set in Nevada, but he wrote several others. He died at Reno.

Charles Brashear, "Remembering Walter Van Tilburg Clark," *Roundup Magazine*, April
2006
Luther, T. N. "Collecting Taos Writers," *Book Talk*, New Mexico Book League, Sept. 1992

Cleaveland, Norman (1901-1997)
Descendant of Catron County Ranchers

Norman was the son of Agnes Morley Cleaveland who wrote *No Life For a Lady*
(1941), an account of Catron County ranch life around the turn of the century
in 1901. Norman attended Stanford University where he studied engineering. He
also won a place on the 1924 Olympic rugby team, a team that won the gold medal
by defeating France. His own life was one of adventure in the mining camps of
Malaya. He became convinced that the death of his grandfather, William Morley,
the official result of an accidental gun discharge, was actually murder at the hands
of the Santa Fe Ring. He endeavored to interest historians in the matter—even addressing the Historical Society of New Mexico at an advanced age—but was never
able to do so. He resided in Santa Fe the last years of his life.

Sharon Niederman, "Interview," *Santa Fe Reporter*, July 28-August 3, 1993
Marc Simmons, "Loss of an Old Warrior," *Book Talk*, New Mexico Book League, July 1997
Marc Simmons, "A Man Steeped in History," *Santa Fe New Mexican*, March 18, 2006

Clever, Charles P. (1827-1874)
New Mexico U.S. Marshal (1857 and 1861), New Mexico Adjutant General (1861-1865 and 1867), New Mexico Attorney General (1862-1867), New Mexico Territorial Representative to Congress (1867-1869)

Clever was born in Cologne, Prussia (now Germany), and educated there and
at the University of Bonn. He immigrated to the U.S. and settled in Santa Fe, New
Mexico, in 1850. He held several jobs, including that of Santa Fe constable, deputy
U.S. Marshal, and U.S. Marshal, while he read law, and was admitted to the bar
in 1861. In addition to the political offices he held, he also served as editor of the
Santa Fe *Weekly Gazette*, which was published in both English and Spanish. He was
a merchant and he practiced law. He died at Tomé, in Valencia County, and is interred at the National Cemetery in Santa Fe. Twitchell (see entry) says of him, "He
was a man of great strength of character; had many friends and many enemies."
Historian Lamar described him as "wily."

Ball, *The United States Marshals*
Lamar, *Far Southwest*
Remley, *Adios Nuevo Mexico*
Twitchell, *Leading Facts*, Vol. II

Clifton, J. M. "Jim" (1903-1932)
Lea County Deputy Sheriff

Lea County Deputy Sheriff Jim Clifton stopped a car near Tatum, New Mexico,
in which he believed were riding three armed robbers. They shortly produced guns
and began shooting, severely wounding the deputy. He was able to return fire and
kill two of the outlaws. The third escaped. Clifton died later the same date, February 24, 1932. The local press said this: "In his passing, law and order in New

Mexico have lost a champion; in his passing a place has been made vacant that cannot be filled…the mould in which he was cast has been broken, and the like of him, in these parts, will never be duplicated. We liked him."
Bullis, *New Mexico's Finest*

Cobos, Dr. Rubén (1911-)
New Mexico Educator/Linguist

Dr. Cobos was born in Mexico and arrived in Albuquerque in 1929. He graduated from Menaul School as valedictorian and then attended the University of New Mexico where he received a Master's degree in Spanish in 1936. He elected to teach at Wagon Mound and remained there for a year before he was recruited to teach at Highlands University. He remained there until he was drafted during World War II. He joined the faculty at the University of New Mexico in 1945 and remained there until he retired in 1976; all the while writing books on languages, particularly Spanish. "The interest," he said, "came from going into all the small villages of northern New Mexico. I'd hear sixteenth-century Spanish. My students spoke it." Among many other works, he wrote *Refranes: españoles del sudoeste* (*Southwestern Spanish Proverbs*) in 1973 and *A Dictionary of New Mexico Southern Colorado Spanish*, Second edition, 2003.
Hughes, *Albuquerque*

Colfax, Schuyler (1823-1885)
U.S. Vice-President

Colfax was born in New York City and moved to Indiana as a young man. He entered the newspaper business and became active in Whig politics. He served in the U.S. House of Representatives from 1854 until 1868, when he was elected Vice-president under President Ulysses S. Grant (see entry). He was not re-nominated in 1872. He was implicated in the Crédit Mobilier of America scandal that became public in 1872-73. Colfax County New Mexico, created in 1869, is named for him.
Julyan, *The Place Names of New Mexico*
New Mexico Blue Book, 2003-2004
Literature abundant

Colyer, Vincent (1824-1888)
New Mexico & Arizona Indian Peace Negotiator

Born in New York, Colyer trained as an artist and became a highly paid portrait and landscape painter. During the Civil War he commanded a regiment of Black troops and later became enamored of humanitarian causes. When President Ulysses S. Grant's (see entry) "Peace Policy" was put into place in 1869, Colyer was named secretary of the Board of Indian Commissioners. He visited New Mexico and Arizona to make peace with the Apaches and to create a system of Indian reservations. He was not successful in brokering a lasting peace, but he was responsible for the reservations pretty much as they exist today. He returned to painting for his livelihood after he left the Indian Commission and died in Connecticut.

Lamar, *The Far Southwest*
Thrapp, *Encyclopedia*
Utley, *Frontier Regulars*

Conklin, A. M. (d. 1880)
Socorro Newspaper Editor

Conklin began publication of the Socorro *Sun* in 1880. He'd shipped his printing press from Albuquerque to Socorro on a raft down the Rio Grande. On Christmas Eve of that year, for no good reason, he was shot and killed by some local toughs as he and his wife left church services. One outlaw was quickly shot to death and another was hanged by local vigilantes, known locally as *"los colgadores"* (the hangers). An Albuquerque newspaper said this in reporting the matter: "Moral: 'Tis a bad thing to assassinate editors in New Mexico."
Bullis, *99 New Mexicans*

Connelly, Henry (1800-1866)
Governor (Territorial) of New Mexico (1861-1866)

Historian Ralph Emerson Twitchell (see entry) indicates that Henry Connelly was born and educated in Kentucky; David Remley says he was born in Virginia but does agree that Connelly was one of the first graduates of the medical school at Transylvania University at Lexington, Kentucky. Connelly soon moved on to Missouri and then to Chihuahua, Mexico, where he entered the mercantile trade. He married there in 1838, but his wife died some years later after producing three children, which he removed to Missouri. He was present in Santa Fe at the time Gen. Stephen Watts Kearny (see entry) occupied New Mexico for the United States (August 1846), and he acted as an agent for Manuel Armijo (see entry), the last Mexican Governor of New Mexico, in negotiations with trader James Magoffin (see entry) and Captain Philip St. George Cooke (see entry). He relocated to Santa Fe in 1848. He

Gov. Henry Connelly. After Twitchell.

married Dolores Perea de Chaves, the widow of Mariano Chaves, and thus became the stepfather of Col. J. Francisco Cháves (see entry). He was so much a part of the Mexican culture that he changed his name to *Enrique Conele*. He became a member of the Territorial Council in 1851 and President Abraham Lincoln (see entry) named him Governor in 1861. Twitchell says this: "He was an intensely loyal man during the Civil War, and it was largely through his influence that the leading citizens of New Mexico refused to ally themselves with the Confederates under General Sibley (see entry). His services to the territory deserve a monument." The lavish home Connelly and his wife shared at Peralta, northeast of Los Lunas, was largely destroyed by retreating Confederate troops in early 1862. A surviving doorway to that house may be viewed at the Albuquerque Museum's Casa San Ysidro facility in Corrales, New Mexico. Bishop Jean B. Lamy (see entry) conducted the

Governor's funeral service. He was interred at Rosario Cemetery.

Lamar, *Far Southwest*

Darlis A. Miller, "Hispanos and the Civil War in New Mexico: A Reconsideration," *New Mexico Historical Review*, April 1979

Simmons, *Albuquerque*

Marc Simmons, "Governor Connelly's Hacienda," *Prime Time*, March 2006

Remley, *Adios Nuevo Mexico*

Twitchell, *Leading Facts*, Vol. II

Cooke, Philip St. George (1809-1895)
U.S. Army Officer/Mormon Battalion Commander

Philip St. George Cooke.
After Twitchell.

A native of Virginia, Cooke graduated from West Point in 1827. His first assignment to the frontier came in 1829 when he and his troops were assigned to guard the Santa Fe Trail at the Arkansas River. He later fought in the Black Hawk War (1832) and was a Captain in General Stephen Watts Kearny's (see entry) Army of the West. He, along with Santa Fe trader James Magoffin (see entry), negotiated with Manuel Armijo (see entry), the governor of New Mexico, before the arrival of Kearny's troops in August 1846. It was rumored that Cooke and Magoffin offered the governor a bribe, but that has never been proved.

The Mormon Battalion—about 400 men in five infantry companies—arrived in Santa Fe in October 1846 and was placed under Cooke's command. The unit continued south along the Rio Grande and then southwest into what became Arizona. The purpose of the battalion's line of march was the establishment of a wagon road from Santa Fe to California. The Mormons arrived in California in late January 1847. Cooke's Canyon, Cooke's Peak, and Cooke's Spring are all named for Philip St. George Cooke. Cooke's Canyon, northwest of Deming, came to be called "the journey of death" by soldiers because of the many Apache Indian attacks along its three-mile length. Cooke wrote two books: *Scenes and Adventures in the Army* and *Conquest of New Mexico and California*. He retired in 1873.

Charles Bennett, "Expedition of Courage, The Mormon Battalion's March to the Pacific," *New Mexico Magazine*, March 2003

Juanita Brooks, ed., "Diary of the Mormon Battalion Mission by John D. Lee," *New Mexico Historical Review*, July 1967

Julyan, *Place Names*

Fugate & Fugate, *Roadside History*

Twitchell, *Leading Facts*, Vol. II

Coolidge, Calvin (1872-1933)
President of the United States (1923-1929)

On October 25, 1923, President Coolidge signed a proclamation that created Carlsbad Cave National Monument.

Barnett, *Carlsbad Caverns*

Cooper, David (1918-2005)
Albuquerque Businessman

Cooper was born in British Columbia, Canada, but raised in Denver. After service in the U.S. Army Air Corps during World War II, he opened Kilroy's, an army surplus store, which evolved into Cooper's Western Wear and then to Western Warehouse. He and his wife, Martha (*née* Rosenblum), were noted for their philanthropic activities. He was the father of noted Albuquerque attorney Roberta Cooper Ramo.

Paul Logan, "Western Warehouse Founder Believed in Charity," Albuquerque *Journal*,
    October 12, 2005
News accounts abundant

Copeland, John N. (c.1851-1903)
Lincoln County Sheriff

A native of Kentucky, Copeland had a somewhat checkered career. He was one of the shortest-serving sheriffs in New Mexico history, serving from April 8, until May 28, 1878. He was appointed to the job after Sheriff William Brady (see entry) was assassinated on April 1 and his service ended when Governor Samuel Axtell (see entry) removed him from office in late May. He was thought to be a McSween (see entry) partisan in the Lincoln County War. Copeland also worked as a butcher, hotelkeeper and lawyer. He died in Lincoln County.

Nolan, *Bad Blood*
Ball, *Desert Lawmen*
Fleming, *J.B. Mathews*

Córdoba, Doña Ana María de (fl. 1693)
Doña Ana County Rancher

Doña Ana María de Córdoba may have inspired the name of Doña Ana County. Robert Julyan cites Adolphe Bandelier, who found 1693 mention of her in a report on Indian raids: "The raiders ... going on to a place called Las Cruces, and stealing stock also at Mesilla, then raiding the ranch of Doña Ana María, Niña de Córdoba." It is also possible that Doña Ana County was named for Doña Ana Robledo (see entry).

Julyan, *Place Names*

Corn, Jasper (1840-1884)
Lincoln County Deputy Sheriff

A Lincoln County deputy under Sheriff John Poe (see entry), Jasper Corn was shot and killed by horse thief Nicholas Aragon during a brief gunfight near Anton Chico. Aragon subsequently killed a second Lincoln County deputy, Johnny Hurley (see entry), in January 1885. Aragon served about ten years in prison for his crimes. Jasper was the brother of Martin Corn (see entry).

Bullis, *New Mexico's Finest*

Corn, Martin Van Buren "Mart" (1841-1915)
Chaves County Pioneer Farmer

Martin Corn was one of the pioneer settlers in the area around what is now Roswell and Chaves County. He arrived there in the late 1870s and became a successful farmer who worked the land up until the time of his death. Married twice, he fathered 21 children between 1868 and 1913. The Corn family remains prominent in southeastern New Mexico.

Larson, *Forgotten Frontier*
Patterson, *The Rock House Ranch*

Coronado, Francisco Vásquez de (1510-1554)
Explorer

Don Francisco de Coronado was the first European to do extensive exploration of what is now New Mexico. Born in Salamanca, Spain, he arrived in the New World in 1535 and by 1538 he had been named governor of Nueva Galicia in western Mexico. When the viceroy of New Spain, Antonio de Estrada, sponsored an expedition north in search of the so-called Seven Cities of Cibola, which had been described by Cabeza de Vaca, Estevánico, and Fray Marcos de Niza (see respective entries), he named Coronado commander. Along with nearly 300 soldiers, mounted and afoot, and nearly 1,000 Mexican Indians driving 1,500 head of cattle, goats and sheep, the army set out in late February 1540. The way north, by way of Zuñi Pueblo in what is now western New Mexico, was slow and arduous. What was probably the first conflict between Europeans and Native Americans took place when Zuñi Indians set upon Coronado and some of his men at the village of Hawikuh in early August 1540. Coronado was injured in the melee. The army continued its march and arrived at Tiguex, near the present town of Bernalillo, in December. Again the indigenous people resisted the occupation of their villages by strangers, and they launched what came to be called the Tiguex War. The Indians were out-matched by Spanish firearms and armor and an estimated 200 of them were killed. In April 1541, Coronado continued his exploration, probably traveling as far to the east as what is now the Palo Duro Canyon in the Texas Panhandle and as far north as central Kansas. He found no riches, of course, and returned to Tiguex for the winter. In the spring of 1542, after Coronado was injured while participating in a horse race, some of his officers petitioned for a return to Mexico and the march south began in April. The expedition had traveled about 4,000 miles and had nothing to show for the effort. After his return, Coronado was charged with a variety of offenses relating to his administration of Nuevo Galicia, including neglect of duty and the use of slave labor. He was convicted and removed from office, although he was later reinstated. In 1543 he was charged with a variety of offenses having to do with his management of the expedition to the north, including waging war and perpetrating "great cruelties" upon the Indians he had encountered. He was cleared of those charges and the matter was dropped. Coronado remained active in public affairs but his health declined and he died in 1554 at the age of 44 years. Historian Dan Thrapp writes this: "Coronado was an able leader, strict though scarcely a martinet. He was bold, brave in action and a man not entirely without mercy toward his enemies, although he could be ruthless in the manner of the day."

Crutchfield, *It Happened in New Mexico*
Ellis, *New Mexico Past & Present*
Etulain, *Beyond the Missouri*
Flint & Flint, eds., *The Coronado Expedition*
Simmons, *New Mexico*
Thrapp, *Encyclopedia*

Couse, Eanger Irving (1866-1936)
Painter, Charter Member of the Taos Society of Artists

A native of Saginaw, Michigan, Couse painted houses as a young man to earn enough money to attend the Art Institute of Chicago. He also studied at the National Academy of Design and at the Julian Académie in Paris. He spent a number of years living and painting in Oregon and on the coast of Normandy. Because Joseph Sharp (see entry) and Ernest Blumenschein (see entry) recommended it, Couse visited Taos in 1902 and thereafter spent his summers in New Mexico. When the Taos Society of Artists was organized in 1915, Couse was elected the first president. He moved to The Land of Enchantment permanently in 1927. Couse spent a lot of time painting Taos Pueblo people. They called him "Green Mountain" because of his stature and because he frequently wore a green sweater. He produced about 1,500 paintings during his lifetime. He died in Albuquerque.

Coke, *Taos and Santa Fe*
Meadowlark Gallery: The Artists Biographies
Nelson, *Legendary Artists of Taos*
Samuels, *The Illustrated Biographical Encyclopedia*
Schimmel & White, *Bert Geer Phillips*
Witt, *The Taos Artists*

Cox, Daniel Ronald "Ronny" (1938-)
Actor, Musician

Ronny Cox was born in Cloudcroft and raised in Portales, New Mexico. He was educated at Eastern New Mexico University, also in Portales. He began a film-acting career in 1972 with *Deliverance* in which he played Drew Ballinger and participated in the famed dueling banjos scene. He has had roles in more than 20 pictures and is probably best remembered for his roles as villain executive in both *Robocop* (1987) and *Total Recall* (1990). He also played on television's *St. Elsewhere* in 1987-88. Cox is

Daniel Ronald Cox

a guitarist and songwriter who tours and regularly appears in theaters and at folk music festivals.

Katz, *Film Encyclopedia*
Maltin, *Movie Encyclopedia*

Cox, William Webb "W.W." (1854-1923)
Doña Ana County Rancher

Cox owned the San Augustine Ranch on the east slope of the Organ Mountains in southern New Mexico. It was adjacent to a ranch owned by Pat Garrett (see entry) in the early years of the 20th century. Some believe that Cox was somehow involved in Garrett's murder in 1908, but no hard evidence has ever been produced. Most of the San Augustine Ranch became part of the White Sands Missile Range after 1945.

Keleher, *Fabulous Frontier*
Pete Ross, "Some Prominent New Mexicans May Have Been Accessories to the Murder of Pat Garrett," *Wild West*, Dec. 2001
Other literature abundant

Crockett, David "Davy" (1853-1876)
Colfax County Rancher/Killer

There is no evidence that Davy Crockett of Alamo fame ever visited New Mexico. His grandson (or maybe he was a nephew) did, though, and left a small mark behind. Young Davy arrived in New Mexico by the mid-1870s and took up a ranch near Cimarron. Ranch work didn't seem to agree with him and he soon gave it up in favor of drunkenness and rowdy behavior. According to Chuck Parsons, in March 1876, Crockett and Gus Hefron shot and killed three Buffalo Soldiers—Privates George Small, John Hanson and Anthony Harvey—in a Cimarron saloon, and he was only convicted of "carrying arms" and fined $50.00. According to Will Keleher (see entry), the shooting took place in May, and the victims were John Black, Charles Morris and Pomeron W. Laughlin. Both agree that Crockett and Hefron spent the next five or six months drinking and harassing the Cimarron citizenry. On October 1 (Bryan says September 30) of the same year, Colfax County Sheriff Isaiah Rinehart and two deputies finally confronted the situation, and when the smoke cleared, young Crockett was dead and Hefron was wounded. One observer of the time wrote that Crockett and Hefron had become "insane from whiskey." (Note: A number of writers have indicated that famed "Shootist" Clay Allison [see entry] was involved in killing the Black troopers. Evidence clearly indicates, however, that he was not.)

Bullis, *99 New Mexicans*
Bryan, *Robbers, Rouges and Ruffians*
Keleher, *The Maxwell Land Grant*
Parsons, *Clay Allison*
Other literature abundant

Crosby, John O. (1926-2002)
Founder of the Santa Fe Opera

John Crosby was born in New York City to wealthy parents. He received his early education in New York and Connecticut and attended the Los Alamos Boys School, near Santa Fe. He served in the U. S. military during World War II and then studied music theory at Yale University. He later attended Columbia University while he worked as a musical arranger on Broadway in New York City. Crosby became aware that opportunities for aspiring opera singers were limited; he undertook to create an opera company, and he chose Santa Fe as the location. He said, "[Santa Fe] was a community that had a flourishing art colony: painters, poets, writers, sculptors. And strangely from that galaxy of the arts, music was rather missing. So it seemed

John O. Crosby

to me that the community would receive this missing link warmly." The original facility, with fewer than 500 seats, was constructed about seven miles north of Santa Fe, and opened on July 3, 1957 with a performance of Puccini's *Madame Butterfly*, conducted by Crosby. Writer Anne Hillerman notes, "The Santa Fe Opera achieved international stature soon after its inception. The fame is due to the high-quality performances and the company's sense of adventure in tackling new and rare works." The structure burned in 1967 and was rebuilt to accommodate nearly 1,900 music lovers. It was completely redesigned and rebuilt again in 1997, to seat more than 2,100. The operating budget for the Santa Fe Opera in 1957 was about $110,000; for 2002, the year of Cosby's death, it was about $14,000,000. The Apprentice Program for Singers was established in 1957 and continues to this day. In 1991, President George Bush awarded Crosby the National Medal of the Arts for "giving young American artists the opportunity to train and perform in their own country." Crosby received numerous awards in his career, including five honorary doctorates and he was guest conductor with many opera companies around the world. He was the longest-serving opera director in the United States when he retired in 2000. Many consider the Opera to be Santa Fe's premier summer attraction, and it is thanks to John Crosby.
Anne Hillerman, *Insiders Guide to Santa Fe*
Tobias & Woodhouse, *Santa Fe, A Modern History 1880-1990*
Other literature abundant

Crumbo, Woodrow Wilson "Woody" (1912-1989)
Taos/Cimarron Artist

Biographer Slim Randles writes: "Woody's father died in 1916 when Woody was four, and Woody's mother, a Potawatomi Indian from Oklahoma, died when he was seven. For several months, [he] lived in a cave on the reservation and made out the best he could…. Then one day he was 'caught' by an older Creek Indian man and taken home with him to be raised. He was sent to the American Indian Institute in Wichita, Kansas, and later to Wichita University. By the time he met Max Evans (see entry) [in Taos in the early 1950s] he was a renowned painter, a well-known crafter of Indian jewelry, a flute player good enough to solo with the Wichita Symphony, and an accomplished dancer." Famed New Mexico painter and writer Max Evans and Crumbo remained friends until Crumbo's death. Crumbo operated a studio and gallery in Cimarron during the last years of his life.
Randles, *Ol' Max*

Cubero, Pedro Rodríguez (1656-1704)
Governor (Spanish) of New Mexico (1697-1703)
Governor Cubero succeeded Don Diego de Vargas (see entry) as Spanish governor of New Mexico. A great antipathy soon developed between the two men and Cubero imprisoned de Vargas for three years on charges filed by the *cabildo* (town council) of Santa Fe. When de Vargas was exonerated and reappointed governor, Cubero announced a campaign against hostile Indians and fled New Mexico, fearing retaliation. The village of Cubero in Cibola County may be named for this governor. Robert Julyan writes, "Cubero passed through here in 1697 on an expedition to Zuñi, and it's possible the name originated then."

Julyan, *Place Names*
Thrapp, *Encyclopedia*
Twitchell, *Leading Facts*, Vol. I

Cuerno Verde "Green Horn" (d. 1779)
Comanche Indian Chief
According to historian Dan Thrapp, Cuerno Verde was "One of the greatest Comanche chiefs of the 18th century." He is said to have hated the Spaniards because they killed his father in battle. He led numerous raids against Spanish colonists in northern New Mexico. Spanish Colonial Governor Juan Bautista de Anza (see entry) wrote of him, "[he] exterminated many towns, killing hundreds and making as many prisoners whom he afterwards sacrificed in cold blood." Anza mounted a campaign against Cuerno Verde in the summer of 1779 and faced him in a significant battle in early September near what is now Walsenburg, Colorado. Cuerno Verde was killed along with his son and several important sub-chiefs. This defeat so dispirited the Comanches that the raiding stopped and they subsequently entered into a long-lasting peace agreement with the Spanish.

Roberts & Roberts, *New Mexico*
Simmons, *New Mexico*
Thrapp, *Encyclopedia*

Cuervo y Valdés, Don Francisco (fl. 1678-1707)
Governor (Spanish) of New Mexico (1705-1707), Albuquerque Pioneer
According to historian Marc Simmons, Cuervo was born into the nobility of northern Spain. He arrived in Sonora, Mexico, in 1678. He was appointed governor in 1704 and arrived in Santa Fe the following year. He wrote this to King Philip V: "I have never seen so much want, misery, and backwardness in my life. I suspect this land was better off before the Spaniards came." One wonders how concerned Philip V could have been with the state of affairs in Santa Fe, on the New World frontier, when Spain was at that time engaged in the War of Spanish Succession (1702-1713) in Europe. It was Cuervo y Valdés who founded Albuquerque on April 23, 1706.

Bryan, *Albuquerque*
García, *Albuquerque*
Julyan, *Place Names*
Simmons, *Hispanic Albuquerque*

Curry, George (1861-1947)
Governor (Territorial) of New Mexico (1907-1910), U.S. Congressman (1912-1913)

George Curry was born in Louisiana and arrived in New Mexico as a teenager in 1879. He worked on a cattle ranch for a couple of years before he became a trader at Fort Stanton. He began a life of public service in 1886 when he became deputy treasurer of Lincoln County. Subsequently he served as assessor, clerk and sheriff and was elected to the territorial council (similar to the modern senate) in 1894, all as a Democrat. He was a member of Teddy Roosevelt's Rough Riders during the Spanish-American War (1898)—although he saw no action in Cuba—after which he became a Republican. He served in several capacities in the Philippines from 1899 to 1907. President Theodore Roosevelt appointed Curry to the governorship of New Mexico in replacement of Herbert J. Hagerman (see entry), and he immediately set about reconciling the rifts within the Territorial Republican Party.

Gov. George Curry. After Twitchell.

Curry became one of New Mexico's first Congressmen, but did not seek re-election to that office. He was the state's historian at the time of his death. Curry County in eastern New Mexico is named for him. Clovis is the county seat.

Curry, *An Autobiography*
Lamar, *Far Southwest*
Robert W. Larson, "Ballinger vs. Rough Rider George Curry: The Other Feud," *New Mexico Historical Review*, October 1968
Paul A. F. Walter, "Necrology," *New Mexico Historical Review*, April 1948
Other literature abundant

Cusey, Mildred Clark "Madam Millie" (1912-1993)
Southern New Mexico Brothel Owner

Millie arrived in New Mexico in the 1920s for the purpose of taking care of her tubercular sister. She soon learned that she could earn more money working as a prostitute than she could as a Harvey Girl. From there it was only a short step into the brothel business. Her Silver City business was "protected" for all of the years it existed. Millie spoke of visits from State Police officers, liaisons with sheriffs and police chiefs. She claimed to have contacts, intimate and otherwise, with judges, legislators, and other high-ranking public officials.

Evans, *Madam Millie*

Cushing, Frank Hamilton (1857-1900)
Zuñi Archeologist/Ethnologist

A native of Pennsylvania, Cushing developed an interest in Indian artifacts and published a paper on the subject when he was only 17. He attended Cornell University before he participated in an expedition to the Southwest in 1879 and became interested in Zuñi Pueblo. During the course of his study of the Pueblo, he mastered the language and sufficiently adopted Indian ways that he was admitted into the tribe, and, according to him, a secret society. The Zuñi people were furious when they learned that Cushing's primary interest was learning their ways so that he could tell the world their secrets, and he did so while he was among them (*Century* magazine Dec. 1882 and Feb. 1883). Beginning in 1884 he spent time in the East, although he returned to the Southwest several times before his death. He wrote no books during his lifetime, but did publish a plethora of scholarly items. In 1941 a volume made up of two of his articles was published as *My Adventures in Zuñi*. In 1979 the University of Nebraska Press published a book, entitled *Zuñi*, that included his selected writings. In 1990 the University of New Mexico published, *Cushing at Zuñi: The Correspondence and Journals of Frank Hamilton Cushing, 1879-1884*, edited by Jesse Green. Cushing died at Washington, D.C., from choking on a fish bone.

Keleher, *Fabulous Frontier*
Thrapp, *Encyclopedia*

Cutting, Bronson Murray (1888-1935)
Santa Fe Newspaper Editor, U.S. Senator (1929-35)

Born in Oakdale, Suffolk County (Long Island) New York, Cutting was educated at the Groton School and Harvard where he was admitted to Phi Beta Kappa. He arrived in New Mexico in 1910, on a stretcher, suffering greatly from tuberculosis. Within two years he was well enough to purchase the Santa Fe *New Mexican*. He also became interested in politics and served as treasurer of the Bull Moose Party, which existed only to support the presidential candidacy of Theodore Roosevelt in 1912. He was also well enough to serve in the army during World War I. He returned to the *New Mexican* after the war and redoubled his political activities. In the 1924 election Cutting supported Democrat Arthur Hannett for governor, but he became disenchanted with Hannett and in the 1926 election he supported Republican Richard Dillon. Dillon won. When U.S. Senator Andrieus A. Jones (see entry) died in office in 1927, Dillon appointed Cutting to replace him. Cutting was elected in his own right in 1929, as a Republican, but that didn't prevent his support of Democrat Arthur Seligman for Governor in 1930. He also supported Franklin Roosevelt for President in 1932. Election of Seligman and Roosevelt put New Mexico in the Democratic column, according to former Republican Congressman George Curry (see entry). Cutting defeated Democratic challenger Dennis Chávez (see entry) in the 1934 general election without a reciprocal endorsement from President Roosevelt. Chávez challenged the election's outcome, but that became academic when Cutting was killed in an airplane crash (TWA Flight 6) near Atlanta, Missouri, on May 6, 1935. Governor

Senator Bronson Murray Cutting

Clyde Tingley (see entry) then appointed Chávez to the seat. That Cutting rose from a virtual deathbed to become one of the most powerful men in New Mexico is a remarkable story.

Albuquerque *Journal*, May 7 – 11, 1935

J. D. Arnold, "Senator Bronson Cutting," *New Mexico Magazine*, May 2003

Congressional Biography

T. Phillip Wolf, "Bronson Cutting and Franklin Roosevelt: Factors in Presidential Endorsement, *New Mexico Historical Review*, October 1977

T. Phillip Wolf, "Cutting vs Chavez Re-Examined," *New Mexico Historical Review*, October 1972 (also see "Cutting vs. Chavez: A Reply to Wolf's Comments," by William H. Pickens; and "The Purge That Failed," by G. L. Seligmann, Jr., in the same issue)

-D-

Da, Popovi "Po" (1923-1971)
San Ildefonso Tribal Governor, Artist, Potter

The son of famed potter, Maria Martínez (see entry), he was named Tony Martinez at birth at San Ildefonso Pueblo, but legally adopted his Pueblo name, Popovi Da, which translates as Red Fox. He graduated from the Santa Fe Indian School in 1939 and served in the U. S. Army during World War II. He was elected Pueblo Governor in 1952 and was later elected Chairman of the All Indian Pueblo Council. Artistically, he painted designs on his mother's pots. He developed a two-color firing process that resulted in the distinctive black-on-black pottery for which is mother was renowned. Popovi Da's own work may be found in a number of collections across the United States, including the Millicent Rogers Museum in Taos. One of his murals may be seen at Maisel's Trading Post in Albuquerque.

Brody, *Pueblo Indian Painting*
Sando, *Pueblo Profiles*

Daily, Bill (1928-)
Television Actor

A native of Iowa, Bill Daily aspired to a musical career but found success playing second banana in several television situation comedies, most notably *I Dream of Jeannie* (1965-1970) with Barbara Eden and Larry Hagman and *The Bob Newhart Show* (1972-1978) with Newhart and Suzanne Pleshette. He also starred in his own sitcom, *Starting From Scratch* (1988-1989) with Connie Stevens. He appeared in two movies, a remake of *In Name Only* (1969) and *The Barefoot Executive* (1971). Daily retired in Albuquerque where he has appeared in a number of Little Theater productions.

Brooks & Marsh, *The Complete Directory*

Daniels, Bill (1921-2000)
Aviator/Businessman/Philanthropist

A native of Hobbs, New Mexico, and a graduate of the New Mexico Military Institute, Daniels enlisted in the U.S. Navy in 1941 and became a fighter pilot,

flying off the carriers U.S.S. Intrepid and U.S.S. Sangamon during World War II. He was awarded both the Bronze Star and the Air Medal before he left the Navy in 1952 with the rank of Commander. Daniels was very successful in the business world; a pioneer in cable television. He was owner of several sports teams, president of the American Basketball Association, and a founder of the U.S. Football League. He founded the Daniels Fund in 1997. It became the largest charity in the Rocky Mountain region. As a resident of Denver, he donated his mansion to the city to become the mayor's official residence. The Sea-Air Operations Gallery of the Smithsonian's National Air and Space Museum is dedicated to his memory.
Smithsonian National Air and Space Museum, Press Release, November 9, 2005

Davis, Oscar (1878-1923)
Raton Chief of Police

When Chief Davis attempted to stop a car driving erratically on the streets of Raton, the driver shot him to death. It turned out that both men in the car were wanted fugitives from Oklahoma, but bootleg whiskey was the immediate cause of the murder. After his capture, the driver said this: "[My brother and I] had both been drinking and were pretty full." Newton Brigance, who did the shooting, was first sentenced to hang, but upon appeal he received 95 years in prison. His brother, Oscar, a passenger in the car, received four to five years in prison. Chief Davis' funeral was one of the largest in Raton history.
Bullis, *New Mexico's Finest*
Pappas, *Raton*

Deagostini, Giovanni Maria (1801-1869)
"Hermit of the Organ Mountains"

(An item in *American Profile*, August 27, 2006, reports the name as Juan Maria Agostini.) Deagostini was born in northern Italy and began his travels around Europe and the Americas by 1820. Described as a "saintly recluse," he was living in a cave near Las Vegas, New Mexico, by the early 1860s. By about 1865 he was living in a cave in the Organ Mountains, east of Las Cruces. The community knew of him because he would occasionally hike into town to trade rosaries and crucifixes for supplies. In 1869 he became concerned that someone wanted to kill him and he made a habit of building a fire outside his cave on Friday evenings to let the people in the valley know that he was alive. On a Friday night in April, there was no fire. Searchers found his body some distance from his cave. Some believed that he was killed by Apaches; others that he was slain by robbers. Local legend held that a man called El Indio Chacon did the deed, or failing that, a priest named Manuel Chavez was the guilty party. No one was ever convicted of the crime. Deagostini is interred at Mesilla.
Aranda, Daniel, "Western Lore," *Wild West*, October 2006

DeLavy, Edmund (1916-1989)
Sandoval County Artist

A native of Maine, DeLavy studied at the Pratt Institute in New York City before World War II. He enlisted in the U.S. Army and served four and a half years before he was discharged and returned to New York. He resumed his art studies at the Art Students League on the G. I. Bill. DeLavy worked as an illustrator in New York, but began traveling in the western United States in 1947. In 1969 he built a house adjacent to Coronado Monument near Bernalillo. For about ten years he illustrated stories in the *New Mexico* Magazine for his friend, and neighbor, John Sinclair (see entry). Upon his death, his home was donated to the Sandoval County Historical Society and today it houses the Society's photo archives, files and library. It also provides a meeting place for the group.

Newsletter, Westerners International, Albuquerque Corral, September 7, 1989

Dempsey, John Joseph (1879-1958)
U.S. Congressman (1935-1941 and 1951-1958), Governor (State) of New Mexico (1943-1946)

Dempsey was born in White Haven, Luzerne Co., Pennsylvania. Early in life he worked as a telegrapher, and later worked for the Brooklyn Union Elevator Co. and served as vice president of the Brooklyn Rapid Transit Co. He entered the oil business in Oklahoma and served as president of the Continental Oil & Asphalt Co. in 1919. He arrived in New Mexico in 1920. A Democrat, he held several appointed positions before he was elected to Congress in 1934. He served until 1941 and was elected governor in 1942 and again in 1944. Dempsey returned to Congress in 1951 and remained in office until his death in 1958, in Washington, D.C. He is interred in Rosario Cemetery in Santa Fe.

New Mexico Blue Book, 2001-2002
Other literature abundant

Denver, John (1943-1997)
Singer/Actor

John Denver

John Denver was born as Henry John Deutchendorf, Jr. on New Year's Eve at Roswell, New Mexico, to a U. S. Army Air Corps officer stationed at the Roswell Army Flying School (later Walker Air Force Base). He traveled widely with his family and dropped out of Texas Tech University at Lubbock in the early 1960s and began a musical career in Los Angeles. In 1965 he joined the Chad Mitchell Trio and in 1969 he became a solo act. In a long career, he released about 300 songs, many of which he had written. He won Grammy Awards, American Music Awards, Country Music Association Awards, an Academy of County Music Award, and an Emmy Award. He was inducted into the Songwriters Hall of Fame in 1996. Among his best-known songs are "Leaving on a Jet Plane" (1969), "Take Me Home, Country Roads" (1971), "Rocky Mountain High" (1975), and "Thank God I'm a Country Boy" (1975). He also had roles in four films: *Oh, God* (1977), *Fire and Ice* (1987), *Foxfire* (1987) and *Walking Thunder* (1994). He was killed when the light aircraft he was piloting

crashed off the coast of California.
Wikipedia Encyclopedia
Other Literature Abundant

Deutschendorf, Henry John, Jr.
See Denver, John

Dietz, Robert Edwin II (c. 1886-1970)
Albuquerque Farmer

Dietz, a native of New York City, moved to Albuquerque in 1910 seeking a cure for the tuberculosis from which he suffered. He married Barbara Johnson in 1914 and they bought land near the Rio Grande and Griegos Road. They later purchased more land and operated a dairy farm and a fruit orchard. His son, Robert III, sold the farm to homebuilder Dale Bellamah in 1959 and Bellamah promptly sub-divided it and named the development Dietz Farms.

Rick Nathanson, Albuquerque *Journal*, November 26, 2005

Dodge, Henry Chee (1856-1947)
Navajo Tribal Chairman (1923-1928)

According to Historian Marc Simmons, Henry Chee Dodge was the son of Henry L. Dodge (see entry) and the grandson of Navajo chief Zarcillos Largo; born in 1856. Rev. Francis Borgman reports that Dodge's father was a "Mexican" named Juan Anaya, and that he was born in 1860. Both agree that he was orphaned at a young age. Simmons says he spent some years with an elderly Navajo man and his daughter, including four years at Bosque Redondo (1864-1868), before an aunt adopted him. Father Borgman asserts that Dodge was raised by an aunt from the beginning. Dodge's aunt later married a trader named Perry Williams who became the guardian of young Chee Dodge. Chee later found work in a trading post where he became fluent in both English and Spanish. He became chief of the Navajos, named to the position by famed Navajo leader Manuelito, according to Father Borgman, when he was 24 years old, in 1884. Simmons reports that he was the first chairman of the Navajo Tribal Council in 1923 and served until 1928. He also prospered in the trading business and in ranching. When he died in 1947, he left an estate of about $200,000.

Francis Borgman, O.F.M., "Henry Chee Dodge, The Last Chief of the Navajo Indians,"
New Mexico Historical Review, April 1948
Marc Simmons, Santa Fe *New Mexican*, October 29, 2005

Dodge, Henry L. (1810-1856)
Navajo Indian Agent (1853-1856)

Dodge was born in Missouri and made his way to New Mexico as a young man. He served briefly as government treasurer of the occupied territory, appointed by General Stephen Watts Kearny (see entry) in 1846. He was later dispatched to Seboyetta (then spelled Cebolleta) where he became enamored of the Navajo people, and he learned their language—a difficult task. He married the niece of Navajo chief Zarcillos Largo and was the father of Henry Chee Dodge (see entry). The

elder Henry Dodge was killed by Apaches near Zuñi.
Marc Simmons, Santa Fe *New Mexican*, October 29, 2005
Twitchell, *Leading Facts*, Vol. II

Dodson, J. L. (fl. 1897)
Albuquerque Bicycle Dealer

Historian Marc Simmons reports that Dodson owned the very first automobile in New Mexico. He had to go to Denver in late 1897 to take delivery on a Locomobile which he then drove to Albuquerque; a trip that took five days.
Simmons, *Albuquerque*

Doheny, Edward Laurence (1856-1935)
Kingston Prospector, Oil Man/Politician

Born in Fond du Lac, Wisconsin, Doheny made his way west as a young man and in the 1880s met Albert Bacon Fall (see entry) in Kingston, New Mexico, where they were prospectors. Doheny was a Democratic candidate for Vice President of the United States in 1920, but is best known as the president of the Petroleum Securities Company. He and Harry F. Sinclair negotiated with Fall, who had been appointed Secretary of the Interior by President Warren G. Harding (see entry), for oil leases at the Teapot Dome reserve in Wyoming, and others. Doheny was accused of giving Fall a $100,000 bribe, but was acquitted of the charge. Fall, however, was convicted of accepting the bribe and sentenced to prison. Doheny died in Los Angeles.
Curry, *Autobiography*
Knappman, *Great Trials*
Owen, *Two Alberts*

Domenici, Pete V. (1932-)
U.S. Senator (1973-)

Senator Pete V. Domenici

Pete Domenici was born in an area of Albuquerque called Los Candelarias. He was educated in the Duke City and graduated from the University of New Mexico, after which he became a minor league pitcher for the Albuquerque Dukes baseball team. He attended law school at the University of Denver and returned to his hometown to practice in 1958. He was elected to the Albuquerque City Commission in 1966 and served for a time as Chairman (ex-officio mayor). A Republican, he ran for Governor of New Mexico in 1970 only to be defeated by Democrat Bruce King (see entry) by about 9,000 votes out of 269,000 votes cast. He was elected to the U.S. Senate two years later when he defeated Democrat Jack Daniels of Hobbs by more than 26,000 votes, the first Republican to serve in the Senate from New Mexico since 1935. He was reelected in 1978 when he defeated former Attorney General Toney Anaya; in 1984 when he defeated Judy Pratt; in 1990 when he defeated Tom Benavides; in 1996 when he defeated Art Trujillo; and in 2002 when he defeated Gloria Tristani. No other New Mexico senator served as long as Domenici (Dennis Chávez served 27 years). The Albuquerque Museum named him a Notable New Mexican in 2005.

Congressional Biography
Hughes, *Albuquerque*
New Mexico Blue Book 2003-2004
News accounts abundant

Doniphan, Alexander William (1808-1887)
Military Officer

Doniphan was born in Kentucky, studied law there and moved on to Missouri in 1830. During the Mexican War he was the commanding officer of 1st Missouri Mounted Volunteers, and he accompanied General Stephen Watts Kearny (see entry) and the Army of the West to New Mexico in 1846. One source says that he "was placed in charge of the territory briefly," but that was not the case. For a short time in the fall of 1846, from September 25 until the following month, he was the highest-ranking U.S. military officer in New Mexico, but Governor Charles Bent (see entry) was in charge. Troops under Doniphan's command won the Battle of Brazito, near the present-day town of Mesquite in southern Doña Ana County, New Mexico, on Christmas day, 1846. He returned to Missouri following the Mexican War. He op-posed secession during the Civil War (1861-1865) and

Alexander William Doniphan. After Twitchell.

took no part in the conflict. A statue in his memory stands at Liberty, Missouri.

Andrew Armstrong, "The Brazito Battlefield," *New Mexico Historical Review*, January 1960
Rathbun & Alexander, *Military Place Names*
Simmons, *New Mexico*
Thrapp, *Encyclopedia*

Dorantes de Carranza, Andrés (fl. 1527-1573)
Spanish Explorer

Dorantes, a Castilian of noble birth, accompanied Cabeza de Vaca (see entry) across the American Southwest between 1527 and 1536. He died in Mexico.
Cabeza de Vaca, *Adventures*

Dow, James Leslie "Les" (1860-1897)
Eddy County Sheriff

Les Dow, a Texan by nativity, took office on January 1, 1897, and was shot to death on Fox Street in Eddy (now Carlsbad) on February 18. His killer, though acquitted at trial, is generally believed to have been Dave Kemp (see entry), the first sheriff of Eddy County. There had been bad blood between them for some time. Before being elected sheriff, Dow had served as a range detective and deputy U.S. Marshal. He also operated a saloon in Seven Rivers, New Mexico: a town now completely covered by the waters behind Brantley Dam. Note: Historian Will

Keleher (see entry) reports that Dow was killed on January 18, 1897. According to the *Pecos Valley Argus* for February 19, 1897, the assassination occurred on February 18.

Bullis, *New Mexico's Finest*
Harkey, *Mean as Hell*
Keleher, *Fabulous Frontier*
Other literature abundant

Dudley, Nathan Augustus Monroe (1825-1910)
U.S. Army Officer, Lincoln County War Figure

Born in Massachusetts, Dudley was commissioned a 2nd Lieutenant in the 10th U.S. Infantry in 1855. While his military career would be considered successful—he retired as a Brigadier General—he benefited greatly by having friends in high office. He was court-martialed three times, and even when convicted he was given light, insignificant sentences. He was also the subject of an inquiry regarding his participation in the Lincoln County War of 1878-81. In the latter case, as commander of Fort Stanton, he engaged U.S. troops in the Five Days Battle in the town of Lincoln in July 1878. As a civil matter, such military action was prohibited under the *posse comitatus* law. The court of inquiry, nonetheless, found in his favor and his career continued until his retirement in 1889. Historian Robert Utley described him thus: "Behind [his] imposing façade…lurked a man whose genuine professional dedication consistently fell victim to a small intellect and huge vanity. He suffered from muddled thought and bad judgment, the result of mediocre endowments impaired by years of dissipation. He got drunk often, and whiskey more or less influenced most of his actions. He compensated…with pomposity, bellicosity, petty despotism, and an extraordinary aptitude for contention."

Thrapp, *Encyclopedia*
Utley, *High Noon*
Other literature abundant

Dummy, The (1870s)
Lincoln County War Figure

Thrapp lists him as a partisan on the side of the Murphy-Dolan faction in the Lincoln County War and indicates that no one, not even Maurice Fulton (see entry), has been able to identify him by name. He was believed to have been deaf and dumb, hence the name, but many believe that he could hear and probably speak. Utley counts him present for the Five Days Battle of July 1878.

Thrapp, *Encyclopedia*
Utley, *High Noon*

Dunigan, James Patrick "Pat" (1925-1980)
Texas Oilman, Sandoval County Land Owner

Born in Muskogee, Oklahoma, Dunigan was raised in Breckenridge, Texas. He graduated from the University of Texas and held a Master's degree from New York University. He was a veteran of World War II. Some sources refer to him as a third generation Texas oilman, but he was also involved in ranching and the restaurant business. Dunigan bought the Valle Grande, a 100,000-acre ranch in the Jemez Mountains of Sandoval County, west of Los Alamos, for $2.5 million in 1963 from the Frank Bond (see entry) family. Dunigan's sons, Michael and Andrew, sold it to the U.S. Government for $101 million in 2000, when it became the Valles Caldera National Preserve.

"Obituary," Albuquerque *Journal*, February 20, 1980
Martin, *Valle Grande*

Dunnahoo, Rufus J. "Rufe" (1879-1931)
Chaves County Deputy Sheriff

Deputy Dunnahoo was shot and killed on Sunday, August 2, 1931, when he and Sheriff John Peck attempted to search the property of one Gilford Welch. Welch was subsequently tried and convicted of voluntary manslaughter and sentenced to four to five years in prison. A local newspaper said, "[Dunnahoo] was well and favorably known."

Bullis, *99 New Mexicans*

Dunton, William Herbert "Buck" (1878-1936)
Painter, Charter Member of the Taos Society of Artists

A native of Augusta, Maine, Dunton was a poor student but a talented sketch artist. By the time he was 16, he was regularly selling his drawings to several newspapers. At age 18 he traveled to Montana and there became enamored of the American West. He returned to the West regularly for about 15 years during which he became an accomplished hunter and a working cowboy. He maintained a home base in New York during this time, where he worked and sold commercial illustrations. Dunton met Ernest Blumenschein (see entry) in 1911 and learned of the wonders of Taos, New Mexico. He moved to Taos the following year, thus becoming the second of the Taos artists to settle there permanently (Bert Phillips [see entry] was first). He turned his back on a lucrative career as an illustrator and turned to paintings of the West: of cowboys and pioneers. He had a strong affinity for the frontier and as one writer noted, "He suffered under the encroachment of people filling up the West." Dunton himself wrote in 1925, "The West has passed—more's the pity. In another 25 years the old-time Westerner will have gone, too—gone with the buffalo and the antelope. I'm going to hand down to posterity a bit of the unadulterated real thing." He died in Taos.

Nelson, *Legendary Artists of Taos*
Samuels, *The Illustrated Biographical Encyclopedia*
Schimmel & White, *Bert Geer Phillips*
Witt, *The Taos Artists*

-E-

Earp, Wyatt Berry Stapp (1848-1929)
Las Vegas Gambler, Kansas & Arizona Lawman

While Wyatt Earp is best known for his activities in Dodge City, Kansas, and Tombstone, Arizona, his historic connection to New Mexico cannot be ignored. He first arrived at Las Vegas, New Mexico, in the early fall of 1879 where he joined his friend John Henry "Doc" Holliday (see entry). Earp stayed but a short time before he and Holliday moved on to Arizona. Of greater historical significance was a visit to Albuquerque—via Silver City and Deming—the Earp brothers and Holliday made in April 1882 after the famed gunfight near the OK Corral in Tombstone (October 26, 1881). They stayed for a couple of weeks during which arrangements were made by railroad officials and Wells Fargo to protect them from extradition to Arizona to face murder charges for the killing of Frank Stilwell at Tucson in March 1882. Even New Mexico Governor Lionel Sheldon (see entry) appears to have been a part of the cabal to protect Earp and Holliday from prosecution. The two of them made it to Colorado where they would be protected from Arizona authorities. Pursuit of them effectively ended by 1883, and if Earp returned to New Mexico after that, it is unrecorded. He died in California in 1929.

Bryan, *Albuquerque*
Metz, *Encyclopedia*
Tanner & Tanner, *Doc Holliday*
Thrapp, *Encyclopedia*
Hornung and Roberts, eds. *True Tales*

Easley, Mack (1916-2006)
New Mexico Political Figure

A native of Oklahoma, Easley was educated there and arrived in southeastern New Mexico in the late 1930s where he worked for the Hobbs *Sun-News* for a time. He served in the Army Air Corps during World War II and attended law school at the University of Oklahoma. He returned to New Mexico with a law degree in 1947. A Democrat, he was first elected to the New Mexico House of Representatives in 1950 and served five non-consecutive terms between 1951 and 1962, including service as Speaker in 1959 and 1960. Easley served as Lieutenant Governor under Governor Jack Campbell (see entry) from 1963 until 1967. He was elected to the State Senate in 1966 and served one term, through 1970. Governor Jerry Apodaca appointed him to the State Supreme Court in 1975, and he was subsequently elected in his own right and retired as Chief Justice in 1982. Easley was one of the very few to serve prominently in all three branches of state government. He died in Albuquerque.

News accounts abundant

Eastlake, William Derry (1917-)
Sandoval County Novelist

Eastlake was born in New York and raised and educated in New Jersey. As a young man he hitchhiked around the U.S., and on the West Coast he became acquainted with such notable writers as William Saroyan, Theodore Dreiser and Nathaniel West. He served in the U.S. Army during World War II, after which he resided in California. He lived for a time on a 400 acre "ranch" near Cuba, in Sandoval County, New Mexico, the result of which was four novels about the Navajo people: *Go In Beauty* (1956), *The Bronc People* (1958), *Portrait of An Artist With 26 Horses* (1963) and *Dancers in the Scalp House* (1975). Eastlake fancied himself the first writer to treat the Indian people as *people*. Many other writers dispute that. Probably his best-known book is *Castle Keep* (1965), which was made into a 1969 movie staring Burt Lancaster. Eastlake moved to Arizona in the 1970s.

David L. Caffey, "Fiction of Northwest New Mexico," *Book Talk*, New Mexico Book League, June 1992

Delbert E. Wylder, "William Eastlake," *A Literary History of the American West*

Eddy, Charles Bishop (1857-1931)
Southeastern New Mexico Rancher/Entrepreneur/Railroad Builder/Promoter

A native of New York, Eddy migrated first to Colorado and then to southeastern New Mexico where he became interested in Pat Garrett's (see entry) vision of harnessing the waters of the Pecos River for irrigation purposes. He also engaged in ranching with his brother, John Arthur Eddy, but became interested in railroad building in addition to the irrigation projects in Eddy County. He and James John Hagerman (see entry) were partners for a time, but parted ways. Eddy also envisioned a railroad from El Paso, north to White Oaks and ultimately to Liberal, Kansas. Carlsbad, New Mexico, was originally named Eddy, and Eddy County is named for Charles Bishop Eddy.

Julyan, *Place Names*
Keleher, *Fabulous Frontier*
Myrick, *New Mexico Railroads*

Edmister, Grace Thompson (1891-1984)
Albuquerque Civic Symphony, Founder and Director

Edmister, a native of Ohio, sought respite from her tuberculosis in Albuquerque, and was in fact cured. She was director of the University of New Mexico

Music Department when she led a group of music enthusiasts who founded the Albuquerque Civic Symphony in 1932. The first concert was held in Carlisle Gymnasium on November 13, 1932, on the University of New Mexico campus. About 2,000 people attended. She was one of the first women in the U.S. to direct a municipal symphony orchestra, and she did so until 1941. While she left New Mexico during the period 1942 to 1970, she returned and in November 1981, at age 91, she directed the New Mexico Symphony Orchestra. She died in Albuquerque. History writer Ollie Reed, Jr., wrote, "She passed her final days much as she had spent all her life, much as she approached that 1981 NMSO concert—with strength, poise and grace, with spirit and motion."

García, *Albuquerque*
Ollie Reed Jr., "She lifted a baton and spirits across the decades," Albuquerque *Tribune*,
        June 29, 2006

Edwards, Ralph (1913-2005)
Broadcasting Personality

Ralph Edwards

Edwards was a pioneer in radio and television broadcasting, beginning his career in 1929. In 1940 he created a quiz show called "Truth or Consequences" in which contestants were asked questions and obliged to perform stunts if they answered incorrectly. For publicity purposes, Edwards invited any town in the U.S. to change its name to Truth or Consequences, and Hot Springs, New Mexico took him up on the offer. By a vote of 1,294 to 295, local citizens approved the name-change. The radio show moved over to television in the fall of 1950, but lasted only one year with Edwards as master of ceremonies. It returned to TV in 1954 with Jack Bailey as emcee; he stayed until 1956. Steve Dunne starred from 1957-58. Edwards and his company produced more than a score of programs over the years, including "This is Your Life" and "The People's Court," the latter of which remained on the air at the time of his death. From 1950 until 1999 Edwards visited T or C, as Truth or Consequences came to be called, each year for the town's fiesta. The civic center auditorium is named for him, as is a city park.

"Obituary," Albuquerque *Journal*, November 17, 2005
Brooks & Marsh, *The Complete Directory to Prime Time*
Julyan, *Place Names*

Elkins, Stephen B. (1841-1911)
U.S. Congressional Representative, Santa Fe Ring Member

Nicknamed "Smooth Steve," Elkins arrived in Mesilla, New Mexico, in 1864. He was elected to the Territorial House of Representatives in the same year, and by 1870 he had been appointed U.S. District Attorney for New Mexico. He and Thomas B. Catron (see entry) became law partners in 1869 and they were both founding members of the Santa Fe Ring. He was elected territorial representative to the U.S. Congress in 1872 and served two terms. Elkins was not present on the floor of the House in 1875 when Representative Julius Burroughs of Michigan declaimed bitterly about events in the South following the Civil War, and the rise of the Ku Klux Klan. Elkins entered the chamber in time to see Burroughs receive adulation from his northern colleagues so he joined in, shaking Burroughs' hand and offering congratulations. Southern representatives didn't appreciate the gesture and the New Mexico statehood bill was as good as dead. It never got out of the House Committee on Territories. The so-called "Elkins handshake" may have contributed to the delay in New Mexico statehood for many years. There are those who believe that Elkins did it on purpose because, as a member of the Santa Fe Ring, he opposed statehood. Elkins left New Mexico in 1877 and moved to West Virginia. He later served as Secretary of War in the administration of President Benjamin Harrison. He was elected to the U.S. Senate from West Virginia in 1895 and served until his death.

Stephen B. Elkins. After Twitchell.

Bullis, *Observer* April 15, 2004.
Keleher, *Fabulous Frontier*
Lamar, *Far Southwest*
Twitchell, *Leading Facts*, Vol. II
Other literature abundant

Estevánico also Estebán & Stephen Dorantes (c. 1510-1539)
Explorer/Guide

Estevánico, a slave throughout his life, is the first Black person to be noted in the recorded history of New Mexico, and he may have been the first non-Indian to enter the land of the Pueblos. Estevánico, a Moroccan, was the slave of Andrés Dorantes (see entry), one of the four survivors of the ill-fated Narváez expedition to Florida in the 1520s. After traversing Texas and much of Mexico with his master, Alonso del Castillo Maldonado, and Cabeza de Vaca (see entry) in the years between 1528 and 1536, he was sold to the viceroy of New Spain, Antonio de Mendoza. Mendoza called upon him to serve as guide for Fray Marcos de Niza (see entry), who set out from New Spain in search of the Seven Cities of Cíbola in what is now New Mexico. Late in 1539, Estevánico reached the Zuñi village of Hawikuh in western New Mexico. He is said to have made unreasonable demands on the villagers, and they killed him, along with several other scouts. Niza's explorations ended at that point. One biographer described Estevánico as "a man of great strength, gaiety, imagination and intelligence, [and] something of a linguist."
Cabeza de Vaca, *Adventures*
Katz, *Black West*
Thrapp, *Encyclopedia*
Other literature abundant

Evans, Max (1924-)
New Mexico Author

(Several sources show the year of birth as 1925. August 29, 1924, is the date provided in Slim Randles' authorized biography of Evans.) Ol' Max Evans was born at Ropes, Texas, southwest of Lubbock. As a youngster he spent time in Humble City (between Lovington and Hobbs), Lamy and later at Des Moines, New Mexico. Much of his youth was spent on horseback, around cattle, as he strove for genuine cowboy status, which he certainly acquired. His first artistic endeavors involved painting, and he moved on to Taos in 1951 where he became well acquainted with Indian painter Woody Crumbo (see entry). In the late 1950s, his interests changed to writing and his first book, *Southwest Wind*, was published in 1958. Probably his most famous novel, *The Rounders*, was published in 1960. Another of his better-known books, *Hi Lo Country*, was published the following year. The *Rounders* and *Hi Lo Country* were both made into movies. Evans wrote books too numerous to list here, but one of his most recent is *Madam Millie: Bordellos from Silver City to Ketchikan* (2002), the biography of New Mexico's last legal madam, Mildred Clark Cusey (see entry). As of 2006, Evans lives and writes in Albuquerque.

Benke, Richard, "Force of nature, force of will…," New Mexico Magazine, September 2004
Max Evans, "Many Deaths—Many Lives," *Book Talk*," New Mexico Book League, June 1994
T. N. Luther, "Collecting Taos Authors," *Book Talk*, New Mexico Book League, Nov. 1992
Randles, *Ol' Max*

-F-

Fall, Albert Bacon (1861-1944)
Legislator/Attorney General/Judge/U.S. Senator/U.S. Secretary of the Interior/ Prison Inmate

Born in Franklin County, Kentucky, a tubercular A. B. Fall made his way to New Mexico by 1883. He was admitted to the bar in 1891, took up the practice of law and entered politics as a Democrat. He was elected to the territorial legislature and appointed to several territorial positions, including Attorney General and Associate Supreme Court Justice. He was involved in some of the major legal actions of the day and in at least one shooting scrape. He was commissioned a captain in the infantry during the Spanish-American War but saw no action before he was mustered out. He became a Republican in 1903. Fall was appointed to the U.S. Senate when New Mexico became a

Senator Albert Bacon Fall

state in 1912. President Warren G. Harding (see entry) appointed him Secretary of the Interior in March 1921. He soon became embroiled in the famed Teapot Dome scandal, and resigned in March 1923. In 1929 he was convicted of accepting a bribe and sentenced to a year and a day in prison; time he served—from July 1931 to May 1932—in the prison at Santa Fe. He was also fined $100,000, an assessment he never paid. Former New Mexico congressman and territorial governor George Curry (see entry) said, "I found it difficult to believe Fall guilty of having accepted a bribe in connection with his official duties.... It was a terrible error in judgment to accept a $100,000 loan while officially negotiating leases of federally owned oil-bearing lands...." Historian William Degregorio, however, states flatly that, "...Albert Fall sold for personal gain the nation's oil reserves at Wyoming's Teapot Dome." Fall died in El Paso, Texas.

Charles Bennett, "Albert Bacon Fall...," *New Mexico Magazine*, October 2003
Bethune, *Race With The Wind*
Bullis, *99 New Mexicans*
Curry, *Autobiography*

Degregorio, *The Presidents*
Ellis, *New Mexico, Past and Present*
Mark Gilderhus, "Senator Albert B. Fall," *New Mexico Historical Review*, October 1973
Owen, *Two Alberts*
Twitchell, *Leading Facts*, Vol. II

Fergusson, Erna (1888-1964)
Albuquerque Author, "The Grand Dame of New Mexico Letters"

Erna Fergusson. Courtesy
The Albuquerque
Museum Photoarchives
PA1978.050.298.

Erna, actually Ernestine, after her grandmother, Ernestine Huning, was born in Albuquerque, the daughter of Harvey B. Fergusson (see entry) and Clara Mary Huning. She graduated from Albuquerque's Central High School in 1906 and began a teaching career while she attended the University of New Mexico and earned a Bachelor of Pedagogy (teaching) degree in 1912. She served with the Red Cross Home Service during World War I and became a reporter for the Albuquerque *Herald* after the war. From 1922 to 1927 she was a principal in Koshare Tour Services, a company that offered tours of Indian country—Navajo and Hopi—which led to a study of New Mexico's three cultures. Her first book, *Dancing Gods*, was published in 1931. She turned her attention to Latin America and wrote several books on the topic before she returned to New Mexico subjects with *Our Southwest* (1940), *Albuquerque* (1947), *Murder and Mystery in New Mexico* (1948), and *New Mexico: A Pageant of Three Peoples* (1951). The Erna Fergusson branch library in Albuquerque is named for her.

Szasz, *Larger Than Life*
University of New Mexico

Fergusson, Harvey (1890-1971)
Author

Harvey Fergusson was the son of New Mexico Congressman Harvey B. Fergusson (see entry), the grandson of Franz Huning (see entry), one of the early German merchants in Albuquerque, and the younger brother of author Erna Fergusson (see entry). He was born in Albuquerque and began his writing career there, but left in 1926, never to return. He wrote a number of historically fictional books, including *Hot Saturday, Wolf Song, Grant of Kingdom, The Conquest of Don Pedro, Home in the West* and *Rio Grande*, all set in, or about, New Mexico. He wrote of Albuquerque: "It is a great city in the making, and I know of no other place where the wilderness is so close to the city, or where the primitive survives so close to civilization." He died at Berkeley, California.

Hillerman, *The Spell of New Mexico*
Ollie Reed, "His Books sang of N. M.—but from exile," Albuquerque *Tribune*, Dec. 28, 2005

Fergusson, Harvey Butler (1848-1915)
Albuquerque Lawyer/Politician, U.S. Congressman

Fergusson was born in Pickens County, Alabama, the son of a Confederate officer who served on the staff of General Robert E. Lee. He was educated at Washington and Lee University. He was admitted to the bar in 1875 and practiced law in West Virginia before he arrived in White Oaks, New Mexico, in 1882, and on to Albuquerque in 1883. He married Clara Mary Huning, the daughter of influential merchant Franz Huning (see entry) in 1887. Two of his children, Erna and Harvey (see entries), became well known writers. Harvey Butler Fergusson was elected New Mexico's delegate to the U.S. Congress and served from 1897 to 1899, losing in an 1898 re-election bid to Pedro Perea of Bernalillo. After statehood in 1912, he served in congress from that year until 1915, losing a bid for re-election in 1914 to B. C. Hernandez (see entry)

Harvey Butler Fergusson.
Courtesy The Albuquerque
Museum Photoarchives
PC1978.050.243.

of Rio Arriba County. Fergusson was among the attorneys, including Albert Bacon Fall (see entry), who defended Oliver Lee (see entry) and Jim Gilliland when they were tried for the murder of Henry Fountain at Hillsboro in 1899. He died in Albuquerque.

Curry, *Autobiography*
García, *Albuquerque*
Simmons, *Albuquerque*
Other literature abundant

Fernández, Antonio Manuel (1902-1956)
U.S. Congressman (1943-1956)

Born in Springer, Colfax County, Fernández was educated in the public schools and at Highlands Normal College in Las Vegas, New Mexico. He attended law school at Cumberland University in Tennessee and was admitted to the New Mexico bar in 1931. He practiced law in Santa Fe. He also served in the state house of representatives in 1935 before he became an attorney for the State Tax Commission. He was an assistant Attorney General from 1937 to 1941 and a member of the Public Service Commission from 1941 to 1942, when he ran for Congress. He was elected to the office eight times, dying the day after his last successful campaign. He is interred at Rosario Cemetery in Santa Fe.

New Mexico Blue Book 2003-2004
Literature abundant

Fisher, Walter Lowrie (1862-1935)
U.S. Secretary of the Interior

Fisher was born in West Virginia, but moved with his family to Indiana as a child. He was educated there and moved on to Chicago where he practiced law. President William Howard Taft appointed him, first to the Railroad Securities

President Taft signed the proclamation that made New Mexico a state on January 6, 1912. Secretary Walter Lowrie Fisher is on the far left behind President Taft.

Commission, and then to Secretary of the Interior. Fisher was present when President Taft signed the proclamation that made New Mexico a state on January 6, 1912. Fisher was instrumental in New Mexico's transition from Territorial status to statehood. He died at Winnetka, Illinois.

Paul Rhetts, Albuquerque, New Mexico

Flipper, Henry Ossian (1856-1940)
Frontier Military Officer/Engineer

Henry Ossian Flipper

Henry Flipper was born into slavery at Thomasville, Georgia. He was not the first Black man to attend the U.S. Military Academy at West Point, but he was the first to graduate, in 1877. He was appointed a 2nd Lieutenant and assigned to the 10th Cavalry, which was made up entirely of Black enlisted men. He served on the Texas frontier and earned a record that was entirely satisfactory until Colonel William Rufus "Pecos Bill" Shafter decided otherwise. Flipper came under suspicion for alleged irregularities in his accounts when he served as Quartermaster. Shafter court-martialed him, and he was dismissed from the service in 1882. Most modern observers agree that Flipper's prosecution was the result of racial bias on Shafter's part.

His sentence was "corrected" in 1976. He worked as an engineer after he left the army. He worked for Albert Bacon Fall (see entry) for a time, and Historian R. E. Twitchell (see entry) writes, "Mr. Henry O. Flipper was employed as special agent and Spanish expert in 1893, having reference to private land claims lying within the Gadsden Purchase. During the seven years Mr. Flipper was connected with this office his fidelity, integrity, and magnificent ability were subjected to tests which few men encounter in life. How well they were met can be attested by the records of the Court of Private Land Claims and the Supreme Court of the United States." Flipper died and was buried at Atlanta, Georgia. He was re-buried with full military honors in 1978 at Thomasville, the place of his birth. Thrapp wrote that Flipper was never married; while William Loren Katz reported that he was indeed married, and he included a photo of Chloe Flipper in his book.

Katz, *Black West*
Thrapp, *Encyclopedia*
Twitchell, *Leading Facts*, Vol. II

Fogelson, E. E. "Buddy" (1900-1987)
Pecos Rancher, Texas Oilman

Born in Nebraska, Fogelson became a Texas wildcatter, searching for oil, as a young man. He later received degrees from Texas Christian University and the University of Virginia. During World War II, he served as a Colonel on the staff of General Dwight D. Eisenhower where he facilitated the delivery of fuel to American military forces as they advanced across Europe. He received several commendations for his work. Fogelson purchased the Forked Lightning Ranch on the Pecos River near Santa Fe in the late 1930s from the estate of Tex Austin (see entry). He met actress Greer Garson (see entry) in the late 1940s and they married in 1949. Over the years they spent a great deal of their time in New Mexico. They were generous with their donations to the College of Santa Fe and the library there was named for him. Notable about Fogelson the rancher is that he introduced the Santa Gertrudis cattle breed to the higher elevation of the Rockies, and he exhibited them at the New Mexico State Fair in 1961. He allowed no hunting or trapping on the ranch. Fogelson and Garson received awards and recognition for their contributions to the Santa Fe Opera and to Pecos National Monument. He died in Dallas and left the ranch to his widow.

Anne Hillerman, "N.M. Philanthropist 'Buddy' Fogelson Dies," Albuquerque *Journal North*, December 2, 1987
Literature abundant

Ford, Alton (1927-2006)
Hunter, Tracker, Conservationist

Alton Ford was born at Silver City to a pioneer family that had homesteaded in southwestern New Mexico late in the 19th century. He began his career as a hunter in 1948 when the New Mexico Department of Game and Fish hired him to hunt mountain lions in the Big Hatchet Mountains of southern New Mexico. He was paid $200 per month and expected to protect the bighorn sheep herd in the area. Ford later worked for the U. S. Fish and Wildlife Service but returned to New Mexico Game and Fish. He was a trapper and the manager of the Red Rock Wildlife area until his retirement in 1987. One of his superiors described him as a dedicated conservationist. Interviewed in 2003, Ford voiced his opinion on subjects related to his career. He said this about Mexican wolves: "Don't let them fool you; they'll kill everything they find… Unlike coyotes, wolves will kill for the sport of it." On wildlife biologists, he opined, "One of the most dangerous things to wildlife is a biologist with a plan." Ford considered Elliott Barker (see entry) his hero. "[Barker] was a good hunter, a real outdoorsman and one of the first really sincere conservationists."

Dan Williams, *New Mexico Wildlife*, Summer 2006

Foreman, Edgar Franklin "Ed" (1933-)
U.S. Congressman from Texas (1964-1968), U.S. Congressman from New Mexico (1969-1971)

Born at Portales, Roosevelt County, New Mexico, Foreman was educated there and attended Eastern New Mexico University and New Mexico State University where he received a B.S. degree in 1955. He served in both the Naval and Air Force Reserves, and became a successful businessman. He was elected to Congress in Texas twice, and in New Mexico once, serving a single term as a Republican between Democratic Congressmen E. S. Johnny Walker (1965-1969) and Harold "Mud" Runnels (1971-1981).

Congressional Biography
New Mexico Blue Book 2003-2004
Literature abundant

Fornoff, Frederick "Fred" (1859-1935)
Bernalillo County Deputy Sheriff, Deputy U.S. Marshal, New Mexico Mounted Police Captain

Capt. Fred Fornoff

Fred Fornoff was the second captain of the New Mexico Mounted Police (the first was John Fullerton of Socorro), appointed by Governor Herbert J. Hagerman (see entry) in April 1906. Fornoff investigated the February 29, 1908 murder of former Sheriff Pat Garrett (see entry) and wrote a report on the matter. For many years historians believed that the report had been destroyed, but historian Chuck Hornung located a copy of it in the early 2000s. It is said to indicate that New Mexico cowboy Billy McNew killed Garrett, and not Texas gunman Jim Miller (see entry), as previously believed. Horung believes that Fornoff's report to Governor George Curry (see entry) was never delivered. Fornoff also served in the Spanish American War and as Albuquerque Town Marshal two different times, 1894 to 1896 and from 1897-98.

Simmons, *Albuquerque*
Hornung, *Fullerton's Rangers*
Hornung, *Thin Gray Line*

Metz, *Pat Garrett*
Thrapp, *Encyclopedia*

Foster, Robert W. "Bob" (1938-)
Albuquerque Boxing Champion

A native of Albuquerque, Foster entered the pro boxing ranks in 1961. He became the light heavyweight champion of the world in 1968 (he knocked out Dick Tiger) holding the title until 1974 (Jorge Ahumada fought him to a draw). He defended his title 14 times. In his career he fought 65 fights, 56 of which he won, 46 by knockouts. The most significant fights Foster lost were against heavyweights Joe Frazier in 1970 and Muhammad Ali in 1972, both by knockouts. He retired from boxing first in 1974, but returned and fought seven more times before he finally quit in 1978. He was inducted into the International Boxing Hall of Fame in 1990. His citation reads in part, "One of the greatest light heavyweight champions in history…." He also owned an Albuquerque nightclub for a time and served for many years as a Bernalillo County deputy sheriff.

Literature abundant

Fountain, Colonel Albert Jennings (1838-1895?)
Doña Ana County Prosecutor, Politician, Man of Mystery

Col. Fountain is best known for the mysterious circumstances that surround his, and his son Henry's, disappearance on or about Feb. 1, 1895 near White Sands in southern New Mexico. No trace of either body has ever been found. In his lifetime, though, he had done much. His biographer wrote: "Between his reported birth date [on Staten Island, NY] in 1838 and 1861, there are twenty-three years—a time span in which a man's life is hardly begun. Yet…this man did more in twenty-three than most men do in several lifetimes." Fountain lived in New Mexico and Texas after 1861. He was a soldier, lawyer, legislator, newspaperman, actor, and prosecutor for the livestock association. Many believe he and young Henry were killed by rancher Oliver Lee (see entry) and a couple of his henchmen, though Lee, defended by Albert Bacon Fall (see entry) and Harvey Fergusson (see entry), was acquitted when tried for young Henry's murder at Hillsboro in 1899.

Col. Albert Jennings Fountain. After Twitchell.

Gibson, *Life and Death*
Metz, *Pat Garrett*
Owen, *Two Alberts*

Fowler, Joel A. "Joe" (c. 1850-1884)
Santa Fe Saloonkeeper, Socorro County Rancher/Killer

There is some dispute about where he was born—one source says Indiana, another Massachusetts—but Fowler spent time in Texas as a young man and arrived in New Mexico by the late 1870s. He operated a saloon at Santa Fe and ranches at White Oaks and Socorro. He killed numerous people, often with a shotgun. In January 1884, a group of vigilantes in Socorro, New Mexico, took him out and hanged him from a tree for the murder of a clothing salesman named James Cale, whom he had stabbed to death while on a drunken spree. Legend holds that Fowler called upon the angels for delivery as he was being hoisted up. One of the vigilantes is alleged to have said, "It's a cold night for angels, Joel. Better call on someone nearer town." Another observer noted that he thought Fowler died of fright even before he was hanged.

Bullis, *99 New Mexicans*
Thrapp, *Encyclopedia*
Other literature abundant

Francis, E. Lee (1913-2001)
Lieutenant Governor (1967-1970)

The son of Lebanese parents, Lee Francis was born in Seboyeta, Valencia (now Cibola) County, New Mexico. He and his wife, the former Ethel Gottlieb, a member of Laguna Pueblo, operated grocery stores and trading posts at Paguate, on the Laguna Reservation, and in the nearby village of Cubero. He was also involved in the cattle, sheep, and wool business; served as the area distributor for Conoco; and was the implement dealer for International Harvester. He had been in the Lieutenant Governor's office for fewer than six months when he was faced with the crisis of the Rio Arriba County Courthouse raid (June 5, 1967) led by Reíes López Tíjerina (see entry). Governor David Cargo (see entry) was out of the state and Francis was acting governor. Francis mobilized the National Guard and dealt with the situation for several days before Cargo returned to the state. (Busto reports that, "Four hundred and fifty National Guardsmen who had been put on alert days earlier by a prescient Governor Cargo were mobilized.") Francis' actions were not well received in some quarters, but his popularity remained high and he was re-elected in 1969. Francis' son attributed his father's political success to the fact that "he was related to half the citizens of New Mexico and the other half liked him." In 1972, Francis ran unsuccessfully for the Republican nomination for the U. S. Senate in a 12-candidate field that included his old boss, Dave Cargo (see entry), and Pete Domenici (see entry). Domenici won. Francis was a longtime member of the Farm Bureau and the Knights of Columbus.

Albuquerque *Journal*, April 5, 1972 & September 13, 2001
Busto, *King Tiger*
Cibola County *Beacon*, September 14, 2001
King, *Cowboy in the Roundhouse*

Franklin, Jimmy Marshall (1948-2005)
Lea County Stunt Pilot

Jimmy Franklin was born and raised on a ranch near Lovington in Lea County, New Mexico. He began flying by age 12 and at age 18 he was an accomplished aerobatics pilot. He was the son of Zip Franklin, for whom the Lea County airport is named. Jimmy Franklin was killed in July 2005 when he collided with another airplane during a performance at Moose Jaw, Saskatchewan. In addition to other aviation performances around the world, Franklin appeared at the Albuquerque Balloon Fiesta in the 1980s.

Lloyd Jojola, "Ceremony to Remember Celebrated Air Show
    Star," Albuquerque *Journal*, October 16, 2005

Jimmy Marshall Franklin

Fulton, Maurice Garland (1877-1955)
Chaves County Historian

Born at Oxford, Mississippi, Fulton received a Master's degree from the University of Mississippi in 1901. He taught college English in Kentucky, North Carolina and Indiana before he arrived at the New Mexico Military Institute (NMMI) at Roswell in 1922. He remained on the staff there until 1948, and in New Mexico until his death in 1955. His interest in the Lincoln County War seems to have been piqued shortly after his arrival at NMMI, and it became a preoccupation throughout the remainder of his life. His friend Ed Penfield reported, "He was… influenced by some of his mild prejudices. He told me that he considered the Tunstall-McSween (see entries) side the superior in right. As he saw it, Tunstall saw the tyranny and corruption in Lincoln County government and…set about to correct the wrongs." Penfield did not agree with that stance. Thrapp reports that Fulton's research was so detailed, and so ongoing, that he could never complete his book on the subject. For that reason, his friend, Robert N. Mullin, edited his papers after his death and in 1968 produced *Maurice Garland Fulton's History of the Lincoln County War*, published by the University of Arizona Press. Along with Paul Horgan (see entry), Fulton also edited *New Mexico's Own Chronicle: Three Races in the Writing of Four Hundred Years* (1937).

Ed Penfield (1911-1986), "Reflections of Maurice G. Fulton, *Book Talk*, New Mexico Book
    League, August 1984
Thrapp, *Encyclopedia*
Other literature abundant

-G-

Gadsden, James (1788-1858)
U.S. Minister to Mexico

Born in South Carolina, Gadsden attended Yale and returned home to enter the business world. He entered the army and served in the War of 1812 and the First Seminole War (1817-1818). He left the army as a Colonel in 1822. He became president of a Carolina railroad company and held a number of governmental positions, both elected and appointed, before President Franklin Pierce appointed him Minister to Mexico in 1853. His instructions were to negotiate a new treaty, as an amendment to the Treaty of Guadalupe Hidalgo (1848), which would call for the purchase of a strip of land across the southern New Mexico Territory (Arizona wasn't created until 1863). The treaty, negotiated in 1853 and ratified by the U.S. Congress the following year, called for the sale of more than 45,000 square miles of Mexican territory for $10,000,000. The land the U.S. acquired by the Gadsden Purchase was considered the ideal latitude for the southern route of the transcontinental railroad. Thus were the modern boundaries of the contiguous United States established.

Beck & Haase, *Historical Atlas*
Encarta Reference Library
Lamar, *Far Southwest*
Twitchell, *Leading Facts*, Vol. II

Gallegos, José Manuel (1815-1875)
Priest of the Albuquerque Parish

Padre Gallegos, a native of New Mexico born at Abiquiú, was the parish priest for Albuquerque, appointed in 1845, when Bishop Jean Baptiste Lamy (see entry) arrived in Santa Fe in 1851. It was rumored at the time that Father Gallegos was considerably more secular than he ought to have been; he was known to gamble, dance, and drink to excess. He was also a businessman who operated a freighting company and a general store. (His net worth was estimated at $8,000 in 1850.) Perhaps worst of all was the fact that his live-in housekeeper was a married woman who had previously been mistress to two Mexican army officers. (There are reports that María de Jesús Trujillo de Hinojos was Gallegos' partner in the general store.) The Padre's conduct soon came to the attention of the Bishop and his Vicar, Joseph Machebeuf. Machebeuf, something of a religious martinet, took grave exception to Gallegos' behavior. He wrote, "It was a great scandal for the people to see a women such as that in the rectory, traveling along with the priest in his coach and active in his business…. The parish administered by a priest so scandalous and so given to business and politics finds itself plunged in the most profound ignominy and corruption." Because he was popular among his parishioners, Gallegos doesn't seem to have taken Lamy and Machebeuf seriously, and in 1852 he went south to Mexico on a trading trip. While he was gone, Lamy suspended him and sent Machebeuf to Albuquerque to take over. Nearly a thousand of Gallegos' parishioners protested to the Bishop, but to little avail. When Gallegos returned to Albuquerque in early 1853, he attempted to re-establish himself but failed. He then left the Church and entered politics. He was elected congressional delegate in 1853, even though Bishop Lamy and many in the "American community" opposed him. One to bear a grudge, Machebeuf wrote, "[Gallegos used] every kind of fraud and intrigue…" to get elected. Gallegos' service in Congress was less than stellar: he spoke almost no English, and when he asked for permission to employ the services of an interpreter on the House floor, his request was denied. Even so, when Gallegos ran for re-election in 1855, against Miguel A. Otero (see entry), he initially won by a slim margin. Otero, however, challenged the results and ultimately won and was seated. Gallegos returned to Albuquerque. He remained active in politics and later served as Speaker of the Territorial House of Representatives and as Territorial Treasurer. He was also one of the incorporators of the Bank of New Mexico, chartered in 1863. Historians Bryan and Sálaz Márquez report Gallegos' date of death as April 21, 1875. Horgan reports that he died in a Santa Fe hospital 1881, after he asked for a priest.

Bryan, *Albuquerque*
Don Bullis, Rio Rancho *Observer*, March 17, 2005
Horgan, *Lamy of Santa Fe*
Lamar, *Far Southwest*
Remley, *Adios Nuevo Mexico*
Sálaz Márquez, *New Mexico*
Simmons, *Albuquerque*
Steele, *Archbishop Lamy*
Twitchell, *Leading Facts*, Vol. II & V

Galusha, J. R. "Chief" (1881-1961)
Albuquerque Police Chief (1916-1925)

Galusha was one of the longest-serving peace officers in New Mexico history. He served as a New Mexico Mounted Policeman, a deputy U.S. Marshal and railroad officer before he joined the Albuquerque Police Department. He was a U.S. Probation Officer for 25 years after he left law enforcement.

Hornung, *Thin Gray Line*

Garcia, Fabian (1871-1948)
New Mexico Educator, "Father of the U.S. Mexican Food Industry"
    Born in Chihuahua, Mexico, Garcia came to the United States as an orphan in 1873. He attended the New Mexico College of Agriculture and Mechanical Arts (NMA&M)—now called New Mexico State University (NMSU)—and was a member of the first graduating class in 1894. He received a Master's degree from Cornell. He became director of the A. & M. Experimental Station in 1923. Garcia was awarded honorary doctoral degrees from both the University of New Mexico and A. & M. In 2005 he was inducted posthumously into the Hall of Fame for the American Society for Horticultural Science. Paul Bosland of NMSU noted that the work he did to standardize chile varieties opened markets and established the state's chile industry.
Norman Martin, "Chile Pioneer is honored," Business Outlook, Albuquerque *Journal*,
        October 3, 2005
Owen, *Las Cruces*

Garcia, Nash Phillip (1913-1952)
New Mexico State Police Officer

    Nash Garcia was the first New Mexico State Police officer to be murdered in the line of duty. Two officers had previously been killed in vehicle accidents. Garcia died after being shot numerous times from ambush by brothers Willie and Gabriel Felipe on the Acoma Pueblo Reservation in what was then Valencia County. The brothers were soon captured and sentenced to long prison terms. One of them died in prison and the other was released in the early 1970s.
Bullis, *New Mexico's Finest*

Officer Nash Phillip Garcia

Garrand, Lewis Hector (1829-1887)
Writer
    Young Lewis Garrand wrote the only eyewitness account of the 1847 trials at Taos of those charged with the crimes associated with the revolt against the American occupation of the previous year. He was a native of Cincinnati, Ohio, who left home at an early age and wandered the Rocky Mountain region. In the fall of 1846 he joined a merchant caravan at Westport Landing, Kansas, under Cerán St. Vrain (see entry) bound for Bent's Fort. Garrand remained there for a time and in early 1847 he joined an army of volunteers led by William Bent (see entry) that set out to avenge the murder of Charles Bent (see entry). Garrand is said to have been sympathetic to the families of those murdered during the uprising, but he seemed to be equally compassionate regarding those standing trial. "It certainly did appear to be a great assumption on the part of the Americans to conquer a country and then arraign the revolting inhabitants for treason," he wrote. Garrand met a num-

ber of notable people during his travels and he penned a narrative of his travels entitled *Wah-To-Yah and the Taos Trail*, published in 1850. He returned to the east and studied both medicine and law and settled in Minnesota in the middle 1850s. He remained there for many years but returned to Cincinnati late in his life. He died at Lakewood, New York.

Crutchfield, *Tragedy at Taos*
Thrapp, *Encyclopedia*
Twitchell, *Leading Facts*, Vol. II

Garrett, Elizabeth (1885-1947)
New Mexico State Song Writer

Elizabeth was the third child born to Patrick Floyd Garrett (see entry) and his wife, Apolinaria (née Gutiérrez). Elizabeth became blind shortly after her birth. A friend of Helen Keller, she became an accomplished musician and song writer, and composed New Mexico's official state song, *O, Fair New Mexico*, in 1915. (Amadeo Lucero, Michael Martin Murphy and Pablo Mares also wrote songs honoring New Mexico.) She moved to Roswell in the 1920s and resided there, earning her living by teaching piano, until she died from a fall on a city street in 1947. She seems to have adored her father. She wrote, "[He shared] all the wonders and beauties and secrets of [the universe]. This intimacy brought me to the tender side of his nature. There was never a time when my questions were rebuffed. Instead he met them with patience and truth as nearly as he knew it." John Nance Garner (1868-1967), U.S. Vice President (1933-1941), who was well acquainted with Garrett at Uvalde, Texas, recalled that Garrett, "gave her [Elizabeth] everything to make her happy and I think finally made quite a musician of her."

Elizabeth Garrett, 1929, by Paul Whitley. Courtesy Historical Society of Southeast New Mexico, No. 4376-A.

Keleher, *The Fabulous Frontier*
Metz, *Pat Garrett*
Roswell *Daily Record*, August 31, 2003

Garrett, Patrick Floyd (1850-1908)
Lincoln County Sheriff (1881-1882), Doña Ana County Sheriff (1896-1900)

Garrett's early fame came during his single two-year term as sheriff of Lincoln County, New Mexico. On July 14, 1881 at Fort Sumner, he killed William H. Bonney (Billy the Kid, see entry). His other adventures in law enforcement and life are too numerous to mention here, but it is significant that it was Garrett who envisioned a vast irrigation project in the Pecos Valley of southeastern New Mexico. He invested heavily in the project, and lost his money before others, notably Charles B. Eddy and J. J. Hagerman (see entries), made the project work. Garrett served as Sheriff of Doña Ana County in the 1890s and as Collector of Customs at El Paso around the turn of the century. He was murdered—shot in the back—along a

wagon road between Organ and Las Cruces on February 29, 1908. Jesse Wayne Brazel (see entry) was charged with the crime, tried and acquitted upon a plea of self-defense. Many theories have been postulated concerning who Garrett's killer really was: Carl Adamson, Jim Miller (see entries), cowboy Billy McNew or rancher W.W. Cox (see entry). None of them were ever charged with the crime, and no one was ever convicted of the murder. For a fanciful version of Garrett's death, see Burns.

Burns, *The Saga of Billy the Kid*
Metz, *Pat Garrett*
Rickards, *Pat Garrett's Last Days*
Pete Ross, "Some Prominent New Mexicans May Have Been Accessories to the Murder of Pat Garrett," *Wild West*, December 2001
Other literature abundant

Garson, Greer (1904-1996)
Actress, Santa Fe Benefactor

Garson was born in County Down, Ireland and educated at the University of London with the intention of becoming a teacher, but she became active in the theater instead. Hollywood boss Louis B. Mayer signed her to a contract in 1934. In a long career, she received seven Academy Award nominations and won the Best Actress Oscar for her 1942 portrayal of *Mrs. Miniver*. In 1948, during the filming of *Julia Misbehaves*, Garson met Texas oilman and rancher E. E. "Buddy" Fogelson (see entry), and they married in 1949. Fogelson owned the Forked Lightning Ranch along the Pecos River near Santa Fe and the couple spent considerable time there, though she continued to act, especially in such notable films as *Sunrise at Campobello* (for which she won a Golden Globe Award in 1961 as best actress). She and Fogelson were generous in their contributions to the College of Santa Fe, and the theater

Greer Garson

there was named for her in 1965, and the library was later named for him. She remained in Dallas, Texas, after Fogelson's death in 1987 because her health was not good. She died there in April 1996. She sold her share of the Forked Lightning to the Conservation Fund, which in turn sold it to the National Park Service. (Note: One source shows Garson's year of birth as 1903; another as 1908. Her tombstone is etched with 1904.)

Literature abundant

Geronimo "Goyalka" (c.1825-1909)
Apache Indian Leader

The Apache name, Goyalka, spelled in several different ways, means "The Yawner." Geronimo was probably born on the Gila River near where modern-day New Mexico and Arizona meet. There is nothing to indicate that he was a great thinker but he was an excellent strategist. His priorities seemed to have changed with some regularity. At times he seemed prepared to fight the encroachment of white men to the very death. Other times he would surrender and return to the reservation. He was not, strictly speaking, a chief; but he was the leader of a warring band, and he in fact led the last significant Apache resistance to white expansionism. He surrendered for the last time in

Geronimo. After Twitchell.

August 1886. His final band amounted to 22 men and 14 women and children. He died, in captivity, of pneumonia at Fort Sill, Oklahoma. Some of his descendants may live on the Mescalero Apache reservation near Ruidoso, New Mexico.

Bullis, *99 New Mexicans*
Robinson, *Apache Voices*
Thrapp, *Encyclopedia*
Other literature abundant

Giddens, Frank D. "Big Frank" (1959-2004)
Carlsbad Football Player

Giddens was born in Lubbock, Texas, but was raised in Carlsbad, New Mexico. There he played high school football and basketball, and wrestled. *Sports Illustrated* listed him as one of the 50 best athletes in New Mexico history. He played college football at the University of New Mexico, and professionally for two years with the Philadelphia Eagles. He played line, and weighed in at over 300 pounds. He became ill at age 27 with type 2 diabetes and high blood pressure. He died at age 45 of an infection exacerbated by the diabetes.

Toby Smith, "Obesity, Football's Lethal Dilemma," Albuquerque
    Journal, November 21, 2005
Literature abundant

Giddings, Marsh (1816-1875)
Governor (Territorial) of New Mexico (1871-1875)

Born in Connecticut, Giddings moved on to Michigan where he became active in Republican politics. President Ulysses S. Grant (see entry) appointed him governor of New Mexico. Lamar comments thus about this era: "By 1868 the governorship had declined to the level where political hacks more often than not held the post. Governor Robert B. Mitchell (see entry)...made little impression on

Gov. Marsh Giddings. After Twitchell.

101

the territory. Governors William Pile (see entry) and Marsh Giddings left even less." Giddings died in office.

Lamar, *Far Southwest*
Other literature abundant

Goddard, Robert Hutchings (1882-1945)
Physicist and Rocket Pioneer

Goddard was born in Worcester, Massachusetts and educated at Worchester Polytechnic Institute. He received a Ph.D. in physics from Clark College in 1911. After conducting experiments in rocketry in the eastern United States, where he developed the first solid-fuel rocket in 1914 and the first liquid fueled rocket in 1923, Dr. Goddard launched a liquid fueled rocket near Roswell, New Mexico, in 1926. He moved his entire workshop and testing facility to Roswell in the early 1930s and conducted some of his most important experiments there until World War II. Goddard liked New Mexico. He once said, "Morning in the desert; when the impossible not only seems possible, but easy." When he died in 1945, he held 214 patents in rocketry.

Clary, *Rocket Man*
Hsi, *Sundaggers*
Other literature abundant

Gonzales, Higinio V. (1842-c.1922)
Santero, Tinsmith and Musician

A native New Mexican, Hinginio Gonzales is known to have resided at San Ildefonso in the 1870s and Rio Arriba County by 1880s. No source consulted offers much in the way of biographical information. Coulter & Dixon write of him: "H. V. Gonzales was an active tinsmith and an accomplished, creative craftsman as well as a gifted painter, musician, poet, teacher and editor. He was quite likely the originator of the Rio Arriba Painted Workshop style [of tinwork]." He is also believed to have written New Mexico's oldest *corrido*—a form of ballad—entitled "Corrido de la Muerte de Antonio Maestas" in 1889.

Coulter & Dixon, *New Mexican Tinwork*
Gavin, *Traditional Arts*
Montaño, *Tradiciones*

Gonzáles, José Ángel (1799-1838)
Governor (Insurrection) of New Mexico (1837-1838)

After the Santa Cruz rebels in the Chimayo Revolt were successful in routing the forces of Governor Albino Pérez (see entry) north of Santa Fe in August 1837, they marched on Santa Fe and took over the government (killing many of the Mexican-appointed officials, and mutilating them most horribly, including Governor Pérez). The rebels then elected José Gonzáles as governor. He was described as "a good honest hunter, but a very ignorant man." His fortunes soon changed. Former Governor Manuel Armijo (see entry), who had initially supported the rebels, reversed himself and managed to re-take Santa Fe for the Mexican government. Four of Gonzáles' lieutenants were captured, but the rebel governor escaped back to Santa Cruz. Early the next year, Armijo, who had by then been installed as official governor, ordered the executions of the four rebels in custody. With a significant number of regular Mexican troops, he crushed the rebellion completely and captured Gonzáles. Armijo immediately ordered him shot. Historian Ruben Sálaz Márquez reports that Gonzáles was granted amnesty. In any event, the Rebellion of 1837 was over. (Note: *The New Mexico Blue Book* does not list Gonzáles as a governor of New Mexico.)

Chávez, *But Time*
Horgan, *Great River*
New Mexico Blue Book, 2003-2004
Prince, *Historical Sketches*
Sálaz Márquez, *New Mexico*
Twitchell, *Leading Facts*, Vol. II

Gonzales, José María "Joe" (1900-1949)
Santa Rosa Night Marshal

Joe Gonzales served as sheriff of Guadalupe County from 1944 to 1948. He became night marshal of Santa Rosa in February 1949. He was killed thirteen days later when Delfido "Fito" Duran stabbed him in the neck, from behind. Gonzales' daughter, Mary Francis, wrote a poem in his memory entitled, "The Violin" which concludes:

Marshal José María
Gonzales

The forty-nine years that he was here
Will live in our hearts from year to year
The road to Heaven is open wide
For he was just too young to die.

Duran was convicted and sentenced to 95 to 99 years in prison. He actually served two years in the penitentiary and eight years at the prison farm before he was released in 1960 and died soon after from cancer.

Bullis, *New Mexico's Finest*

Gorman, Rudolph Carl "R. C." or "Rudy" (1931-2005)
Taos Painter, "The Picasso of American Art"

R. C. Gorman, born at Chinle, Arizona, on the Navajo Reservation, became world-renowned for his paintings. Legend holds that he began drawing pictures when he was three years old; and a teacher, Jenny Lind, of the Ganado Presbyterian Mission School, taught him about art history and mediums. "I guess she was the most influential teacher that I ever had," he said. He also acknowledged the influence of Mexican artists José Clemente Orozco (1883-1949), Diego Rivera (1886-1957), David Alfaro Siqueiros (1896-1974) and Rufino Tamayo (1899-1991); and of course the Spaniard Pablo Ruiz y Picasso (1881-1973). Gorman moved to Taos, New Mexico, in 1968 and maintained a studio and gallery there until his death from an infection. He once commented, "If I am remembered at all, I'd be very surprised and amused." His father, Carl Gorman, was one of the famed Navajo "Code Talkers" of World War II. R. C. was buried on private land near El Prado, New Mexico. He was posthumously recognized with Southwest Association for Indian Arts 2006 Lifetime Achievement Award.

Albuquerque *Journal*, November 4 & 8, 2005
Albuquerque *Tribune*, November 4, 2005
S. Derrickson Moore, "Remembering R. C., Bon Vivant, Trailblazer," *New Mexico Magazine*, June 2006
Other literature abundant

Grant, Ulysses S. (1822-1885)
Mexican War Officer, Civil War General, President of the United States (1869-1877)

As a general, Grant figured out how to defeat the Confederacy during the Civil War (1861-65). He served as President of the U.S. from 1869-1877. President Grant established a "Peace Policy" toward the nomadic Indians of the American West, which was generally unpopular. Grant County in western New Mexico is named for him. Silver City is the county seat.

Literature abundant

Gray, Clifford "Slick" (1920-2006)
Southwestern New Mexico Lawman

Gray was a native of Gadsden, Arizona, who joined the Deming, New Mexico, Police Department in the early 1940s. He served two terms as Luna County Sheriff (1967-1970) and as Chief of the Lordsburg Police Department (1970-1977). His final law enforcement position was as Chief of the Deming Police Department (1977-1991). Gray was legendary as a lawman in southwestern New Mexico.

"Obituary," Albuquerque *Journal*, February 28, 2006
Kuehl, William, conversation, March 2006

Gregg, Josiah (1806-1850)
Trader, Writer

Gregg was born in Tennessee but raised in Howard County, Missouri. He was bookish as a child and studied surveying as a teenager. He taught school for a time before he studied both medicine and law. His health was not good, and he hoped that the climate on the plains of northern Mexico—now New Mexico—would prove salubrious. He joined a mercantile caravan bound for Santa Fe in 1831 and subsequently made three round trips via the Santa Fe Trail. He became fluent in Spanish and a couple of Indian tongues. In 1839 he opened a new mercantile route from Van Buren, Arkansas, to Santa Fe, the importance of which was that caravans could leave from the east a month earlier each year than they could from Missouri. Gregg's place in New Mexico history was secured in 1844 with the publication of his book, *Commerce of the Prairies: Life on the Great Plains in the 1830's and 1840's*. He also published a reliable and comprehensive map of the western prairies in 1845. His writings are important not just because he wrote about what he saw, but also because his observations reflect the prevailing American attitudes of the day. He was anti-Catholic and anti-Mormon. He deplored the primitive state of Mexican agriculture but he was fond of the Mexican people. "The Mexicans," he wrote, "are remarkable for their politeness and suavity of manners." Crutchfield says that Gregg died during the Mexican War while Thrapp reports that he died after being thrown from a horse in California.

Crutchfield, *Tragedy at Taos*
Etulain, *New Mexican Lives*
Thrapp, *Encyclopedia*

Gurule, Leopoldo C. "Leo" (1943-1980)
Santa Fe County Deputy Sheriff

Deputy Leo Gurule was shot and killed while responding to a domestic violence call in Santa Fe. His killer then committed suicide. The deputy had requested assistance before he responded to the call, and his request was refused. Department officials later denied that Gurule had made any such request, but other law enforcement officers had in fact heard the radio transmission. The entire matter was compounded by the fact that Gurule had been given notice of termination from his job, for political reasons. The Santa Fe County Detention Center was named in honor of Deputy Gurule. His wife, Beverly (Len-

Plaque at Santa Fe County Detention Center honoring Deputy Sheriff Leopoldo C. Gurule

nen), joined the Santa Fe Police Department after her husband's death. She later became Santa Fe Chief of Police, and retired from that position in early 2006.

Bullis, *New Mexico's Finest*
Beverly Lennen, conversation, November 2005

Gutierrez, Juan (fl. 1765)
Las Huertas Founder

For want of money to pay his debts, Juan Gutierrez of Bernalillo was obliged to sell his ranch to the Santa Ana Indians in 1765. The extent of his debt and the size of the ranch are not known, but the change in ownership resulted in the displacement of eight families that had been tenants on his land. Gutierrez was not insensitive to the needs of the families and he soon petitioned Governor Tomas Veles Cachupín for a grant of land at a place called Las Huertas, east of Bernalillo. The grant was finalized in 1768, and by then 21 families resided there. The modern-day village of Placitas occupies a part of what was the original Las Huertas grant. The Land Grant still exists.

Bullis, *99 New Mexicans*

Gutierrez, Sidney McNeill (1951-)
Albuquerque Astronaut

Born in Albuquerque, Gutierrez graduated as valedictorian from Valley High

Sidney McNeill Gutierrez

School in 1969 and from the U.S. Air Force Academy in 1973. He received a Master of Arts degree in management from Webster College in 1977. He was a U.S. Air Force test pilot before he became a National Aeronautics and Space Administration (NASA) astronaut in 1984. He is a veteran of two space flights and spent more than 488 hours in space. He was the pilot of the Columbia on its 11th flight, June 1991. He retired from the Air Force in 1994 and was inducted into the International Space Hall of Fame in 1995. He resides in Albuquerque.

International Space Hall of Fame: Inductee Profile

NASA Biographies
Sálaz Márquez, *New Mexico*

Gylam, Lewis Jacob "Jackicito" (c.1837-1873)
Lincoln County Sheriff

Some sources show his middle initial as "G" and others refer to him simply as Jack. He was elected sheriff of Lincoln County in 1871, defeating Juan Patrón. Alexander Hamilton Mills in turn defeated Gylam in 1873. He was out of office on December 1 when he was killed, along with Ben Horrell (see entry) and Dave Warner, in a gunfight fueled by whiskey, on the streets of Lincoln. Town Constable Juan Martínez (see entry) was also killed. A native of Ohio, Gylam had been a farmer before he became sheriff. After his death, he was accused of stealing county tax money, but that was probably a ploy by local political strongman Lawrence Murphy (see entry) to explain away some cash shortages in the county's coffers.

Ball, *Desert Lawmen*
Bullis, *99 New Mexicans*
Nolan, *Bad Blood*
Wilson, *Merchants, Guns & Money*
Other literature abundant

-H-

Hagerman, Herbert James (1871-1935)
Governor (Territorial) of New Mexico (1906-1907)

The son of J. J. Hagerman (see entry), who was one of the movers and shakers in the agricultural development of the Pecos Valley in southeastern New Mexico, Herbert was born in Milwaukee, Wisconsin, and educated at Cornell University. He entered the diplomatic service and served as assistant secretary to the U.S. Ambassador to Russia. He left the State Department to accept appointment as governor of New Mexico, appointed by President Theodore Roosevelt. Hagerman was not well versed in territorial administrative matters and made the mistake of challenging Holm O. Bursum (see entry), the territory's leading Republican. The result was the brevity of Hagerman's administration. Roosevelt removed him from office, allegedly for selling public lands without proper authority, even though the charges were vague and politically motivated and even though his father and Roosevelt were personal friends. Herbert settled in Roswell where he led the "progressive" Republicans who contributed to the defeat of Bursum for Governor in 1911 by throwing their support to Democrat William C. McDonald.

Lamar, *Far Southwest*
Other literature abundant

Gov. Herbert James Hagerman. After Twitchell.

Hagerman, James John "J. J." (1839-1909)
Pecos Valley Entrepreneur

At the behest of Charles B. Eddy (see entry), Hagerman became involved in irrigation projects in the Pecos Valley of southeastern New Mexico; an involvement that cost him millions of dollars. He and Eddy parted ways and

James John Hagerman. Courtesy Historical Society of Southeast New Mexico, No. 555-B.

became business rivals. At one point, Hagerman offered Eddy a deal: "If you will quit lying about me, I will quit telling the truth about you." On the demise of Hagerman, Historian Will Keleher (see entry) wrote this: "The man who had done more, single-handed, for New Mexico than any other man, although he owed it nothing and it gave him little in return, was at rest. John James Hagerman knew nothing of six-shooters, or of yearling steers, or of cow camps or trails up and down the Pecos River. He had taken the dreams of Pat Garrett (see entry), Charles B. Eddy and many other[s]... and by intelligence, force of character and determination, had translated them into actualities." The town of Hagerman in Chaves County is named for him. He was the father of New Mexico Governor Herbert J. Hagerman (see entry).

Julyan, *Place Names*
Keleher, *Fabulous Frontier*

Hall, Arthur W. (1889-1981)
Watercolor Artist and Etcher

Reared in Texas and Oklahoma, Hall attended the Art Institute of Chicago and studied in Scotland and France. He moved to Santa Fe in 1946 and operated the Southwest School of Painting. He held memberships in several etching societies, the Southern States Art League, Prairie Printers Association, and American Water Colors League. He died in Albuquerque.

Albuquerque *Journal*, February 14, 1981

Hall, Thomas "Tom" (d. 1886)
Grant County Deputy Sheriff

While in pursuit of killers and kidnappers, Deputy Hall was shot in the back and left alongside a mountain road between Silver City and Pinos Altos on March 16, 1886. He was found late that evening, but efforts to save him were unsuccessful and he died the following day. His killer, Pilar Saiz, aka Pilar Perez, was captured the following year and tried for the crime. Saiz denied that he had kidnapped the girl in question, but claimed that he had "won her away by love." The girl, however, was not moved by this assertion and told authorities who had killed Deputy Hall. According to the Silver City *Enterprise*, Siaz's lawyer "...could not say anything in favor of the defendant." Saiz was convicted and hanged on July 6, 1888.

Alexander, *Six-guns*
Bullis, *New Mexico's Finest*
Gilbreath, *Death on the Gallows*

Hall, Thomas H. "Tom" (d. 1911)
Luna County Deputy Sheriff

On November 11, 1911, with the help of two masked men, Irvin Frazier escaped from the Luna County Jail at Deming where he was being held on a burglary charge. Sheriff Dwight Stephens (see entry) and a posse that included Tom Hall took up a pursuit that lasted eight days before Frazier and his friends were discovered in an adobe house on the VXT Ranch in the Black Mountains of Socorro County. The bandits immediately opened fire on the posse and killed both Deputy

Hall and posseman A. L. Smithers (see entry) on the spot. One of the outlaws was killed at the scene. Frazier escaped only to be captured a couple of weeks later in El Paso. Tried and convicted of murder, he was hanged at Socorro on April 25, 1913. The third man was never captured. One newspaper reporter wrote this about the fallen officers: "A home in Deming is desolate. A wife and mother's heart is bleeding at every pore. Five orphan children…are bowed in grief and go forth into the world to battle without the counsel, and strong protecting arm of a father."

Bullis, *New Mexico's Finest*
Gilbreath, *Death on the Gallows*

Hammer, Armand (1898-1990)
Industrialist/Philanthropist, San Miguel County School Founder

A native of New York City, Hammer completed medical school, but made his money as the president of Occidental Petroleum. He was also known for his cozy relationship with the USSR beginning in the 1920s and continuing into the years of the Cold War (1946-1991), an activity frowned upon by many Americans. Of significance to New Mexico is Hammer's founding the United World College of the American West at Las Vegas in 1982. The College was installed in the Montezuma Castle northwest of town. The school's mission is "to teach international understanding by bringing together young men and women of diverse ethnic and social backgrounds, in an environment in which they must work together for success." About 200 students are enrolled in the school at any given time, representing 80 to 90 countries.

Literature abundant

Harding, Warren Gamaliel (1865-1923)
U.S. Senator (Ohio), President of the United States (1921-1923)

A newspaperman by profession, Harding was elected President of the United States in 1920 and died in office on August 2, 1923. It was he who appointed New Mexican Albert Bacon Fall (see entry) Secretary of the Interior, a position Fall abused in the Teapot Dome scandal. Harding County in eastern New Mexico is named for him. Mosquero is the county seat.

Julyan, *Place Names*
Other literature abundant

Harkey, Daniel R. "Dee" (1866-after 1949)
Eddy County Lawman

Dee Harkey moved to New Mexico from Texas in 1890 and became a lawman soon afterward. He remained in public life until 1911. He claimed to have "been shot at more times than any man in the world not engaged in a war." When he was 83 years old he wrote a book called *Mean as Hell* that purported to detail his adventures. Many historians consider it fanciful at best and downright dishonest at worst. His recollections are certainly subjective, his dates often confused. Still, it is entertaining reading.

Harkey, *Mean as Hell*

Harper, Ashby (1917-1992)
Educator, Swimmer

A 1939 graduate of Princeton University, Ashby Harper became headmaster of Albuquerque Academy in 1964. During his tenure, the school moved from a small facility at Edith and Osuna Road, to the 300-acre campus on Wyoming NE that it occupies today. Enrollment grew from about 160 when he took over to 800 when he retired in 1985. Harper was also known for his athletic prowess. In 1982, at age 65, he swam the 21 miles across the English Channel, the oldest person to do it. He later swam 29 miles around Manhattan Island in New York, and 26 miles across Santa Barbara Channel in California. He was inducted into the Albuquerque Sports Hall of Fame in 1988. He had participated in a one-mile swimming race only a few hours before he died.

Albuquerque *Journal*, July 13, 1992

Harrison, Will (1907-1965)
Newspaperman

Will Harrison was born at Madisonville, Tennessee. His first job in New Mexico journalism was with the Gallup *Independent* in 1934. He worked for free to gain experience and also worked as a musician to earn a living. A couple of years later he owned and operated the Grants *Review*, a weekly that only lasted a year. He also worked for the Associated Press, the New Mexico *Sentinel*, the Santa Fe *New Mexican*, and the Albuquerque *Journal*. In 1952 he initiated a column called "Will Harrison's Inside the Capital." He became one of the most widely read columnists in the state, and Governor Jack Campbell (see entry) said, "Will Harrison...was probably New Mexico's best-known citizen at the time of his death." Harrison gained national attention in 1964 when District Court Judge Paul Tackett of Albuquerque cited him for contempt for a series of columns he wrote about a case involving an Eddy County Assistant District Attorney who was involved in an auto accident that claimed five lives. Tackett ruled that since the case remained pending when Harrison wrote his columns, the commentary amounted to contempt of court. He sentenced Harrison to 10 days in jail. Harrison appealed and the New Mexico Supreme Court found in the journalist's favor only months before his death. U. S. Senator Clinton P. Anderson (see entry) said upon learning of Harrison's death, "I did not always agree with him, but I always read his column. He was a good personal friend...."

Santa Fe *New Mexican* November 19, 1965

Harwood, Thomas (1831-1917)
Methodist Minister/Educator

A native of Wisconsin, Harwood served in the Union Army during the Civil War, rising to the rank of regimental chaplain and suffering a bullet wound to the shoulder. He arrived in New Mexico in 1869 and served for a time as a circuit-riding missionary in the northern part of the territory. Early in his labors, he concerned himself with only English-speaking folks, but later learned to speak Spanish so that he could "broaden his field for missionary and educational work."

Harwood wrote a book about his experiences on the New Mexico Frontier called *History of New Mexico Spanish and English Missions* (1908). He arrived in Albuquerque in 1883 and served as president of the Boy's Biblical and Industrial School, which came to be popularly known as the Harwood School. His wife, Emily, operated the Harwood Girls School, a Methodist institution. She also had a long and distinguished teaching career. Dr. Harwood died in Albuquerque of neuralgia of the stomach, a disorder that had kept him bedridden for two and a half months. He is interred at Fairview Cemetery. Note: The Harwood Foundation is not named for Thomas Harwood, but for Burt Harwood of Taos.

Thomas Harwood. After Twitchell.

Albuquerque *Journal*, January 1, 1917
Bryan, *Albuquerque*
Mondragón & Stapleton, *Public Education*
Marc Simmons, "The Lone Missionary," *Prime Time*, March 1998

Hatch, Carl Atwood (1889-1963)
U. S. Senator (1933-1948), Federal District Court Judge (1949-1962)

Carl Hatch was born in Phillips County, Kansas, and attended the public schools there and in Oklahoma. He graduated from Cumberland University in Tennessee in 1912 and entered the practice of law the same year at Eldorado, Oklahoma. He moved to Clovis, New Mexico, in 1916 and served as assistant attorney general in 1917-1918. He held several public offices, including District Court Judge from 1923 to 1929. In 1933, Governor Andrew W. Hockenhull appointed Hatch to the U. S. Senate to fill a vacancy created by the resignation of Sam G. Bratton (see entry). Hatch was elected to the office in 1934, 1936, and

Carl Atwood Hatch

1942. He did not stand for re-election in 1948. Senator Hatch is best remembered as the author of "An Act to Prevent Pernicious Political Activities," also called the "Hatch pure politics bill," but best known as the Hatch Act of 1939 (not to be confused with the Hatch Act of 1887 which had to do with agricultural experimental stations). The 1939 act prohibited political campaign activities by federal employees, and state employees who were paid largely with federal funds. Senator Hatch became concerned when he learned that Works Progress Administration (WPA) money had been used to secure votes for Democratic candidates in the 1938 elections. Himself a Democrat, Hatch considered this corruption and he believed that it should not be tolerated. Efforts to water down the act were rebuffed by the U. S. Supreme Court in both 1947 and 1974. In 1993, however, Congress amended the act so that Federal employees can take an active part in political campaigns for Federal offices. President Harry S. Truman appointed Hatch to the Federal Court in 1949 and he served until a year before his death from pulmonary emphysema.

Judge Sam Bratton's comment upon the death of Hatch was typical of the many accolades he received: "The public has lost a great member of its family."
Albuquerque *Journal*, September 16, 1963
Congressional Biography
New Mexico Blue Book, 2003-2004

Hatch, General Edward (1832-1889)
New Mexico Military District Commander (1876-1881)
Hatch, a native of Maine, commanded the U.S. Army in New Mexico during the most tumultuous years of the Apache Indian Wars. He was primarily vexed by Mimbres Apache Chief Victorio (see entry) from 1877 to 1880. The press criticized him for not being aggressive enough in capturing or killing the hostiles. He was posted to Nebraska after he left New Mexico and died there after a fall from a buggy. The town of Hatch in northern Doña Ana County is named for him.
Julyan, *Place Names*
Thrapp, *Encyclopedia*
Utley, *Frontier*
Other literature abundant

Haut, Walter (1922-2005)
Roswell Army Air Field Military Spokesman

Walter Haut. Courtesy Historical Society of Southeast New Mexico, No 2441.

As a young lieutenant in the U.S. Army, Walter Haut was the man who, in July 1947, announced to the world that space aliens had crash-landed near Roswell in southeastern New Mexico. He had been instructed to do so by his boss, Col. William Blanchard, the commander of the Roswell Army Air Field (which became Walker Air Force Base in 1949). The army quickly repudiated the story and claimed that the wreckage was only that of a weather balloon. The controversy, of course, has continued from that day to this. Haut was a native of Chicago, but made Roswell his home after he left the Army in 1948. In 1991, he was one of the founders of the International UFO Museum in Roswell, and served as the museum's president until 1996. He was inducted into the New Mexico Tourism Hall of Fame in 2002. Haut was also the first president of the Roswell YMCA.
"Lt. Announced UFO Wreck in Roswell," Albuquerque *Journal*, December 14, 2005
Roswell *Daily Record*, December 19, 2005

Heady, Ferrel (1916-2006)
University of New Mexico President (1968-1975)
A native of Missouri, Heady was educated at Washington University in St. Louis, where in 1940 he received a Ph.D. in Political Science. He served as a research fellow at the Brookings Institution and worked for the Department of Agriculture, both in Washington D. C., before World War II during which he served in the U.S.

Navy. He saw action in the South Pacific. From 1946 to 1967 he was Professor of Political Science and Director of the Institute of Public Administration at the University of Michigan. The University of New Mexico named him Vice President of Academic Affairs in 1967 and in 1968 he became President, succeeding Thomas L. Popejoy (see entry). He served as President until 1975. His tenure included some of UNM's most tumultuous events: the Viet Nam war protests beginning in the late 1960s, the "Love Lust" poem controversy of 1969 (in which an allegedly obscene poem was assigned reading for freshman English students), the student strike of 1970, during which the New Mexico National Guard was called out, and others. When Heady announced his intention to retire, the Albuquerque *Journal* noted editorially, "The school has continued to grow, both in student enrollment and in physical plant: strides have been made in connection with student relations and faculty freedom; and even the big school's image before the legislature has improved. Heady took his lumps during student riots but in retrospect it is plain that he handled the situation as well or better than similar situations were handled elsewhere." Heady remained at UNM as professor of Political Science and Public Administration until 1981 when he became professor emeritus. The awards Heady received and the recognition for professional excellence are too many to list here. His book, *Public Administration: A Comparative Perspective* (1991), is a standard graduate school text. Heady's autobiography is titled *One Time Around* (1999).

Albuquerque *Journal*, September 19, 1974 & August 23 & 27, 2006
Albuquerque *Tribune*, August 23, 2006
Davis, *Miracle on the Mesa*
Horn, *The University in Turmoil*

Heard, J. H. "Jay" (1881-1932)
Hidalgo County, U.S. Customs Service Inspector
Jay Heard and a ranchman named Claude Gatlin became engaged in a dispute over a flock of turkeys owned by Heard. At one point, Heard administered a beating to Gatlin. Later, Heard visited a ranch in New Mexico's boot-heel region, near Hachita, as a part of his work as a Custom's Inspector and Gatlin was present. Gatlin promptly grabbed a rifle and shot and severely wounded the Inspector, who died later. Gatlin was never captured. One source says he lived a "squalid" life after the murder and died drunk in a snow bank in northern Mexico.

Bullis, *New Mexico's Finest*
Hilliard, *Adios Hachita*

Henderson, Alice Corbin (1881-1949)
Santa Fe Poet/Editor/Librarian
As a poet, she was known as Alice Corbin; as prose-writer, Alice Corbin Henderson. She was born in St. Louis and resided variously in the Midwest and South before she and her husband, William Penhallow Henderson, an illustrator, moved to Santa Fe in 1916. She was tubercular and sought relief in the high and dry air of New Mexico. She had published several volumes of poetry before she arrived in the Land of Enchantment, and she had served as associate editor of *Poetry: A*

113

Magazine of Verse. She is credited with helping along the careers of such notable writers as Carl Sandburg and Edgar Lee Masters. After she turned her attention to the Southwest, she produced *Red Earth: Poems of New Mexico* (1920), *The Turquoise Trail* (an anthology published in 1928), and *The Sun Turns West* (1933). Her last book, *Brothers of Light: The Penitentes of the Southwest,* was probably most important to New Mexicans. She also served for a time as librarian and curator of the Museum of Navaho Ceremonial Art. Corbin Henderson associated with some of the leading poets and writers of her day, including Mary Austin (see entry), Witter Byner (see entry), Willa Cather (see entry), Paul Horgan (see entry) and D. H. Lawrence (see entry), to mention only a few.

T. N. Luther, "Collecting Santa Fe Authors: Alice Corbin Henderson," *Book Talk*, New Mexico Book League, April 1997

Rudnick, *Mabel Dodge Luhan*

Henson, Lou (1932-)
New Mexico State University Basketball Coach

A native of Oklahoma, Henson arrived in 1953 at New Mexico State University (NMSU) where he played guard under Coach Presley Askew. After graduation, he coached Las Cruces High School to a record of 145-23 and state championships in 1959, 1960, and 1961. He moved to Hardin-Simmons University in 1962 and in four years posted a record of 67-36. He returned to NMSU in 1966 and became Aggie head coach for the next nine seasons. In 1970 the Aggies went to the Final Four for the only time in their history. Henson coached the University of Illinois for 21 seasons and returned to NMSU in 1997 and coached the team for a salary of $1 per month. In eight seasons at Las Cruces he posted four 20-win seasons. He retired in 2005 as the sixth all-time winningest coach with a career 779 wins. His NMSU teams won 289 games. Henson was well regarded by his players and by other coaches as well. He was inducted into the New Mexico Sports Hall of Fame in 2005.

Lou Henson

Brad Moore, "Hall of Fame Inducts Four…." *Albuquerque Journal*, December 7, 2005

New Mexico State University, January 22, 2005

Hernández, Benigno Cárdenas "B. C." (1862-1954)
Lumberton Merchant, Rio Arriba County Sheriff (1904-1906), U.S. Congressman (1915-1917 & 1919-1921)

Born in Taos, Hernández was educated in public and private schools, and entered the mercantile trade as a young man. He moved on to Lumberton in Rio Arriba County in 1896 and continued to work as a merchant, becoming involved in local Republican politics. He served as sheriff of Rio Arriba County from 1904 to 1906 and treasurer and tax collector from 1908 to 1912. He ran for, and was elected to, Congress in 1914, defeating Democrat Harvey B. Fergusson (see entry). He was himself defeated for re-election in 1916 by William B. "Billy" Walton (see entry). He ran again in 1918, defeating Walton. He did not seek re-election in 1920. President Warren G. Harding (see entry) appointed Hernández collector for the Internal Revenue Service for the District of New Mexico, a position he held until 1933. He also served on the Selective Service Board during World War II. He died in California.

New Mexico Blue Book 2003-2004
News accounts abundant

Hibben, Frank C. (1910-2002)
New Mexico Archaeologist, Anthropologist

A native of Lakewood, Ohio, and Princeton educated, Hibben first arrived in New Mexico in the 1930s, collecting specimens for the Cleveland Museum of Natural History. He became so enamored of the state that he returned and completed his Master's degree at the University of New Mexico (UNM) in 1936, in zoology. He went on to earn a Ph.D. from Harvard in archaeology—in just one year—and returned to UNM, where he taught for the remainder of his life, except for the years in served with the military during World War II. He attained full professor status in 1952. He variously served as chair of the Albuquerque Zoological Board (1960-70) and director of the Zoo (1977); and chair of the New Mexico Game and Fish Commission (1961-1971). He made numerous trips to Africa and worked with such notables as Louis and Mary Leakey. He was also a renowned big-game hunter. The books and scholarly articles he wrote are too numerous to list here. It was largely because of Hibben's efforts that the Maxwell Museum at UNM was established, and he served as director from 1961 to 1971. In 1994, Hibben was recognized by UNM with the Zimmerman Award, given to an alumnus who has "made a significant contribution to the world and has brought fame and honor to the university and state." He died in his sleep in his Albuquerque home.

"Obituary," Albuquerque *Journal*, June 12, 2002
Other literature abundant

Higgins, Frederick "Fred" (1860-1941?)
Chaves County Lawman

Born in White County, Georgia, Higgins left home at a young age and made his way west to El Paso, Texas, where he worked on a goat ranch. He arrived in Roswell, New Mexico in about 1890 and married the same year. He was soon involved in law enforcement and was a deputy to Sheriff Charles W. Haynes by 1896 when he participated in the hanging of murderer Antonio Gonzales. Higgins also served as a deputy U.S. Marshal under Edward Hall, and others. He was involved in the pursuits of such notable outlaws as George Musgrave and the Christian brothers. Higgins led the posse that chased down and killed William T. "Black Jack" Christian (see entry) in April 1897 in eastern Arizona. Higgins was elected sheriff of Chaves County in 1898 and held the office until 1905. He also served about two years in the New Mexico Mounted Police. He was present when Roswell town marshal Roy Woofter (see entry) was shot and killed by bootlegger Jim Lynch in 1910; and, as a member of the New Mexico Mounted Police, Higgins accidentally shot and killed Tranquilino Lopez, a Doña Ana County jailer, in 1911. Note: Fleming indicates that Higgins died in 1924. Tanner indicates that he died in 1941.

Bullis, *New Mexico's Finest*
Fleming, *Treasures of History IV*
Gilbreath, *Death on the Gallows*
Tanner & Tanner, *Musgrave*

Hill, Janaloo (1939-2005)
Historian/Owner of Shakespeare, New Mexico, the Ghost Town

Janaloo was the daughter of Frank and Rita Hill who purchased the ghost town of Shakespeare, in far southwest New Mexico in 1935. In the late 1960s, she gave up a career as a model and returned home. "It became obvious that if I wanted to keep Shakespeare I had to return and help my parents," she said. She died of cancer in 2005. Janaloo's widower, Manny Hough, offers tours of the ghost town on selected weekends or by special arrangement. As a town, Shakespeare dates to the 1870s and at one point it reached a population of about 3,000 souls.

Don Bullis, Rio Rancho *Observer* June 9, 2005 & July 14, 2005
Hill, Janaloo & Rita, *New Mexico Historical Review*, July 1967
Hill, Janaloo, *The Hill Family*
Jenkinson, *Ghost Towns*
Marc Simmons, *New Mexican*, July 2, 2005

Hillerman, Anthony G. "Tony" (1925-)
Writer

There is no better, or better-known, writer living in New Mexico in the early years of the 21st century than Tony Hillerman. Born in Sacred Heart, Oklahoma, his life's journey has taken him from the Dust Bowl of the 1930s, to Europe in World War II—where he received a Silver Star for heroic action against the enemy—into the field of journalism, and then to the halls of academe at the University of New Mexico where he taught journalism and served as unofficial assistant to president Tom Popejoy (see entry); all before he became a very successful novelist and non-fiction writer. An item titled "About the Author" at the beginning of his autobiography, *Seldom Disappointed* (2001), best sums up the recognition he has received in a long writing career: "Tony Hillerman is the former president of the Mystery Writers of America and has received their Edgar and Grand Master awards. His other honors include the Center for the American Indian's Ambassador Award, the Silver Spur Award for the best novel set in the West, the Navaho Tribe's Special Friend Award, the National Media Award from the American Anthropological Association, the Public Service Award from the U.S. Department of the Interior, the Nero Wolfe Award, the Lifetime Achievement Award from the Oklahoma Center for the Book, an honorary lifetime membership in the Western Literature Association, and the Grand Prix de Littérature Policière. In addition to his election to Phi Beta Kappa, [he] has been named Doctor of Humane Letters at Arizona State University and at Oregon's Portland State University...." The dedication in the same book speaks volumes about him: "To Marie, who wanted me to do this, and to all you other writers, wannabes, shouldbes, willbes, and hadbeens included, I dedicate this effort. You're the ones who know it ain't easy. May you get as lucky as I have been." Hillerman is the creator of Navajo policemen Jim Chee and Joe Leaphorn and has written nearly 20 novels about them. He has also written nearly a dozen non-fiction books. In terms of encouraging and helping aspiring writers, Hillerman is generous to a fault. Tony and Marie live in Albuquerque's North Valley.

Literature abundant

Hilton, Conrad (1887-1979)
San Antonio, New Mexico, Native, New Mexico Legislator (1912-1913), International Hotelman

Hilton was born in San Antonio, New Mexico, on Christmas day in 1887. Early in life he started his own bank, and was elected to the first New Mexico state legislature in 1912. He served in France during World War I, and returned to New Mexico briefly before he moved on to Texas where he entered the hotel business. He built the Albuquerque Hilton in 1939 (it later became La Posada). Hilton went on to become an international hotelier with properties in major cities around the world, but he never forgot his New Mexico roots. Both of his sons, Nick and Barron, attended the New Mexico Military Institute; and when he married Zsa Zsa Gabor in 1942, he did it in Santa

Conrad Hilton

Fe (they were divorced in 1947). He also contributed significantly to the construction cost of a new gymnasium for the Sisters of Loretto in the town of Bernalillo.

Don Bullis, "Conrad Hilton of New Mexico," *New Mexico Historical Notebook*, February 11, 2005
Bullis, *99 New Mexicans*
Hilton, *Be My Guest*

Hindman, George (d. 1878)
Lincoln County Deputy Sheriff

Hindman was shot and killed, along with Sheriff William Brady (see entry), on April 1, 1878, on the main street in the town of Lincoln, murdered by a band of cowards, including William H. Bonney (Billy the Kid, see entry) hidden behind an adobe wall.

Literature abundant

Hinójos, Blas (d. 1835)
Mexican Soldier

In 1834, Captain Blas Hinójos was *comandante-principal* of New Mexico. He was killed in an engagement with Navajos in 1835.

Twitchell, *Leading Facts*, Vol. II

Holliday, John Henry "Doc" (1851-1887)
Las Vegas, New Mexico Saloonkeeper/Gambler
Arizona Gunman/Dentist

Holliday is usually associated with Dodge City, Kansas, and Tombstone, Arizona, but he also left a mark on Las Vegas, New Mexico. He arrived in Las Vegas in 1878 and established a dental practice, but also spent considerable time gambling. He opened his own saloon in the summer of 1879 and operated it for a few months. Legend holds that Holliday killed an army scout named Mike Gordon in July 1879 but modern biographers discount the story. He did engage in a gunfight with bartender Charlie White in Las Vegas in 1880, but neither man was killed. Holliday died of tuberculosis at Glenwood Springs, Colorado, and is buried there. His tombstone reads, "He Died In Bed."
Tanner & Tanner, *Doc Holliday*
True West Magazine, April 2006
Other literature abundant

Holley, Charles Hardin "Buddy Holly" (1936-1959)
Recording Artist

Buddy Holly

Holly was born at Lubbock, Texas, and became interested in music at a young age. Early in his career, he was signed to a recording contract with Decca Records, but the company decided that he was not ready for the big time, so they sent him home. In 1956, Holly contacted the Norman Petty (see entry) recording studio in Clovis, New Mexico, and Petty agreed to record the young Texan. One of those recordings was *That'll Be the Day*, which again attracted the attention of Decca Records. Holly and Petty remained closely associated until 1958 when they parted ways after a dispute about who got credit for what. Holly was killed in an airplane crash near Mason City, Iowa, along with artists Ritchie Valens and J. P. Richardson (The Big Bopper).
News accounts abundant

Holly, Buddy
See Holley, Charles Hardin

Hoover, Herbert (1874-1964)
President of the United States (1929-1933)

On May 14, 1930, President Hoover signed legislation that created Carlsbad Caverns National Park.
Barnett, *Carlsbad Caverns*

Horgan, Paul George Vincent O'Shaughnessy (1903-1995)
New Mexico Writer/Historian/Librarian

Paul Horgan was born in Buffalo, New York, but along with his family moved to Albuquerque in 1915. He was educated there and at the New Mexico Military Institute (NMMI) at Roswell, where he struck up a lifelong friendship with famed painter Peter Hurd (see entry). He began his writing career in 1921 as a reporter with the Albuquerque *Morning Journal*. He later served as librarian at NMMI for a number of years. Horgan was a prolific writer throughout his life. He began receiving critical attention in 1933 when he won a Harper Prize for *The Fault of Angels*. Over the years he wrote 17 novels and more than a dozen works of non-fiction. He won Pulitzer prizes for *Great River: The Rio Grande in North American History* (1955) and for *Lamy of Santa Fe: His Life and Times* (1975).

Bryan, *Albuquerque*
Horgan, *Peter Hurd*
M. Bruce McLaren, "The Reporter and the Poet," *New Mexico Magazine*, January 2004
Marc Simmons, "Two Writers Lost," *Trail Dust*, August 9-15, 1995
Other literature abundant

Horn, Calvin (1918-1996)
Albuquerque Businessman/Philanthropist/Publisher/Author

Horn was born in Kentucky, but arrived in New Mexico with his family at the age of three. His mother suffered from tuberculosis and by age 15 both of his parents had died. He and his older brother, H. B., fended for themselves by selling newspapers. The two of them founded the Horn Oil Company in 1939. Horn served in World War II and attained the rank of captain. He continued in the oil business after the war and at one time operated 26 filling stations. Horn also engaged in politics, beginning in the late 1940s when he was elected to the state House of Representatives, serving as Speaker in 1951. He also served one term in the state Senate. He and William S. Wallace of Highlands University formed Horn & Wallace Publishing in 1959. They specialized in reprints of important Southwest books: Twitchell's (see entry) five volume *The Leading Facts of New Mexico History*, Bancroft's *History of Arizona and New Mexico* and Sanchez's *Forgotten People*. Horn & Wallace also published Horn's *New Mexico's Troubled Years: The Story of the Early Territorial Governors*. Horn, who served on the UNM Board of Regents for ten years (1970-1980), also wrote *The University in Turmoil and Transition: Crisis Decades at the University of New Mexico* (1981), which dealt with the upheaval of the 1960s and 1970s. At the encouragement of Professor Richard Etulain, he underwrote the Calvin P. Horn Lectures in Western History at the University of New Mexico. In an item about Horn, written after his death, Dr. David V. Holtby cited a quote from Horn's book about early governors: William Carr Lane said in his inaugural address, "I have come amongst you with two objects in view: namely, to employ my time honorably to myself, and usefully to the people of this Territory." Horn himself might have said the same thing.

David V. Holtby, "Calvin Horn: Publisher, Author, Patron," *Book Talk*, New Mexico Book
        League, January 1997
Horn, *The University in Turmoil*
Paul Logan, "'Super Citizen' C. Horn Dies," Albuquerque *Journal*, December 20, 1996

Horrell Family (1800s - 1900s)
Lincoln County Ranchers/Killers

Family patriarch Samuel Horrell (d.1869) settled in Lampasas, Texas, in 1857. He had seven sons: William (c.1839-c.1862-65), John (c.1841-1869), Samuel (c.1843-1936), James Martin—called Mart—(c.1846-1878), Thomas (c.1850-1878), Benjamin Franklin—called Ben—(c.1851-1873), and Merritt (c.1853-1877). He also fathered one daughter, Sally Ann (c.1857). All except Sally Ann and the younger Samuel were destined to die violent deaths.

William "Bill" was the first, killed during the Civil War, date and place unknown.

John was next. Acting as trail-boss, he drove a herd of cattle to Las Cruces, New Mexico, in 1869, and there he got into a quarrel with one of his employees, who killed him. The exact date is not known.

"Old" Sam was killed by Apaches in the Organ Mountains, east of Las Cruces in January 1869. Son Tom and John's widow survived the attack.

Benjamin "Ben" was shot to death on December 1, 1873, in the town of Lincoln along with Jack Gylam (see entry) and Dave Warner. This marked the beginning of the "Horrell War" in New Mexico that resulted in the deaths of many innocent Hispanic citizens.

Merritt was next in line. On January 22, 1877, he was shot to death in the Gem Saloon in Lampasas, Texas, by "Pink" Higgins. The Horrell War had ended in New Mexico and the Higgins-Horrell Feud had started up in Texas.

Mart and **Tom** were last. They became involved in the robbery business, and after four of their henchmen robbed and killed a merchant at Rock School House on Hog Creek in Bosque County, Texas, an indignant citizenry displayed its righteous wrath on December 15, 1878, and killed them. After the Horrells had been arrested and locked up, estimates are that 150 citizens formed the crowd that protected another 50 who actually entered the Bosque County Jail and shot the brothers numerous times. One witness reported that he "...found the bodies...and enough buckshot on the floor to fill the crown of a good-sized hat." No doubt somewhat exaggerated, but the coroner's jury reported that Mart was shot 11 times and Tom ten times, with "...pistols and guns fired by parties unknown to us."

"Young" Sam is reported to have resided at several locations in the American West, and died at Eureka, California, in 1936 at the age of 99. His obituary did not mention his violent days in Texas more than 60 years earlier. Historian Fred Nolan (see entry) says that "Young" Sam was not 99 years old when he died, but that exact birth dates for members of the clan are hard to pin down.

It is generally reported that citizens who had occasion to live around the Horrells did not mourn their passing. It would be nearly impossible to tally up the number of people who died at their hands, and at the hands of their henchmen and relatives. Young Sam did well to get away from Texas and New Mexico; neither place wanted him around.

Nolan, *Bad Blood*
Wilson, *Merchants*

Houghton, Joab (1811-1877)
Judge

Born in New York and educated as a civil engineer, Houghton arrived in New Mexico in 1845 where he served as U. S. Consul at Santa Fe. He soon entered into the merchandising trade with Eugene Leitensdorfer. After the American Occupation of New Mexico the following year, General Stephen Watts Kearny (see entry) appointed Houghton to the Superior Court. Why the General made the appointment is not clear, except that Houghton was closely associated with Charles Bent (see entry), who was appointed governor, and Carlos Beaubien (see entry) who was also appointed to the bench. Houghton was not well regarded as a jurist. Twitchell wrote: "He was not educated to the bar and the records of his court, from 1846 to 1850 fairly demonstrate, from the crude manner in which the entries are made and from the decidedly peculiar and irregular method of entering orders, judgments, and decrees, that his experience in dispensing justice in those turbulent and troublous times was anything but satisfactory either to himself or to litigants." He was off the bench from 1850 to 1865 but his second term was no improvement over the first, according to The Santa Fe *New Mexican* which opined thus: "It is now clear that Judge Houghton is wanting in all the essentials necessary to a speedy and satisfactory administration of justice...." The judge left the bench in 1869. He married in 1876 and died in 1877.

Crutchfield, *Tragedy at Taos*
Lamar, *Far Southwest*
Remley, *Adios Nuevo Mexico page 139*
Sálas Márquez, *New Mexico*

Huning, Frank "Franz" (1827-1905)
Albuquerque Merchant

A native of Hanover, Germany, Huning and his younger brother, Charles, arrived in New Mexico in the late 1840s. Franz was soon engaged in the mercantile trade as an employee of Simon Rosenstein who ran a store in Albuquerque (now Old Town). In the late 1850s he established his own mercantile establishment, and began hauling goods over the Santa Fe Trail. He also operated a flourmill and a sawmill. He was quite successful and became an important man in a growing Albuquerque. Along the way he purchased land east of Albuquerque, and when the railroad arrived in 1880, he profited considerably from the sale of town lots. He constructed what was called Castle Huning at the intersection of Central Avenue and Fourteenth Street in Albuquerque in 1883, and resided there until his death. The two-story home, which contained

Frank Huning. Courtesy The Albuquerque Museum Photoarchives PA2004.013.001

about 14 rooms, was demolished in 1955. Huning was the grandfather of famed writers Erna and Harvey Fergusson (see entries). The Huning-Highland area, east of Albuquerque's downtown, is named for Franz Huning.

Bryan, *Albuquerque*
Simmons, *Albuquerque*

Hurd, Peter (1904-1984)
San Patricio Artist

The name given to him soon after his birth at Roswell, New Mexico, was Harold Hurd, Jr., but he was called "Pete." He legally changed his name to Peter when he was in his 20s. Peter came from a family with a strong military tradition—a Hurd had fought in every American conflict dating back to the French and Indian War (1754-1763)—and he studied at the New Mexico Military Institute before he entered the U.S. Military Academy at West Point at age 17. Two years later he resigned—leaving the Academy on good terms—and entered Haverford College, Pennsylvania, where he studied painting. He left there to study at the Pennsylvania Academy of Fine Arts. He became acquainted with famed painter N. C. Wyeth in 1923 and soon fell in love with Wyeth's oldest daughter, Henriette. They married in 1929. His work gained national fame by the late 1930s and he served as an artist and war correspondent for *Life* Magazine during World War II. He built the Sentinel Ranch at San Patricio, west of Roswell in the 1930s, and some of his best work was done there. Hurd received national attention in January 1967 when President Lyndon B. Johnson declared that an official portrait of him, done by Hurd at the President's request, was "the ugliest thing I ever saw." The Johnson family rejected it. Hurd, for his part, retorted that he had only one session with the president during which Johnson fell asleep. The painting, though, was sold to the Smithsonian Institution and hangs today in its National Portrait Gallery. Hurd died near Roswell of Alzheimer's disease, which had effectively prevented him from painting for the last ten years of his life. His final painting was a watercolor called "The Three Horsemen," completed in 1975.

Albuquerque *Journal*, July 10, 1984
Handbook of Texas Online, s.v. "Hurd, Peter"
Horgan, *Peter Hurd*
Metzger, *My Land*
Tulsa *World*, Jan. 6, 1967

Hurley, John (1848-1885)
Lincoln County Deputy Sheriff

Hurley was shot and killed by the same horse thief, Nicholas Aragon, who shot and killed Deputy Jasper Corn (see entry) the previous year.

Bullis, *New Mexico's Finest*
Other literature abundant

Hurley, Patrick Jay (1883-1963)
U.S. Army Officer/ Ambassador to China, New Mexico Candidate for U.S. Senator (1946 & 1948)

Hurley was born in Oklahoma. He rose to the rank of Colonel during World War I and Major General during World War II. He also served as Secretary of War in the administration of President Herbert Hoover (1929-1933), and Ambassador

122

to China in the administration of Franklin D. Roosevelt (1944-1945). A Republican, he ran for the U.S. Senate from New Mexico twice and lost both times, to Dennis Chávez (see entry) in 1946 and to Clinton P. Anderson (see entry) in 1948. Only about 1,800 votes separated Chávez and Hurley in the 1946 election, but a quick recount gave Chávez about a 5,000-vote margin of victory. Hurley then had the ballots impounded pending a second re-count, but before that could be done, ballots in Lincoln, Doña Ana and Otero counties were burned. Hurley then appealed to the U.S. Senate's Privileges and Elections Committee, which investigated and found in Hurley's favor. A vote on the Senate floor, however, went for Chávez by a narrow margin, and he was seated.

New Mexico Blue Book, 2003-2004
Santa Fe *New Mexican*, July 31, 1963

Hurricane, Al (1936-)
See: Sanchez, Alberto

Hyde, Benjamin Talbot Babbitt (1872-1933)
Santa Fe Scientist/Boy Scout Leader

Hyde attended St. Paul's Military School on Long Island, and then studied at Harvard. After a career in industry, he retired in 1912 and devoted his life to science, particularly natural history. He was one of the first to explore the ruins of Pueblo Bonito in Chaco Canyon. He was also interested and active in Boy Scout work. Hyde Memorial State Park near Santa Fe, one of New Mexico's oldest parks, was named for him in 1938. His widow donated it to the State of New Mexico after his death.

Davis, *Historical Encyclopedia*
Julyan, *Place Names*

-I-

Irick, John B. (1924-1988)
Albuquerque Political Figure

John Irick was born at Stroud, Oklahoma, and raised there during the Dust Bowl days of the 1930s. He served in the Pacific Theater of Operations during World War II as a B-25 pilot. He arrived in New Mexico after the war in 1946 and moved to Albuquerque in 1949 where he entered the insurance and real estate businesses. A Republican, he was first elected to the state senate in 1971, and served until 1980. He served as minority whip for eight of his ten years in the legislature. Irick ran for mayor of Albuquerque in 1974, and lost to Harry Kinney and in 1982 he ran for governor of New Mexico, and lost to Toney Anaya. He worked on the fund-raising drive for the New Mexico Museum of Natural History, and Governor Garrey Carruthers appointed him to the Mortgage Finance Authority, a position from which he resigned to accept appointment to the Governor's Organized Crime Prevention Commission, a position he held at the time of his death. He was well regarded by members of both political parties. The Albuquerque *Journal* editorialized after his death: "Irick was a genuinely nice person as well as an effective legislator and politician—a rare combination. From the Natural History Museum to a myriad of little things, New Mexicans will long enjoy the fruits of his public service."

Albuquerque *Journal*, August 2, 1988
Rio Rancho *Observer*, August 17, 1988

-J-

Jaffa, Nathan (1863-1945)
Mayor of Roswell (1903), Territorial Secretary (1907-1909 & 1911)

Born in Germany, Jaffa came to the United States about 1877 and settled briefly in Trinidad, Colorado. As a young adult he moved on to Las Vegas, New Mexico, where he managed Jaffa Brothers, a mercantile establishment. He established the firm of Jaffa-Prager in Roswell after 1886. Jaffa served on the first Roswell Board of Town Trustees in 1891 and as Chaves County Commissioner (1895-1897). He was the first Republican to be elected in the county. He was particularly interested in public office and served as Territorial Secretary—appointed by President Theodore Roosevelt—because of his friendship with Governor George Curry (see entry). When he was mentioned as a candidate for governor upon New Mexico statehood in 1912 (the election was in 1911), he declined to allow his name to go before the Republican convention. He resided at Las Vegas at the time of his death. Twitchell said this about him: "He occupies a high position in the social and business life of New Mexico and his standing is owing to his own efforts. He is a type of the self-made American citizen."

Nathan Jaffa. After Twitchell.

Curry, *Autobiography*
Fleming, *Captain Joseph C. Lea*
"Obituary," Albuquerque *Tribune*, September 13, 1945
Twitchell, *Leading Facts*, Vol. II
Other literature abundant

Jencks, Clinton "El Palomino" (1918-2005)
Grant County Labor Organizer

A native of Colorado and a World War II veteran, Jencks was employed by the International Union of Mine, Mill & Smelter Workers Local 557 in Denver in 1947.

125

He was dispatched to Silver City, New Mexico, to assist the Amalgamated Bayard District of the UMM&SW Local 890, a union made up largely of Hispanic workers. In 1950, he was a principal organizer of the so-called "Salt of the Earth" strike against Empire Zinc. It lasted 15 months and won a number of concessions for workers from the company. A movie of the same name was shot in Silver City in 1953. These events occurred during the peak of Wisconsin Senator Joe McCarthy's communist witch-hunts, and both of these projects suffered because of it. Jencks was charged with perjury in 1954 when it was alleged that he'd lied on an affidavit declaring that he was not a communist. He was convicted, but the U.S. Supreme Court reversed that decision in 1957, before he was sent to prison. Jencks earned a Ph.D. from Berkeley and taught economics at San Diego State University from 1964 until his retirement in 1988. He died in 2005.

Steve Boisson, "The Movie Hollywood Could Not Stop," *American History Magazine*, February 2002

David A. Fryxell, "Solidarity in Paint," *Desert Exposure*, June 2005

Myrna Oliver, "Organizer Led Mine Strike," Albuquerque *Journal*, Dec. 24, 2005 (reprinted from the Los Angeles *Times*)

Jenkins, Dr. Myra Ellen (1916-1993)
New Mexico State Historian

Dr. Jenkins was born in Elizabeth, Colorado, and received her B.A. and M.A. degrees from the University of Colorado. She taught in the Colorado public schools for some years before earning a Ph.D. from the University of New Mexico in 1953. She became an archivist when the New Mexico State Records Center and Archives were created in 1960. She served as New Mexico State Historian from 1969 until 1980. John Grassham of the Historical Society of New Mexico wrote: "Myra Ellen, an authority on numerous topics relating to New Mexico's past, specialized in land grants, water rights, and Pueblo Indian research…." Some of her published works include: "The Baltasar Baca 'Grant': History of An Encroachment," *El Palacio* (1961); "Taos Pueblo and Its Neighbors, 1540-1847" (1966) and "Spanish Land Grants in the Tewa Area" (1972), both in the *New Mexico Historical Review;* "Oñate's Administration and the Pueblo Indians," in *When Cultures Meet: Remembering San Gabriel Del Yougue Oweenge*, (Sunstone Press, 1987); and *A Brief History of New Mexico* which she wrote with Albert H. Schroeder (see entry), published by the University of New Mexico Press in 1974. Her work earned her many honors, including the New Mexico Woman's Hall of Fame, and as Grassham wrote, "A large void was created with the death of Myra Ellen Jenkins."

John Grassham, "In Passing: Myra Ellen Jenkins, 1916-1993, *New Mexico Historical Review*, October 1993

Jerrell, W. L. (d. 1884)
Doña Ana County Deputy Sheriff

Billiard hall owner W. L. Jerrell became a deputy to Sheriff Guadalupe Ascarte for the purpose of chasing down George Hester, who had allegedly robbed Barncastle's Store in the town of Doña Ana on New Year's Eve, 1883. Jerrell trailed Hester into Texas, where he boarded a stagecoach at San Angelo bound for Abilene. Also aboard the stage was Texas Ranger L. S. Turnbo. Along the way the coach was robbed and Jerrell and Turnbo, the only armed passengers, resisted the thieves. Jerrell was shot and killed in the gun battle. The people of San Angelo paid to have Jarrell's body returned to New Mexico. A local newspaper described Jarrell as "a man of nerve and brave as a lion."

Bullis, *New Mexico's Finest*

Johnson, Charley (1938-)
New Mexico State University Football Player/College Professor

A native of Big Spring, Texas, Johnson became starting quarterback at New Mexico State University (NMSU) in 1958 and led the Aggies to an 11-0 football season in 1960. He went on to pro football and played nine seasons with the St. Louis Cardinals, two seasons with the Houston Oilers, and four seasons with the Denver Broncos. He also acquired advanced degrees in chemical engineering along the way. In 1999 he returned to NMSU to teach chemical engineering. As of late 2005, he was chairman of the department.

Jeff Berg, "Charley Johnson," *New Mexico Magazine*, December 2005

Johnson, Hezekiah S. (fl. 1849-1876)
Albuquerque Newspaper Publisher, District Court Judge (1879-1876)

A native of Pennsylvania, Johnson arrived in New Mexico about 1849. He practiced law in Albuquerque and served as a deacon in the Episcopal Church. He is said to have preached in an Albuquerque hotel lobby on Sunday mornings. Johnson began publishing the *Rio Abajo Weekly Press* on January 20, 1863. It was a newspaper without pretense. The issue dated March 22, 1864 contained no news. The editor explained, "The news from the East by the last mail is unimportant." The *Rio Abajo Weekly Press* ceased publication by 1864 and was succeeded by *The New Mexico Press.* Johnson served a term in the Territorial Legislature before he became District Court Judge from New Mexico's Second District, a position he held at the time of his death.

Hezekiah S. Johnson. After Twitchell.

Bryan, *Albuquerque*
Simmons, *Albuquerque*
Other literature abundant

Johnson, Thomas "Tom" (d. 1933)
Santa Fe Murderer

Tom Johnson was the first man to be executed by electrocution in New Mexico, on July 21, 1933. He was convicted and sentenced to die for the stabbing death of Angelina Jaramillo on November 15, 1931, in her Santa Fe home. Johnson is the only African-American to be executed by electrocution in New Mexico. Santiago

Garduno was executed on the same date, for the poisoning death of his 14-year-old stepson. Until 1929, executions in New Mexico were done by means of hanging, and were the responsibility of each county's sheriff.
Albuquerque *Journal*, July 21, 1933

Jones, Andrieus Aristieus (1862-1927)
U.S. Senator from New Mexico (1917-1927)

Senator Andrieus Jones

A native of Tennessee, Jones began his New Mexico career by teaching school in Las Vegas from 1885 to 1887. He was admitted to the bar in 1888 and became something of an authority on land grant issues and water rights. He served as undersecretary of the Department of the Interior during the Woodrow Wilson administration (1913-1917). He became a recognized authority on income tax law during his ten years in the Senate. He died in office in December 1927; and Governor Richard C. Dillon appointed Bronson Cutting (see entry) to replace him.
Congressional Biography
Keleher, *Maxwell Land Grant*

Jones, Thomas W. "Tom" (1898-1935)
Lincoln County Chief Deputy Sheriff

Texas bank robbers and killers Ed "Perchmouth" Stanton and his cohort, Glen Hunsucker, were hiding out on a dry-land farm between Corona and Ramon, New Mexico. Lincoln County Sheriff A. S. McCamant organized a posse to seek them out. As the officers pursued the outlaws into rugged country, Stanton and Hunsucker ambushed them and Deputy Tom Jones was shot and killed immediately in the fight. Hunsucker was also killed. Stanton was captured and ultimately executed at Huntsville prison on September 28, 1934. Tom Jones' widow, Ola, was the superintendent of the Lincoln County Schools.
Bullis, *New Mexico's Finest*

Jonva, Nicolas de la Cruz (fl. 1680)
Tewa Indian Leader

Nicolas de la Cruz Jonva was a member of San Ildefonso (Po-soheh) Pueblo who worked with Po'pay (see entry), and others, in planning the Pueblo Revolt of 1680.
Sando, *Po'pay*

Joy, Christopher Carson "Kit" (1860-1936)
Grant County Train Robber

Joy was a working cowboy before he took up train robbery as an avocation. He, along with cowboys Mitch Lee, Frank Taggart and George Cleveland, robbed a train at Gage, New Mexico, on November 28, 1883, during which they killed the engineer. They were all eventually arrested and jailed, but managed to escape custody in early March 1884. A posse took up pursuit and when the dust settled, Cleveland was dead of a gunshot wound and Lee and Taggart were dead of lynching. Joy avoided capture for a short while, but was tracked down and shot by a rancher. His leg was amputated as a result of his wound, and in November 1884 he was convicted of second-degree murder and sentenced to life in prison. Territorial governor William T. Thornton (see entry) pardoned him in March 1896. He spent the remainder of his life at Bisbee, Arizona, where he died in 1936.

Alexander, *Lynch Ropes & Long Shots*
Alexander, *Whitehill*
Metz, *Encyclopedia*
Thrapp, *Encyclopedia*

-K-

Kearney, Kent (d. 1898)
Doña Ana County Deputy Sheriff
Kent Kearney was a schoolteacher by trade, but became a deputy to Doña Ana County Sheriff Pat Garrett (see entry). He was a member of the posse Garrett organized to capture Oliver Lee (see entry) and Jim Gilliland at Wildy Well in the summer of 1898. Both men were suspects in the disappearance of Albert Jennings Fountain (see entry) in 1895. Kearney was shot and killed in the gunfight. Garrett's posse was obliged to retreat and Lee and Gilliland were not arrested. No one was ever prosecuted for Kearney's murder.

Bullis, *New Mexico's Finest*
Gibson, *Life and Death*
Metz, *Pat Garrett*

Kearny, Stephen Watts (1794-1848)
U.S. Army of the West, Commander

Gen. Stephen Watts Kearny. After Twitchell.

Kearny was born in New Jersey and commissioned a 1st Lieutenant in the U.S. Army Infantry in 1813, in time for him to participate in the War of 1812 during the course of which he was slightly wounded. He remained in the army and was posted to the West on several occasions. Kearny was promoted to General at the end of June 1846 and given command of the U.S. Army of the West that occupied New Mexico in August of the same year. He made the first attempt at establishing civil government in the occupied territory, which remained a part of Mexico at the time. Kearny marched on to California in late September 1846, and after several skirmishes he occupied Los Angeles in January 1847. He marched on to Mexico and reached Vera Cruz—where he received the brevet rank of Major General—before he returned to Fort Leavenworth and then to St. Louis, where he died the following year from yellow fever, which he had contracted in

Mexico.
Thrapp, *Encyclopedia*
Other literature abundant

Keleher, William A. (1886-1972)
New Mexico Historian

Without doubt, Will Keleher is one of New Mexico's most important historians. His works on the last half of 19th century New Mexico are comprehensive and authoritative. Born in Lawrence, Kansas, he arrived in Albuquerque at the age of two years in 1888. He began his career as a newspaperman, and then in 1915 became a lawyer. This combination made him both a good writer and a meticulous historian. His books include: *Maxwell Land Grant* (1942), *The Fabulous Frontier* (1945), *Turmoil in New Mexico, 1846-1868* (1952), and *Violence in Lincoln County, 1869-1881* (1957).
Literature abundant

Kemp, David Leon (1862-1935)
Eddy County Sheriff/Killer

Born in Coleman County, Texas, Kemp killed a man during an altercation when he was 15 years old. He was first sentenced to hang, then his sentence was commuted to life, and then he was pardoned because of his age. He moved on to southeastern New Mexico. When Eddy County was created in 1890, he was elected sheriff and served four years in that position. He also operated a saloon in Phenix [sic], a wet village a few miles from the town of Eddy, which was dry. In 1897, Kemp killed James Leslie Dow (see entry), one of his successors as sheriff, but was acquitted of the charge. He eventually moved back to Texas where he died of a heart attack many years later. Much controversy has surrounded Kemp's life and adventures. Dee Harkey (see entry) wrote that Kemp was an outlaw and cattle rustler, but then Harkey was one of Kemp's enemies. Historian Bill O'Neal paints a much more positive picture of him. In his *True West* item he notes that Kemp did not drink, smoke or cuss; his only vice was chewing gum (Note: the Kemp entry in O'Neal's *Encyclopedia of Western Gunfighters* is much closer to Harkey's version. He seems to have changed his mind between 1979 and 1991.)
Harkey, *Mean as Hell*
Dennis McCown, "The Last Shooting of the Old West," *Quarterly of the National Association for Outlaw and Lawman History*, undated
O'Neal, *Encyclopedia*
O'Neal, "They Called Him Mister Kemp," *True West*, April 1991
Other literature abundant

Kendall, George Wilkins (1809-1867)
New Orleans Newspaperman

A native of New Hampshire, he and Horace Greeley (1811-1872) learned printing together in New York City. In 1837 Kendall traveled west and soon became one of the founders of the New Orleans (Louisiana) *Picayune* newspaper. Kendall accompanied the so-called Texan Santa Fe Expedition to New Mexico in

1841, and as a result of that unhappy experience—he spent nearly a year in a Mexican prison—he wrote *Narrative of an Expedition Across the Great South-western Prairies from Texas to Santa Fe: Narrative of the Texan Santa Fe Expedition* (1844). He denied in his writings that the Texans were anything but "pioneers" with peaceful intentions, even though they were heavily armed and equipped with cannons. He decried the treatment of the Texans by Governor Manuel Armijo (see entry). R. E. Twitchell (see entry) later wrote: "The Mexicans and Armijo have been the subjects of great abuse for their conduct and treatment of the Texans, but generally speaking, all fair-minded people must admit that the invaders were simply out of luck and received the same sort of treatment that would have been accorded by their own people had Texan territory been invaded by a hostile force...." It was Kendall who perpetrated the myth that Armijo was born of low and disreputable parentage, and early in life was an illiterate sheep thief and killer. One historian has written that Kendall's "writings have undeservedly been credited as reliable sources of his [Armijo's] biography." In 1847, Kendall returned to Mexico as a Texas soldier in the Mexican War, in which he was wounded. In the late 1840s he published *The War Between the United States and Mexico*. Kendall County, Texas, is named for him. He died there.

Laune, Paul, "Reporter on the Spot," *The American West*, November 1974

LeCompte, Janet, "Manuel Armijo's Family History," *New Mexico Historical Review*, July 1973

Sálaz Márquez, *New Mexico*

Thrapp, *Encyclopedia*

Twitchell, *Leading Facts*, Vol. II

Kent, James I. "Jim" (1875-1909)
Union County Deputy Sheriff

Kent was born in Texas (a newspaper of the day reported that he was born in "Bartols County," but no source consulted shows any such county in Texas). He arrived at Folsom, New Mexico, in 1904 and married Gladys Hittson in 1905. He probably became a deputy when D. W. Snyder took office on January 1, 1909. While investigating horse thefts around Union County, Deputy Kent learned that the Jamison brothers were responsible for the crimes. They were known to maintain a "camp" in eastern Colfax County, near the Union County line. Kent, along with deputies H. M. (or perhaps I. F. or I. P. or Sam, depending on the source) Williams and Gay Melon set out to arrest the Jamisons. Kent entered the small adobe house in which the outlaws were hiding and ordered them to put up their hands. He was immediately shot to death and Deputy Williams was badly wounded. A newspaper at the time reported that the Jamesons finished eating breakfast, stepping around Kent's body as they did so, before they bothered to flee. Melon ran for help and soon reached the John King ranch. King rode to the town of Folsom and telegraphed Union County Sheriff Snyder who sent out a posse. The posse captured the Jamisons only about 20 miles from the scene of the shooting and returned them to Clayton. George Jamison was later convicted of manslaughter and sentenced to five years in prison. Most sources report that Deputy Williams survived his wounds, but one reports that he died of his wounds at Trinidad, Colorado. Kent was well regarded. His obituary read, in part, "His untimely death we greatly deplore and realize that one has been called from our midst whose place in our community will be hard to fill."

Albuquerque *Journal*, July 3 & 4, 1909
Bullis, *New Mexico's Finest*
Clayton *Citizen*, July 2 & 9, 1909
Click, *Us Nesters*

Ketchum, Samuel W. "Black Jack" (1854-1899)
Train Robber

A Texan by birth, Sam Ketchum was the older brother of Tom "Black Jack" Ketchum (see entry). Some historians report that Sam used the name "Black Jack" too, and no one is sure why. (Outlaw Will Christian [see entry] also went by the name "Black Jack.") Sam, along with Elza Lay and Harvey Logan, robbed the Colorado and Southern passenger train Number 1 about five miles south of Folsom, New Mexico, in Union County on July 11, 1899. A posse pursued the thieves to Turkey Creek Canyon north of Cimarron and a sharp fight ensued. Sheriff Ed Farr of Colorado was killed, and several possemen were wounded; one of them, Henry Love (see entry) died four days later. Sam was so severely wounded that his arm was amputated, although there are several versions of that story. He was captured and died in the Santa Fe Penitentiary on July 23, 1899.

Bullis, *99 New Mexicans*
Metz, *Encyclopedia*
Metz, *Shooters*
Other literature abundant

Ketchum, Thomas Edward "Black Jack" (1863-1901)
Train Robber

The younger brother of Sam Ketchum (see entry), on August 16, 1899, Tom tried to rob the same train that Sam had robbed on July 11 of the same year. As an indirect result of the first robbery, Sam had died. Tom's luck was no better. He was severely wounded and subsequently captured. On September 8, 1900, he was convicted of "Assault on a Railroad Train" and sentenced to hang. His execution was badly botched, and his head was severed from his body. Tom Ketchum is the only man in U.S. history to have been hanged for train robbery.

Bullis, *99 New Mexicans*
Metz, *Encyclopedia*
Metz, *Shooters*
Other literature abundant

Kilburn, William Harvey (1864-1904)
Silver City, New Mexico, Town Marshal

Five cowboys from the nearby Diamond A ranch rode into Silver City in late August 1904, and two of them, Howard Chenowth and Mart Kennedy, proceeded to imbibe to drunkenness. When the ranch foreman, Pat Nunn, confronted them and ordered them back to the ranch, a fight flared up and Chenowth shot the foreman, but the first bullet hit Nunn's pocket watch and thus his life was saved. A further struggle followed in which Constable Perfecto Rodriguez attempted to intercede, only to be shot to death. Marshal Kilburn hurried to the scene, only to be shot, too. He died a week later. Chenowth was captured, tried and convicted, and sentenced to 50 years in prison. On Christmas day, 1905, he escaped jail and fled to South America. He was never recaptured. New Mexico Governor Richard Dillon pardoned him in 1927 and he spent his final years in the U.S.

Alexander, *Lawmen, Outlaws*
Bullis, *New Mexico's Finest*

King, Bruce (1924-)
Governor (State) of New Mexico (1971-74, 1979-82, 1991-94)

Gov. Bruce King

A native of Stanley, in southern Santa Fe county, a rancher and a Democrat, Bruce King served more years, twelve, as governor of New Mexico than anyone else in the state's history. Beginning in 1970, he was the first governor to serve a four-year term without the ability to succeed himself. Roberto A. Mondragón served as his Lieutenant Governor during his 1971-74 and 1979-82 terms. Casey Luna filled that position for his 1991-94 term. Always popular, and beginning with service on the Santa Fe County Commission and in the New Mexico House of Representatives, he only lost one election—the Democratic primary for Governor in 1968—until Republican Gary Johnson defeated for Governor him in the 1994 general election. His autobiography is entitled *Cowboy In The Roundhouse: A Political Life.*

Sue Major Holmes, "Former Governor Still Going Strong," Albuquerque *Journal*, February 5, 2005
New Mexico Blue Book 2003-2004
Other news accounts abundant

Kinney, Harry (1924-2006)
Mayor of Albuquerque (1974-1977, 1981-1985)

Harry Kinney was born at Trinidad, Colorado, but received a public education at Raton, New Mexico. He graduated from the University of New Mexico in 1945 with a degree in engineering. He served in the U. S. Navy during both World War II and the Korean Conflict and remained in the Naval Reserve until 1970. He operated an appliance store in Albuquerque for a time and joined Sandia Laboratory (later Sandia National Laboratories) in 1956. He was first elected to public office when he ran for Bernalillo County Commission in 1956. He served until 1958, and was elected to the Commission a second time in 1960 and served until 1964. He served on the Albuquerque City Commission from 1966 to 1973, as chairman from 1971 to 1973. This was at a time when the Chairman of the Commission was the *de facto* mayor, even though the position didn't carry the title. When Albuquerque

134

changed its charter and created a mayoral form of government, Kinney was the first one elected to the office, in 1974. He was defeated by David Rusk when he ran for re-election in 1978 but was elected again in 1981 and succeeded in office by car dealer Ken Schultz. For want of something to do, Kinney drove an Albuquerque taxicab for about five years after his political career ended. A Republican, Kinney was well regarded by politicians in both parties. He was responsible for helping to get the Albuquerque International Balloon Fiesta started. During his term, land was purchased for the Rio Grande Nature center. He supported bike trails and he oversaw the opening of Albuquerque's first senior citizen center. Senator Pete Domenici (see entry) said, "Harry knew more about city and county government than any other person around. I have never known a more honest, forthright and reputable and involved public person." Albuquerque Mayor Martin Chávez said, "Much of what is right with our city today can be traced back to planning and foresight during [his] time of public service."
Albuquerque *Journal*, May 10, 11 & 13, 2006
Albuquerque *Tribune*, May 10, 2006

Kinney, John (1847-1919)
Lincoln County War Figure, Doña Ana County Cattle Rustler
One historian described Kinney's gang as the "most dangerous band of rustlers ever to operate in New Mexico." A native of New Hampshire, Kinney arrived in New Mexico in 1875. He participated in the Lincoln County War (1878-81), and then set up a butcher shop in Las Cruces where he sold stolen beef. Beginning in early 1883, Major Albert Jennings Fountain (see entry) and the New Mexico Volunteer Militia set their sights on the Kinney gang and succeeded in putting it out of business. Kinney was sentenced to five years in prison, but served considerably less time than that. He operated a feedlot in Arizona after his release from prison.
Bullis, *99 New Mexicans*
Metz, *Encyclopedia*

Kirker, James "The King of New Mexico" (1793-1853)
Scalp Hunter
Born in Belfast, Ireland, Kirker arrived in New York by 1812 and participated in the War of 1812. He moved on to St. Louis by 1817 and to Santa Fe, New Mexico, in 1824. He called himself "The King of New Mexico," but no one seems to know why. His claim to fame was that he slaughtered literally hundreds of Apache, Comanche, Navajo and Ute Indian people in the 1830s and 1840s for the bounty paid by the Mexican government for Indian scalps: $100 for men, $50 for women, and $25 for children. He became a naturalized Mexican citizen, but in 1846 he hired out to the U.S. Army under Colonel Alexander Doniphan (see entry) during the Mexican War (1846-1848). He returned to the scalp hunting trade in 1849, again for the Mexican government, after the war. He led a wagon train to California in the early 1850s and died there, of alcoholism, according to some.
Gregg, *Commerce*

Ralph A. Smith, "The 'King of New Mexico and the Doniphan Expedition," *New Mexico Historical Review*, January 1963
Thrapp, *Encyclopedia*

Knapp, Lewis Alexander "Alex" (c. 1862-1912)
Albuquerque Police Officer

Alex Knapp was the first New Mexico peace officer to be mortally wounded in the line of duty after statehood. The very day that New Mexico officially became a state of the Union, January 6, 1912, a drunk by the name of Fred Watson, aka Theodore Goulet, shot Knapp on Copper Ave. in Albuquerque. Knapp, unarmed when he was shot, died on January 15. Goulet was sentenced to 10 years to life in prison.

Bullis, *New Mexico's Finest*

Kusz, Charles L., Jr. (1849-1884)
Manzano, New Mexico, Newspaper Editor

(Another source indicates that Kusz's middle initial was "G.") Kusz was a native of New York State, but arrived in Colorado in the middle 1870s. He managed to earn the respectable fortune of $150,000 in a few years. One source reports that he lost most of it to an absconding wife. Whatever the reason, Kusz arrived in Manzano, New Mexico, about 1880 and there he began publishing a newspaper he called *The Gringo and the Greaser*, one of the most interesting publications in New Mexico history. Kusz, it appears, was against much more than he favored, and stated his opinions in writing twice every month. He didn't like Roman Catholics, the Penitentes in particular; he opposed rustlers and rustling and the entire educational system. He soon made a plethora of enemies, and on March 26, 1884, someone shot him to death. One source says he was having dinner with a friend when he was killed; another that he was in his print shop at the time. Although no one was ever prosecuted for the killing, one historian has written, "…the killer was most likely a gringo, a greaser, a Roman Catholic, a rustler, or a school teacher…."
It is interesting that a book entitled *Red Blood and Black Ink: Journalism in the Old West* (see bibliography) makes no mention of Kusz or his publication.

Dary, *Red Blood*
McLoughlin, *Encyclopedia*
Fugate & Fugate, *Roadside History*
Thrapp, *Encyclopedia*

-L-

La Farge, Oliver Hazard Perry (1901-1963)
New Mexico Writer

A native of New England, a great-great-great-grandson of Commodore Perry, and a graduate of Harvard (1924), La Farge led a somewhat eclectic life before he arrived in New Mexico. His educational background was in anthropology and as an undergraduate he did field work in Arizona. After graduation, he involved himself in expeditions to Chiapas in Mexico and to Guatemala. His first novel was *Laughing Boy* (1929) about a Navajo silversmith, set in 1915. Many critics consider it his best work. It was issued by the Literary Guild and it won the Pulitzer Prize. His other book about the Navajo was *The Enemy Gods* (1937), again considered one of his best. T. N. Luther writes, "Overall he did much to help the American Indian. Although sometimes in his personal dealings he was regarded as snobbish, perhaps even arrogant, at his best he made many friends. Perhaps his greatest achievement was to publicize the plight of the ... Indians...."
Hillerman, *The Spell of New Mexico*
Luther, *Collecting Santa Fe*

La Lande, Jean Baptiste (fl. 1790-1821)
Santa Fe Merchant

La Lande, a French Creole, is believed to have been a native of Illinois. He crossed the plains to Santa Fe early in the 19th century and arrived in Santa Fe in 1804. As an agent of William Morrison, a merchant of Kaskaskia, Illinois, his purpose was to determine what market for eastern goods existed in Spanish New Mexico. He seems to have promptly forgotten about returning to the East—the trek was too arduous—and he ignored the debt for merchandise that he owed to Morrison. He received a grant of land from the Spanish government, married and settled down in Santa Fe. One of the chores American explorer Zebulon Pike (see entry) had, upon reaching Santa Fe in 1807, was to collect this debt, and apparently Pike tried to do so, but unsuccessfully. La Lande pled poverty. La Lande died in Santa Fe in 1821, quite wealthy, leaving behind a large family. He is one of the first to traverse the vast country between U.S. Territory (Illinois was a part of the

Indiana Territory at the time) and Spanish New Mexico for the purposes of trade. William Becknell (see entry) did not open the Santa Fe Trail as a regular trade route until 1821, and by then New Mexico was under Mexican Rule.

Thrapp, *Encyclopedia*
Twitchell, *Leading Facts*, Vol. II

Lamy, Jean Baptiste (1818-1888)
Santa Fe Bishop and Archbishop (1851-1885)

Lamy was a French Catholic cleric who became the first Bishop of New Mexico in 1851 and retired as Archbishop in 1885. A cover blurb on Paul Horgan's (see entry) *Lamy of Santa Fe* says this in part: "Lamy's accomplishments, including the endowing of hospitals, orphanages, and English-language schools and colleges, formed the foundation of modern-day Santa Fe and often brought him into conflict with corrupt local priests." Modern historians such as Fray Angélico Chávez (see entry), and his nephew, Dr. Thomas E. Chávez (see entry), take exception to the characterization of the Mexican priests as "corrupt." There is thus a recent reconsideration of the Bishop's relationship to those priests. Lamy built the cathedral in Santa Fe. He was the model upon which the protagonist of Willa Cather's (see entry) 1927 novel *Death Comes for the Archbishop* was based, but LaTour had Cather's personality.

Archbishop Lamy. Courtesy Archdiocese of Santa Fe

Chávez, *But Time and Change*
Chávez y Chávez, *Wake for a Fat Vicar*
Horgan, *Lamy*
Steele, *Archbishop Lamy*
Other literature abundant

Lane, William Carr (1789-1863)
Governor (Territorial) of New Mexico (1852-53)

Lane was a physician, former mayor of St. Louis and Missouri legislator when President Millard Fillmore appointed him governor of New Mexico. He was a Whig and his tenure did not extend far into the Franklin Pierce Democratic administration. One historian wrote this about what Lane faced: "The post [governor of New Mexico] was just about as undesirable as one could be. So far as Washington was concerned, New Mexico might just as well have been on another planet, and no one there took the slightest interest in its voteless inhabitants, white or red." After leaving the governor's office, Lane ran for delegate to Congress in 1853, but lost to Padre José Manuel Gallegos in a contested race.

Gov. William Carr Lane. After Twitchell.

"William Carr Lane, Diary," *New Mexico Historical Review*, July 1964
Lamar, *The Far Southwest*

Larrazolo, Octaviano Ambrosio (1859-1930)
Governor (State) of New Mexico (1919-1920), U.S. Senator from New Mexico (1928-1929)

Born in the Mexican state of Chihuahua, Larrazolo migrated to Tucson, Arizona, in 1870 with Bishop Jean Baptiste Salpointe, who educated the boy in Spanish, English and Latin. (Salpointe became Archbishop of Santa Fe in 1885.) Larrazolo was further educated at St. Michael's College in Santa Fe. His education complete, he returned to Tucson to teach school for a year before he moved on to San Elizario, Texas, where he became a school principal. He became a U.S. citizen in 1884 and became active in politics about then, too. He served in several appointed positions in Texas while he studied law, and was admitted to the bar. He moved on to Las Vegas, New Mexico, in 1895 and continued to be active in Democratic politics.

Senator Octaviano Larrazolo

He ran for delegate to Congress in 1900, 1906 and 1908, losing each time. In 1910 he changed his party affiliation to Republican. In 1918 he was elected governor, but was not re-nominated in 1920. It was Larrazolo who pardoned the prisoners captured after Pancho Villa's (see entry) raid on Columbus, New Mexico; that is, he pardoned those who had not already been hanged. He was elected to the New Mexico House of Representatives in 1926 and to the U.S. Senate to fill out the term of Andrieus A. Jones (see entry), who had died in December 1927. He served briefly in Washington, but became ill and returned to Albuquerque, where he died in April 1930. He was the first and only native Mexican to be elected governor and the first to be elected to the United States Senate.

Curry, *Autobiography*
Hurst, *Villista Prisoners*
New Mexico Blue Book, 2003-2004
Twitchell, *Leading Facts*, Vol. II

Lawrence, David Herbert Richards "D. H." (1885-1930)
English Novelist

At the behest of Mabel Dodge Luhan (see entry), Lawrence lived at the Kiowa Ranch near Taos, New Mexico, for a couple of years in the 1920s. As the story goes, Mabel traded the ranch to Lawrence's wife, Frieda, for a copy of the manuscript of one of Lawrence's novels, *Sons and Lovers* (1913). Three other works came of his visit to New Mexico: *The Plumed Serpent*, a novel published in 1926, *David*, a play, also written in 1926, and *Mornings in Mexico*, a travel item published in 1927. Some of Lawrence's biographers fail to mention that he spent time in New Mexico, and, if they do, it is only in passing, even though the only home he ever owned is the one near Taos and his ashes repose there.

Fugate & Fugate, *Roadside History*
Ousby, *Literature*
Rudnick, *Mabel Dodge Luhan*
Other literature abundant

Lea, Joseph Callaway "Capt. Lea" (1841-1904)
Chaves County Pioneer

Generally considered "The Father of Roswell" (see entry for Van Smith), Capt. Lea arrived in the Pecos Valley in the early 1880s. He was born in Tennessee, but lived in Missouri at the beginning of the Civil War. He is said to have ridden with Confederate guerrilla William Clarke Quantrill during the war. His efforts changed Roswell from a cluster of buildings along the Rio Pecos into a genuine town that was incorporated in 1903. He died of pneumonia in Roswell shortly after he was elected the town's first mayor. Lea County in far southeastern New Mexico was named for him. Lovington is the county seat.

Joseph Callaway Lea and John W. Poe. Courtesy Historical Society of Southeast New Mexico, No. 3326-J.

Fleming, *J. C. Lea*
Julyan, *Place Names*
Larson, *Forgotten Frontier*

Lee, John D. (1812-1877)
Utah Mormon Leader

At the behest of Brigham Young, Lee joined the Mormon Battalion in the Mexican War after the death of its commander, Capt. James Allen, for the purpose of collecting tithes from the soldiers. He did so when the troops were paid at Santa Fe (1846). Late in his life, Lee was held accountable for the Mountain Meadows Massacre in southwestern Utah (1857), and was executed by firing squad for the crime on March 23, 1877. He was restored to fellowship in the Mormon Church in 1961.

Juanita Brooks, ed., "Diary of the Mormon Battalion Mission by John D. Lee," *New Mexico Historical Review*, July 1967

Lee, Oliver Milton (1865-1941)
Otero County Rancher/Accused Killer

Lee arrived in New Mexico from Texas in 1884, and soon set up a ranching operation at Dog Canyon south of modern-day Alamogordo. He was believed to have been involved in several killings over the ensuing ten years, but he was not prosecuted. In 1899, he, along with Jim Gilliland, was tried for the murder of Henry Fountain, son of Albert Jennings Fountain (see entry), both of whom had disappeared in late January 1896. He was acquitted. Lee was elected to the State Senate in 1922 and 1924 and was noted for always carrying a gun on his person, even in the legislative chambers. Territorial Governor and Congressman George Curry (see entry) said of Lee, "[he had] a well-earned reputation as a good citizen, expert rancher, and efficient public servant."

Curry, *Autobiography*
Keleher, *Fabulous Frontier*
Owen, *Two Alberts*
Other literature abundant

Lee, Stephen Louis (c. 1808-1847)
Taos County Sheriff

Lee was one of the first sheriffs appointed after the American occupation of New Mexico in August 1846. The exact date of his appointment is unclear, but he is known to have been collecting taxes in October 1846. Mexican nationalists and Taos Indians who opposed the American occupation of New Mexico killed him and several others on January 19, 1847. A native of Kentucky, he was first a trapper, then a trader/merchant, before Gov. Charles Bent (see entry) appointed him sheriff. His brother, Elliott, was saved from death during the rebellion by Padre Antonio Martínez (see entry).

Ball, *Desert Lawman*
Chávez, *But Time*
Crutchfield, *Tragedy*
Other literature abundant

Leopold, Rand Aldo (1886-1948)
New Mexico Conservationist

Leopold was born at Burlington, Iowa, and grew up there. He received a Master's degree from the Yale University School of Forestry and went to work for the U.S. Forest Service in 1909. He was assigned to the New Mexico/Arizona district where it is said that he recognized the need for the Forest Service to do more than manage timber production. He campaigned for the preservation of wildlife habitats on public lands. He served as secretary of the Albuquerque Chamber of Commerce in 1918 and urged development of a city park that eventually became the zoo. In 1924 he developed a plan to exclude roads and to require additional use permits, except for grazing, in the Black Mountains of western New Mexico. His plan only allowed trails and telephone lines for fire protection. In 1933 he published *Game Management*, which set standards for the science of wildlife management. He became a professor at the University of Wisconsin in 1933 and remained there until his death. The Aldo Leopold Wilderness in the New Mexico's Gila National Forest, established in 1980, is named for him.

Encarta Reference Library
Hsi, *Sundaggers*
Other literature abundant

Liebert, Martha (1933-)
Sandoval County Librarian, Archivist, Historian

Liebert was born at Grand Forks, North Dakota. She received a B. A. from the University of North Dakota and a Master's in Art from the University of New Mexico. In 1965 she started a public library in the town of Bernalillo

Martha Liebert

in Sandoval County. She worked at building it into a popular and useful facility until her retirement in 1989. The library was named for her in 1986. In the years since, she has served as president of the Sandoval County Historical Society and as the organization's archivist. She remains active in a number of historical organizations, including the Albuquerque Corral of Westerners International. Her husband, Joe, is an expert on, and avid collector of, historical tools.
Carol A. Myers, ed., *Biographical Sketches, Westerners Newsletter*, Albuquerque Corral, 1995

Lincoln, Abraham (1809-1865)
President of the United States (1861-1865)
Lincoln was President during that crisis of democracy called the U.S. Civil War. Important to New Mexico, though, were a number of appointments he made, including that of Henry Connelly as governor (see entry). Lincoln County, New Mexico, was named for him four years after his assassination. Carrizozo is the county seat.
Julyan, *Place Names*
Literature abundant

Longabaugh, Harry Alonzo "The Sundance Kid" (1867-??)
Western Outlaw
A member of the so-called Wild Bunch, or the Hole In The Wall Gang, along with Robert Leroy Parker (Butch Cassidy, see entry), Longabaugh occasionally hid out in southwestern New Mexico. According to the legend that he and Parker were *not* killed in South America in 1909 or 1911, Sundance returned to the United States and resided in an unnamed New Mexico town, living under an unknown alias, until his death on an unrecorded date.
Betenson, *Butch Cassidy*
Other Literature abundant

Looney, Ralph (1924-2000)
Albuquerque *Tribune* Editor
Looney served as editor of the Albuquerque *Tribune* from 1973 to 1980. He wrote *Haunted Highways*, about New Mexico ghost towns, and *O'Keeffe and Me: A Treasured Friendship*, about his acquaintance with famed artist Georgia O'Keeffe (see entry). He won the 1971 Robert F. Kennedy journalism award for a nine-part series he wrote on the Navajo Indians. After he left Albuquerque he served as editor of the *Rocky Mountain News* in Denver until he retired in 1989.
Albuquerque *Tribune*, September 4, 2000

Lopez, Lucy "Mama Lucy" (1914-1994)
Las Vegas, New Mexico, Restaurant Owner and Political Symbol
A native New Mexican, she operated the Plaza Hotel and Mama Lucy's Restaurant in Las Vegas, New Mexico for about three decades. Over the years, many students at Highlands University stayed in her rooms and ate her sumptuous meals. Her restaurant became a gathering place for politicians, most of them young and of a liberal bent. She became a symbol when New Mexico *Independent* editor Mark

Acuff (see entry) observed a group of young Democratic state representatives gathered around a table in Santa Fe's Bull Ring Restaurant and commented that it looked like "a meeting at Mama Lucy's." He thereafter in his editorial columns referred to the group as the "Mama Lucy Gang," and the sobriquet stuck. The group was significant in New Mexico politics in the 1970s in that they managed to wrest power away from conservatives and elect Walter Martínez of Grants Speaker of House in 1971 (Martínez was defeated in 1979). Their influence spread to the state senate, and they were instrumental in the election of Jerry Apodaca to the governor's office in 1974. Upon the occasion of her death, Albuquerque *Journal* columnist Larry Calloway wrote, "'Mama Lucy' became a symbol of New Mexico liberalism in its vintage."

Larry Calloway, "Mama Lucy is Dead: ¡Viva Mama Lucy!" Albuquerque *Journal*, June 2, 1994

Lanny Tonning, conversation, April 11, 2006

Love, Henry (d. 1899)
Colfax County Cowboy/Posseman

Henry Love was an unlucky man. He was a part of the posse that pursued train robbers Sam Ketchum (see entry), Elza Lay and Harvey Logan into Turkey Creek Canyon near Cimarron, New Mexico, in July 1899. In the course of the gun battle, Colorado Sheriff Ed Farr was killed and Love and another posseman were wounded, as were outlaws Sam Ketchum and Elza Lay. The bullet that hit Love took him in the thigh, struck a pocketknife he carried in his pocket and drove the blade into his leg. He had previously used the knife to treat cattle afflicted with blackleg, a form of anthrax. Love died four days later from the disease.

Bryan, *Robbers*
Bullis, *New Mexico's Finest*
Other literature abundant

Lovelace, William Randolph "Uncle Doc" (1883-1968)
Albuquerque Medical Doctor

Suffering from tuberculosis, Lovelace arrived in New Mexico from Missouri in 1906 and took up the practice of medicine and surgery in Sunnyside (now Fort Sumner), where he practiced for about seven years. He moved to Albuquerque in 1913 and in 1922 formed a partnership with Edgar Lassetter that marked the beginnings of the Lovelace Clinic. By 1947, the clinic boasted of 16 doctors. The Lovelace Medical Center on Gibson Blvd. was constructed in 1952 and scheduled for closure over several years beginning in 2006. Doc was the uncle of William Randolph Lovelace II (see entry).

Garcia, *Three Centuries*
New Mexico Museum of Space History, December 5, 2005
Ollie Reed, Jr., Albuquerque *Tribune* November 30, 2005

Lovelace, William Randolph II "Randy" (1907-1965)
Albuquerque Medical Doctor

A New Mexico Museum of Space History biographical note indicates that

Lovelace II was a native New Mexican. Ollie Reed, Jr., however, writing in the Albuquerque *Tribune*, reports that Lovelace was born in Springfield, Missouri. Both agree on the year and that he earned a Medical Degree from Harvard in 1934; and that he worked at the Mayo Clinic and Bellevue Hospital in New York City before he relocated to Albuquerque in 1946 to join his uncle's (see entry) medical clinic. He was a pioneer in aviation medicine, and in 1943 he won the Distinguished Flying Cross for testing oxygen equipment by jumping from an airplane at more than 40,000 feet. So well respected in aviation medicine was he that the first seven American astronauts were selected from a field of 32 at the Lovelace Clinic in Albuquerque. The William Randolph Lovelace II Award recognizes outstanding contributions to space science and technology and is awarded annually. He, his wife, Mary, and his pilot, Milton Brown, were killed in a plane crash near Aspen, Colorado, in December 1965.

New Mexico Museum of Space History, December 5, 2005
Ollie Reed, Jr., Albuquerque *Tribune* November 30, 2005

Luhan, Mabel Ganson Evans Dodge Sterne (1879-1962)
Taos Patron of the Arts and Artists

A native of Buffalo, New York, Mabel Dodge Sterne (once widowed and once divorced) dabbled in letters in Italy, France and Greenwich Village in New York. Described as bored and rich, she arrived in Taos, New Mexico, in 1917 while still married to artist and sculptor Maurice Sterne, who wished to "save the Indians, their art-culture." Sterne returned to New York, but she remained in Taos and soon divorced again. She associated with the members of the Taos Society of Artists (created in 1915). In 1923 she married Tony Lujan, a Taos Indian. She took his name, but Anglicized it. At her beckoning, Georgia O'Keeffe (see entry) visited New Mexico as did several writers and artists, some of whom joined the creative clique in Taos. British writer D. H. Lawrence (see entry) was among them, and early on, Mabel owned the property that came to be known as the Lawrence Ranch, north of Taos, now owned by the University of New Mexico.

New Mexico Blue Book, 2003-2004
Rudnick, *Mabel Dodge Luhan*
Literature abundant

Lujan, Manuel, Jr. (1928-)
U.S. Congressman

Manuel Lujan was born on a farm near San Ildefonso in northern New Mexico. He attended St. Michael's High School in Santa Fe and graduated from the College of Santa Fe in 1950. He engaged in his family's insurance business for a number of years and frequently served as delegate to Republican National Conventions. The first Hispanic Republican to be elected to the U.S. Congress, he served from 1969 until 1989. He did not seek re-election in 1988. President George H. W. Bush named him

Congressman Manuel
Luján

Secretary of the Interior in 1989 and he served until 1993.
Congressional Biography
News accounts abundant

Lummis, Charles Fletcher (1859-1928)
New Mexico Writer

Lummis was born in Massachusetts and educated at Harvard (although he did not graduate) with Theodore Roosevelt. He edited a weekly newspaper at Cincinnati for a time before he walked from Ohio to Los Angeles in 1884, covering more than 3,500 miles in 143 days. As he walked, he sent dispatches to the Los Angeles *Times*. He became city editor of the *Times* and remained in Los Angeles for a couple of years. He covered General George Crook's campaign against the Apache leader Geronimo (see entry), in 1886 before he retired to Isleta Pueblo, near Albuquerque, to recover from a stroke he suffered, "from overwork," according to historian Marc Simmons (see entry). One of the books Lummis wrote was called *Pueblo Indian Folk Stories*. It got him into trouble with the Isleta Indian people when they discovered that the book revealed some tribal secrets. Simmons reports that he was able to patch up his relationship through the intercession of Pablo Abeita (see entry). Probably his best-known book was *The Land of Poco Tiempo* (1893). Abeita's son, Lummis (named for the writer), said late in his life, "he [Charles Lummis] had many strange ways about him." Erna Fergusson called Lummis "The first propagandist to trumpet the news [about New Mexico's unique qualities] abroad."

Fergusson, *New Mexico*
Marc Simmons, "Early Writer of Pueblo People," *Prime Time*, July 2005
Thrapp, *Encyclopedia*

Luna, Solomon (1858-1912)
Valencia County Sheep-raiser, *Patrón*, Albuquerque Banker

Luna was born at Los Lunas, New Mexico, to a prominent and well-established family. He was educated at St. Louis University and entered the sheep-raising business upon his graduation and return to New Mexico. He was variously elected probate clerk, sheriff, and treasurer of Valencia County and to the National Republican Committee. He was passed over for appointment to the office of U.S. Marshal in 1897, some said because of his association with the Tom Catron (see entry) and the Santa Fe Ring. Luna was the most powerful Republican leader at the state constitutional convention in 1910. He was a strong supporter of Holm Bursum (see entry) for governor in New Mexico's 1911 election that led up to statehood. Bursum lost to William McDonald. He also served as vice-president of the First National Bank of Albuquerque. Marc Simmons (see entry) points out that in his role as *Patrón*, he succeeded

Solomon Luna. After Twitchell.

admirably: in one Valencia County election, about 4,300 votes were cast at a time when the county only had about 1,800 residents.

Simmons, *Albuquerque*
Twitchell, *Leading Facts*, Vol. II

Lusk, Thomas Eugene "Gene" (1920-1969)
Eddy County Legislator/Gubernatorial Candidate

Gene Lusk was born in southeastern New Mexico and educated in the Lovington and Santa Fe schools. He graduated from the New Mexico Military Institute at Roswell in 1937 and earned a Bachelor's degree in political science from UNM in 1941. He served in the U.S. Army Air Corps as bombardier during World War II and entered the University of Michigan law school upon release from military service. He entered the practice of law at Carlsbad and was a member of the McCormick, Lusk, Paine and Freezer law firm. Lusk was elected to the New Mexico senate in 1952 and re-elected in 1956. He served as Senate Majority Leader from 1957 to 1959. He ran for the U.S. Congress in 1960 but lost in the Democratic primary to Joseph M. Montoya (see entry). In 1966 he defeated former New Mexico Governor John Burroughs in the Democratic primary race for governor, only to lose to Republican David Cargo (see entry) in the general election. He returned to the practice of law. On Friday afternoon, February 14, 1969, Gene Lusk committed suicide by shooting himself in the head in his wife's hospital room in Carlsbad. The son of Congresswoman Georgia Lusk (see entry), Lusk was also a cousin to New Mexico Attorney General Boston Witt (1965-1968).

Albuquerque *Journal*, February 15, 1969
Other news accounts abundant

Lusk, Georgia Lee (1893-1971)
Lea County Rancher, Educator, U.S. Congresswoman (1947-49), New Mexico State Superintendent of Schools

Congresswoman Lusk was born in Carlsbad, New Mexico, educated at New Mexico Highlands Normal College and Colorado State Teachers College and graduated from Western New Mexico University in 1914. She became superintendent of the Lea County Schools while she operated the family ranch. She served as State Superintendent of Public Instruction from 1931 to 1934 and from 1943 to 1946. An active Democrat, she was delegate to several national conventions, and in 1946 she was elected to Congress. She was not re-nominated for the office in 1948. She also served on the War Claims Commission from 1949 to 1953 and as New Mexico Superintendent of Public Instruction again from 1955 to 1958. She died in Albuquerque and is buried in Carlsbad. She was the mother of T. E. "Gene" Lusk (see entry).

Congresswoman Georgia Lusk

Mondragón & Stapleton, *Public Education*
News accounts abundant

-Mc-

McCarty, Henry (1859-1881)
See Bonney, William H.

McCarty Gallegos, Frankie (1928-2005)
Albuquerque Newspaper Editor

Born in Amarillo, Texas, McCarty moved with her family to Denver in the 1940s. She graduated from the University of Denver late in that decade with a degree in journalism. She worked for the *Raton Range* before she joined the staff at the Albuquerque *Journal* in 1954. Her first assignments were obituaries and re-writes. She remained with the *Journal* until 1994 when she retired as managing editor. She was one of the first women in the country to hold that position. McCarty was widowed in 1962 when her husband, Tony Gallegos, died in a boating accident at Vallecitos Reservoir in Colorado. "She was a groundbreaking journalist who cared deeply about the newspaper and her community," said *Journal* publisher T. H. Lang. "She mentored a whole generation of New Mexico journalists." Among the awards she won in a long career were the Women of Achievement Award from the New Mexico Press Women (1961), the first "sweepstakes" prize from the New Mexico Press Association (1968), the Dan Burrows Award from the New Mexico Society of Professional Journalists (1987), and the governor's award for Outstanding New Mexico Women (1989).
Albuquerque *Journal*, October 27, 2005
Dave Smoker, conversation, March 2006

McClure, J. A. (c.1871-1911)
Atchison, Topeka & Santa Fe Railroad Police

While investigating theft from slow-moving trains along the Belen Cutoff, between Belen and Mountainair, Officer McClure was shot from ambush and his body dumped into a well. The Howe family—father and two sons—were suspected, and were pursued into Texas, where they chose to shoot it out with a posse of New Mexico lawmen and Texas Rangers near Sierra Blanca. The father, F. B. Howe, and son Guy were killed. McClure was the first railroad officer to be killed in the

line of duty in New Mexico.
Bullis, *New Mexico's Finest*

McDonald, Thomas F. "Tommy" (1934-)
Albuquerque Football Player

Born at Roy, New Mexico, McDonald was an all-state football player at Albuquerque's Highland High School and all-American at the University of Oklahoma (1956). He was drafted by the Philadelphia Eagles in 1957 where he was a three-time all-pro. He played for the Dallas Cowboys in 1964, the Los Angeles Rams in 1965 and 1966, the Atlanta Falcons in 1967 and the Cleveland Browns in 1968. He is the only New Mexico native to be named to the Pro Football Hall of Fame, inducted in 1998.
www.HickokSports.com

McDonald, William C. (1858-1918)
First Statehood Governor of New Mexico (1912-1916)

McDonald was born in Herkimer County, New York, where he was educated. He taught school there for three years, and studied law, although he never practiced. He arrived in White Oaks, New Mexico, in the spring of 1880 where he found employment as an engineer. In 1890 an English syndicate hired him to manage the Carrizozo Cattle Company. While in White Oaks, he became well acquainted with two other young men who would play prominent political roles in New Mexico during the late territorial and early statehood days: Albert Bacon Fall and Harvey Butler Fergusson, (see entries). McDonald served in the Territorial Legislature and as Lincoln County assessor before he was named chairman of the Democratic Central Committee. He was elected governor in 1911 when a bloc of "Progressive" Republicans, led by Herbert J. Hagerman (see entry), rejected the candidacy of Holm Bursum (see entry), bolted their party and supported the Democratic candidate. Republican George Curry (see entry), who had served as territorial governor, gave McDonald generally high marks: "He had given New Mexico a sound business administration. His appointments, with a few minor exceptions, had been good. His economical administration has been popular with the people, but unpopular with influential Democratic politicians." McDonald declined to seek re-election in 1916, and died a couple of years later. He is interred at White Oaks.
Curry, *Autobiography*
Lamar, *Far Southwest*
Simmons, *Albuquerque*
Twitchell, *Leading Facts*, Vol. II & V

McGuire, Robert (c. 1846-1886)
Albuquerque City Marshal

On November 20, 1886, Marshal McGuire and his deputy, E. D. Henry, went to Martíneztown, northeast of Albuquerque, in search of two outlaws—Charlie Ross and John "Kid" Johnson—for whom they held arrest warrants. A gunfight took place at the outlaw hideout, and both McGuire and Henry died as a result of it. The outlaws escaped punishment and lived to old age. As a result of this incident, the Albuquerque city council gave peace officers a bit more latitude in the use of firearms: "Hereafter any criminal may be shot by police if he makes a show of his arms or attempts to use them."

Albuquerque *Journal*, November 23, 1886
Bullis, *New Mexico's Finest*
Simmons, *Albuquerque*

McJunkin, George "Nigger George" (1856-1922)
Union County Ranch Foreman, Discoverer

McJunkin was born into slavery in Texas. He moved on west as a young man, freed after the Civil War, and was working on the Crowfoot Ranch near Folsom, New Mexico, by the late 1870s. In 1908, he discovered the deposit of ancient animal bones in Dead Horse Arroyo that came to be called the Folsom Site in the 1920s. McJunkin, self-educated in many sciences, and a musician as well, received no credit for his find during his lifetime, and is yet today often overlooked.

Hillerman, *The Great Taos Bank Robbery* ("Othello in Union County")

McKinney, Thomas L. "Tip" (fl. 1881)
Lincoln County Deputy Sheriff

A deputy to Sheriff Pat Garrett (see entry) of Lincoln County, New Mexico, McKinney was present in Fort Sumner on the evening of July 14, 1881, when Garrett shot and killed William H. Bonney (Billy the Kid, see entry). McKinney is known to have been a member of a well-known Texas family, but historians do not provide dates of birth and death.

Keleher, *Violence*
Metz, *Pat Garrett*
Other literature abundant

McMullan, John J. (1917-2005)
Albuquerque Realtor, New Mexico House of Representatives (1977-1995), Part Owner, Albuquerque Dukes Baseball Team

Born in Kansas City, Missouri, McMullan moved to New Mexico and graduated from UNM in 1941. He served in the U.S. Army during World War II. He arrived back in Albuquerque after the war, suffering from tuberculosis. He entered the real estate business. It is estimated that he built 700 homes and 900 apartment units in a 60-year career. He became a part owner of the Albuquerque Dukes in 1960 and retained an interest in the team until 1979. In the state legislature, McMullan, a Republican, became a part of the conservative "Cowboy Coalition" which unseated Speaker Walter Martínez and the liberal "Mama Lucy Gang" from power in the House of Representatives in 1979.

News accounts abundant

McSween, Alexander A. "Alex" (c. 1843-1878)
Lawyer, Lincoln County War Figure

Alex McSween was destined to be at the wrong place, at the wrong time. The circumstances surrounding his birth are unknown. He was probably born in Canada and adopted by a Scottish emigrant named Murdock McSween, with whom he remained to adulthood when he moved to the U.S. He married Susan Hummer at Atchison, Kansas, and the two of them soon migrated to Lincoln County, New Mexico, arriving there in 1875. A deeply religious man—he studied for the Presbyterian ministry for a time—Alex practiced law in the frontier community. Early on, Lawrence Murphy (see entry) was his client, but that didn't last. He was soon aligned with cattleman John Chisum (see entry) and English entrepreneur John Tunstall (see entry). After Tunstall's murder by Murphy men in February 1878, McSween became *de facto* leader of the so-called "Regulators" who opposed Murphy's minions. This all led to the Lincoln County War (1878-1881). McSween was shot to death during the Five Day Battle at Lincoln in July 1878. According to Burns, he never carried a gun and was, for all practical purposes, murdered in cold blood. Utley says he was shot five times and died instantly. His widow went on to become the "Cattle Queen of New Mexico" (see entry).

Burns, *Billy the Kid*
Keleher, *Violence*
Nolan, *Lincoln County*
Thrapp, *Encyclopedia*
Utley, *High Noon*

McSween, Susan Hummer (1845-1931)
Lincoln County War Figure, "The Cattle Queen of New Mexico"

Susan Hummer was born at Gettysburg, PA. She moved to Kansas as a young woman and married Alexander McSween there in 1873. The two of them moved on to New Mexico and arrived in Lincoln in March 1875, just in time for Alex to get involved in the circumstances that led up to the Lincoln County War (1878-1881). When the shooting ended, Alex was dead. Susan went on to experience numerous adventures; and she married George Barber in 1880. Together they started ranching at Three Rivers and at one time had a herd of 8,000 head. She divorced Barber in 1892 and operated the ranch until 1917, when she sold it to Albert Bacon Fall (see entry). She moved to White Oaks where she resided for the remainder of her life. She was buried there.

Burns, *Billy the Kid*
Keleher, *Violence*
Nolan, *Lincoln County*
Thrapp, *Encyclopedia*
Utley, *High Noon*
Other literature abundant

-M-

MacGillivray, Finlay (1918-2006)
University of New Mexico Regent (1956-1962), State Fair Manager (1963-1980)

A native New Mexican, MacGillivray was born in Socorro, of Scottish ancestry. His family farmed in the Estancia Valley and he moved into Albuquerque in the late 1930s. He served as a pilot during World War II and returned from the Pacific Theater of Operations to enter the family business in Albuquerque, Comer Oil Companies. Governor John Simms (see entry) appointed him to the University of New Mexico Board of Regents in 1956. He served as president for his last two years during which the initial appropriation for the creation of the University's Medical School was made. Governor Jack Campbell (see entry) appointed him manager of the State Fair and he retained the job under governors David Cargo (see entry), Bruce King (see entry) and Jerry Apodaca (see entry). Attendance at the State Fair grew from about a half million when MacGillivray took the job to over a million when he retired. He served as General Manager of Ruidoso/Sunland Park Inc. from 1980 to 1983.

Albuquerque *Journal*, August 23, 2006
Hughes, *Albuquerque in Our Time*

Mackenzie, General Ranald Slidell (1840-1889)
New Mexico Military District Commanding Officer (1881-1883)

A native of New York City and a West Point graduate (1862), Mackenzie made most of his reputation for Indian fighting in Texas where he emerged victorious at the Battle of Palo Duro Canyon during the Red River War of 1874. His mental health began to fail about the time he was named commander of the New Mexico District in 1881. He was retired from active service in 1884, and died at Staten Island, NY.

Thrapp, *Encyclopedia*
Utley, *Frontier*
Other literature abundant

Maestas, Frank (1936-2006)
Albuquerque Sports Writer

A native of Las Vegas, New Mexico, Maestas joined the Albuquerque *Journal* as a sports writer in 1962, and over a long career he was named New Mexico sports writer of the year three times: 1966, 1968 and 1970. Sports editor Ed Johnson said, "He [Maestas] was the last of the classic sports writers. He got to the heart of the story." Maestas died of a rare lung disease.

"Legendary New Mexico Sports Journalist Dies," Albuquerque *Journal*, March 9, 2006

Magee, Carlton Cole "Carl" (1873-1946)
Albuquerque Newspaper Editor, Oklahoma City Inventor

Carlton Cole Magee.
Courtesy The Albuquerque Museum Photoarchives PC1978.050.497.

Magee, an attorney and editor, arrived in New Mexico from Oklahoma in 1917. He made the move in hopes of improving his wife's health. He purchased the Albuquerque *Morning Journal*, a Republican-leaning newspaper, in 1920. He soon felt called upon to attack, editorially, the state's Republican leadership and quickly lost their support. Albert Bacon Fall (see entry), in particular, took steps to terminate Magee's bank funding. He lost the *Morning Journal* and by early 1923 he was editor of the New Mexico *State Tribune*, which, late the same year, was purchased by the Scripps-Howard newspaper chain. It was Magee who coined the Scripps-Howard slogan: "Give Light, and the People Will Find Their Own Way." By 1923, he was into a political feud with the Republican leadership of San Miguel County—Judge David Leahy and Secundino Romero—which resulted in a shooting in a Las Vegas hotel lobby which left Leahy wounded and an innocent bystander dead. Magee was tried but found not guilty in the matter, several times. Magee returned to Oklahoma City and continued his journalistic career as editor of the Oklahoma City *News*. He also invented the parking meter (patent number 2,118,318) and became president of Magee-Hale Park-O-Meter Co. He died of pneumonia in Oklahoma City and is buried at Rose Hill Memorial Park in Tulsa, OK.

Bryan, *Albuquerque*
Bullis, *99 New Mexicans*
Susan Ann Roberts, "The Political Trials of Carl C. Magee," *New Mexico Historical Review*, October 1975
Simmons, *Albuquerque*

Magoffin, James Wiley (1799-1868)
Santa Fe Trail Merchant, Presidential Secret Agent

A native of Kentucky, Magoffin was engaged in the Mexican trade by the 1820s. In 1825 he was named American Consul at Saltillo in the Mexican state of Coahuila and later in Chihuahua. He was summoned to Washington, D.C., in the early summer of 1846 and met with President James K. Polk. The President designated Magoffin as his agent with the task of persuading Mexican authorities in New Mexico, namely Governor Manuel Armijo (see entry) and Colonel Diego Archuleta (see entry), to not oppose military occupation by the U.S. Army of the West. Magoffin, along with U.S. Army Captain Philip St. George Cooke (see entry), was successful in negotiations with Armijo and Archuleta. The U.S. Army under General Stephen Watts Kearny (see entry) marched into Santa Fe in August of 1846 without firing a shot. Magoffin attempted the same kind of negotiations in Chihuahua later the same year, but was not successful. In fact, he was arrested by Mexican authorities as a spy and nearly executed. One source holds that Magoffin was rescued by none other than General Manuel Armijo. Magoffin settled in El Paso in the late 1840s and built a large estate. He was the cause of the so-called "Magoffin Salt War" in December 1853. He died at San Antonio, Texas, and is buried there.

Horgan, *Great River*
Lamar, *Far Southwest*
Metz, *Shooters*
Sálaz Márquez, *New Mexico*
Simmons, *New Mexico*
Thrapp, *Encyclopedia*

Magoffin, Susan Shelby (1827-1855)
Diarist of the Santa Fe Trail

Susan Shelby was born into a wealthy Kentucky family and educated by private tutors. She married into another Kentucky family, the Magoffins. Her husband was Samuel and her brother-in-law was James (see entry); both were involved in the Mexican trade after the opening of the Santa Fe Trail in 1821. In 1846 and 1847 she and Samuel traversed the Trail from Independence, Missouri, to Santa Fe, and then well into Mexico. Along the way she kept a diary in which she recorded what she saw, and her impressions. It was published as *The Diary of Susan Shelby Magoffin, 1846-1847: Down the Santa Fe Trail and Into Mexico* (1926). Her trek was quite arduous and some historians believe that it broke her health. She died at a young age at St. Louis, Missouri.

Chávez, *Illustrated History*
Drum, ed. *Down the Santa Fe Trail*
Literature abundant

Marcy, William Learned (1786-1857)
U.S. Secretary of War (1845-1849), U.S. Secretary of State (1853-1857)

Marcy was born in Massachusetts, but became a New York conservative Democratic politician and supporter of Martin Van Buren. His wing of the Democratic Party was called the Hunkers. He was elected governor of New York and served from 1833 to 1839. He is primarily remembered as a strong advocate of the spoils system of patronage in government hiring as originally practiced by President Andrew Jackson. During the late 1840s he

Secretary William Learned Marcy

153

served as Secretary of War in the James K. Polk administration, and for that reason New Mexico's first military installation after the American Occupation of 1846 was Santa Fe's Fort Marcy. Of further significance to New Mexico is the fact that he served as Secretary of State in the Franklin Pierce administration and therefore approved the Gadsden Purchase of 1853. Marcy died on July 4, 1857.

Degregorio, *The Complete Book of Presidents*
Encarta Reference Library
Other literature abundant

Marron, Owen N. (1861-1945)
Albuquerque Mayor/Lawyer

Born in Essex County, New York, Marron originally studied to become a teacher and when he arrived in Albuquerque it was to become assistant superintendent of the U.S. Indian School. A year later he was transferred to the Indian School in Santa Fe. While engaged in his educational duties, he read law with William Burr Childers, a well-known attorney of the day, and was admitted to the bar in 1891. When his career as an educator ended, he entered into a law partnership with Needham C. Collier. President Grover Cleveland appointed Collier to the Second Judicial District bench in 1893, and Marron became the Clerk of Courts. Upon his return to private law practice, Marron became active in Democratic politics and was elected mayor of Albuquerque for three consecutive terms in 1899, 1900 and 1901. He was a strong supporter of New Mexico statehood and a leading contender for Governor as that appeared in the offing by 1911. He declined the nomination and supported William C. McDonald of Carrizozo who won election as New Mexico's first governor under statehood. He remained active in public affairs in the years afterward, serving as president and board member of the Albuquerque Commercial Club (which later became the Chamber of Commerce). He was an organizer and the first president of Albuquerque's State National Bank, and he held a financial interest in a number of enterprises. He is said to have been dictating his memoirs at the time of his death. Among his pallbearers were some of Albuquerque's best-known citizens: businessman and school board president S. Y. Jackson (see entry), Attorney and Historian William A. Keleher (see entry) and U.S. Appeals Court Judge Sam Bratton (see entry) among them.

"O. N. Marron Dies; Pioneer Attorney, Former Mayor," Albuquerque *Journal*, January 3, 1945

Martínez, Antonio José (1793-1867)
Taos Priest

Padre Martínez was born at Abiquiú. By 1821, he was a widower and studying for the priesthood in a Durango, Mexico, seminary. He became the priest at Taos in 1826. Some historians, notable among them Ralph Emerson Twitchell (see entry), believed that Padre Martínez was one of the organizers of the Taos Revolt of 1847, during which 15 or so Americans, and Mexicans sympathetic to the Americans, were murdered. It is a fact that Padre Martínez and Governor Charles Bent (see entry)—one of those murdered—were long-standing foes, but later re-

154

search by historians such as Father Juan Romero indicates that Martínez was actually opposed to the rebellion. Father Romero flatly states, "Padre Martínez was not a participant in the plans to overthrow American rule in New Mexico." Padre Martínez had been active in New Mexico politics after American Occupation. The arrival in Santa Fe of Bishop Jean Baptiste Lamy (see entry) in 1851 did not bode well for the Padre's future. The Bishop considered Martínez far too secular and first suspended him in 1856 and then excommunicated him in 1858. (There is some question about whether or not Bishop Lamy had the authority to excommunicate Padre Martínez in the way he did.) Martínez built his own chapel and continued his ministry. On the occasion of his death, the territorial legislature had inscribed upon his tombstone, *La Honra de Su País,* "A Credit to His Country."

Padre Antonio José Martínez. Courtesy The Albuquerque Museum Photoarchives PC1998.27.29

Chávez, *But Time and Chance*

E. K. Francis, "Padre Martínez: A New Mexican Faith," *New Mexico Historical Review,* October 1956

Romero, Father Juan, speaking at the annual convention, Historical Society of New Mexico, April 2006.

Steele, *Archbishop Lamy*

Father Juan Romero, "Begetting the Mexican American: Padre Martínez and the 1847 Rebellion" *Seeds of Struggle*

Twitchell, *Leading Facts,* Vol. II

Martínez, Donaldo "Tiny" (1924-2006)
San Miguel County Political Figure

Ezequiel C. de Baca (see entry), New Mexico's first Lt. Governor, and second Governor, after statehood, was Tiny Martínez's grandfather, thus his own predisposition for politics. Martínez graduated from Georgetown University Law School, a protégé of Senator Dennis Chávez (see entry) in the late 1940s and returned home to San Miguel County. Over the years he served as District Attorney for 16 years, as a member of the West Las Vegas Board of Education for 18 years and Chairman of the San Miguel County Democratic Party for 12 years. According to his obituary, his real goal was to "liberate politics from patronage." Jesus Lopez of Las Vegas said, "He was one of the great sons of New Mexico. He was the first to really start championing the cause of Hispanic people." One observer reported that he was called Tiny because of his large ears, but his niece reported that was not so. "The fact is," she wrote, "he was called 'Tiny' because he was the tiny baby until Carmen, his sister and my mother, came along eight years later."

Gabriela D. Guzman, "Obituary," Albuquerque *Journal,* March 2, 2006

María Elena Alvarez Luk, "Dear Readers," *Prime Time,* April 2006

Martínez, Esther, (P'oe Tsáwä) (1912-2006)
Storyteller and Linguist

Esther Martínez

She was born at Ohkay Owingeh (San Juan Pueblo) and named P'oe Tsáwä (Blue Water). Among her many friends she was referred to as Kó'ôe Esther (Aunt Esther). Within her family was simply called Sa'yaâ (Grandmother). As a child she was obliged to attend the Santa Fe Indian School where speaking her native Tewa language was forbidden. That unfortunate experience left a lasting mark on P'oe Tsáwä. She graduated from the Albuquerque Indian School in 1930 and worked at menial jobs—cleaning woman, cook and janitor—while she raised ten children. She was in her early 50s when she met linguist Randy Speirs and she became interested in the subject. She studied linguistics and became a major conservator of the Tewa language. She was also renowned as a teacher and storyteller. She compiled Tewa dictionaries in the language's several dialects and she participated in the translation of the New Testament into Tewa. P'oe Tsáwä published three books: *The San Juan Tewa Dictionary* (1983), *The Naughty Little Rabbit and Old Man Coyote* (1992), and *My Life in San Juan Pueblo: Stories of Esther Martínez* (2004). She received the Teacher of the Year award from the National Council of American Indians in 1997 and the New Mexico Arts Commission presented her with the Governor's Award for Excellence in 1998. In September 2006, the National Endowment for the Arts (NEA) named her a National Heritage Fellow, one of only 11 in the United States. On her way home from receiving that award in Washington, DC, she was killed in an automobile accident in Española.

Albuquerque *Journal*, September 18, 2006
Matthew Martínez, Artist Biography, VG, English Department, University of Minnesota
NEA, *National Heritage Fellowships Biography*

Martínez, Juan (d. 1873)
Lincoln Constable

Ben Horrell (see entry), Dave Warner and Jack Gylam (see entry) rode into the town of Lincoln on December 1, 1873. Some said they were just looking for a good time, others that they intended to "run the town." Whichever it was, they were soon drunk and making nuisances of themselves. Constable Martínez confronted the men and relieved them of their guns. A while later, the three had re-armed themselves and were shooting up a brothel. Martínez and several members of the police guard confronted them again. Dave Warner had some long-standing quarrel with Martínez and he pulled his gun and shot the constable, who fell dead. The police guard promptly killed Warner as Horrell and Gylam fled. The lawmen chased them down and killed them. This marked the beginning of what was called the Horrell War (1873-1874) in Lincoln County that left a number of Hispanic citizens dead.

Bullis, *New Mexico's Finest*
Nolan, *Bad Blood*
Wilson, *Merchants*

Martínez, Julián "Paddy" (1881-1969)
McKinley County Uranium Pioneer

In 1950, Paddy Martínez, a Navajo Indian living near Haystack Mountain in McKinley County, found a yellow rock near his hogan. Historian Abe Peña writes, "He had heard that yellow rocks might contain a valuable mineral." What Martínez had heard was correct. The rock contained uranium oxide: "yellowcake." This marked the beginning of a huge mining industry in western New Mexico—the first mine was the Haystack—with underground as well as open pit mines, in McKinley and Valencia Counties. Grants, New Mexico, came to be called "The Uranium Capital of The World" and by the 1960s half the uranium produced in the U.S. came from the area. Martínez was hired by the Anaconda mining company and paid $400 per month for the remainder of his life. He was a remarkable man who spoke three languages—Navajo, Spanish and English—and loved storytelling in all three. His tombstone in Grants identifies him simply as, "Uranium Pioneer."

Julyan, *Place Names*
Peña, *Memories*
This Is Grants-Milan, Manly W. Lutz Publications, 1969

Martínez, Maria Antonia Montoya (1887-1980)
San Ildefonso Pueblo Potter

Generally regarded as one of the most famous among American Indian potters, Maria was born at San Ildefonso, a Tewa Pueblo, probably in 1887 (some sources show her birth as early as 1884, or as late as 1889). She grew up around potters and learned the art at a time when it was not a necessary part of Pueblo life as mass-produced utensils and vessels were readily available. Her black-on-black work was so good that she and her husband, Julian Martínez, displayed the work at the St. Louis World's Fair in 1904 and the Panama-California Exposition in 1915. Her first pottery was signed "Poh-ve-ha" but by 1923 she used "Marie" and after 1925 Julian's name was added to the signature. The two of them worked together until his death in 1943. Maria then worked with her daughter-in-law, Santana, and the two of them did two European tours, which created an even greater demand for their work. Beginning in 1956, she signed her work, "Maria

María Antonia Montoya Martínez. Courtesy The Albuquerque Museum Photoarchives PA1968.12.312-1.

Poveka." She also worked with her son, Popovi Da (see entry), and he added yet another dimension to her work and created a numbering system. As one source says, Maria's ability to make beautiful, perfectly symmetrical shapes by hand is still unparalleled. Popovi Da died in 1971, but his son, and Maria's grandson, Tony Da continues the tradition.

Sando, *Pueblo Profiles*
Spivey, Richard L., "Maria's Legacy," *New Mexico Magazine*, August 2003
New Mexico Blue Book, 2003-2004
Other literature abundant

Mason, Barney (fl. 1880)
Lincoln County Lawman/Outlaw Associate

Pat Garrett (see entry) biographer Leon C. Metz writes this about Mason: "Very little is known about Mason's life and career. He and Garrett knew each other at Fort Sumner and in fact were each other's best man at a double wedding [when Garrett married Apolinaria Gutiérrez, January 14, 1880 at Anton Chico]. In the early days of Garrett's pursuit of Billy the Kid, Mason was Garrett's constant companion. However, their relationship cooled quickly thereafter for reasons which have never been stated. Probably Garrett tired of Mason's lies, cold-bloodedness, small-time criminal activities, and general lack of dependability. Mason is reported to have died when the roof of an adobe house caved in on him." William A. Keleher (see entry) says that Mason and Garrett were brothers-in-law. Walter Noble Burns goes so far as to suggest that Mason was a coward who hid at the sight of Billy the Kid (see entry).

Burns, *Billy the Kid*
Keleher, *Violence*
Metz, *Pat Garrett*
Other literature abundant

Masterson, James P. "Jim" (1855-1895)
Colfax County Militia Leader

Jim Masterson was the younger brother of famed Dodge City, Kansas, lawman Bat Masterson. Jim served in several law enforcement positions in Kansas before New Mexico Governor Lionel Sheldon (see entry) hired him to lead Militia Company H, the purpose of which was to evict squatters from the Maxwell Land Grant. The 35 members of the group seem to have taken their work a bit too seriously; and public pressure obliged Governor Sheldon to disband Company H. About 300 vigilantes then marched Masterson and his bunch to the Colorado line and admonished them never to return to New Mexico. George Curry (see entry), who was involved in the affair, reported that he did not think any of them ever did.

Curry, *Autobiography*
Other literature abundant

Mather, David "Mysterious Dave" (1845-?)
Las Vegas, New Mexico, Lawman/Gunman

A native of Connecticut, Dave Mather was said to have been a direct descendant of 17th century religious leaders, Increase and Cotton Mather, both of Boston. By the early 1870s, Dave was living in Arkansas where he was regarded as a cattle thief and "general nuisance." He later moved on to Dodge City, Kansas, where he was likewise a gambler and general ne'er-do-well, though he served for a time as a deputy marshal. He and Wyatt Earp became friends and the two of them entered into a fraudulent scheme to sell fake gold brick to suckers in Mobeetie, Texas. They were caught and sent packing. Mather moved on to Las Vegas, New Mexico, where he became a deputy town marshal under Hyman Neill, aka, Hoodoo Brown (see entry). Mather was present in the Close and Patterson Saloon in January 1880, when four thugs—Tom Henry, Jim West, John Dorsey and "Big" Randall—shot and killed Marshal Joe Carson (see entry). Mather took a hand in the matter and killed Randall and wounded Jim West and Tom Henry. Mather was uninjured. Many believe that Mather led the mob that lynched Henry, West and Dorsey a few weeks later. He left Las Vegas not long afterwards and drifted around the American West, engaging in a plethora of petty criminal activities. He was last reliably seen in Nebraska in 1887, and then disappeared from history. That's why they called him "Mysterious Dave."

Bullis, *99 New Mexicans*
Metz, *Shooters*
O'Neal, *Encyclopedia*
Other literature abundant

Mathews, J. B. "Billy" (1847-1904)
Lincoln County Deputy Sheriff, Lincoln County War Figure

Mathews was a participant in New Mexico's famed Lincoln County War (1878-1881). A partisan on the side of the Murphy-Dolan faction, he participated in most of the significant events in the conflict. He was present when William H. Bonney (Billy the Kid, see entry) and his friends murdered Sheriff William Brady (see entry) and his deputy, George Hindman (see entry), on April 1, 1878. Bonney claimed that he was more interested in killing Mathews than he was Sheriff Brady, but Mathews was uninjured in the fight, and fired a shot that wounded young Billy. After the shooting and gun smoke of the Lincoln County War cleared away, Mathews became a farmer and rancher in southeastern New Mexico.

Burns, *Billy the Kid*
Fleming, *J. B. Mathews*

Mauldin, William Henry "Bill" (1921-2003)
World War II Cartoonist

Bill Mauldin was born at Mountain Park in south-central New Mexico. He studied at the Chicago Academy of Fine Arts before he entered the U. S. Army early in World War II. Early on he was assigned to the 45th Infantry Division where he began drawing cartoons featuring the front-line soldiers, Willie and Joe. After he was assigned to *Stars and Stripes*, the GI's newspaper, his cartoons became popular with American troops all over Europe. At one point, General George Patton confronted Mauldin and threatened to "throw his ass in jail" in response to a cartoon that poked fun at Patton's order that required all soldiers be clean shaven, even in combat. General Eisenhower interceded on behalf of Mauldin and that ended the matter. Eisenhower considered Mauldin's cartoons morale boosters. Mauldin's initial efforts to continue working as a cartoonist after the war were unsuccessful and he worked for a time as an actor, writer and illustrator. He returned to cartooning in 1958 when he joined the St. Louis *Post-Dispatch*. He moved on to the Chicago *Sun-Times* in 1962 and remained there until his retirement in 1991. He won two Pulitzer Prizes: one in 1945 for his Willie and Joe cartoons and another in 1959 for a cartoon in the *Post-Dispatch*. Historian Stephen Ambrose wrote, "More than anyone else, save only Ernie Pyle (see entry), [Mauldin] caught the trials and travails of the GI. For anyone who wants to know what it was like to be an infantryman in World War II, this book is the place to start—and finish." He died from Alzheimer's disease.

Mauldin & Ambrose, *Up Front*
Other literature abundant

Maxwell, Deluvina (d. 1927)
Fort Sumner Adopted Daughter, Billy the Kid Associate

Deluvina was an Indian child who had been captured by Mexicans at Canyon de Chelly. Lucien Maxwell (see entry) ransomed her for ten dollars and she remained with the Maxwell family for the remainder of her life. She is said to have been an admirer of William H. Bonney (Billy the Kid, see entry) and she was present in Fort Sumner in July 1881 when Sheriff Pat Garrett (see entry) killed the outlaw.

Burns, *Billy the Kid*
Serna, *Tessie Maxwell*
Other literature abundant

Maxwell, Lucien Bonaparte (1818-1875)
Northeastern New Mexico Land Baron

Maxwell probably reached New Mexico by the middle 1830s. He was well acquainted with Kit Carson (see entry), Ceran St. Vrain (see entry) and other American trappers and traders living in what was then a part of Mexico. His most important acquaintance, though, was Carlos Beaubien (see entry) who was a partner in the Beaubien-Miranda Land Grant of northeastern New Mexico. In 1842 Maxwell married Beaubien's daughter, María de la Luz, who was called simply Luz. By the 1850s Beaubien had signed most of his land holdings over to Maxwell, who then managed to buy out most of the other of Beaubien's partners and heirs. Thus was formed the huge—1.7 million acres—Maxwell Land Grant. A sizable portion of the original land grant is now the Vermejo Park Ranch, owned by Ted Turner. Maxwell created the town of Cimarron, but died at Fort Sumner.

Lucien Bonaparte Maxwell.
After Twitchell.

Keleher, *Maxwell*

Lawrence R. Murphy, "Master of the Cimarron: Lucien B. Maxwell," *New Mexico Historical Review*, January 1980
Serna, *Tessie Maxwell*
Other literature abundant

Maxwell, Peter Menard "Pete" (1848-1898)
Fort Sumner Rancher

Pete Maxwell was the son of land baron Lucien Bonaparte Maxwell (see entry). Pete's claim to fame is that he witnessed the shooting death of William H. Bonney (Billy the Kid, see entry) by Sheriff Pat Garrett (see entry) on July 14, 1881 at Fort Sumner. The killing took place in Pete's bedroom.

Metz, *Pat Garrett*
Serna, *Tessie Maxwell*
Other literature abundant

Medina, Mariano (1810-1878)
Taos Mountain Man

There were not many Mexicans among the mountain men of the early 19th Century, but Medina was the exception. A native of Taos, New Mexico, he trapped in the Rocky Mountains and lived for a time with the Flathead Indians. He is said to have killed an Indian and fled to Bent's Fort where he became a scout for the Army. In the late 1850s he opened a trading post near Loveland, Colorado. He died there after receiving some recognition as a pioneer.

Thrapp, *Encyclopedia*
Robert G. McCubbin, "Hardy as Bears, Historic Photos of notable, but grizzly, Mountain Men," *True West*, March 2006

Mechem, Edwin Leard "Big Ed" (1912-2002)
Governor (State) of New Mexico (1951-54, 1957-58, 1961-62)

Senator Edwin Mechem

Mechem was born at Alamogordo, New Mexico, and educated there and in Las Cruces. He attended New Mexico State University briefly but graduated from Law School at the University of Arkansas in 1939. He was admitted to the New Mexico bar the same year. He worked as agent for the Federal Bureau of Investigation from 1942 to 1945. Mechem, a Republican, was first elected governor of New Mexico in 1950, again in 1952, once more in 1957 and one final time in 1961; more times than anyone in the state's history. (Bruce King [see entry] was elected three times, but served more total years, twelve, than Mechem, eight.) Governor Mechem made New Mexico history when he resigned from the office of governor on November 30, 1962, which elevated Lieutenant Governor Tom Bolack to the Governor's chair. Bolack, on the same date, appointed Mechem to the U.S. Senate to fill the vacancy created by the death of Senator Dennis Chávez (see entry), on November 18. Mechem was not elected to the office in 1964 (Bolack served but one month as governor). Mechem was appointed to the U.S. District Court Bench in 1970 and served until his death.

Congressional Biography
New Mexico Blue Book, 2003-2004
Literature abundant

Meem, John Gaw IV (1894-1983)
New Mexico Architect

Meem was born in Brazil to parents who were Episcopalian missionaries. He graduated from the Virginia Military Institute in 1914 with a degree in civil engineering. He worked for a time in New York City and served in the Army during World War I, attaining the rank of Captain. He contracted tuberculosis in 1919 and arrived in New Mexico in the early 1920s seeking a cure. He was admitted to Sunmount Sanatorium in Santa Fe. While there, he met Carlos Vierra who introduced Meem to the "Santa Fe Style." By the early 1930s, he had developed a reputation for his Spanish Pueblo Style. He was the University of New Mexico architect from 1933 until 1959, and in designing more than 30 buildings, including Zimmerman Library, he was largely responsible for the Pueblo-style architecture that makes the UNM campus unique. He also designed such landmarks as the Albuquerque Little Theater, Lovelace Clinic, the visitors' center at Coronado State Park in Bernalillo, and Fuller Lodge in Los Alamos, among others. One of the most interesting facts about Meem's life is that he held no degree in architecture, although he was awarded an honorary Master of Arts degree from Colorado College and also awarded a Silver Medal by the Fifth Pan-American Congress of Architects for excellence in design.

Arthur L. DeVolder, "John Gaw Meem, F.A.I.A.: An Appreciation," *New Mexico Historical Review*," July 1979
Garcia, *Albuquerque*
Simmons, *Albuquerque*
Taylor, *Southwestern Ornamentation*
Other literature abundant

Melgares, Facundo (1775-?)
Governor (Spanish) of New Mexico (1818-1822)

At the very time that Zebulon Pike (see entry) and his troop of 22 U.S. soldiers was moving west toward New Mexico in 1806-07, Lt. Facundo Melgares was traveling east with a large military contingent of Spanish soldiers which consisted of 100 dragoons and 500 mounted militia. Some said that he was looking for Pike. Others said that he was exploring into U.S. territory for the Spanish government. In any event, he did not find Pike and returned to Santa Fe. After Pike was arrested by Spanish authorities in 1807 and removed to Santa Fe, Melgares was assigned to escort Pike south, and the two of them became good friends. Melgares was one of the last Royalists on the Spanish frontier and he became the last Spanish governor of New Mexico before Mexico became independent of Spain in 1821 (some sources indicate that he remained in office until 1822).

Arthur Gómez, "Royalist in Transition: Facundo Melgares, the Last Spanish Governor of

New Mexico, 1818-1822," *New Mexico Historical Review*, October 1993
New Mexico Blue Book, 2003-2004

Mendizábal, Bernardo López de (d. c. 1662)
Governor (Spanish) of New Mexico (1659-1661)

Governor Mendizábal was one of several New Mexico governors who attempted to wrest power away from the 17th century Catholic Church. At one point he invited Indians from Tesuque to dance in Santa Fe. He said, "Look there, this dance contains nothing more than this hu-hu-hu and these thieving friars say it is superstitious." He also charged the clergy with failing to observe the rules of chastity, poverty and obedience. The friars, in turn, charged the Governor with being a crypto-Jew and with having sexual relations with a slave girl, an offense punishable by life in a slave galley, according to historian Ruben Sálaz Márquez. Mendizábal began an investigation into charges against the friars and was himself arrested by the Inquisition for "impinging on ecclesiastical privilege." He was taken to Mexico City in chains where he died in prison. The Inquisition posthumously exonerated him.

Sálaz Márquez, *New Mexico*

Mentzer, Gus (1858-1882)
Colfax County Killer

Gus Mentzer was hanged by a Raton mob on the evening of June 26, 1882, after a shooting spree that resulted in four deaths, including those of a judge and deputy sheriff. It was after this incident that local citizens issued a statement which read in part: "...all professional gamblers, footpads, thieves, cappers, dance hall men, bunko men, and all these [sic] who have no visible means of support, as well as all dance house girls and prostitutes generally, are hereby notified and publicly warned to leave this town within 48 hours from 12 o'clock at noon on the first day of July 1882, and never return under penalty of incurring the just wrath of an indignant and outraged people."

Bryan, *Robbers*
Bullis, 99 *New Mexicans*
Other literature abundant

Meriwether, David (1800-1893)
Governor (Territorial) of New Mexico (1853-1855)

The name as spelled above is from his congressional profile. Twitchell (see entry), in *Leading Facts*, spells it "Merriwether." The *New Mexico Blue Book*, published by the Secretary of State's Office in 2004, spells it "Meriweather." Meriwether was born in Virginia but reared in Kentucky. As a young man, he had been a part of an effort, along with a party of Pawnee Indians, to open trade negotiations with Spanish New Mexico (1819). His party was set upon by Spanish soldiers and most of the Indians

Gov. David Meriwether.
After Twitchell.

were killed. Meriwether was captured and taken to Santa Fe where he was confined. He was ultimately released and had several adventures with Indians as he returned to the American settlements. When Meriwether arrived in Santa Fe to assume his duties as governor, more than 30 years later, the roof over the room in which he'd been confined collapsed. "This the people interpreted as a favorable omen," according to Twitchell. Most of Meriwether's administration was taken up by addressing problems with the Utes and Jicarilla Apaches.

Lamar, *The Far Southwest*
Twitchell, *Leading Facts*, Vol. II

Mickey, Lewis H. (d. 1925)
Curry County Railroad Special Officer

A Clovis, New Mexico, newspaper explained: "[Mickey] was shot and mortally wounded by Leslie Starr, sixteen year old youth, about 2 a.m. last Saturday morning and Starr in turn was shot to death by Officer Mickey as he lay in a dying condition, as a result of the officer's attempt to arrest the boy. When they were found by other officers, they were lying on the top of a freight car about ten feet apart, Starr dead and Mickey dying." Mickey was the third, and last, railroad officer to be killed in the line of duty in New Mexico.

Bullis, *New Mexico's Finest*

Miera y Pacheco, Bernardo (c. 1713-1785)
Soldier, Mapmaker, Sculptor

(One source shows a birth year as 1713; another as c. 1719.) Born in Santibánez in the northern Spanish province of Santander, Miera y Pacheco arrived in the New World in 1743 and Santa Fe in 1756. Two years later, New Mexico Governor Francisco Antonio Marín del Valle submitted to the Viceroy of New Spain a map prepared by Miera y Pacheco which detailed Spanish villages and Indian pueblos. This is believed to be the first map of New Mexico. Miera y Pacheco was also a talented carver of saints, a mathematician and a painter. One historian writes, "His remarkable aptitude produced a unique stone-carved altar screen for the military chapel of Nuestra Señora de la Luz, constructed in 1760 on the south side of the Santa Fe plaza." It is the earliest known example of the baroque estípite column in New Mexico. His sculptures and paintings were also found in churches at San Felipe, Santa Clara and Zuñi Pueblos and the Spanish Village of Truchas. Miera y Pacheco's painting of Santa Rosa de Lima still hangs in the church at Abiquiú in northern New Mexico.

Esquibel & Carrillo, *Tapestry*
Gavin, *Traditional Arts*
Montaño, *Tradiciones*
Donna Pierce & Felipe Mirabal, "The Mystery of the Cristo Rey Altar Screen and Don Bernardo de Miera y Pacheco," *Spanish Market*, Vol. 12, No.1, 1999

Miles, John Esten "Johnny" (1884-1971)
Governor (State) of New Mexico (1939-1942), U.S. Congressman (1949-1951)

Miles was born in Rutherford County, Tennessee, and attended school there.

164

He moved to Fannin County, Texas, and took up farming in 1902. He moved on to Granite, Oklahoma, in 1905 and on to Quay County, New Mexico in 1906 where he homesteaded near Endee (a town named for a cattle brand). A Democrat, he began his political career as a member of the school board. He also served as postmaster of Endee before he moved to Tucumcari in 1920. He served as county assessor from 1920-24; secretary of the State Tax Commission 1925-27 and again from 1931-34. After his term as governor, he served as chairman of the Public Service Commission, 1943-1945, and as Commissioner of Public Lands, 1945 to 1948. He did not seek re-election to Congress in 1950, but did run for governor only to be defeated by Republican Ed Mechem (see entry). He remained active in party politics until his death.

Julyan, *Place Names*
News accounts abundant

Miller, James B. "Killin' Jim" (1861-1909)
Texas Gunman/Killer

Miller was born in Van Buren, Arkansas, according to one source, and at McCulloch County, Texas, according to another. Metz gives his year of birth as 1861 while O'Neal reports 1866. From age one, he spent his life in Texas. Historian Metz says this: "[Miller] lived to raise the art of bushwhacking and ambush practically to a science. By some accounts, he killed between 20 and 50 men, although such figures defy documentation." Miller's significance in New Mexico history is that some suspected that he was responsible for the murder of former Sheriff Pat Garrett (see entry) near Las Cruces on February 29, 1908. New Mexico Mounted Policeman Fred Fornoff (see entry) is said by some to have proven that Miller was involved in Garrett's murder, but his report to Governor George Curry (see entry) has allegedly been lost to history (Curry, in his autobiography, failed to mention that such a report was ever made). Historian Chuck Hornung reports that a copy of Fornoff's report did survive; and that it concluded Garrett was murdered by cowboy Billy McNew. Miller was lynched by an Oklahoma mob in April 1909 for the murder of rancher Gus Bobbitt. There is no doubt about his date of death.

Curry, *Autobiography*
Hornung, Chuck, presentation at the annual convention, Historical Society of New
        Mexico, April 2006
McLoughlin, *Wild & Woolly*
Metz, *Encyclopedia*
Metz, *Pat Garrett*
O'Neal, *Encyclopedia*
Pete Ross, "Some Prominent New Mexicans May Have Been Accessories to the Murder of
        Pat Garrett," *Wild West Magazine*, December 2001

Mills, Alexander Hamilton "Ham" (c. 1837-1882)
Lincoln County Sheriff

Mills served as sheriff of Lincoln County, New Mexico, in 1873 and 1874, and briefly as Justice of the Peace. He proved himself to be completely ineffective against the Horrell Brothers during the Horrell War of those years. A large man and a fine pistol shot, history records that he was frequently drunk. He was accused of embezzlement at one point and murder at another, but he never served prison time. He abandoned his wife and took to the road in the late 1870s. He was murdered by "Mexicans" at Georgetown, near Silver City, in 1882.

Ball, *Desert Lawmen*
Klasner, *My Girlhood*
Nolan, *Bad Blood*
Thrapp, *Encyclopedia*

Mills, William Joseph (1849-1915)
Governor (Territorial) of New Mexico (1910-1912)

Mills was the last of New Mexico's territorial governors. He was born in Yazoo City, Mississippi, but after the death of his father when he was but a child, his mother moved to Connecticut where she remarried. Mills attended law school at Yale and practiced in both Connecticut and New Mexico before President William McKinley appointed him Chief Justice of the New Mexico Supreme Court in 1898. He remained on the court until President William Howard Taft (see entry) appointed him governor. During his brief tenure, he generally continued the policies of his predecessor, George Curry (see entry), and in fact retained all but one of Curry's appointments.

Gov. William Joseph Mills.
After Twitchell.

Curry, *Autobiography*
Twitchell, *Leading Facts*, Vol. II

Milne, John (1880-1957)
Albuquerque Superintendent of Schools (1911-1956)

Born in Scotland, he arrived in the U.S. at a young age and was raised on a farm in Illinois. He was educated at Milwaukee State Teachers College and taught for a year in Wisconsin before he moved on to New Mexico in 1906. He held teaching and administrative positions before he was appointed Superintendent in 1911. (Note: Bryan says Milne's tenure began in 1911; Simmons says 1910.) During his 45-year tenure, enrollment in the Albuquerque schools rose from about 1,500 to almost 40,000. Milne had the foresight to purchase plots of land in the various quadrants of the city; land upon which future schools could be constructed. Albuquerque's Milne Stadium is named for him. His 45-year tenure in office was reportedly the longest for any superintendent of schools, in any large school system, in the United States.

Bryan, *Albuquerque*
Simmons, *Albuquerque*

Milton, Hugh M. II (1897-1987)
Doña Ana County Educator/Military Man

Born in Kentucky, Milton served in World War I as an enlisted man before being promoted to 2nd Lieutenant. He returned home and graduated from the University of Kentucky in 1919 and earned a Master's degree in 1922. He became an assistant professor of mechanical engineering at the New Mexico College of Agriculture & Mechanical Arts (now New Mexico State University) in 1924, Dean of Engineering in 1933, and university president in 1938. He was recalled to active military duty in 1941 during World War II, and served in the Pacific Theater of Operations; and was promoted to Brigadier General in 1945. After the war, he served an additional year as president of NMA&M before assuming the office of president of the New Mexico Military Institute (NMMI) in 1947, a position he held until he was again recalled to active military duty in 1951. He was promoted to Major General and served as Assistant Secretary, and later as Under Secretary, of the Army. He returned to southern New Mexico in 1961 and went to work for the First National Bank of Doña Ana County as Vice President for Public Relations. He remained active in civic affairs, including leading the effort to preserve Fort Selden. That effort led to the creation of the Doña Ana Historical Society. A statue of General Milton stands near Milton Hall on the NMSU campus at Las Cruces. After his death, a neighbor said he was "A true southern gentleman, a man with an abiding faith in and concern for his fellow man, and most certainly a distinguished American."

John Porter Bloom, Correspondence, February 2006

Lee Geomets, "Hugh M. Milton II, Educator Soldier—Distinguished American," *Southern New Mexico Historical Review*, January 1994

Owen, *Las Cruces*

Mitchell, Robert Byington (1823-1882)
Governor (Territorial) of New Mexico (1866-1869)

Born in Ohio and educated in Pennsylvania, he practiced law in Ohio until he joined the U.S. Army during the Mexican War, being mustered out as a 1st Lieutenant. He returned to Ohio for a time, and then moved on to Kansas where he became active in the free state issue and was elected to the Kansas territorial legislature. He reentered the U.S. Army during the Civil War and rose to the rank of Brigadier General. President Andrew Johnson appointed him Governor of New Mexico in 1866. His administration was marked by controversy and conflict with the territorial legislature. Historian Jane C. Sanchez (see entry) calls Mitchell "one of the most disliked men ever appointed to territorial office." The Santa Fe *Daily New Mexican* reported on February 9, 1869, "Governor Mitchell having left the Territory without leave of absence, thereby abandoning the Gubernatorial chair....Mitchell left here on the 4th

Gov. Robert Byington Mitchell. After Twitchell.

instant, in a two-wheeled coach, for the States—it is supposed." He returned to Kansas upon his departure from New Mexico.

Jane C. Sanchez, "Agitated, Personal, and Unsound..." *New Mexico Historical Review*, July 1966

Twitchell, *Leading Facts*, Vol. II

Montoya, Joseph Manuel "Joe" (1915-1978)
U.S. Senator

Senator Joseph Montoya

Born in Pena Blanca, Sandoval County, New Mexico, to a politically active family, Montoya attended Regis College in Denver and graduated from Georgetown University Law School in 1938. He was admitted to the bar in 1939. A Democrat, he was elected to the New Mexico House of Representatives in 1936, re-elected in 1938, and served as majority leader in 1939 and 1940. Montoya served in the state senate from 1940 to 1946 and as lieutenant governor from 1947 to 1951 under the administration of Governor Thomas J. Mabry. He ran for U.S. Congress in 1950 and lost. He returned to the state senate in 1953 and 1954 and served again as lieutenant governor from 1955 to 1957 under the administrations of John F. Simms and Edwin L. Mechem (see entries). (Note: Montoya served as Lieutenant Governor at a time when candidates for that office ran independently of the candidate for Governor. Mabry and Simms were both Democrats, but Mechem was a Republican. Legend holds that Mechem was afraid to leave the state lest Montoya do great mischief in his absence.) Montoya was elected to Congress on April 9, 1957, in a special election to fill the vacancy created by the death of Antonio M. Fernandez (see entry). Montoya remained in Congress until he was elected to the United States Senate in November 1964. He was re-elected in 1970 but defeated in 1976 by Republican Harrison "Jack" Schmitt (see entry), a former astronaut. Montoya died in Washington, D.C., and is interred in Rosario Cemetery in Santa Fe. Senator Montoya is remembered by many New Mexicans for his participation in the Watergate hearings of the Richard Nixon administration in the early 1970s.

New Mexico Blue Book, 2003-2004
News accounts abundant

Montoya, Nestor (1862-1923)
Santa Fe, Albuquerque Newspaperman, U.S. Congressman (1921-23)

Born in Albuquerque, Montoya graduated from St. Michael's College in Santa Fe in 1881. As a young man he worked as assistant postmaster in Santa Fe, and as a court interpreter. In 1888 he and Enrique H. Salazar founded *La Voz del Pueblo* ("The Voice of the People"). In 1901 he founded *La Bandera Americana* ("The American Flag") newspaper in Albuquerque. He served in the Territorial House of Representatives from 1892 to 1903. He also served in the Territorial Council (Senate) in 1905 and 1906. He was a member of the 1910 state constitutional conven-

tion, a regent of the University of New Mexico from 1916 to 1919, Bernalillo County Clerk in 1919 and 1920. He was also president of the State Press Association for many years. Elected to Congress in 1920, he died in Washington in January 1923, before completing his term.
Congressional Biography
Sálaz Márquez, *New Mexico*

Congressman Nestor
Montoya. After Twitchell.

Moore, Jim (1941-)
Albuquerque Museum Director
A graduate of Highland High School and the University of New Mexico, Moore taught art history at Wichita State University and was the director of the Toledo (Ohio) Museum before he became director of the Albuquerque Museum in 1979 at a time when the museum was in the process of moving from its original airport location to its present location on Mountain Road near Old Town. He was also instrumental in the museum's multi-million dollar expansion project that was completed in 2005, the year he retired.
David Steinberg, "Albuquerque Museum thrived under Moore," Albuquerque *Journal*,
        November 27, 2005
News accounts abundant

Morrell, David (1943-)
Santa Fe Novelist
Morrell was born in Canada, but raised and educated in the eastern U.S. He received both M. A. and Ph.D. degrees from Penn State. His first novel was about a Viet Nam veteran who returned to the U.S. only to come into serious conflict with a small-town police chief. The vet's name was Rambo, and the title of the novel was *First Blood*, published in 1972. This book was the genesis of the several Rambo movies. Morrell, considered by many the "father" of modern action novels, was a professor at the University of Iowa at the time. He continued teaching there until 1986 when he moved to Santa Fe to devote full time to writing. He is the author of 28 books, including *Last Reveille* (1977), which is set at Columbus, New Mexico, at the time of Pancho Villa's (see entry) raid in 1916. *Extreme Denial* (1996) is set near Santa Fe.
www.davidmorrell.net
Luther, T. N., "Collecting Santa Fe Authors, Part IX," Book Talk, New Mexico Book League,
        April 2000

Morris, Thomas Gayle (1919-)
U.S. Congressman (1959-1969)
Born in Eastland County, Texas, he moved to New Mexico as a young man. He served in the U.S. Navy during World War II, engaged in farming and ranching in Quay County after 1944, and graduated from the University of New Mexico in 1948. A Democrat, he was elected to the New Mexico House of Representatives in

1952 and served from 1953 to 1958. He was elected to Congress in 1958. He was defeated in a bid for re-election in 1968 by Republican Manuel Luján (see entry). He also lost a bid for the Democratic nomination for the U.S. Senate in 1972.
News accounts abundant

Morrow, John (1865-1935)
U.S. Congressman (1925-1929)
Born in Lafayette County, Wisconsin, he attended the public schools and the normal university. He taught school in several states before he arrived in New Mexico. He was the superintendent of schools in Colfax County from 1892 to1896. He became a member of the New Mexico bar in 1895 and practiced in Raton. He engaged in banking, acquired large ranch holdings and conducted a large livestock operation. Elected to the U.S. Congress in 1922, 1924 and 1926, his re-election bid in 1928 failed when he lost to Republican Albert G. Simms (see entry). He died at Raton and is interred there.
New Mexico Blue Book, 2003-2004
News accounts abundant

Muñoz, Edward (1928-2006)
Gallup Mayor
A native of Gallup, Muñoz became involved in local politics after service in the military during World War II. He was elected mayor and served from 1958 to 1969, and again from 1987 to 1991. It was during his second stint as mayor that he took decisive action regarding the alcohol abuse problems in Gallup. He worked to close the town's liquor store drive-up windows, something that later became state law. He was also an early supporter of lowering the state's presumptive level for drunken driving from .10 to .08. That, too, became state law. He closed Gallup's drunk tank and initiated alcohol treatment programs. He also banned Sunday liquor sales in Gallup. Robert Rosebrough, Gallup's mayor at the time of Muñoz's death, said, "He [Muñoz] was a remarkably determined man and he was a real fighter. He was the only man strong-willed enough to take on Gallup's alcohol problems."
Albuquerque *Journal*, March 3, 2006

Murphy, Lawrence Gustav (1831-1878)
Lincoln County Empire Builder, Lincoln County War Figure
Born in Ireland, Murphy immigrated to the U.S. as a young man and entered the military service. He arrived in New Mexico in 1860 and was appointed Lieutenant in the 1st New Mexico Volunteers. By 1866 he was stationed at Fort Stanton and held the rank of Major. He left the Army that year and became the post sutler. His mercantile endeavors led to the creation of the store called "The House of Murphy," or more familiarly, just "The House." It was this monopolistic enterprise that became the target of John Tunstall, Alex McSween and John Chisum (see entries) in the Lincoln County War (1878-1881). Upon Murphy's death, Frank Coe of Lincoln County said, "[He] was sick and was put in the hospital and the Sisters

of Charity would not let him have whiskey, and that cut his living off. He died in a short time and everybody rejoiced over it."

Keleher, *Violence*
Lamar, *The Far Southwest*
Utley, *High Noon*
Wilson, *Merchants*
Other literature abundant

Myers, Dwight Andrew (1931-1995)
New Mexico Book League Executive Director (1972-1995)

Dwight Myers was employed for many years by publishers such as Prentice Hall and Simon & Schuster. He and his wife Carol started the New Mexico Book League (NMBL) in 1972 and the first edition of *Book Talk*, Vol. I, No. 1, appeared in April of that year. He remained in charge of the publication until his death on September 16, 1995. The by-laws of NMBL read: "The object of the New Mexico Book League shall be to enrich the cultural life in New Mexico through the popularization of reading; to make books available to all the people of New Mexico; to encourage creative writing and the publication of books ...; to promote understanding and cooperation between the membership and the general public; to promote fa-

Carol and Dwight Andrew Myers

vorable legislation relating to books; to conduct workshops in the field of creative writing, bookselling, publishing, and librarianship; to sponsor literary events in the public interest; and to engage in such other activities as may further the objectives of the League." *Book Talk* continued publication, after Myers' death, until October 2001, Vol. XXX, No. 4. Carol Myers served the Book League and *Book Talk* for all of its 30 year run. Robert R. White served as Executive Director from 1995 until 2001. Marc Simmons (see entry) wrote in the final edition, "As a charter member and subscriber, as well as an occasional contributor, I've maintained a loyal attachment [to *Book Talk*] from the start.... The contribution that both [Dwight and Carol Myers] made to our regional world of books will not be forgotten."

Carol A. Myers, "A Farewell to All My Dear Friends," *Book Talk*, New Mexico Book League, Oct. 2001

Newsletter, Westerns International, Albuquerque Corral, October 1995

-N-

Nakai, Raymond (1919-2005)
Navajo Tribal Chairman

Nakai served as chairman of the Navajo Nation from 1964 to 1971. Some considered him the first modern tribal leader. It was under his administration that the Navajo reservation came to be called the Navajo Nation. He was also instrumental in the establishment of the Navajo Community College, now called Diné College, the first such school in the U.S. to be tribally operated and controlled.

"Obituary," Albuquerque *Tribune*, August 16, 2005

Nakayama, Roy "Mr. Chile" (1923-1988)
Doña Ana County Agricultural Researcher/University Professor

Nakayama was born in Doña Ana County, New Mexico, and received his early education there, graduating from Las Cruces High School in 1941. He briefly attended the New Mexico College of Agriculture and Mechanical Arts (now New Mexico State University) before he enlisted in the U.S. Army during World War II. He finished college after the war, graduating in 1948. He later received both Masters and Ph.D. degrees from Iowa State University. He became an associate professor at New Mexico State University in 1960 and remained on the faculty there until 1986. His research into "improving" chile led to the development of "Nu Mex Big Jim" in 1974, "Española Improved" and "R Naky" strains of New Mexico's state vegetable. By the 1980s, New Mexico produced more chile than all other states combined. One of his students commented, "Roy Nakayama was the best researcher I've ever known...the best horticulturist State [New Mexico State University] ever had."

Szasz, *Larger Than Life*
Nancy Tod, "The Deeds of Roy Nakayama: Chile and Pecans; Research and Teaching,"
  Southern New Mexico Historical Review, January 1994

Naranjo, Domingo (fl. 1680)
Tewa Indian Leader

Domingo Naranjo, said to have been half Black, was a member of the Santa

Clara (Ka-'p-geh) Pueblo. He, among others, worked with Po'pay (see entry) in planning the Pueblo Revolt of 1680.
Sando, *Po'pay*

Narbona (c.1768-1849)
Navajo Headman

A significant leader of the Navajo, Narbona had spent years in negotiating peace agreements with Spanish, Mexican and American military leaders. He met with yet another American officer, Colonel John M. Washington (see entry), at the Chusca Valley in 1849. There arose some sort of dispute over a horse and the Navajos felt disposed to flee. They were fired upon as they did so, and Narbona was killed. He was allegedly shot several times and then scalped, even though he was more than 80 years old. Narbona was the father-in-law of Manuelito who served as Navajo headman in the 1870s and 1880s.

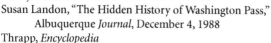
Narbona. After Twitchell.

Susan Landon, "The Hidden History of Washington Pass," Albuquerque *Journal*, December 4, 1988

Thrapp, *Encyclopedia*

Neill, Hyman G. "Hoodoo Brown" (fl. 1879)
Las Vegas Justice of the Peace (and corrupt to the core)

Neill arrived in Las Vegas, New Mexico, about the same time the railroad did, and the railroad arrived on April 4, 1879. He got himself elected Justice of the Peace and appointed a bunch of Dodge City, Kansas, criminals as his constables. During his months of dominating the community of East Las Vegas, outlawry prevailed. County authorities finally caught up with him when he tried to pilfer the estate of a man murdered by one of his deputies. He fled in early 1880 and disappeared from history.

Bryan, *Wildest*
Otero, *My Life*

Nelson, David Cooper (1921-1960)
Valencia County Murderer

On January 8, 1960, Nelson became the only person to be executed in New Mexico by means of lethal gas. The method of execution was changed from electrocution to gas in 1956. It was changed again, to lethal injection, in 1980. Nelson, a hitchhiker, was convicted of the 1956 killing of Ralph Henderson Rainy who had picked him up near Flagstaff, Arizona. Rainy's body, shot twice in the head, was found in Valencia County, New Mexico.

News accounts abundant

Nelson, Martin (d. 1885)
Bonito City Killer

One night in May 1885, Martin Nelson shot and killed seven residents of the town of Bonito City, New Mexico, in the Sacramento Mountains. Motives for the killings of four members of the Mayberry family, and three other men, were never determined. Nelson was shot and killed by townsman Charles Berry the morning after the murders. The town of Bonito City now lies under the waters of Bonito Lake, near Ruidoso in Lincoln County.

Raynor, *The Gold Lettered Egg*
Simmons, *Ranchers, Ramblers & Renegades*

Niza, Fray Marcos de (c. 1495-1558)
Spanish Explorer

A Frenchman and Franciscan friar, Niza arrived in the New World in the early 1500s. It was Niza, along with the Moor, Estevánico (see entry), who ventured into what is now western New Mexico in search of the Seven Cities of Cibola in 1539. Zuñi Indians at Háwikuh killed Estevánico, and Niza ventured no further north. He did get a look at the adobe village and mistook the yellow adobe-plastered walls for gold. His reports of a golden city prompted further exploration, and Niza accompanied Coronado to the north in 1540, but soon returned to Mexico, presumably after Coronado discovered that the walls at Háwikuh were not made of gold. Niza died in a monastery at Xochimilco near Mexico City.

Thrapp, *Encyclopedia*
Other literature abundant

Noggle, Anne (1922-2005)
Albuquerque Aviator/Photographer

Noggle began her career during World War II flying for the Woman's Air Corps Service Pilots, one of the first women to do so. She later acquired an interest in art and photography and moved to Albuquerque where she graduated from the University of New Mexico with a degree in art history. She taught at the University of New Mexico from 1970-1984. Noggle produced three books: *For God, Country, and the Thrill of It*; *A Dance With Death: Soviet Airwomen in World War II*; and *Silver Lining*.

"Obituary," Albuquerque *Journal*, August 29, 2005
Szasz, *Larger Than Life*

Nolan, Frederick "Fred" (1931-)
New Mexico Historian

Fred Nolan was born in Liverpool, England, and was educated there and at Aberaeron, Wales. As a young man he worked as a shipping clerk, salesman of several items, and a squiggler (whatever that is!) in a chocolate factory. "Somehow in the process," he writes, "I became an authority on the history of the American frontier." He was founder of the English Westerner's Society. Later, while working as a publishing executive, he published 14 western novels and six children's books. Over the years he has written numerous books, including westerns, biographies and thrillers. Nolan is certainly the leading living expert on New Mexico's famous Lincoln County War (1878-1881), and the people associated with it. His books on that subject include *The Life and Death of John Henry Tunstall* (1965), *The Lincoln County War: A Documentary History* (1992), *Bad Blood: The Life and Times of the Horrell Brothers* (1994) and *The West of Billy the Kid* (1998). He is currently at work on an

Frederick Nolan

anthology called *The Billy the Kid Reader* expected out in 2007. The awards he has received over the years are too many to mention here.

Nolan, Fred, *biographical sketch*

Nordhaus, Robert "Bob" (1909-)
Albuquerque Attorney/Ski Enthusiast

Nordhaus was born in Las Vegas, New Mexico, the son of one of the state's pioneer merchants, Max Nordhaus. Robert arrived in Albuquerque with his family in 1912, where he received a public and boarding school education. He then attended Yale and Yale Law School and returned to Albuquerque in 1935. He was a part of the creation of the Albuquerque Ski Club in 1936. The group cleared runs in the Sandia Mountains and then added a rope tow made from old auto parts to create La Madera Ski Area (now Sandia Peak). A lift ticket was 50 cents. World War II interrupted his skiing enterprise. He served in the 10th Mountain Division—Ski Troops—and after the war he formed a company that bought out the Albuquerque Ski Club and

Robert Nordhaus

installed a 4,200-foot T-bar lift. He formed the law firm of Nordhaus and Moses in 1955. His specialty was water, oil and gas law, and he represented several Indian groups. From 1958 to 1971, he prosecuted a land claim for the Jicarilla Apache tribe before the Indian Claims Commission against the U.S. government. He won the claim. His firm is recognized as one of most prominent Indian law firms in the country. In partnership with Ben Abruzzo (see entry), Nordhaus participated in the construction of the Sandia Peak Tramway in the early 1960s. According to Nordhaus, about 8,000,000 people have ridden the Sandia Tram through the end of 2005. He retired from the practice of law in 1987. He is the author of *Tipi Rings: A Chronicle of the Jicarilla Apache Land Claim* (1995).

Hughes, *Albuquerque*

Newsletter, Westerners International, Albuquerque Corral, January 1990

Salmon, *Sandia Peak*

-O-

O'Folliard, Tom "Bigfoot" (c. 1858-1880)
Lincoln County Outlaw, Billy the Kid Associate

Born in south Texas, O'Folliard arrived in New Mexico by 1878 and soon became associated with William H. Bonney (Billy the Kid, see entry). O'Folliard was present during the Five Days Battle at Lincoln in July 1878. He was shot and killed, probably by Pat Garrett (see entry), at Fort Sumner, New Mexico, in December 1880. He is interred there along with Charles Bowdre (see entry) and Bonney. Describing the three of them, their tombstone is simply inscribed "PALS."
Literature abundant

O'Grady, Patrick F. "Pat" (1875-1945)
Albuquerque Police Chief (1925-1945)

Born on St. Patrick's Day, Pat O'Grady was a native of Waterford, Ireland. Early in life he worked on the docks in Ireland, but followed his brothers to the U.S. in the early 1900s. He settled first in Chicago where he worked as an officer in the Chicago & Northwestern Railroad freight yards. He arrived in Albuquerque, New Mexico, in 1906 and went to work as a gateman at American Lumber Co. He joined the police department in 1908 as a night patrolman. The night police headquarters at the time was in the White Elephant Saloon at the corner of Second Street and Central Avenue (then called Railroad Ave.), where the Sunshine Building is located today. The saloon had a telephone. When an important call came in, the bartender would go into the street and whistle for a cop (another story held that the bartender would bang on a lamp post with a meat cleaver to get the cop's attention). In 1909 O'Grady was named Night Captain (or marshal), and Chief of Police in 1925. He served in that capacity until his death. He once claimed that he worked as Albuquerque's night cop for 18 years without a day off. When he joined the department, it was made up of fewer than a dozen officers who responded to calls on horseback or by buckboard. It was O'Grady who put motor vehicles into general use; with radios installed by the middle 1930s. He also created a fingerprinting department. About 50 officers served in the department by 1945. O'Grady, who rarely carried a gun, was liked and respected by a broad spectrum

of citizens. Chairman of the Albuquerque City Commission Clyde Tingley (see entry) said, "There never has been even the slightest hint of any kind of scandal in our [police] department during all the years that Pat O'Grady served as chief, and the credit is due to him. Albuquerque won't seem the same without Pat O'Grady." "O'Grady Born Policeman; Served 37 Years on Force," Albuquerque *Journal*, June 20, 1945
Bryan, *Albuquerque*

O'Keefe, Sister Vincent (fl. 1865)
Sister of Charity
At the behest of Santa Fe Bishop Jean Baptiste Lamy (see entry), Sister Vincent and three other Sisters of Charity—Catherine Mallon, Theodosia Farn and Pauline Leo—arrived in Santa Fe from Cincinnati, Ohio, in 1865 and established St. Vincent Hospital and Orphanage.
Hammett, *Santa Fe*
Sálaz Márquez, *New Mexico*

O'Keeffe, Georgia (1887-1986)
New Mexico Artist
O'Keeffe was born on a farm near Madison, Wisconsin, in 1887. In 1905 and 1906 she studied at the Art Institute of Chicago. She also studied at the Art Students League in New York City. She worked as a commercial artist for a time and also taught art. In 1915, some of her work came to the attention of Alfred Stieglitz (1864-1946), a pioneer in photography as an art form, and an ardent promoter of modern art. O'Keeffe moved to New York in 1918 and Stieglitz promoted her work. The two married in 1924; she was 28 years old, he was 52. Beginning in 1929, as a guest of Mabel Dodge Luhan (see entry) of Taos, she began visiting New Mexico, and subsequently spent summers in the northern part of the state. She purchased a house at Ghost Ranch, north of Abiquiú, in 1940 and a house in Abiquiú in 1945. In 1946, after Stieglitz died, she moved permanently to New Mexico. (Stieglitz rarely joined O'Keeffe in New Mexico, preferring to remain in New York.) O'Keeffe authority Barbara Buhler Lynes says, "In New Mexico, she discovered an environment that was particularly appealing to her and where she could continue to develop her work. I doubt that she could have done so effectively if she had stayed in New York." Late in her life, O'Keeffe's eyesight began to fail, but she continued to be creative even then by working in clay. The Georgia O'Keeffe Museum in Santa Fe offers, "An ongoing tribute to the journey of one remarkable woman, and others who share her spirit."
Emily Drabanski, "Confronting the O'Keeffe myths," *New Mexico Magazine*, March 2006
Eisler, *O'Keeffe and Stieglitz*
Lynes & Paden, *Maria Chabot*
Rudnick, *Mabel Dodge Luhan*
Carol Cooper Zdeba, "Georgia on my mind," *New Mexico Magazine*, June 2004
Other literature abundant

O'Leary, Dennis (1878-1901)
New Mexico Frontier Soldier

Tombstone of Pvt. Dennis O'Leary. Courtesy Don Bullis.

The body of Dennis O'Leary lies beneath one of the few tombstones in the Santa Fe National Cemetery that is not a simple white marble-slab marker. Instead it is a sandstone statue of a soldier reclining against a tree, and, it is said, it was actually sculpted by O'Leary himself. The young soldier was stationed at Fort Wingate in western New Mexico at the turn of the century in 1901. He absented himself from the fort and went into the mountains where he is believed to have carved his own tombstone, including the date of his own death (April 1, 1901). History writer Ollie Reed reports that he may have committed suicide, although the official cause of death is listed as tuberculosis. Exclusive of suicide, it seems unlikely that he could predict his day of demise so precisely. The unusual grave marker was placed on his grave at Fort Wingate initially, but when the fort closed in 1911, the marker, along with O'Leary's remains, were moved to the Santa Fe National Cemetery.

Ollie Reed, Jr., "Written in Stone" Albuquerque *Tribune*, November 11, 2005

Olinger, Robert Ameridth "Pecos Bob" "Big Indian" (c.1841-1881)
Lincoln County War Figure, Doña Ana County Sheriff's Deputy, Deputy U.S. Marshal, Killer

Deputy U.S. Marshal Robert Ameridth Olinger

Olinger and his brother, Wallace, were natives of Ohio. They arrived in New Mexico about 1876 and settled at Seven Rivers in what is now Eddy County. The two became associated with the "Seven Rivers Warriors" led by outlaw Marion Turner, and both participated in the Five Day Battle in Lincoln (July 1878). In 1881, Bob Olinger and Lincoln County Deputy J. W. Bell (see entry) were assigned to guard William H. Bonney (Billy the Kid, see entry) after Bonney was convicted and sentenced to hang for the murder of Sheriff William Brady (see entry). Bonney shot and killed both Olinger and Bell when he escaped custody for the last time on April 28, 1881, from the Lincoln County Courthouse. Olinger was generally disliked; most people of the day considered him a loudmouth and a bully. He was known to have killed three men in cold blood, most agreed. Simmons (see entry) reports that after his death, his mother said of him, "Bob was a murderer from the cradle and if there is a hell, I know he is in it." It must be noted, however, that Lily Klasner in her book, *My Girlhood Among Outlaws* (1972), described Bob, and his brother Wallace, as "decent, industrious folk who had come to New Mexico because of business opportunities." It should also be noted that Lily and Bob, according to rumors of the day, were engaged to be married.

Bullis, *New Mexico's Finest*

Klasner, *My Girlhood*
Metz, *Encyclopedia*
Simmons, *Six-Guns*

Ollito, Francisco El (fl. 1680)
Tewa Indian Leader
Francisco El Ollito was a member of San Ildefonso (Po-soheh) Pueblo who worked with Po'pay (see entry), and others, in planning the Pueblo Revolt of 1680.
Sando, *Po'pay*

Oñate y Salazar, Juan de (c. 1552-1626)
Colonizer, Governor (Spanish) of New Mexico (1598-1608)
(Note: one historian shows his birth year as 1549). Oñate was born at Zacatecas, Mexico, the son of one of the town's founders. He had a twin brother named Cristóbal. He married Isabel Cortéz Tolosa, the granddaughter of Mexico's conqueror Hernán Cortez. Isabel died in the late 1580s. (Historian Thomas E. Chávez [see entry] says that Oñate did not have a twin, and that Isabel did not die until sometime in the early 17th century.) Oñate began his journey north in February 1598 with a large group of colonists, the estimated number of which varies, but ranges up to nearly 600. The caravan reached San Gabriel, near San Juan Pueblo, in July of the same year. Oñate began exploration of the region and soon had problems with some of the Pueblo people, particularly the Acomas. In January he ordered retaliatory action against Acoma and some sources estimate that as many as 800 Indians were killed and the remainder sold into slavery. His other major problem was desertions among his colonizers; some estimates running as high as 400 of them returning to Mexico. He managed to hang on until 1608 when he was replaced. In 1614, Mexican authorities tried him for misconduct in office. He was acquitted of some charges and convicted of others. He was pardoned for his crimes before his death at Guadalcanal, Spain, in 1626. In spite of it all, the Spanish Colonial period began with Oñate's *entrada*.
Ellis, *New Mexico, Past and Present*
Roberts & Roberts, *New Mexico*
Simmons, *New Mexico*
Simmons, *Spanish Pathways*
Snow, *New Mexico's First*
Thrapp, *Encyclopedia*

Oppenheimer, J. Robert "Oppie" (1904-1967)
"Father of the Atomic Bomb"
Oppenheimer was born in New York City and educated at Harvard, Cambridge University in England and Göttigen University in Germany. His intellectual capabilities were considerable and by the 1930s he had established himself as a theoretical physicist and had published more than a dozen articles on the subject. In 1941 he was named to head the atomic bomb project and he selected Los Alamos, New Mexico, as the location of the weapons laboratory. He was named director in 1942.

Before it was all over, he supervised more than 3,000 people and yet retained a role in addressing theoretical and mechanical problems associated with development of the atomic bomb. He was present when the first bomb was detonated at Trinity Site, between Socorro and Alamogordo, New Mexico, on July 16, 1945. The force of the explosion was equal to that of 18,000 *tons* of TNT. Afterwards he quoted the *Bhagavad-Gita*: "I am become death: the destroyer of worlds." After World War II, Oppenheimer was appointed chairman of the General Advisory Committee of the Atomic Energy Commission and he voiced his opinion against the development of a hydrogen bomb, a program supported by physicist Edward Teller (see entry). In the early 1950s, at the time of the great Red Scare, Oppenheimer's past association with left-wing groups and Communists came to the fore. In June 1954, the Atomic Energy Commission voted against reinstating his access to classified information, thus ending his influence over science policy. He returned to teaching and died of throat cancer in 1967. There is a research center and one street, a very short one, named for him in Los Alamos.

Hsi, *Sundaggers*
Rhodes, *Making the Atomic Bomb*
Other literature abundant

Orchard, Sarah Jane Creech "Sadie" (1860-1943)
Hillsboro-Kingston Businesswoman

Sadie Jane Creech Orchard

Legend holds that Sadie Creech was born in London, England, and made her way to the U.S. and arrived in Kingston, New Mexico by the mid-1880s. More recent research, however, indicates that she was born in Mills County, Iowa. There is some question about when she was born: the 1870 census indicates that she was born in 1860; her birth certificate shows her birth year as 1862; and her tombstone shows 1865. Historian Glenda Riley concluded that 1860 is probably correct, but the exact date is unknown. Sadie stayed a short time in Kingston—where she worked as a prostitute—before she moved down the road a few miles to Hillsboro. There, in 1895, she married James W. Orchard and became well known as Sadie Orchard. She was also noted for driving Orchard's stagecoach over the rocky roads between Kingston, Hillsboro and Lake Valley to the south, but it is unlikely that she did it very often. She operated a brothel in Hillsboro after 1901 when she and Orchard divorced. She also owned a hotel in Hillsboro. She was well regarded in the community for her many good works and she remained in Hillsboro until her death in 1943. She was interred in Hot Springs, now known as Truth or Consequences. Historian Riley wrote, "Morally, it might matter to some that Madame Sadie ran a brothel. For others, however, Sarah Jane Creech Orchard—or Sadie—was a hard working woman who contributed a lifetime of good humor, energy and altruism to New Mexico and to the Old West, and for that she is remembered."

Fergusson, Erna, *New Mexico*

Riley & Etulain, *Wild Women of the Old West*
Rakocy, *Ghosts of Kingston*

Ortiz, Alfonso (1939-1997)
San Juan Pueblo Educator/Indian Affairs Activist

Born into poverty at San Juan Pueblo in northern New Mexico, Alfonso Ortiz overcame numerous obstacles to gain an education, and ultimately earned a Ph.D. in anthropology. He taught at the University of New Mexico from 1974 until the year before his death. Among his writings are *The Tewa World: Space, Time, Being, and Becoming in a Pueblo Society* (1969), *New Perspectives on the Pueblos* (1972), *Myths and Legends of North American Indians* (1984) and *The Ethnohistory and Social Anthropology of Native North American Peoples* (1996). Ortiz also served as Southwest editor of the *Handbook of American Indians North of Mexico*, volumes nine and ten, sponsored by the Smithsonian Institution, published in 1979 and 1983. As a part of his eulogy to Dr. Ortiz, Keith Basso said, "Alfonso, in fundamental ways, helped to change the moral, educational, and political conscience of this nation in its dealings with the Indian people. That was Alfonso's greatest hope and that was his greatest challenge. That, in a sense, was his spirit—and that, in the end, is his greatest legacy."
Basso, Keith, "Alfonso Ortiz," *Book Talk*, New Mexico Book League, April 1997
Sando, *Pueblo Profiles*

Ortiz, Filimon J. (1898-1952)
New Mexico Department of Corrections Officer

Officer Ortiz's body was found in the early morning hours of June 11, 1952, face up and cold inside the New Mexico state penitentiary at Santa Fe. Investigation revealed the following: There was no blood around the body even though he'd obviously been stabbed and beaten with a pipe; all prisoners in the cell block were accounted for and locked in their respective cells; Ortiz carried no keys so he could not have freed any of them under any circumstances; an autopsy determined that he had died at about 1:00 a.m. but another officer reported seeing Ortiz alive at 4:00 a.m.; and while a penknife and a length of pipe were found near the body, no one could explain how they got there. The crime was never solved.
Bullis, *New Mexico's Finest*

Ortiz y Pino de Kleven, María Concepción "Concha" (1910-2006)
"The Grande Dame of New Mexico"

It is interesting that Concha Ortiz y Pino was born into a prominent Spanish family at Galisteo, in Santa Fe County, at the very time that the Constitutional Convention was meeting to draft a document that would lead to statehood for New Mexico. Spanish was her first language and she didn't learn English until she was ten years old. Home schooled, she attended the Loretto Academy for girls in Santa Fe before she returned home and established a school of Colonial New Mexican arts and crafts. A Democrat, Concha was elected to the state house of representatives from Santa Fe County, District 4, in 1936. She was the youngest woman to ever serve in the New Mexico Legislature, and only the third woman. Concha was re-elected in 1938 and 1940 and in 1941 she was named the majority whip for the House of Representatives, the first woman to hold that position anywhere in the United States. She did not seek re-election in 1942. She married college professor Victor Kleven in 1943. In 1951, when her father became too ill from Parkinson's disease to continue, Concha took over the operation of her family's 100,000 ranch, Agua Verde; a spread that covered parts of Santa Fe, San Miguel and Torrance counties. Victor died unexpectedly in 1956 at the age of 59. "With that tragedy," her biographer, Kathryn Córdova, has written, "Concha lost her desire to remain at Agua Verde. She put it up for sale." It soon sold to oilman/rancher Robert O. Anderson (see entry), leaving Concha quite wealthy. "Concha never went back." Córdova quotes an Albuquerque *Journal* article: "When talking with Concha Ortiz y Pino de Kleven, it quickly becomes clear that in her mind, her greatest accomplishments aren't necessarily reflected in the myriad certificates and awards covering her walls. It's in the memories of friendships formed and the

people she helped along the way." And Concha says, "Life is so interesting, if you don't sit on it. The worst thing, to me, is the accumulation of goods that don't help anyone. It's stinginess of the heart." No one could ever accuse Concha of that.

Córdova, *¡Concha!*
Other literature abundant

Mariano Sabino Otero.
After Twitchell.

Otero, Mariano Sabino (1844-1904)
Delegate to the U.S. Congress

Mariano Sabino Otero was the son of Juan Otero, the nephew of Miguel Antonio Otero I (see entry), and the cousin of Miguel Antonio Otero II (see entry); a family long active in New Mexico public affairs. Mariano served as delegate to the U.S. Congress in 1879-1881. Twitchell (see entry) says "He wielded great influence during his career, was shrewd in business affairs, of progressive ideas and in every sense a representative New Mexican." He married the daughter of José Leandro Perea (see entry) of Bernalillo.

Twitchell, *Leading Facts*, Vol. II

Otero, Miguel Antonio I (1829-1882)
Delegate to the U.S. Congress

A native of Valencia County, New Mexico, Otero served in the Territorial House of Representatives from 1852 to 1854, as attorney general in 1854, and as delegate to Congress from 1856 to 1861. He also served as Secretary of the New Mexico Territory in 1861 and 1862. He was the father of New Mexico Governor Miguel Antonio Otero II (see

Miguel Antonio Otero.
After Twitchell.

entry) and the uncle of Mariano Sabino Otero (see entry), also a delegate to Congress. Otero was a Southern sympathizer in the years leading up to the Civil War, and supported a fugitive slave act for New Mexico, which the legislature passed but Governor Abraham Rencher (see entry) vetoed. He lost in a re-election bid in 1861 to John S. Watts, a strong Union supporter. New Mexico remained with the Union during the Civil War.
Lamar, *Far Southwest*

Otero, Miguel Antonio II "Gillie" (1859-1944)
Governor (Territorial) of New Mexico (1897-1906)

Gillie, as he was called, was the longest-serving of New Mexico's territorial governors (1897-1906) and the first and only Hispanic to hold the office. His grandparents arrived in New Mexico sometime in the late 18th Century. His father, Miguel Antonio Otero I (see entry) served as New Mexico's delegate to the U.S. Congress and his son served as Attorney General and State Auditor. He wrote two books about his colorful life: *My Life on The Frontier, 1864-1882* (1935) and *My Nine Years as Governor of the Territory of New Mexico* (1940). Otero County was named for him as a part of a political compromise. Alamogordo is the county seat.

Gov. Miguel Antonio Otero.
After Twitchell.

Julyan, *Place Names*
Otero, *My Life*
Otero, *My Nine Years*
Other literature abundant

-P-

Palen, Joseph G. (1812-1875)
Chief Justice, New Mexico Territorial Supreme Court (1869-1875)

Joseph G. Palen. After Twitchell.

Palen was born in Greene County, New York, and educated at Amherst and Harvard. He practiced law in New York for many years before President U.S. Grant (see entry) appointed him Chief Justice of the New Mexico Supreme Court. Historian Howard Lamar reported that Palen was an uncompromising member of the Santa Fe Ring. R. E. Twitchell (see entry) wrote, "Among his closest friends [were] Messrs. Elkins (see entry), Catron (see entry), Breeden, and Waldo." No doubt about Ring membership. Palen doesn't seem to have done anything remarkable during his six years on the bench, but control of the territorial judiciary was important to the Ring.

Lamar, *Far Southwest*
Twitchell, *Leading Facts*, Vol. II

Parker, Robert (or George) Leroy "Butch Cassidy" "Jim Lowe" (1866-??)
Western Outlaw

Robert Leroy Parker

No one seems quite sure about his first name. Thrapp reports that Butch himself said that his real first name was George. His father and his sister, though, called him Robert. Speculation as to how he came to be known as Butch Cassidy is far too extensive for inclusion here. Cassidy was a leader of the so-called Wild Bunch or Hole in the Wall gang that ranged widely in the American West, especially in Wyoming and Montana. They robbed banks and trains in the late 1890s. Cassidy and other gang members occasionally hid out at the WS Ranch near Alma in southwestern New Mexico. Cassidy went by the name Jim Lowe while there. He and his friends stole a herd of horses when they left the area about 1900. The Pinkerton Detective Agency reported that Cassidy, along with Harry Longabaugh (see entry), was killed in Bolivia in 1909. Members of the Parker family believe that he was *not* killed in South America, but returned to the U.S. and died as late as 1937, perhaps in Spokane, Washington.

Betenson, *Butch Cassidy*
Daniel Buck and Anne Meadows, "Butch & Sundance: Still Dead?" *Quarterly of the National Association for Outlaw and Lawman History*, April-June 2006
Kelly, *Outlaw Trail*
Other literature abundant

Patrón, Juan Bautista (1850-1884)
Lincoln County Teacher, Probate Judge, Legislator

Born in Santa Fe, New Mexico, Patrón was, according to Thrapp, a protégé of Bishop Jean Baptiste Lamy (see entry) who studied at Notre Dame. By 1875 he had arrived in Lincoln County and was a clerk for Lawrence Murphy (see entry), but that apparently did not last long. He inquired into the murder of two "Mexicans" and organized a citizen's posse to address the matter. As a result of his efforts, John Riley, one of Murphy's minions, shot him in the back. The wound crippled him for life. Riley was acquitted. Patrón served in the Territorial Legislature in 1877 and 1878. He sided with the McSween faction in the Lincoln County War. He and John Tunstall (see entry) were friends. A Texan named Mike Maney, aka Mike Manning, murdered Patrón at Puerto de Luna in 1884. Maney, like Riley, escaped punishment.

Nolan, *Bad Blood*
Thrapp, *Encyclopedia*

Pattie, James Ohio (1804-after 1833)
Gila River Mountain Man, Trapper

A native of Kentucky, along with his father, Sylvester (1782-1828), he arrived in Santa Fe, New Mexico, in 1824 by way of Missouri. After he and his father assisted in the rescue of the daughter of an important Mexican official, they received a license from the Mexican government to trap along the Gila River in southwestern New Mexico. They had many additional adventures before they made their way west to San Diego, California, where they were jailed by Mexican authorities. Sylvester became ill and died in jail there. James either escaped or was released and made his way to New Orleans. *The Personal Narrative of James O. Pattie, of Kentucky*, a somewhat embellished account of his exploits, was published at Cincinnati in 1831. There is some mystery about his last years, after 1833.

Dennis Goodwin, "Westerners," *Wild West*, June 2005
Thrapp, *Encyclopedia*
Twitchell, *Leading Facts*, Vol. II

Peña, Lee Vicente (1895-1944)
Taos City Marshal

Marshal Lee Vicente Peña

That police work can be unexpectedly dangerous was sadly proven in the case of Taos Town Marshal Lee Peña. On a Wednesday evening, only a few days before Christmas in 1944, the marshal was summoned to a tavern in town where a drunk had been causing a disturbance. The miscreant offered no resistance when Peña asked the man to step outside; but only seconds later he produced a gun and shot the lawman in the upper left chest. Peña was dead on arrival at a local hospital. The killer was an army deserter by the name of Henry Gonzales, 24. He was soon captured and convicted and sentenced to 120 to 150 years in prison. According to a news story of the day, the judge "voiced a request that the state board of pardons and the present and future governors deny any appeals for Gonzales to be pardoned." Gonzales served 14 years before he was released from prison after Governor John Burroughs commuted his sentence. A native of Texas, Peña arrived in New Mexico in 1915 and volunteered for military service in World War I in 1917. According to his son, he "walked across France." Lee Peña was survived by a wife and seven children.

"150 Years Given in Taos Slaying," Albuquerque *Journal*, June 5, 1945

Bullis, *New Mexico's Finest*

John O. Peña, Correspondence, November, 1999 & May 2006

Peñalosa, Diego Dionisio de (d. 1687)
Governor (Spanish) of New Mexico (1661-1664)

Historian Tom Chávez (see entry) reports that Peñalosa had been convicted of murder in Perú before he was appointed governor of New Mexico. He forcefully opposed the power of the 17th century Catholic Church in New Mexico. Involved in a dispute over livestock with one Pedro Durán y Cháves, Peñalosa ordered him arrested. Before that could be accomplished, Durán y Cháves took sanctuary in a church. The governor was not dissuaded and had him physically removed. The clergy, in the person of Fray Alonso de Posada, strongly objected and threatened Peñalosa with excommunication. The governor did not seem to be impressed, but perhaps he should have been. In March 1664 he went to Mexico City where he was promptly arrested and imprisoned, charged with more than 230 counts of malfeasance. His trial took two years and his reputation was ruined. He fled to England first, then France. (Historian Chávez says he was "deported" from the Spanish empire.) He called himself the Count of Santa Fe and he consorted with Robert LaSalle (1643-1687) in planning the establishment of a French settlement in Spanish territory, along the Gulf of Mexico in what is now Texas. That effort failed when LaSalle's own men mutinied and killed him.

Chávez, *New Mexico*

Sálaz Márquez, *New Mexico*

Twitchell, *Leading Facts*, Vol. I

Peppin, George Warden "Dad" (1841-1904)
Lincoln County Sheriff, Lincoln County War Figure

Born in Vermont, Peppin made his was to New Mexico by means of the 5th Infantry of the so-called California Column in 1862. He was discharged at Fort Stanton, in Lincoln County, in 1864. He made his living as a stonemason for many years. Peppin's claim to fame came with the Lincoln County War. After Sheriff William Brady (see entry) was murdered on April 1, 1878, and his successor, John Copeland (see entry), was removed after a month or so in office, Peppin became sheriff. Since he was staunchly on the side of Murphy and Dolan (see entries), some local folks called him the "quasi-sheriff." His appointment came in time for him to be the representative of the law at the time of the Five Day Battle at Lincoln in July 1878. He handled the situation badly by allowing the Murphy-Dolan faction to control events, and he hid behind a detachment of regular army troops as the killing spun out of control. He was not re-elected in the November election. Investigator Frank Angel (see entry) described him as a "weak Murphy man—partisan not reliable." He later became a butcher at Fort Stanton.

Ball, *Desert Lawmen*
Burns, *Billy the Kid*
Thrapp, *Encyclopedia*

Peralta, Pedro de (c. 1584-1666)
Governor (Spanish) of New Mexico (1610-1614)

Pedro de Peralta is best remembered as the founder of Santa Fe. He was born in Spain and migrated to the New World as a young man. He was appointed governor of New Mexico, probably in 1609, but didn't arrive to take the post until 1610. He was one of several 17th century governors described as "contentious" toward the Franciscans. The question seems to have centered on who, churchman or governor, was in charge. The conflict during Peralta's administration culminated in May 1613 when the governor sent a troop of soldiers to Taos to collect the tribute owed by the Indians under the *encomienda*. Fray Isidro Ordóñez stepped in. The cleric prevented the soldiers from collecting and disbursed a group of Indians who had arrived to make payment. Ordóñez also demanded that Governor Peralta cease using Indian labor in the construction of the Palace of the Governors in Santa Fe. Peralta was outraged at the Franciscan's interference, but continued to govern as he had, undeterred. Ordóñez responded, one gathers, with equal outrage. He called the governor "a heretic, a Lutheran and a Jew" and excommunicated him. The dispute became so acrimonious that at one point Peralta took a shot at the churchman, but missed. Ordóñez then managed to capture and imprison Peralta until a new governor, Bernardo de Ceballos, arrived. Peralta returned to Mexico City and, according to Thrapp, "served the king in various capacities in Mexico and South America." He died in Spain. (Note: Thrapp also says that Peralta spent nine years as governor. Other sources are unanimous in reporting that his tenure began in 1610 and ended in 1614.)

Broughton, William H., "The History of Seventeenth-Century New Mexico: Is It Time for New Interpretations? *New Mexico Historical Review*, January 1993

Fugate & Fugate, *Roadside History*
Horgan, *Great River*
Roberts & Roberts, *New Mexico*
Thrapp, *Encyclopedia*

Perea, José Leandro (1822-1883)
Sandoval County Benefactor, "The Sheep King of New Mexico"

José Leandro Perea.
Courtesy Sandoval County
Historical Society.

Perea was born in the village of Bernalillo. By the time of his death, he was one of the richest man, if not the richest, in New Mexico Territory. He reportedly owned more than 200,000 sheep at one time. It was Perea who, in 1878, prevented the railroad from constructing its shops, marshaling yards and roundhouse in the town of Bernalillo, the result of which was that Albuquerque became New Mexico's largest city, not Bernalillo. He was a community benefactor in that he spent his own money to build schools and provide teachers for Bernalillo. He was the father of 13 children and many of his descendants continue to live in Sandoval County.

Bullis, *99 New Mexicans*
Simmons, *Albuquerque*

Pérez, Albino (d. 1837)
Governor (Mexican) of New Mexico (1835-1837)

Governor Pérez issued a detailed proclamation in July 1836 entitled, "Plan of Regulation of Public Instruction." He wrote that this was necessary because "Running the streets are children who ought to be receiving the education so necessary at the fitting and proper age; youths of evil disposition, abandoned to laziness and licentiousness, practicing vices; useless aims which only serve to corrupt, like the plague, the city that tolerates and feeds them; and above all, what are the results? Robbery, immorality, poverty, desertion, and the most humiliating shame of the city...." This was not well received. First of all, that Pérez was not a New Mexican but a Colonel in the Mexican army caused some resentment. Second, it was a part of a general tax increase imposed from Mexico City by President Antonio López de Santa Anna (1794-1876). Also, according to historian Marc Simmons (see entry), Pérez had an illicit affair with his maid—which produced a son, Demetrio—and a weakness for gambling, neither of which endeared him to Santa Feans. In August 1837 Pérez marched north toward Santa Cruz to put down what he perceived as a rebellion. His small force of regular army troops and Indian volunteers was routed near Black Mesa. Pérez himself was chased down, captured and beheaded. Legend holds that his head was carried back into Santa Fe where it was used as a football in a game of the day.

Horgan, *Great River*

Marc Simmons, Santa Fe *New Mexican*, "Rebellion makes quick work of 'outside governor,'" March 11, 2006
Twitchell, *Leading Facts*, Vol. II

Perkins, Don (1938-)
Football Player

Perkins was born in Waterloo, Iowa, but played football at the University of New Mexico where he was a three-time All-Skyline selection from 1957 to 1959. He joined the Dallas Cowboys in 1961—when he was named rookie of the year—and played for eight seasons, until 1969, when he retired from football. In 2005, he ranked third on the Cowboy rushing list behind Emmitt Smith and Tony Dorsett. He was the first Cowboy to rush for 6,000 yards. Perkins was named to the Pro Bowl six times, and was All-Pro once, in 1962. He was inducted into the Cowboys Ring of Honor in 1976, along with quarterback Don Meredith.

News accounts abundant

Perry, Charles C. "Charlie" (fl. 1890s)
Roswell Town Marshal, Chaves County Sheriff (1895-96), Thief

Perry had a fearsome reputation with a gun and had killed several men, among them cowboys George Griffin and B. Champion. As Chaves County Sheriff, in 1896, Perry absconded with tax collections, amounting to $7,639.02. He went first to Mexico where he met a woman; but he ended up in South Africa where he was killed in a casino. None of the money was recovered.

Ball, *Desert Lawmen*
Fleming, *Treasures of History IV*
Klasner, *My Girlhood*
Larson, *Forgotten Frontier*

Charles C. Perry. Courtesy Historical Society of Southeast New Mexico, No. 1386.

Pershing, General John Joseph "Black Jack" (1860-1948)
U.S. Army Soldier

Pershing graduated from West Point in June 1886 and was soon assigned to the 6th U.S. Cavalry and was posted to Fort Bayard, New Mexico, near Silver City, arriving there in September. Apache leader Geronimo, had already surrendered but Pershing did participate—unsuccessfully—in the pursuit of another Apache leader, Mangas Coloradas. Pershing's unit was reassigned to Fort Stanton, near Lincoln, in 1887 and moved again to Fort Wingate, near present day Gallup, in 1889. He was transferred back to Fort Stanton later the same year and back to Fort Wingate in 1890. Such was life on the frontier. He and his troop left New Mexico for South Dakota in December 1890, but took no part in the fight at Wounded Knee (December 29, 1890). After Mexican revolutionary Pancho Villa's raid on Columbus, New Mexico on March 9, 1916, General Pershing was back in New Mexico, assigned the task of pursuing Villa's troops deep into Old Mexico. This expedition was unsuccessful and Villa was never captured. The effort was valuable to the Americans, however, because many of the tactics used—deployment of a mechanized army and the use of airplanes—would be used again in Europe during World War I, only year or so later. Pershing won a Pulitzer Prize for his 1931 book, *My Experiences in the World War*. Those who knew him reported that he was well-liked, and well-respected, by both his superiors and his subordinates throughout his career. He earned the name "Black Jack" because he commanded a company of the 10th Cavalry (Negro) for ten years that included the Spanish American War (1898). Pershing wrote this: "It has been an honor which I am proud to claim to have been at one time a member of that intrepid organization of the Army which as always added glory to the military history of America—the 10th Cavalry."

Katz, *Black West*

Donald Smythe, S. J., "John J. Pershing: Frontier Cavalryman," *New Mexico Historical Review*, July 1963

Other literature abundant

Petty, Norman (1927-1984)
Musician, Record Company Owner

Norman Petty

Norman Petty was born in Clovis and educated there. A piano player, Petty and his wife, Vi, and guitarist Jack Vaughn formed the Norman Petty Trio in 1948. In 1956, their version of *Mood Indigo* sold half a million copies, which allowed Petty to expand his recording studio. The following year, their *Almost Paradise* hit number 18 on the charts. Petty is best known for recording some of music's best-known artists: Buddy Holly (see entry), Buddy Knox, Roy Orbison, Waylon Jennings, and others. One source reports that some of Holly's best work was recorded at Petty Studios, and it was a Petty recording of Holly's *That'll Be the Day* that led to a recording contract with Decca Records. Petty died of leukemia. His original studio is now the Norman & Vi Petty Performing Arts Center, operated by Eastern New Mexico University.

Norman Petty Studios

Other literature abundant

Phillips, Bert Geer (1865-1956)
Painter, Charter Member of the Taos Society of Artists

A native of Hudson, New York, Phillips studied art at the National Academy of Design and the Art Students League. He also worked and studied in both London and Paris. He met Joseph Henry Sharp (see entry) in Paris and heard all about the wonders of Taos, New Mexico. In 1898, Phillips and Ernest Blumenschein (see entry) set out by wagon from Denver en route to Mexico. According to legend, the wagon broke down near Taos, and Phillips waited while Blumenschein carried the broken wheel into to town for repair. When Phillips entered the town a short time later and took a look around, he became certain that the village would be his home. He thus became the first of the Taos artists to settle there permanently (Sharp is often considered the "Spiritual Father" of the Taos Art Colony because he was the first to visit the town, but Phillips was the first to live there). Phillips wrote, "Nothing could be more natural than that a distinctive American art idea should develop on a soil so richly imbued with romance, history and scenic beauty as is to be found in the far famed beautiful Taos Valley and the Poetic Indian Village of Taos Pueblo." When the Taos Society of Artists was created in 1915, Phillips was elected the first Secretary/Treasurer, and it was in his home that the Society was unanimously voted out of existence in March 1927. Phillips resided in Taos until 1952, only a short time before his death.

Nelson, *Legendary Artists of Taos*
Samuels, *The Illustrated Biographical Encyclopedia*
Schimmel & White, *Bert Geer Phillips*
Witt, *The Taos Artists*

Pike, Zebulon Montgomery (1779-1813)
U.S. Military Officer, New Mexico Explorer

In 1806, Pike and a party of 22 soldiers set out from St. Louis to find the head-waters of the Arkansas and Red Rivers; at least that was the officially stated pur-pose of the expedition. In early 1807 he found himself at the confluence of the Rio Grande and the Rio Conejos, where he constructed a blockhouse. He was within Spanish territory and was soon arrested and taken to Santa Fe. He was well treated—his captors allowed him to retain his weapons—and finally released and returned to New Orleans. Many thought at the time that his purpose all along was to get a look at the northern Spanish frontier, and if that is so, he was certainly successful. In 1810 Pike wrote a book about his adventures in Nuevo México called *The Southwestern Journals of Zebulon Pike, 1806-1807*, that was published in the U.S. and Europe. (Note: The University of New Mexico Press republished Pike's book in 2006, edited by Stephen Harding Hart and Archer Butler Hulbert. See Bibliography.) The book stimulated interest in Spanish North America at a time when Mexico was striving for independence from Spain. Pike advanced in rank to Brigadier General, but was killed near York, Ontario, during the War of 1812. Pike's Peak, Colorado, is named for him. Note that he never climbed the peak, and he did not name it for himself.

Literature abundant

Pile, William Anderson (1829-1889)
Governor (Territorial) of New Mexico (1869-1871)

Born in Indiana and educated as a Methodist Epis-copal minister, he moved on to Missouri and joined the Union Army during the Civil War, attaining the rank of brevet Major General. He served in the U.S. Congress in the late 1860s before being named Governor of New Mexico. His single claim to fame was that he sold as waste

Gov. William Anderson
Pile. After Twitchell.

paper——some say unintentionally——a significant portion of the old Spanish and Mexican archives he found in Santa Fe. Not all of the documents were lost. He became Minister to Venezuela after leaving New Mexico.
Congressional Biography
Twitchell, *Leading Facts*, Vol. II

Pío, Fray Juan (d. 1680)
Tesuque Pueblo Priest
Fray Pío is said to have been the first Spanish casualty in the Pueblo Revolt of 1680. Pueblo Indian historian Joe Sando writes, "The Pueblo Revolt began the instant Padre Pío was killed." Pío's companion, a soldier named Pedro Hidalgo, managed to escape back to Santa Fe.
Sando, *Po'pay*
Sálaz Márquez, *New Mexico*

Pipkin, Daniel "Red" (1876-1937)
New Mexico/Arizona Outlaw, McKinley County, New Mexico, Deputy Sheriff
Pipkin was a member of a gang that included William "Bronco Bill" Walters and William "Kid" Johnson when they robbed a train near Belen, New Mexico, in May 1898. He was present, but escaped, at a gunfight near the Black River in eastern Arizona in late July 1898 when Johnson was killed and Walters wounded and captured. Pipkin was at last captured and served seven years in prison. After his release, he resided in Gallup, New Mexico, where he became a deputy to Sheriff Bob Roberts. He committed suicide in 1937 rather than wait for death from cancer of the throat.
Tanner & Tanner, "Red Pipkin, Outlaw From the Black River Country," *Wild West Magazine*, Oct. 2003
Thrapp, *Encyclopedia*

Poe, John W. (c. 1851-1923)
Lincoln County Sheriff, Chaves County Banker/Rancher

Joseph Callaway Lea and John W. Poe. Courtesy Historical Society of Southeast New Mexico, No. 3326-J.

(Thrapp shows his date of birth as October 17, 1851. Twitchell shows the year as 1850.) Poe, a Kentuckian by nativity, became a Texas buffalo hunter by 1875, then a lawman at Fort Griffin, Texas. He arrived in New Mexico in 1881, in time to become a deputy to Lincoln County Sheriff Pat Garrett (see entry) and to join in the pursuit of William H. Bonney (Billy the Kid, see entry). Poe was present in Fort Sumner on the evening of July 14, 1881, when Garrett killed Bonney. Poe succeeded Garrett as Lincoln County sheriff in 1883, but gave up law enforcement at the end of 1885 and began a career in ranching and banking. He died at Roswell. Twitchell incorrectly states that Poe was Lincoln County Sheriff at the time

Bonney was killed.
Keleher, *Violence*
Thrapp, *Encyclopedia*
Twitchell, Vol. II
Other literature abundant

Polk, James Knox (1795-1849)
President of the United States (1845-1849)

Polk probably had more direct impact on New Mexico than any other president until Franklin Roosevelt was elected in the 1930s. Under Polk's administration, and because of his policies, a huge segment of the Southwest became part of the United States, and that included what is now New Mexico. Polk, a Democrat, was helped along in his political career by former President Andrew Jackson to the extent that he was sometimes called "Young Hickory" (Andy was "Old Hickory"). While Jackson had encouraged Indian removal from the southeastern United States to lands west of the Mississippi, Polk supported the annexation of Texas and the concept of Manifest Destiny which held that the U.S. should occupy all lands between the Atlantic and Pacific oceans. The Mexican War (1846-1848) was waged during his administration, and the Treaty of Guadalupe Hidalgo was signed in 1848. The result was that, for about $18 million, the U.S. acquired more than a half-million square miles of territory, or about half of Mexico. That acquisition included what became New Mexico. Not all Americans supported Polk and the Mexican War. Whig Congressman Abraham Lincoln (see entry) said this: "I more than suspect that he is deeply conscious of being in the wrong,—that he feels the blood of this war, like the blood of Abel, is crying to Heaven against him.... He is a bewildered, confounded, and miserably perplexed man." Polk had promised to serve only one term and did not seek re-election in 1848. He left office the following year and died soon afterwards, probably of cholera.
Degregorio, *Presidents*
Other literature abundant

Po'pay (c. 1630-c. 1690)
Pueblo Indian Revolutionary Leader

The Pueblo Revolt of 1680 is the only instance in which the indigenous people of North America drove the European interlopers away from their country. Po'pay gets the credit for leading the revolt, but several others were also instrumental. He was born at San Juan Pueblo (Ohkay Owingeh) north of Santa Fe, and raised there. He took positions of responsibility in his Pueblo and became the war captain. In an effort to destroy the native religion—to root out the devil—Spanish Governor Juan de Treviño (see entry) ordered the arrest of 47 Pueblo *caciques*, Po'pay among them. Four were hanged, one committed suicide, and the rest flogged on charges of "practicing sorcery." Po'pay joined with other Indian leaders in planning the rebellion, which began on August 10, 1680, coincidentally, the feast day of St. Lawrence, a Spanish Christian martyr. Pueblo Indian historian Joe Sando writes: "After eighty-two years of silent submission and resentment, the Pueblo people had had enough. Their pent-up hatred for the Spanish soldiers, suppressed for so long, had been released." About 400 Spanish settlers and 20 priests were killed, and about 2,100 Spaniards were driven into exile near what is now El Paso, Texas. An estimated 300 of the Indians were killed; 47 were captured and executed. New Mexico remained in the hands of Pueblo Indians until Diego de Vargas (see entry) and the Spaniards returned in 1692. In 2005, a statue of Po'pay by Cliff Fragua of Jemez Pueblo was installed in Statuary Hall in the U.S. Capitol in Washington, D.C.

Stefanie Beninato, "Popé, Pose-yemu, and Naranjo: A New Look at Leadership in the
    Pueblo Revolt of 1680," *New Mexico Historical Review*, October 1990
Sálaz Márquez, *New Mexico*
Sando, *Po'pay*
Simmons, *Spanish*

Popejoy, Thomas L. "Tom" (1902-October 24, 1975)
University of New Mexico President (1948-1968)

With 20 years of service, Tom Popejoy was the longest serving of the University of New Mexico presidents, and he was the first native New Mexican to hold the office. Popejoy was born on a ranch in Colfax County, east of Raton where he attended public school. He arrived at UNM in 1921 to begin his undergraduate studies. He graduated in 1925 with a degree in economics and in 1929 earned a master's degree, also in economics. He joined the UNM faculty as an instructor and worked his way up to the rank of associate professor. In 1937 he was named comptroller and later served as assistant to Presidents Zimmerman (see entry) and Wernette. When President Zimmerman died in 1944, there was talk of elevating Popejoy to the presidency, but the Board of Regents decided on outsider J. Philip Wernette, a Harvard Ph.D. Some faculty people had been critical of Popejoy because he had spent as much time in university administration as he had in teaching, and, besides, he didn't have a Ph.D. Wernette's tenure was short and Popejoy became President on July 1, 1948. His accomplishments in a long tenure are too many to include here, but it is noteworthy that UNM enrollment when he took office was fewer that 5,000 students; and more than 14,000 when he retired. William E. Davis, who served as UNM President from 1975 to 1982, wrote this: "In many ways [Popejoy] was like a hero out of pulp fiction, bigger than Kit Carson, but smaller than a New Mexican grizzly. His visage was somewhere between Benjamin Franklin and Sam Houston, his personal demeanor someplace between Andrew Jackson and Abe Lincoln. Best of all, though, he was New Mexican to the bone. He was the stuff legends are made of, and there never was or will be a lack of tall tales about Tom Popejoy." Popejoy Hall, UNM's outstanding 2,000-seat performance venue, was named for Tom Popejoy upon the occasion of his retirement in 1968. He died in Albuquerque.

Davis, *Miracle on the Mesa*
García, *Albuquerque*
Hillerman, *Seldom Disappointed*
Horn, University in Turmoil

Price, Sterling "Old Pap" (1809-1867)
Governor (Military) of New Mexico (1847-1848)

Price was born in Prince Edward County, Virginia. He was educated there, studied law and was admitted to the bar before he moved to Missouri about 1830. He was active in politics there and resigned from the U.S. Congress to accept appointment as Colonel in the Missouri Infantry on August 12, 1846, early in the Mexican War. He arrived in Santa Fe, after the American Occupation of August 1846, with reinforcements. General Stephen W. Kearny (see entry) had already departed for California and Colonel Alexander Doniphan (see entry) soon also departed for Chihuahua, leaving Price in command.

Gov. Sterling Price. After Twitchell.

Price led the American forces and mountain men who put down the Taos Revolt of January 1847, and he thus became military governor of New Mexico. He served until the following year, and was discharged in November 1848. He later became governor of Missouri and served as a Major General in the Confederate Army during the Civil War. It is interesting that his Congressional biography makes no mention of his service in New Mexico.

Congressional Biography
Crutchfield, *Tragedy*
New Mexico Blue Book, 2003-2004
Twitchell, *Leading Facts*, Vol. II

Prince, LeBarron Bradford (1840-1922)
Governor (Territorial) of New Mexico (1889-1893)

Prince was a New England blueblood, a descendant of Governor William Bradford (1590-1657) of Plymouth Colony who had arrived in America on the Mayflower. His grandfather and great-grandfather both served as governor of Rhode Island. L. Bradford Prince was born in Flushing, New York, and graduated from Columbia Law School. He soon became active in Republican politics. In 1878, President Rutherford B. Hayes appointed him Chief Justice of the New Mexico Supreme Court, a position he held until 1882. Twitchell (see entry) reports that Prince was an impartial justice. President Benjamin Harrison appointed Prince governor of New Mexico. Even though he was nominally a part of the Santa Fe Ring, he and Tom

Gov. LeBarron Bradford Prince. After Twitchell.

Catron (see entry) loathed each other and Prince fought Catron for control of the Republican Party. Prince wrote this: "A Territory with bad officials is a despotism, and not a republic; it is ruled by men named by an authority 2,000 miles away, who are not responsible to any local instrument of power." Prince, of course, was one of those so appointed. He and his wife entertained frequently and lavishly, "people of all classes" at the Palace of the Governors. He retired to Rio Arriba County where he farmed and from whence he served in the Territorial Council (Senate). Prince wrote widely about New Mexico, including his 1883 book, *Historical Sketches of New Mexico*, and his 1910, *New Mexico's Struggle for Statehood: Sixty years of Effort to Obtain Self Government*. He also served for many years as president of the Historical Society of New Mexico. He died, however, in Queens, New York.

Lamar, *Far Southwest*
Twitchell, *Leading Facts*, Vol. II
Other literature abundant

Pyle, Ernest Taylor "Ernie" (1900-1945)
World War II Correspondent

Ernest Taylor Pyle. Courtesy The Albuquerque Museum Photoarchives PA2003.031.002.

A native of Indiana and a well-known and respected reporter and columnist on the national scene in the 1930s, Ernie Pyle and his wife Jerry built a house in southeast Albuquerque in 1940. He went on to become one of the most famous correspondents of World War II. He covered military action in North Africa, Italy, France and in the Pacific, and wrote two books: *Here Is Your War* (1943) and *Brave Men* (1944). He won a Pulitzer Prize for his work in 1943. Pyle was killed by Japanese gunfire on the island of Ie Shima on April 18, 1945. He was referred to by the newspapers of the day as "The wiry little columnist, beloved by GIs throughout the world." The Ernie Pyle Branch of the Albuquerque Public Library is located in his former home at 900 Girard SE.

"Ernie Pyle Killed on Pacific Isle...," Albuquerque *Journal*, April 19, 1945
Bryan, *Albuquerque*
Melzer, *Ernie Pyle*
John E. Miller, "Ernie Pyle, From Hoosier Farm Boy to the GIs' Friend," *American History*, Oct. 2005
Garcia, *Three Centuries*
Hillerman, *The Spell of New Mexico*
Simmons, *Albuquerque*

-Q-

Quay, Matthew Stanley (1833-1904)
U.S. Senator from Pennsylvania (1887-1904)

A Union Civil War hero, Quay served in a number of public offices before he was elected to the United States Senate as a Republican. He is said to have been a strong supporter of statehood for New Mexico, so when a new county was created in east central New Mexico in 1903, it was named for him. Julyan points out that he was invited to visit New Mexico, but did not, "possibly because he was ill; he died the following year."
Julyan, *Place Names*
New Mexico Blue Book, 2003-2004

Senator Matthew S. Quay

-R-

Rainbolt, William "Will" (1876-1901)
Chaves County Chief Deputy Sheriff

Chief deputy Will Rainbolt was standing in as Chaves County sheriff while Sheriff Fred Higgins (see entry), his brother-in-law, was out of town. Rainbolt heard that a young cowboy named Oliver Hendricks was packing a gun at a dance being held in the southern part of Roswell, and he set out to investigate. Rainbolt managed to arrest Oliver, but then Oliver's brother, Nathan, appeared on the scene. Unable to convince Rainbolt not to arrest his brother, Nathan pulled his own gun and shot the deputy, who died on the spot. Nathan avoided arrest for several years, and when he was captured, returned to Roswell and tried for the crime, he was acquitted. The local newspaper pontificated thus: "The pernicious habit of carrying a gun is responsible for more murders than either whiskey or women, the great promoters of crime."

Bullis, *New Mexico's Finest*
Fleming, *Treasures of History IV*

Ralston, William C. (1826-1875)
Grant County Mining Speculator

Ralston was a wealthy mining promoter who had prospered by his participation in Nevada's Comstock Lode. He founded the Bank of California before he invested in mining properties around Grant (later called Ralston and finally Shakespeare), New Mexico. He was duped by the Great Diamond Hoax of 1872. He drowned in San Francisco Bay in 1875, some said of his own doing.

Sherman, *Ghost Towns*

Read, Benjamin M. (1853-1927)
Santa Fe Attorney/Historian

Read was born in Las Cruces, educated at St. Michael's College in Santa Fe and then taught there. From 1875 to 1880 he "had charge" of the Santa Fe schools. Read served as secretary to Governor Lionel A. Shelton (see entry), studying law at the same time. He was admitted to the bar in 1885. He was elected to the territorial legislature in 1900 and served as Speaker. His first love seems to have been New Mexico history. He produced several books on the subject, among them, *The Mexican American War* (1910), *Illustrated History of New Mexico* (1911), *Hernán Cortés and His Conquest of México* (1914), and *Popular Elementary History of New Mexico* (1914). According to John Porter Bloom, "In writing historical works, Read laid great emphasis upon use of original documentary sources. At considerable expense of time and money, he had research done for him in Spanish and Mexican archives.... His work did not enjoy the popularity that his zeal and intelligence seemed to warrant." He died at Santa Fe, survived by seven children.

John Porter Bloom, "Read to Prince: My Dear Friend and Colleague, Your Book is Simply Wretched," *Book Talk*, New Mexico Book League, Oct. 1998.
Montaño, *Tradiciones*
Twitchell, *Leading Facts* Vol. II

Rencher, Abraham (1798-1883)
Governor (Territorial) of New Mexico (1857-1861)

Born near Raleigh, North Carolina, Rencher served in the U.S. Congress from 1830 to 1834 as a Jacksonian; from 1834 to 1838 as an Anti-Jacksonian, and from 1838 to 1840 as a Whig. He was minister to Portugal from 1843 to 1847. His administration as governor of New Mexico, like that of his predecessor, David Meriwether (see entry), was made difficult by problems with nomadic tribes, primarily the Navajo. During his administration, nearly 300 citizens were killed by Indians; and Navajos attacked Fort Defiance on February 7, 1860. The Historical Society of New Mexico was created during his administration. Some sources report that Rencher was neutral, while others indicate that he supported the Union, as the Civil War approached; even though he was a southerner, and, in fact, owned slaves even as he served as Governor of New Mexico. President Abe Lincoln (see entry) replaced him with Henry Connelly (see entry), a staunch Unionist.

Gov. Abraham Remcher.
After Twitchell.

Lamar, *The Far Southwest*
Remley, *Adios Nuevo Mexico*
Twitchell, *Leading Facts*, Vol. II

Rhee, Lawrence "Larry" (1917-2005)
Albuquerque Holocaust Lecturer

Rhee was born in Germany, and along with his family, fled Hitler and Nazi rule and arrived in the United States in 1936. He joined the U.S. Army in 1942 and served in combat intelligence because of his fluency in German. He also participated in the Nuremberg War Trials after the war, as a translator and as a member of the photo evidence unit. He spent several years in Mexico after the war and returned to Albuquerque, New Mexico, in 1959, where he worked for the Duke

City Lumber Co. After his retirement in 1982, he spent much of his time in lecturing on the Holocaust and the Nuremberg Trials. Andrew Lipman, president of the New Mexico Holocaust and Intolerance Museum, said, "That he was an eyewitness was very important because he supplied the photographic evidence and had actual proof of what happened. He felt that was important because there are people out there who don't know about it, and there are others who don't believe it."
"Obituaries," Albuquerque *Journal*, November 2, 2005

Rhodes, Eugene Manlove "Gene" (1869-1934)
New Mexico Writer

Gene Rhodes was born in Nebraska, but by age 12 was living in New Mexico, near Engle, where his father, Col. Hinman Rhodes, had acquired ranching property. One source says he was working as a cowboy by age 13, but Will Keleher (see entry) quotes Mrs. H. G. Graham, wife of a rancher for whom Gene worked: "Gene Rhodes was never really qualified as a cowboy; at most he was a horse wrangler, a fair hand at watching and rounding up horses for the cowboys to use on the roundups." While working for the Grahams, Gene had an opportunity to make the acquaintance of such frontier luminaries as Oliver Lee (see entry), Bill McNew and Sheriff Pat Garrett (see entry). Rhodes received an elementary education at Eagle Creek in Lincoln County, and later attended school in Mesilla. He also briefly attended Pacific College in California. He began a writing career in 1902. He subsequently wrote numerous short stories and novels, among them, *Good Men and True* (1910), *The Stepsons of Light* (1921), and *Beyond the Desert* (1934). Gene lived in New York and California for a number of years but returned to New Mexico before his death. He is interred at Rhodes Pass in the San Andres Mountains of Socorro County (now a part of the White Sands Missile Range). Inscribed upon his tombstone is: *Pasó Por Aqui*, "He passed by here." This was also the title of his best-known short story.
Keleher, *Fabulous Frontier*
C. L. Sonnichsen, "Gene Rhodes and The Decadent West," *Book Talk*, New Mexico Book
League, Sept. 1990
Thrapp, *Encyclopedia*

Rhodes, Virgil (1924-2005)
State Legislator (1971-1974), Candidate for Lieutenant Governor (1974)

Born in Hale County, in the Texas Panhandle, he was a farmer and contractor before he moved to Albuquerque in 1964 and began building apartments and developing commercial property. A Republican, he was elected to the state House of Representatives in 1970 and served until 1974 when he ran for Lieutenant Governor as running mate to Joe Skeen (who would be elected to congress in 1980). The ticket lost by fewer than 4,000 votes. He later served in the state Senate.
Rio Rancho *Journal*, Jan. 3, 2006

Richter, Conrad Michael (1890-1968)
Albuquerque Novelist/Essayist

Richter was born in Pine Grove, Pennsylvania, and entered into a journalism career by 1910. He married Harvena Achenbach in 1915 and by 1928 she had developed tuberculosis making a move to a higher and dryer climate necessary. They moved to Albuquerque. They only lived in New Mexico for ten continuous years—from 1928 to 1938—but returned often. Probably his best-known novel is *The Sea of Grass* (1937) but he wrote two others set in the West: *Tacey Cromwell* (1942) and *The Lady* (1957). He won a Pulitzer Prize for *The Town* (1950) the final book in his Ohio trilogy. The other two were *The Trees* (1940) and *The Fields* (1946). His daughter, Harvena Richter, taught creative writing at the University of New Mexico from 1969 to 1989.

Hillerman, *The Spell of New Mexico*
Johnson, *Conrad Richter*
Harvena Richter, "Conrad Richter in New Mexico," *Book Talk*, New Mexico Book League, Oct. 1997
Elibrary, University of New Mexico

Rittenhouse, Jack D. (1912-1991)
New Mexico Bookman

Born in Kalamazoo, Michigan, he spent a part of his youth in Arizona but returned to the Midwest and attended Indiana State Teachers College at Terre Haute. After a short tenure as a teacher, he ventured east to New York City where he became involved in the publishing industry. He later entered the advertising business in Houston, Texas, and retired from it in 1960 when he moved to New Mexico. Among his books are *A Guide Book to Highway 66* (1946), *American Horse-Drawn Vehicles* (1948), *The Man Who Owned Too Much*, (about Lucien Maxwell, see entry) (1958), *Cabezon, A New Mexico Ghost Town* (1965), *The Santa Fe Trail: A Historical Bibliography* (1971) and *Maverick Tales* (1971). An entry in *Literary New Mexico* says this: "Jack was a newspaper reporter; book reviewer; bookstore and library employee; book copywriter; editor; advertising manager; mail boy for Alfred Knopf; manual and catalog writer; author of over ten books; director of the Museum of New Mexico Press; publisher and owner of Stagecoach Press; UNM Press's Western Editor and Business Manager; instructor; printer; bibliographer; bookbinder. He was everyone's final authority on books of the West, especially the Southwest." Tony Hillerman wrote, "[Rittenhouse is] my nominee for New Mexico's most erudite citizen."

Hillerman, *The Spell of New Mexico*
Myers, *Literary New Mexico*
Smith & Polese, *Passions in Print*
Newsletter, Westerners International, Albuquerque Corral, September 12, 1991

Roberts, Andrew L. "Buckshot" (1837-1878)
Lincoln County War Figure

Roberts claimed to be a southerner, born in 1837, but documentation for most aspects of his life is lacking. Some sources claim that he was a part of the posse that killed John Tunstall (see entry), but he denied it. His main claim to fame is that he alone, perhaps inadvertently, confronted a gang of outlaws, The Regulators, at Blazer's Mill, 30 or so miles southwest of Lincoln. William H. Bonney (Billy the Kid, see entry) was a member of the gang that numbered somewhere between 14 and 20 riders. In the course of the battle, Roberts shot and wounded Regulators Charlie Bowdre (see entry), George Coe and John Middleton; and killed Dick Brewer (see entry). He was himself shot and severely wounded, probably by Bowdre; although Bonney claimed to have shot him, too. Roberts died the following day and was buried beside Brewer. W. C. Jameson writes that Roberts had no intention of confronting the outlaws, but stumbled into a bad situation. Keleher (see entry) reports, however, that Roberts went to Blazer's Mill in search of members of The Regulators in order to capture or kill them and claim the reward. Roberts was called "Buckshot" because, he said, earlier in his life he had been wounded by a shotgun blast, perhaps fired by a Texas Ranger, which left numerous buckshot in his right shoulder. He thus had only limited use of his right arm and was obliged to fire his rifle from the hip; something he apparently did with considerable accuracy.

Jameson, W. C. "Westerners," *Wild West* Magazine, June 2006
Keleher, *Violence*
O'Neal, *Encyclopedia*
Utley, *High Noon*
Wilson, *Merchants*

Robledo, Doña Ana (d. 1680)
Doña Ana County

Doña Ana may have been the inspiration for Doña Ana County, New Mexico. She is said to have been the granddaughter of Pedro Robledo, who died along the trail as a part of the Juan de Oñate *entrada* of 1598. As the story goes, she, along with many others, was obliged to flee south after the Pueblo Revolt of 1680. When she saw the place where her grandfather had died so many years before, she experienced great anguish and died. The area came to be named for her burial place. Robert Julyan believes it is more likely that Doña Ana County is named for Doña Ana María de Córdoba (see entry).

Julyan, *Place Names*

Rodey, Bernard Shandon (1856-1927)
"Father of the University of New Mexico"
Albuquerque Attorney/Legislator

Born in Ireland, he and his family migrated to Canada in the early 1860s. He arrived in Albuquerque in the early 1880s after having read law in Boston. Admitted to the New Mexico bar in 1882, in 1883 he founded the law firm that bears his name and became one of the largest in New Mexico. He was elected to the Territorial Council (Senate) in 1889 and was instrumental in drafting legislation that created the University of New Mexico. He served as representative to the U.S.

Congress from 1901 to 1905. He died in Albuquerque and is interred in the Fairview Cemetery. Rodey Theater at the University of New Mexico is named for him.

Congressional Biography
Garcia, *Three Centuries*
Bart Ripp, "Father of UNM was cigar-smoking Irishman," Albuquerque *Tribune*, February 27, 1989
University of New Mexico
Other literature abundant

Bernard Shandon Rodey. Courtesy The Albuquerque Museum Photoarchives. PA1978.50.510.

Rogers, Dick (c.1857-1885)
Colfax County Gunfighter

Probably a native of Texas, Dick Rogers was elected captain of the vigilantes who opposed Militia Company H during the troubles in Colfax County, New Mexico, in the mid-1880s. He was killed in an assault on the jail at Springer in mid-March 1885. His reputation was a mixed bag. One source referred to him as "a fearless cowboy;" another as an "outlaw-vigilante." He is reported to have made Jim Masterson (see entry) dance by shooting around his feet in a Raton saloon. His career was short in any event.

Bullis, *99 New Mexicans*
Curry, *Autobiography*

Romero, Doña Antonia (fl. 1804)
Seboyetta Heroine

In 1804, a large band of Navajos attacked the village of Seboyetta (then spelled Cibolleta), west of Albuquerque at the foot of Mt. Taylor in what is now Cibola County. Doña Antonia observed a warrior who had breached the wall and was in the act of removing the bar that held the great door closed. She killed the Indian by hitting him on the head with a *metate* (a flat stone used to grind corn), thus saving the day.

Peña, *Memories*

Romero, Juan (d. 1884)
Cabezón Rancher

Juan Romero operated a ranch near the town of Cabezón, northwest of Bernalillo. In March 1884 the Castillo brothers, Candido and Manuel, set out from Seboyetta to rustle cattle in the area and local folks resisted the thievery. Romero was killed in the gunfight that followed. His murder so incensed the citizenry that a large reward was offered; and a posse led by deputy sheriff Jesús Montoya tracked down the Castillo brothers. One of them was killed and the other was sentenced to prison.

Bullis, *99 New Mexicans*
Rittenhouse, *Cabezon*

Rooke, Sarah J. "Sally" (d. 1908)
Folsom Telephone Operator, Heroine

Sally Rooke arrived in Folsom, New Mexico, around 1905 and so liked the place that she stayed. Her date of birth is not reported, but she was in her 60s when the events described here occurred. The rain began as a summer shower on the afternoon of August 27, 1908. The wind picked up and it rained harder by dark or a little later, and then it became a deluge. Mrs. Ben Owen, a rancher's wife on Johnson Mesa, called the telephone switchboard in Folsom and warned: "It's raining so hard up here the wash tubs are running over with water. You better get out before you're swept away." But Sally Rooke didn't run. She began cranking the phone and she warned more than 40 families that the flood was coming down the valley. Then the wall of water struck. Mrs. Rooke was in a three-way conversation with Allcutt McNaghten and his mother when her voice ceased. Her body was found some time later about 16 miles south of town. No one knows how many lives she saved, but fatalities would certainly have been greater than the 17 known to have perished that night. Sally Rooke was a true heroine.

Bullis, *99 New Mexicans*

Rosas, Luis de (d. 1642)
Governor (Spanish) of New Mexico (1637-1641)

New Mexico Pueblo Indian historian Joe Sando says that Rosas was "perhaps the most notorious of the governors who made a practice of enslaving native people for personal enrichment." Rosas was responsible for the slaughter of Apaches who would not submit to slavery. He was also determined to wrestle power from the church friars in favor of the civil authority. Rosas was placed under house arrest by his successor, Juan Flores de Sierra y Valdés, after a preliminary review of his administration. Rosas was killed by a jealous husband in January 1642.

Sálaz Márquez, *New Mexico*
Sando & Agoyo, *Po'Pay*

Rosenbloom, Robert "Bob" (1943-1971)
New Mexico State Police Officer

Officer Robert Rosenbloom

On the evening of November 8, 1971 New Mexico State Police Officer Robert Rosenbloom made what he might have thought was a routine traffic stop on Interstate Route 40, about 15 miles west of Albuquerque. His last radio transmission to the Albuquerque dispatcher indicated that he was stopping a rental vehicle with California plates and containing three Black males. Exactly what happened next is not known, but when Sgt. C. A. Hawkins arrived on the scene he found Officer Rosenbloom face down on the ground with his pistol beside him. He had been shot twice. The perpetrators of the crime, Robert Finney, Ralph Goodwin and Charles Hill, members of a group called The Republic of New Africa, made it into Albuquerque where they hijacked an airliner, and forced it to take them to Cuba. One of them died there, but as of 2005, the other two remained free, protected by the Fidel Castro regime.

Bullis, *New Mexico's Finest*

Ross, Edmund G. (1826-1907)
Governor (Territorial) of New Mexico (1885-1889)

Born in Ohio and a printer by trade, Ross first migrated to Wisconsin and then on to Kansas. His performance for the Union cause during the Civil War was heroic. He was appointed to the U.S. Senate in 1865 and was elected in his own right in 1867. In June 1868, Ross cast the deciding vote that acquitted President Andrew Johnson of impeachable offenses. This act destroyed his political career in Kansas, and he moved on to New Mexico when his term expired in 1871. He was employed by the Santa Fe *New Mexican* and the Deming *Headlight*. President Grover Cleveland appointed Ross territorial governor, the first Democratic governor in 24 years. Ross wrote in 1887: "From the Land Grant Ring grew others, as the opportunities for speculation and plunder were developed. Cattle Rings, Public Land Stealing Rings, Mining Rings, Treasury

Gov. Edmund G. Ross. After Twitchell.

Rings, and rings of almost every description grew up, till the affairs of the Territory came to be run almost exclusively in the interest and for the benefit of combinations organized and headed by a few longheaded, ambitious and unscrupulous Americans." He died in Albuquerque and is interred at Fairview Memorial Park.

Kennedy, *Profiles*
Lamar, *Far Southwest*
Twitchell, *Leading Facts*, Vol. II

Rowe, Truett Eugene (1904-1937)
Federal Bureau of Investigation Agent

Truett Rowe was assigned to the FBI's El Paso, Texas, Field Office, the jurisdiction of which then included New Mexico. He learned that an Oklahoma car thief named George Guy Osborne was likely hiding out at his brother's place, south of Gallup. Rowe traveled by bus to Gallup, where he prevailed upon police chief Kelsey Pressley to drive him to the Osborne place. Osborne did not initially resist arrest, but when Rowe allowed him to go into a bedroom to change clothes, the thief produced a gun and shot the agent. Rowe died while en route back to Gallup. Officers soon arrested Osborne, who was convicted and sentenced to life in prison. Rowe is the only FBI agent to be killed in the line of duty in New Mexico.

Agent Truett Eugene Rowe

Albuquerque *Journal*, June 2, 1937

Bullis, *New Mexico's Finest*
James W. Nelson, Albuquerque FBI, Special Agent in Charge, Correspondence, October
    24, 1989
Bart Ripp, "The day that Truett Rowe was shot," *Albuquerque Tribune*, May 25, 1987

Rudabaugh, Dave (1854-1886)
Las Vegas Outlaw/Killer/Peace Officer, Billy the Kid Associate

Born in Illinois, Rudabaugh made his way west as a young man, arriving first in Kansas, although he may have spent some time in Arkansas and east Texas. He was arrested for train robbery in Kansas in 1878. He turned state's evidence and got off. He is known to have spent some time at Ft. Griffin, Texas. He was accused of both stagecoach and train robbery in 1879. He arrived in Las Vegas, New Mexico, late the same year, where he became a policeman under Hyman G. Neill, aka Hoodoo Brown (see entry). He remained in Las Vegas after Brown fled, and in late April he killed jailer Antonio Lino Valdez (see entry) in an attempt to free prisoner J. J. Webb. Rudabaugh was with William H. Bonney (Billy the Kid, see entry) when Sheriff Pat Garrett (see entry) captured the Kid and his gang on December 21, 1880. Rudabaugh was tried for the murder of Valdez, convicted and sentenced to hang. He escaped custody, however, and fled to Mexico. In Parral, Chihuahua, Rudabaugh killed two Mexicans over a card game, and local Mexican citizens in turn killed him. Legend holds that Rudabaugh's head was mounted on a stick and paraded about the town.

Bullis, *99 New Mexicans*
Keleher, *Violence*
Metz, *Pat Garrett*
Thrapp, *Encyclopedia*
Other literature abundant

Runnels, Harold Lowell "Mud" (1924-1980)
U. S. Congressman (1971-1980)

Mud Runnels was one of New Mexico's most colorful politicians. Born in Dallas, Texas, and educated at Cameron State Agricultural College in Lawton, Oklahoma, he served in the Army Air Corps Reserves during World War II, and was employed by the Federal Bureau of Investigation during the same period. He moved to Lovington, New Mexico, in 1951 and formed the Runnels Mud Company in 1953, hence his sobriquet. (The "mud" in this case is a lubricant used in oil well drilling.) A Democrat, he was elected to the New Mexico State Senate in 1960 by defeating Donald Hellam in the Democratic primary election, and to the U. S. Congress in 1970 by defeating Republican Ed Foreman (see entry) in the general election. While serving in the state senate in the late 1960s, Runnels attracted a great deal of attention to himself by his strong and vocal reaction in the "Love Lust" poem controversy; a hullabaloo over the reading assignment of an allegedly obscene poem for freshman students at the University of New Mexico. On the matter of campus unrest in the early 1970s, Runnels said, "I cannot, nor will not, subscribe to a society that lets a militant, debased, depraved, mocking group of radicals take advantage of the very people who make it possible for those radicals to have freedom to express themselves." The congressman remained popular in the second district, and in the 1978 election cycle he was unopposed in both the primary and general elections; the first time in the history of the state that a congressional race was uncontested. Runnels had stated his intention to run for Governor of New Mexico in 1982. He died at Memorial Sloan-Kettering Cancer Center in New York City. He had a long history of lung problems, including cancer, but doctors said he was cancer-free at the time of his death. His demise was attributed to pleurisy and emphysema. His congressional seat remained vacant until January 1981 when Republican Joe Skeen (see entry) occupied it.

Albuquerque *Journal*, August 6, 1980.
Congressional Biography
New Mexico Blue Book, 2003-2004

Rush, Olive (1873-1966)
Santa Fe Artist/Muralist

Born into a Quaker family in Fairmount, Indiana, Rush left home as a teenager to attend the Corcoran Art School in Washington, D. C. She went on to study at the Art Students League in New York. She became an illustrator and worked for 20 years for several publishers and popular magazines. She traveled widely and studied in Europe before she relocated to Santa Fe, New Mexico, after World War I. By 1925, she had created a large enough body of work on New Mexico subjects to organize her own show that was hosted by the Art Institute of Chicago and the Denver Art Museum, among others. Notably, she painted the mural in the foyer of the Women's Board of Trade Library in Santa Fe in 1933, a product of the Public Works of Art Project. The building today houses the Fray Angélico Chávez History Library and Photo Archives. The mural is still there. She also did murals in the Public Library, the Post Office, and in La Fonda, and others. She was once quoted as saying, "You must learn your own best way of living and creating. You are an individual in art as in life." Rush taught at the Santa Fe Indian School (now the Institute of American Indian Art). She died at Santa Fe.

Coke, *Taos and Santa Fe*
Cuba, *Olive Rush*
Hammett, *Santa Fe*
Nestor & Robertson, *Artists of the Canyons and Caminos*
Tobias & Woodhouse, *Santa Fe*

Rusk, J. B. "Jerry" (c. 1872-1912)
New Mexico Mounted Police Officer

Private Rust was transporting a prisoner from Denver to New Mexico when he contracted pneumonia and died. He is the only member of the New Mexico Mounted Police, which existed from 1905 to 1921, to die as a result of performing his duties.

Hornung, *The Thin Gray Line*

Russian Bill (c.1850-1881)
See Tettenborn, William Rogers

Rutherford, William L. "Bill" (1880-1923)
Otero County Sheriff

A native of Missouri, Rutherford arrived in Otero County, New Mexico, in 1906. He entered the cattle and sheep raising business and by 1916, or so, he owned about 3,000 head, counting both. He was elected to the state legislature in 1914 and served two terms before he was elected sheriff in 1922. On February 13, 1923, Sheriff Rutherford received a telephone call from the Lincoln County Sheriff's office, which advised him that two thieves and escapees were headed his way. Rutherford soon observed the suspects near the corner of 10th St. and New York Ave. in Alamogordo. The sheriff was shot and killed as he attempted to question them. One of the things that puzzled investigators was what had become of the Sheriff's hat; it was nowhere to be found. The killers, William LaFavers and Charles Hollis Smelcer, fled the town, only to be captured the next day after a massive manhunt. One of them was wearing the Sheriff's hat. Both were sentenced to be hanged; but Governor Arthur Seligman (see entry) pardoned Smelcer in 1931 and Governor John E. Miles (see entry) pardoned LaFavers in 1939. Bill Rutherford had served as sheriff for only six weeks at the time of his death.

Historical Files, transcriptions of audiotapes, Alamogordo Public Library
Bullis, *New Mexico's Finest*
Twitchell, *Leading Facts*, Vol. III

Ruxton, George Frederick (1821-1848)
Observer/Writer

Ruxton, a native of Kent in England, arrived at Vera Cruz, with British diplomatic credentials early in the Mexican War, in 1846. He remained there a short time before journeying to Albuquerque, Santa Fe and points north. He was probably the *least* objective observer/writer of his day. He did not like Mexicans—although he made an exception in regard to Mexican women—or Americans either. Historian Dan Thrapp quotes an unnamed source: "He [Ruxton] scorned the tight-fisted Yankee traders, the filthy, illiterate emigrants, and the American soldiers' lack of discipline." He also did not like Mormons or Catholics, priests in particular. He described Santa Fe as a "prairie dog town." He died of dysentery in St. Louis 1848. A number of historians cite Ruxton's descriptions of New Mexico and New Mexicans. Many others do not.

Thrapp, *Encyclopedia*
Twitchell, *Leading Facts*, Vol. II

Rynerson, William Logan (1828-1893)
New Mexico Legislator/District Attorney

Rynerson was born in either Mercer or Hardin County, Kentucky, depending on the source. He migrated first to California in the 1850s, and then to New Mexico as a part of the California Column during the Civil War in 1862. He mustered

out at Mesilla and purchased interests in mining properties around Pinos Altos, near Silver City. He also entered
politics and was elected to the Territorial legislature. He
became engaged in a dispute with the Chief Justice of the
New Mexico Supreme Court, John P. Slough (see entry),
That resulted in an altercation in which Rynerson shot
and killed the jurist. Rynerson was acquitted of murder
upon a plea of self-defense. He served as District Attorney in the third district, Las Cruces and southern New
Mexico, but was a partisan on the side of Murphy-Dolan-
Riley (see entries) and the Santa Fe Ring throughout the
Lincoln County War. It was Rynerson who successfully
prosecuted William H. Bonney (Billy the Kid, see entry)
for the murder of Sheriff William Brady (see entry). He
died in Las Cruces.

William Logan Rynerson.
After Twitchell.

Thrapp, *Encyclopedia*
Twitchell, *Leading Facts*, Vol. II
Utley, *High Noon*

-S-

Saavedra, Louis E. "Lou" (1933-)
Albuquerque Technical-Vocational Institute, President, (1964-1989), Albuquerque City Commission (1967-1974), Chairman (1973), Albuquerque Mayor (1989-1993)

Mayor Louis Saavedra

Lou Saavedra was born in Tokay, New Mexico, a small coal-mining community located southeast of Socorro that no longer exists. Educated in Socorro, he worked his way through Eastern New Mexico University—where he earned both Bachelor and Master's degrees—by working as a typesetter for the Portales *News-Tribune*. Saavedra joined the Albuquerque Public Schools in 1960 as a teacher at Valley High School. In 1961 he became Associate Public Information Director, a position he held until 1964 when he became the first employee of the Albuquerque Technical-Vocational Institute. His first title was "principal" but that soon changed to President, and he occupied the position until 1989. While employed by T-VI, he served on the Albuquerque City Commission from 1967 to 1974. After his retirement, he ran for, and was elected, Mayor of Albuquerque. He served from 1989 to 1993 and did not seek re-election. Thirty-five students were enrolled in T-VI when Saavedra began his tenure there; when he retired it was New Mexico's second largest postsecondary school. By 2000, enrollment was about 20,000 on four campuses. Graduates have a 96% placement rate. The name of the school was changed to Central New Mexico Community College in 2006.

Garcia, *Albuquerque*
Bryan, *Albuquerque*
Dave Smoker, Correspondence, April 2, 2006

Sanchez, Alberto "Al Hurricane" (1936-)
New Mexico Musician

Alberto Sanchez was born in Dixon, New Mexico, and arrived in Albuquer-

210

que in 1947, where he attended high school. He began his musical career by playing guitar for coins in Old Town before he was asked to become a troubadour in a local restaurant. Along with his brothers, Mauricio (Tiny Morrie) and Gabriel (Baby Gaby), Alberto created the "Albuquerque Sound" which features trumpet and saxophone arrangements. He reports that his mother called him "Hurricane" because he knocked things over, and he adopted the sobriquet as his professional name. Over the years he has played with such notables as Fats Domino, James Brown, and Chuck Berry. His recording company, Hur-

Albert "Al Hurricane" Sanchez

ricane Records, has produced more than 50 LPs or CDs. His popularity, and that of his son, Al Hurricane, Jr., as Latin and pop music performers continues into the early 21st century.

Hughes, *Albuquerque*
Montaño, *Tradiciones*

Sanchez, Jane Calvin (1930-2006)
New Mexico Historian

Born at Cerrillos, Jane Sanchez had an abiding interest in New Mexico history and in the lives of early explorers. She also did extensive research into the history of New Mexico land grants. She graduated from the University of New Mexico in 1950, majoring in languages. Sanchez worked for the *New Mexico Historical Review* for many years. The *Review* published several of her articles. She was an active member of the Albuquerque Corral of Westerners International, the Historical Society of New Mexico and the New Mexico Jewish Historical Society. She died in her home in Albuquerque while working at her computer on yet another historical item.

Jan Jonas, "Obituary," Albuquerque *Tribune*, February 17, 2006
New Mexico Historical Review, July 1966

Sánchez, Juan Amadeo (1901-1969)
Artist

Born near Taos, Sánchez was raised in the hamlet of Colmor (named for Colfax and Mora counties because the county line ran through the community, which is now abandoned), southwest of Springer. He was a prolific artist in the Federal Arts Project, a part of the Works Progress Administration in the 1930s. In 1937, a significant exhibition of his work was presented at the San Miguel Federal Arts Center in Las Vegas. He continued working until his death at Raton. Many of his works can be found in permanent collections at the Palace of the Governors and the Museum of International Folk Art in Santa Fe.

Boyd, *Portfolio*
Nunn, *Sin Nombre*
"People and Places," *New Mexico Magazine*, June 1966.

Sando, Joe Simon (1923-)
Historian

Joe Simon Sando

Joe Sando is New Mexico's senior historian on Pueblo Indians. He was born at Jémez Pueblo and graduated from Santa Fe Indian School in 1941. He attended college briefly before he entered the U.S. Navy and served aboard the aircraft carrier USS Corregidor, in the Pacific Theater of Operations throughout World War II. He suffered a unilateral hearing loss as a result of his service in the military. He entered Eastern New Mexico University after his discharge from the military in 1946, and graduated in 1949. Because of his hearing loss, he attended graduate school at Vanderbilt University studying Audiology and speech pathology. In 1970, Sando began teaching Pueblo Indian history at the University of New Mexico. He also taught South, Central, and North American Indian history at the Institute of American Indian Arts in Santa Fe. While teaching he became aware that books on Indian history did not exist, and he set about correcting that. His first book was *The Pueblo Indians* (1976); followed by *Pueblo Indian Biographies* (1978); then *Nee Hemish* "We Jemez" (1982), *Pueblo Nations: Eight Centuries of Pueblo Indian History* (1992), *Pueblo Profiles* (1995) and finally, he edited, along with Herman Agoyo, *Po'Pay: Leader of the First American Revolution* (2005). "I live and operate in two worlds," Sando writes. "My Indian world continues to bring me much pleasure as I am fluent in my native language and participate in the ceremonials and feast days of the Pueblo Indian people. I also feel at home reading, writing and listening to good music." He is an active member of the Albuquerque Corral of Westerners International.

"Biography," Albuquerque Corral, Westerners International

Sandoval, Alejandro (1845-1919)
Albuquerque Prominent Citizen

A life-long resident of Bernalillo County, Sandoval served in several elective positions, most importantly in the Constitutional Conventions of 1889 and 1910. According to one source, "Sandoval county [sic] bears his name to his honor and his influence." The *New Mexico Blue Book* (2003-2004) reports that the county, created in 1903, was named for "the distinguished family who lived in the region in the 18th century." A year and a half after Alejandro's death, a news item in the Albuquerque *Morning Journal* reported that his widow had purchased, and placed upon his grave in Calvary Cemetery, a statue of the Virgin Mary measuring five feet six inches in height. It stood atop a pedestal that was nine feet high, for a total of 14 feet six inches. It was said to have been one of the tallest and most expensive tombstones in the state of New Mexico.

"One More Formal Tribute to Honorable Alejandro Sandoval..." Albuquerque *Morning Journal*, February 13, 1921

New Mexico Blue Book, 2003-2004

212

Schaefer, Jack Warner (1907-1991)
Cerrillos Author

Jack Schaefer was born in Cleveland, Ohio, and studied Greek and Latin at Oberlin College in that state. He also studied English and American literature at Columbia University in New York. His early career was in the field of journalism, and by the late 1940s he was living and working in Westport, Connecticut, while he wrote his first, and probably most famous, novel, *Shane*. Completed in 1945, it was published in 1949. The book, initially successful, was made more so by the 1953 movie of the same name, which starred Alan Ladd in the title role, and was directed by George Stevens. By the middle 1950s, Schaefer was able

Jack Warner Schaefer.
Courtesy Dick Ruddy.

to sell his Connecticut farm and move to a small New Mexico ranch near Cerrillos in Santa Fe County. He remained a resident of New Mexico until his death. He wrote numerous books, both novels and historical items, during his lifetime, although *Shane* and *Monte Walsh* (1963) are probably the most famous. Significant, though, is *New Mexico*, a history Schaefer wrote for young people. It is interesting that Schaefer changed his mind about *Shane*. He said, late in his life, "Today I wouldn't put Shane on the side of the homesteaders because they were destroying the West. But I couldn't really put him on the side of the ranchers either, because they were no better."

John C. Allred, *Book Talk*, New Mexico Book League, Feb. 1989
Marc Simmons, *Book Talk*, New Mexico Book League, July 1999
Norman Zollinger, *Book Talk*, New Mexico Book League, March 1991
"Obituary," Albuquerque *Journal*, January 25, 1991

Schaefer, R. J. (1936-2005)
Albuquerque Real Estate Developer

A native of New York City, Schaefer served in both the U.S. Army and Air Force before he settled in Roswell, New Mexico, in the 1960s and began his real estate career. He moved on to Albuquerque in the early 1980s and continued real estate development. He was also noted for the time and money he volunteered to churches and homeless shelters. Schaefer was murdered in his Albuquerque home in November 2005 by drug addicts seeking money with which to purchase methamphetamine. His wife, Olga, was severely wounded in the attack. Five suspects were arrested within hours of the killing.

Albuquerque *Journal* & Albuquerque *Tribune*, November 23, 2005

Schiff, Steven Harvey "Steve" (1947-1998)
U.S. Congressman (1989-1998)

Schiff was born in Chicago and received his early education there. He graduated from the University of New Mexico Law School and entered practice in Albuquerque in 1972. He was active in the New Mexico Air National Guard. A Republican, he was elected Bernalillo County District Attorney and served from 1980 to

Congressman Steven H. Schiff

1988, when he was elected to Congress. He was re-elected four times. He died of squamous-cell skin cancer and is interred in the Jewish section of Fairview Cemetery in Albuquerque.

Congressional Biography
News accounts abundant

Schmitt, Harrison Hagan "Jack" (1935-)
Moon Walker (1972)
U.S. Senator (1977-1983)

Schmitt, a native of Santa Rita, Grant County, New Mexico, received a public education before he attended the California Institute of Technology and Harvard, from which he received a Doctorate in geology in 1964. He was an astronaut for the National Aeronautics and Space Administration (NASA) from 1965 to 1975, during which time, as lunar module pilot on Apollo 17, he walked on the moon, the only civilian, and the last American, to do so. A Republican, he was elected to the U.S. Senate from New Mexico in 1976 by defeating incumbent Democrat Joseph M. Montoya (see entry). He was defeated for re-election in 1982 by Democrat Jeff Bingaman (see entry). He wrote a book entitled *Return to the Moon: Exploration, Enterprise and Energy in the Human Settlement of Space.*

Senator Harrison Schmitt

Congressional Biography
Dianne Edwards, "Harrison Schmitt Still Living the Big Adventure, *Prime Time*, March 2006
News accounts abundant

Scholes, France Vinton (1898-1979)
Scholar

Scholes arrived at the University of New Mexico in 1925 with both undergraduate and graduate degrees from Harvard University. He was initially hired on a part-time basis for $45.00 per month. He rose to the rank of professor of history by 1930 and earned his Ph.D. from Harvard in 1943. He served as dean of the UNM graduate school from 1946 to 1949, as academic vice president from 1949 to 1956 and as research professor of history until his retirement in 1962. He wrote widely on the period of New Mexico history from the arrival of Oñate (see entry) in 1598 to the Pueblo Revolt of 1680, as well as on other subjects related to Latin American colonial history. The Albuquerque *Journal* editorialized after Dr. Scholes death, "…[He] was most comfortable, and is best remembered, in the role for which his native talents and training qualified him: as a superb historian, scholar and teacher." Scholes Hall on the UNM campus is named for France V. Scholes. He died in Albuquerque.

Albuquerque *Journal*, February 13, 1979

214

Schroeder, Albert H. (1914-1993)
New Mexico Archaeologist/Ethnohistorian

Albert Schroeder was born in Brooklyn, New York. He received his B. A. (1938) and M. A. (1940) degrees from the University of Arizona. He served in the U.S. Army during World War II, after which he began a career with the National Park Service that would last for 30 years. During the 1950s and 1960s, he served as an expert witness on Apache Indian land claims before the Indian Claims Commission. He also did research work on the Spanish *entrada* (entrance). He participated in the translation of *A Colony on the Move: Gaspar Castaño de Sosa's Journal, 1590-91*, published by the School of American Research in 1965. He also co-authored, with New Mexico State Historian Myra Ellen Jenkins (see entry), *A Brief History of New Mexico*, published by the University of New Mexico Press in 1974. It is interesting to note that Schroeder died only one month after Jenkins.
Joseph P. Sánchez, "In Passing: Albert H. Schroeder, 1914-1993," *New Mexico Historical Review*, Oct. 1993

Scott, Winfield Townley (1910-1968)
Santa Fe Poet

A native of New England, Scott arrived in New Mexico in 1954 and spent his last years in Santa Fe. Considered a major American poet by some, and second tier by others, he had previously served as literary editor of the *Providence Journal*. After his death, the University of Texas published, *The Literary Notebooks of Winfield Townley Scott: 'A Dirty Hand'*, in 1969.
Hillerman, *The Spell of New Mexico*
Luther, *Collecting Santa Fe*

Segale, Sister Blandina (1850-1941)
Santa Fe/Albuquerque Sister of Charity

Sister Blandina was born in Genoa, Italy. She took her vows and became one of the Sisters of Charity of Cincinnati, Ohio. At the request of Bishop Lamy (see entry), she was posted to the American West where she served in Colorado and New Mexico from 1872 to 1894. Her first chore was the construction of a new St. Vincent's hospital in Santa Fe. Construction began on the feast day of St. Blandina, June 2, 1877. The roof went on three years later. She arrived in the Albuquerque parish from Santa Fe in 1880 to take over its educational program. Progress in building the facilities was slow, so Sister Blandina went to Santa Fe and engaged the services of a stonecutter who had worked on the cathedral there. Under her direction, the convent was completed the following year. It remains today on the northwest corner of the Albuquerque Old Town plaza, next to the San Felipe Neri church. Late in her life, in 1932, she wrote a memoir entitled *At the End of the Santa Fe Trail*. It was most recently re-issued in 1999.
García, *Three Centuries*

Johnson, *Old Town, Albuquerque*
Simmons, *Albuquerque*
Steele, *Historical Sketch*

Seligman, Arthur (1871-1933)
Governor (State) of New Mexico (1931-1933)

A Santa Fe banker, Seligman was active in public affairs in New Mexico for many years. As early as 1909 Gov. George Curry (see entry) appointed him to a committee that worked on statehood matters. A Democrat, he was swept into office as governor with other Democrats as a result of the Great Depression, which began in 1929. Seligman created the New Mexico Motor Patrol, predecessor to the State Police, in 1933. He died on September 25, 1933, and was succeeded by Andrew Hockenhull.

New Mexico State Police 60ᵗʰ Anniversary Year Book
Curry, *Autobiography*
Other literature abundant

Seligman, Milton S. (1914-2005)
Albuquerque Attorney

Admitted to the bar in 1937, he was the longest-practicing attorney in New Mexico when he retired after 65 years. He was a member of one of New Mexico's pioneer Jewish merchant families. He was instrumental in bringing electricity to rural New Mexico. Milton Seligman was not related to Governor Arthur Seligman.

Obituary, Albuquerque *Journal*, September 6, 2005

Selman, John Henry "Uncle John" or "Old John" (1839-1896)
Lincoln County Killer, El Paso, Texas, Lawman

Very little good can be said about John Selman. He was born in Arkansas but moved to Texas with his family by the early 1860s. He joined the Confederate Army but later deserted. He became associated with Sheriff John Larn at Fort Griffin, Texas, and the two of them entered into the cattle rustling business. Selman is believed to have killed a couple of people around Fort Griffin, and probably participated in several lynchings. Larn was arrested and summarily executed; but Selman fled to New Mexico where he and his brother, "Tom Cat," became involved in the Lincoln County War. After the war's Five Day Battle of July 1878, the Selman brothers and a band of thieving cutthroats roamed southeastern New Mexico and murdered, raped and robbed at will. They left at least six Hispanic citizens dead, all of them unarmed and shot down in cold blood. Selman continued his murderous ways in West Texas and was at last arrested on Texas charges. No jurisdiction wanted to prosecute him, and he was allowed to escape before he could begin naming some prominent people who had participated in the Ft. Griffin lynchings. He was never arrested or charged for the crimes he committed in New Mexico. ("Tom Cat" was probably hanged somewhere along the way, but not in New Mexico.) After spending some time in Old Mexico, John Selman returned to El Paso about 1885. In 1892 he was elected constable. His only real claim to fame is that on August 19, 1895 he shot and killed famed murderer John Wesley Hardin by shooting him in the back as he stood at the bar in the Acme Saloon in El Paso. Less than a year later, Selman himself was shot and killed by Deputy U.S. Marshal George Scarborough outside the Wigwam Saloon in El Paso. One source says, Selman "was very intelligent, very cunning, a skillful talker, persuasive and logical, an expert gambler, but his death was no loss to anyone."

DeArment, *George Scarborough*
Metz, *John Selman*
Thrapp, *Encyclopedia*

Sharp, Joseph Henry (1859-1953)
Painter, Charter Member of the Taos Society of Artists

A native of Ohio, Sharp was educated at Cincinnati. As a result of a swimming accident as a teenager, Sharp became completely deaf. He became an accomplished lip-reader and he always carried a pad and pencil with him. He attended the Cincinnati Art Academy and also studied in Europe. In the early 1880s, he first visited Santa Fe, and other places in the American West. He returned to Europe before he became an instructor at the Cincinnati Art Academy. He first visited Taos in 1893 and was greatly impressed with the "unspoiled" life of the Taos Pueblo people. He regaled his artist friends, including Bert Phillips and Oscar Berninghaus (see entries), with tales of Taos. He began spending summers in Taos in 1909 and purchased an abandoned Penitente *morada* (chapel) that he used as a studio. He relocated permanently to Taos in 1912. He is considered the father of the Taos Art Colony, as he was one of the very first to make much of northern New Mexico's potential for artistic endeavor. He was a charter member of the Taos Society of Artists that existed from 1915 to 1927. Over the years, he traveled widely and purchased a second home in Pasadena, California. At age 93, in 1953, he closed his Taos studio and retired to Pasadena where he died later the same year. His life's work amounted to literally thousands of paintings, "an unparalleled visual of the Native American," according to one source.

Bickerstaff, *Pioneer Artists*
Fugate & Fugate, *Roadside History of New Mexico*
Meadowlark Gallery: The Artists Biographies
Nelson, *Legendary Artists of Taos*
Samuels, *The Illustrated Biographical Encyclopedia*
Schimmel & White, *Bert Geer Phillips*
Witt, *The Taos Artists*

Shaver, Paul A. (1910-2005)
Albuquerque Police Chief (1948-1971)

Shaver was born in Salisbury, North Carolina, but moved to Albuquerque at the age of four years because of his mother's tuberculosis. After service in the U.S. Army in 1929 and 1930, he returned to Albuquerque and joined the police department in 1935. The department had 27 officers at the time. "When I came here as an officer," he said, "I was given a gun and a nightstick and told to get into uniform.

Now we have the police academy and FBI school, and there is training where there used to be only common sense." He was responsible for starting the department's fingerprint bureau, the Chaplaincy Program, the School Crossing Guard Program, and others. Shaver was one of the longest-serving municipal police chiefs in New Mexico history.

"Obituary," Albuquerque *Journal*, December 11, 2005; news item, December 10, 2005

Shaw, James Madison "Jim" (fl. 1897-1899)
New Mexico/Arizona Outlaw/Turncoat

Jim Shaw, a train robber in his own right, was a marginal member of the High Fives outlaw gang, which ranged widely around New Mexico and Arizona in the late 1890s. Shaw, for reasons not entirely clear, told authorities where the gang was hiding, in a cave near Cole Creek, Arizona. A posse, led by Deputy U.S. Marshal Fred Higgins (see entry) of Roswell, New Mexico, moved in early on the morning of April 28, 1897. The scene of the confrontation was somewhat confused, but when the smoke cleared away, William "Black Jack" Christian (see entry) was dead. Other gang members escaped. Attempts were made on Shaw's life in the months afterward, but they may not have had anything to do with his betrayal. Shaw was reported killed in October 1897, but it was in error. He was known to have been alive in January 1899 when he was arrested for participation in a Nevada train robbery. He was acquitted of that charge and seems to have disappeared from history thereafter.

DeArment, *George Scarborough*
Tanner & Tanner, *Musgrave*
Thrapp, *Encyclopedia*

Sheldon, Lionel Allen (1828-1917)
Governor (Territorial) of New Mexico (1881-1885)

Lionel Sheldon moved around a lot. He was born in Otsego County, New York, and raised in Lagrange, Ohio. He was educated at Oberlin College in Ohio and Fowler Law School in Poughkeepsie, New York. He served as General of Union volunteers during the Civil War and settled in New Orleans, Louisiana, after the war. He was elected to Congress from Louisiana twice (he served from 1869 to 1875 during which time he would have been considered a "Yankee Carpetbagger"), and then failed at re-election. He returned to Ohio. He served as Governor of New Mexico from 1881 to 1885. He was an active member of the Santa Fe Ring, and appointed Tom Catron's (see entry) law partner, William Breeden, to the office of Attorney General, thus solidifying Ring control of the New Mexico legal system. According to the media of the day, "Sheldon has the reputation of being one of the best poker players that ever came to the territory."

Gov. Lionel Allen Sheldon.
After Twitchell.

218

Keleher, *Violence*
Lamar, *Far Southwest*
Other literature abundant

Sherwin, Ted B. (1918-2006)
Public Relations Expert

A native of Wyoming, and a graduate of the University of Wyoming with a degree in journalism, Ted Sherwin arrived in Albuquerque after a stint in the U. S. Army during World War II. He joined Sandia Laboratory in 1948 (which was then operated as a branch of the Los Alamos Labs, but which became Sandia Corporation, a wholly owned subsidiary of Western Electric, late in 1949, and a national laboratory in 1979) and remained employed there for 34 years. He started as a technical writer but over the years was responsible for the creation of the Lab's public relations programs and served as spokesman. Sherwin also founded the New Mexico Chapter of the Public Relations Society of America.

Albuquerque *Journal*, August 30, 2006
Sandia National Laboratories, Historian

Sibley, General Henry Hopkins (1816-1886)
New Mexico's Confederate Invader

Gen. Henry Hopkins Sibley. After Twitchell.

A native of Louisiana, Sibley graduated from West Point in 1838 and served in the U.S. Army until 1861. He was stationed at Fort Union, New Mexico Territory, when he deserted to accept a commission as Colonel in the Confederate Army. (Some Southerners take exception to the use of the term "deserted" in this context. They suggest that Sibley was within his rights to resign his commission in the U.S. Army and then take up arms against the nation he had previously served.) He was soon promoted to Confederate Brigadier General. Sibley was the commander of the Texas Confederates who invaded New Mexico in 1862 and scored initial successes at Valverde, Albuquerque and Santa Fe, only to be turned back at the Battle of Glorieta in March of that year. Historian Don Alberts (see entry) suggests that Sibley was the wrong man for the job, if for no other reason than he was a drunkard. His troops referred to him as a "walking whiskey keg." Alberts adds, "…Sibley was, without doubt, one of the Confederacy's worst generals." After the war he served as a General in the Egyptian army for a few years, but his drinking habits caught up with him and he was dismissed. He died in poverty in Virginia. Note: C.S.A. General Henry Hopkins Sibley should not be confused with U.S. Army General Henry Hastings Sibley, who led military forces in the State of Minnesota at the time of the Sioux uprising of 1862. They were not related.

Alberts, *Battle of Glorieta*
Thompson, *Confederate General of the West*
Thrapp, *Encyclopedia*

Sierra, Mateo (1918-2005)
Albuquerque Builder

Mateo Sierra was born in Sombrerete, Mexico, and moved with his family to Albuquerque when he was seven. He served in the Pacific Theater of Operations during WWII. He became a superintendent with Lembke Construction Company and supervised the construction of such notable structures as Albuquerque Convention Center, Zimmerman Library and Popejoy Hall on the University of New Mexico campus, and more than 100 others. The Convention Center, he said, was the toughest to build.

Paul Logan, "Builder Put Up Important Sites," Albuquerque *Journal*, October 6, 2005

Silko, Leslie Marmon (1948-)
Laguna Pueblo Author

Silko was born of mixed blood: Laguna and Plains Indian, German and Hispanic. She was raised at Laguna Pueblo west of Albuquerque by her great grandmother. She attended reservation school, Manzano High School in Albuquerque, and the University of New Mexico. Her first novel was *Ceremony* (1977). Her second was *Almanac of the Dead* (1991). Her father is Lee Marmon.

Literature abundant

Silva, Vicente (1845-1893)
Las Vegas Outlaw Gang Leader

Born near Albuquerque, Silva moved to Las Vegas, New Mexico, and opened the Imperial Saloon near the plaza in 1875. He prospered as a businessman but greed seems to have consumed him. By late in the 1880s he was the boss of a large gang of robbers and rustlers called *La Sociedad de Bandidos de Nuevo Mexico* (The Society of Bandits of New Mexico) while he kept up a respectable front. For several years the gang pillaged almost at will. Finally, though, they rustled cattle from a rancher named José Esquibel, who took grave exception to the thievery. He learned who had stolen his herd, and where the cattle had been taken. He and his son first recovered the herd and then rode to Las Vegas where he swore out a warrant for Silva. Silva fled to the hills and successfully hid out for a time. But then he turned on gang member Patricio Maes and hung him from a bridge in Las Vegas because he thought Maes had betrayed him. Then he killed his brother-in-law for imagined treachery. And finally, he killed his own wife for the same reason. That was more than even the criminals in his gang could abide. One of them, Antonio Valdez, shot Silva in the head and killed him in May 1893. The gang continued to operate for a time, but fell apart after a while, much to the relief of everyone living in that part of New Mexico.

Bryan, *Wildest*
Simmons, *Six-Guns*
Other literature abundant

Simmons, Marc (1937-)
New Mexico Historian

Often called New Mexico's historian laureate, a book entitled *Marc Simmons of New Mexico, Maverick Historian* (2005), has been written about him and his work. It lists the more than 40 books, more than 1,400 newspaper and magazine articles, and the more than 50 scholarly articles he has written. His eclectic knowledge includes tales of Spaniards and Mexicans; outlaws and lawmen, the Indians of New Mexico's many tribes and every curve and stop on the Old Santa Fe Trail. Simmons earned a Ph.D. in history from the University of New Mexico in 1965. In addition to his academic pursuits, he has worked as a cowboy and farrier. He lives in a small adobe house in rural New Mexico, near Cerrillos, that he built himself.

Marc Simmons

Simmons won the 1983 Western Writers of America Spur Award for his definitive *Albuquerque, A Narrative History*. Highly respected, he is certainly New Mexico's most prolific living historian.

Mark L. Gardner, "Marc Simmons," *New Mexico Magazine*, June 2005
Morgan, *Marc Simmons of New Mexico*
Other literature abundant

Simms, Albert Gallatin (1882-1964)
U.S. Congressman (1929-1931)

Albert Simms was born in Hampsted County, Arkansas; he attended private schools and the University of Arkansas. He arrived in Silver City, New Mexico in 1912. He was admitted to the bar in 1915 and practiced in Albuquerque. He engaged in the banking business and served on both the Albuquerque City Council and the Bernalillo County Commission before he was elected to the U.S. Congress in 1928. His bid for re-election in 1930 failed, but he did serve on the Republican National Committee from 1932 to 1934. While serving in Congress, he met Ruth Hanna McCormick (see entry), whom he married in 1932. He became a farmer and rancher and died at Albuquerque. He is interred in Fairview Park Cemetery.

Congressional Biography

Simms, John F. Jr. (1917-)
Governor (State) of New Mexico (1955-56)

John Simms was then-youngest man to assume the office of Governor at age 38 in 1955. (Dave Cargo [see entry], elected Governor in 1966 was younger than Simms at age 37.) Simms defeated Alvin Stockton of Raton and succeeded Republican Edwin Mechem (see entry) who had completed his allotted two consecutive two-year terms. He was the son of New Mexico Supreme Court Justice John Simms Sr. (see entry). His tenure only lasted two years. Mechem defeated him in the 1956 election.

New Mexico Blue Book, 2003-2004

Simms, John Sr. (1885-1954)
New Mexico Supreme Court Chief Justice (1929-1930)

Arrived in New Mexico from Arkansas in 1913 suffering from tuberculosis. He entered the practice of law in 1915. He was the father of Governor John Simms, Jr. (see entry).

Garcia, *Three Centuries*

Simms, Ruth Hanna McCormick (1880-1944)
Albuquerque Political Figure/Benefactress

Born to Senator Marcus A. Hanna of Ohio, who was often called the "maker of presidents," Ruth Hanna had an active personal and political life before she met Congressman Albert G. Simms (see entry) of New Mexico in 1930. She was married to Illinois U.S. Senator Joseph Medill McCormick who died in 1925 the result of suicide after a failed re-nomination bid. She served in Congress from 1929 to 1931, but lost an election bid to fill her late husband's seat in the Senate in the 1930 election. She met Albert G. Simms during his single term in the U.S. Congress (1929-1931). They were married in 1932. She left her mark during the years that she lived in Albuquerque by contributing greatly to the Albuquerque Little Theatre, and founding two educational institutions: Manzano Day School and the Sandia School. She was also active in Republican circles and contributed substantially to the New Mexico Republican Women. The Albuquerque *Journal* editorialized after her death, "Mrs. Simms' wide range of interests in civic, educational, and political matters was whole-hearted. Her leadership and support in these varied activities will be missed. That is why her death is a distinct loss to the community and the state."

"Mrs. A. G. Simms Dies In Chicago Hospital," Albuquerque *Journal*, January 1, 1945
Miller, *Ruth Hanna McCormick*

Sinclair, John L. (1902-1993)
Sandoval County Cowboy/Writer

John Sinclair was born in New York City and orphaned at a young age. His heritage was Scottish, so he was sent back to Scotland to be raised and educated in the discipline of animal husbandry. He returned to America in 1923, sent by his Scottish relatives to set up a farm and ranch in British Columbia. Along the way he stopped off at Clovis, New Mexico, and he went no further. His relatives disowned him and he became a working cowboy. For a few years he worked on ranches from Roswell to Capitan and by 1930 he was living in what he called Red Cabin in the Capitan Mountains. He published his first piece in 1937, in the *New Mexico Magazine*. It was called "Shepherds on Horseback." His days of riding the chuck line were about over. He served as a research assistant for the Museum of New Mexico from 1938 to 1940, as curator at the Lincoln County Courthouse Museum from 1940 to 1942 and as superintendent at the Coronado State Monument near Bernalillo from 1944 to 1962; when he retired. His best-known novel was *In Time of Harvest* (1943).

Clark Kimball, "John L. Sinclair: Epiphany on The Mountain," *Book Talk*, New Mexico
    Book League, April 1989
John L. Sinclair, "The Bookshelf at Red Cabin," *Book Talk*, New Mexico Book League, June
    1991
Sinclair, *Memoirs*

Siringo, Charles Angelo (1855-1928)
New Mexico Cowboy/Range Detective/Writer

Born in Texas, Siringo spent his early life working as a cowboy. He then spent
more than 20 years working for the Pinkerton National Detective Agency, during
which time he pursued such notable outlaws as Butch Cassidy and the Sundance
Kid (see entries). He wrote several books: *A Texas Cowboy or Fifteen Years on the
Hurricane Deck of a Spanish Pony* (1885); *A Cowboy Detective* (1912); *Two Evil
Isms: Pinkertonism and Anarchism* (1915); *A Lone Star Cowboy* (1919); *Billy the Kid*
(1920); and *Riata and Spurs* (1927). Siringo resided in New Mexico for many years
but died in California. Siringo Road in Santa Fe is named for him.

Lamar, *Charlie Siringo's West*
Other literature abundant

Skeen, Joseph Richard "Joe" (1927-2003)
U. S. Congressman (1981-2003)

Joe Skeen was born in Roswell but graduated from
high school in Seattle, Washington. He served in the
United States Navy in 1945 and 1946, and graduated
from Texas A&M University in 1950. He operated a sheep
ranch near Picacho in Lincoln County. Skeen served in
the New Mexico Senate from 1960 to 1970. When Pete
Domenici (see entry) ran for governor in 1970, Joe Skeen
was his running mate. The Domenici/Skeen ticket lost to
the Bruce King/Roberto Mondragón ticket. Skeen ran for
governor in 1974 and lost to Jerry Apodaca (see entry)
and again in 1978 when he lost to Bruce King (see entry).

Congressman Joe Skeen

When Democratic Congressman Harold Runnels (see entry) died in the summer
of 1980, Attorney General Jeff Bingaman (see entry) ruled that the Democrats
could replace him on the ballot, but that the Republicans could not name an opponent since they had not previously—in 1978 or 1980—fielded a candidate to oppose Runnels in the general election. The Democrats then named David King, the
nephew of the sitting governor, Bruce King, as their candidate. Skeen announced
that he would seek the office as a write-in candidate. Annoyed at the Democrats,
Dorothy Runnels, the Congressman's widow, announced that she would do the
same thing. When the dust settled, Skeen polled 38% of the vote to King's 34%
and Runnels' 28%. Skeen became only the third U. S. Congressman in history to
win office as a write-in candidate. He was re-elected 10 consecutive times, and did
not seek re-election in 2002 because of illness (Parkinson's disease). Skeen was a
likable man who was generally well regarded by members of both political parties.

He died in Roswell.
Congressional Biography
News accounts abundant

Slough, John P. (c.1830-1867)
Chief Justice, New Mexico Supreme Court

John P. Slough was probably born in Ohio. He moved to Denver in the 1850s and practiced law there. When the Civil War began, at the request of Colorado Gov. William Gilpin he organized the 1st Colorado Volunteers and became the regimental commander. Slough's troops were instrumental in turning back the Confederate invasion of New Mexico at Glorieta Pass in early 1862. His military star was on the rise after that. He traveled to Washington, D.C., where he was promoted to Brigadier General and ultimately became military governor of Alexandria, Virginia. He was a pallbearer at the funeral of President Abraham Lincoln (see entry). President Andrew Johnson appointed him Chief Justice of the New Mexico Supreme Court after the Civil War. One observer described Slough as an "abrasive, quick-tempered, highly-opinionated jurist with numerous bitter political enemies." Another says he "had an exceptional command of abusive language, which he used masterfully and willingly against any opponent." He became involved in a dispute with legislator William Rynerson (see entry); and Rynerson shot him to death in Santa Fe's La Fonda Hotel. Rynerson was acquitted at trial upon a plea of self-defense.

John P. Slough. After Twitchell.

Alberts, *Rebels*
Twitchell, *Leading Facts*, Vol. II
Other literature abundant

Smith, Guthrie "Gloomy Gus" (1877-1945)
Santa Fe Newspaperman

Guthrie Smith was born in Pickens County, Alabama. He was educated at a private school in Huntsville, Alabama, and graduated from West Point. He later studied at Cumberland University in Lebanon, Tennessee. For all of that education, by 1903 he found himself working as a telegraph operator at Santa Rosa, New Mexico. He continued in that line of work until 1908 and in 1910 he became editor of the Alamogordo *News*. He moved on to Santa Fe where he became a correspondent for several New Mexico papers. When Holm Bursum (see entry) was appointed to the United States Senate in 1921, Smith went to Washington with him. He served as a correspondent to several Southwestern newspapers. Upon his return to New Mexico he became editor of the Santa Fe *Record*, a weekly newspaper, which position he held for many years. Because of his dour outlook, he was known to many of his readers as "Gloomy Gus." He died at Santa Fe.

"Guthrie Smith, Newsman, Dead," Albuquerque *Journal*, January 10, 1945

Smith, Jedediah S. (1799-1931)
Santa Fe Trader, Mountain Man

A native of New York, Smith arrived in St. Louis in 1822. He is best known for his mountain man activities all over the Rocky Mountain West, and for setting a record with the number of pelts amassed in one season: 668 in 1824-25. In 1831, he entered the Santa Fe trade and set out for New Mexico from St. Louis with 22 wagons. He misjudged water requirements for his caravan, and while searching for a stream he was set upon by Comanche Indians. In the fight that followed, he killed the leader of the band and was himself killed. Smith was unusual among mountain men: he didn't smoke or drink, and, as an ardent Methodist, he frequently read the Bible and pontificated.

Time-Life Books, *The Trailblazers*
Twitchell, *Leading Facts*, Vol. II
Other literature abundant

Smith, Van Ness Cummings "Van" (1837-1914)
Chaves County Pioneer, Gambler

Born in Vermont, Van Smith arrived in Arizona in 1863 and became the territory's first sheriff, appointed by the governor to the job in Yavapai County in 1864. He later tried his hand at mining and gambling, unsuccessfully, before he moved on and arrived in New Mexico's Pecos Valley in 1869. He built a hotel and store where Roswell now stands and named the town after his father. Historian Frederick Nolan (see entry) wrote: "[Smith is] arguably more entitled than Joseph C. Lea (see entry) to be remembered as the 'father of Roswell.'"

Fleming, *J. C. Lea*
Larson, *Forgotten Frontier*
Frederick Nolan, "Van C. Smith: A Very Companionable Gentleman." *New Mexico Historical Review*, April 1997

Smithers, A. L. (d. 1911)
Luna County Deputy Sheriff

Killed by jail escapees on November 18, 1911. See entry on Thomas H. Hall.

Smokey Bear (c. 1950-1975)
Forest Fire Prevention Symbol

The best-remembered monument in Elliot Barker's (see entry) memory had nothing to do with his literary accomplishments. In May 1950, a huge fire broke out on Capitan Mountain, New Mexico. A fireman rescued a small bear cub, badly burned, clinging to a charred tree. The cub was flown to Santa Fe and nursed back to health. On behalf of the New Mexico Department of Game and Fish, Barker donated Smokey to the Forest Service in Washington, D.C., specifying that the cub should become a symbol of forest-fire prevention and wildlife conserva-

Smokey Bear

tion. Smokey lived for more than 26 years at the National Zoo and became one of the most recognized animals in the world.

Literature abundant

Speight, William Thomas (1911-1949)
New Mexico State Police Officer

Officer William Thomas Speight

Bill Speight died of a heart attack as he struggled to service a generator that provided power to a 200-foot radio tower on a mountain near Cloudcroft during a February snowstorm. His State Police career is noteworthy. In 1939 he engaged in a gunfight in Alamogordo, and was shot in the leg with a shotgun. He killed his assailant. Doctors were unable to remove all of the buckshot from his leg and the wound caused him discomfort for the rest of his life. In 1947, as he assisted the Border Patrol in a search for illegal aliens, his leg gave out and he fell off a boxcar. He broke his neck and injured his spine. He recovered but suffered occasional blackouts. After he wrecked a State Police car during such a spell, he was allowed to continue his police duties, but only if he used his own personal car. The State Police at the time did not offer health care benefits to officers.

Bullis, *New Mexico's Finest*

St. Vrain, Cerán (1802-1870)
Taos Trapper, Trader, Merchant, Soldier

Ceran St. Vrain. After Twitchell.

St. Vrain was a trapper, freighter over the Santa Fe Trail, merchant and military leader during the period of Mexican Rule (1821-1846) and during American Territorial days. He was closely associated with Charles Bent (see entry) and Kit Carson (see entry). He led a band of mountain men, called the Avengers, against the Mexican nationalists and Taos Indians who had rebelled against American occupation in January 1847 and killed Bent and several others. Later in life he operated a mill and store at Mora. Remley reports that St. Vrain died in 1855; while Crutchfield, Julyan and Thrapp agree on 1870 as his year of death. The community of St. Vrain in Curry County may have been named for him.

Crutchfield, *Tragedy*
Julyan, *Place Names*
Remley, *Adios Nuevo Mexico*
Twitchell, *Leading Facts*, Vol. II

226

Staab, Abraham (1839-1913)
New Mexico Frontier Merchant

Staab was born in Westphalia, Germany, and made his way to the United States at age 15; settling for a time in Norfolk, Virginia, where he found employment in mercantile establishments. He learned the basics of business and accounting during his two years there before he moved on to Santa Fe. In 1858 Abraham and his brother, Zadoc, opened their own general merchandising business. Early on, they engaged in the retail trade, but by the middle 1860s Zadoc Staab and Brother had become the largest wholesale company in the Southwest; their operations reaching into Colorado, Utah, Arizona and as far south as Chihuahua in Mexico. Historian Will Keleher (see entry) referred to Abraham as "The Merchant Prince of Santa Fe." He served in a number of important positions including Chairman of the Santa Fe County Commission.

Abraham Staab. After Twitchell.

He was well regarded by all who knew him, and contributed significantly to the construction costs of the Santa Fe Cathedral by forgiving notes that Bishop Lamy (see entry) had signed for cash advances. Keleher relates the story of the transaction. It is interesting that Staab's name is not mentioned by Lamy's biographer, Paul Horgan (see entry), nor is it cited in several other accounts of the Cathedral's construction.

Floyd S. Fierman, "The Triangle and the Tetragrammaton," *New Mexico Historical Review*, October 1962

Keleher, *Fabulous Frontier*

William J. Parish, "The German Jew and the Commercial Revolution in Territorial New Mexico, 1850-1900," *New Mexico Historical Review*, January 1960

Stanton, Edward L. "Perchmouth" (1888-1934)
New Mexico/Texas Killer

Perchmouth Stanton was a small Texan with a large gun. A petty thief, he had served prison time in Huntsville, Texas, prison and in the federal correctional system. He was released in late 1932; and in January 1933 he and an accomplice, Glen Hunsucker, shot and killed Swisher County, Texas, Sheriff John Mosley at Tulia rather than submit to arrest. A week later, at Rhome, Texas, they killed Wise County Deputy Sheriff Joe Brown. They hid out on a dry-land homestead between Corona and Ramon, in Lincoln County, New Mexico. Sheriff A. S. McCamant located them there in July 1933. In the pursuit that followed, Lincoln County Deputy Tom Jones (see entry) was shot and killed from ambush. Glen Hunsucker was also killed in the battle. Stanton was captured and subsequently executed by electrocution at

Edward L. Stanton

227

the Huntsville, Texas, prison on September 28, 1934.
Bullis, *99 New Mexicans*

Stapp, Col. John Paul (1910-1999)
Alamogordo Scientist, "The Fastest Man on Earth"

Col. John Paul Stapp

A U.S. Air Force officer who held both Ph.D. (in biophysics) and medical degrees, Col. Stapp was the first man to ride a rocket sled in the southern New Mexico desert. The tests were done to help determine the tolerance limitations for pilots who were forced to eject while in flight. In 1954 he rode a vehicle that accelerated from zero to 632 miles per hour in five seconds, and then was brought to a stop in 1.4 seconds. In all he rode the sled nearly 30 times, proving that man could withstand 40 times the pull of earth's gravity. He died at Alamogordo.
Albuquerque *Tribune*, Nov. 16, 1999

Steele, S.J., Thomas J. (1933-)
Catholic Priest, New Mexico Historian

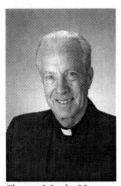
Thomas J. Steele, S.J.

Father Steele was born and raised in the St. Louis, Missouri, area, and educated at St. Louis University where he earned undergraduate, graduate and post graduate degrees. He was ordained a priest in 1964. He arrived at the University of New Mexico to work on a doctorate in English and American literature, and, he says, fell in love with the *santos* of New Mexico, and everything New Mexican "except the politics." He taught at Regis University in Denver for 29 years, and part time at UNM for 20 years. He is the curator of the Regis collections of *santos* and pueblo pottery. In 1999, Father Steele was awarded the UNM alumni Zia Award for his contributions to New Mexican cultural research. His written works over the years are too many to list here, but a representative sampling includes *Santos and Saints: The Religious Folk Art of Hispanic New Mexico* (1974, 1982, 1994), *A Guidebook to Zen and the Art of Motorcycle Maintenance* with Ronald DiSanto (1990), *The Regis Santos: Thirty Years of Collecting 1966-1996* (1997), *Seeds of Struggle: Harvest of Faith, The Papers of the Archdiocese of Santa Fe Catholic Cuarto Centennial Conference—The History of the Catholic Church in New Mexico*, editor, with Paul Rhetts and Barbe Awalt (1998), *Archbishop Lamy: In His Own Words* (2000), and *Religious Architecture of Hispano New Mexico*, with Thomas Lucero (2005). Father Steele lives at Immaculate Conception Parish in Albuquerque and continues to do research and writing.
Paul Rhetts, correspondence, August 2006

Stephens, Dwight B. (1873-1916)
Luna County Sheriff

A native of Ohio, first appointed sheriff of Luna County, New Mexico, in 1904, Stephens was killed in a gunfight with five jail escapees near Rincon in Doña Ana County in February 1916. One of the escapees was killed and the other four eventually captured. In 1911, Sheriff Stephens had been involved in a gunfight, also with jail escapees, that resulted in the deaths of deputies Tom Hall and A. L. Smithers (see entries). He was one of the longest-serving of early New Mexico sheriffs. Fred Fornoff (see entry), former captain of the New Mexico Mounted Police, said, "Sheriff Stephens was not a gunman in any sense to which odium might attach. The Luna County Sheriff was a fearless man and had a high sense of duty."

Bullis, *New Mexico's Finest*
Deming *Graphic*, February 25, 1916
Deming *Headlight*, February 25, 1916
Other newspaper accounts abundant

Stern, Richard Martin "Dick" (1915-)
Santa Fe Novelist

Dick Stern was born in California and educated at Harvard. He began selling stories to magazines in 1942. He lived in New York and Texas, and then back in California, before he and his wife moved to Santa Fe in 1950. He is the author of at least 30 novels, which represent several genres and geographical areas. Of particular interest to New Mexicans is his Johnny Ortiz mystery series that features an Apache-Anglo-Hispanic policeman. The series includes *Murder in the Walls* (1971), *You Don't Need an Enemy* (1971), *Death in The Snow* (1973), *Tangled Murders* (1989), *Missing Man* (1990), and *Interloper* (1990).

Betty Ann Parker, "The Case of the Literary Chameleon," Book *Talk*, New Mexico Book League, Nov. 1991

Stockton, Isaac T. "Ike" (1852-1881)
New Mexico Saloonkeeper/Rancher/Gunman

Ike and his brother Port (see entry) were considered by Ramon Adams to be "bad men of the first order." Ike managed to get involved to some extent in all of New Mexico's wars: the Lincoln County War, the Colfax County War and the San Juan County War. He was shot in the leg by a Colorado deputy and died after the limb was amputated. He spent a considerable amount of time as an adult in getting his younger brother out of trouble.

Adams, *Six Guns*
Bullis, *99 New Mexico*
Other literature abundant

Stockton, William Porter "Port" (1854-1881)
New Mexico Gunman

Port was the younger brother of Ike Stockton (see entry). Said to have killed his first man at age 12, with a shotgun, Port killed at least three other men in his short lifetime—men who were generally unarmed. Historian Dan Thrapp says "He was involved in assorted shootings and mayhem." A rancher named Alfred Graves put an end to the matter when he killed Port in a gunfight near Farmington.

Adams, *Six Guns*
Bullis, *99 New Mexicans*
Thrapp, *Encyclopedia*

Sumner, Col. Edwin V. "Bull," "Bull of the Woods" (c.1797-1863)
New Mexico Military District Commander (1851-1853)

Col. Edwin V. Sumner. After Twitchell.

Born at Boston, Massachusetts, Sumner was a career military man with more than 30 years of service when he arrived in New Mexico. His impression of the 9th District was not at all positive. He wrote, "The New Mexicans are thoroughly debased and totally incapable of self-government, and there is no latent quality about them that can ever make them respectable." Sumner referred to Santa Fe as "that sink of vice and extravagance." He advocated that the U.S. Government abandon New Mexico and leave the people to their own devices. Sumner built Fort Union and several other New Mexico forts before he was relieved of his command and transferred, "no doubt to his complete satisfaction," one historian wrote. Gen. James Carleton (see entry) named Fort Sumner in eastern New Mexico for him. Sumner died at Syracuse, New York.

Don Bullis, "New Mexico's Bull of the Woods: Col. E. V. Sumner," Rio Rancho *Observer*, July 22, 2004
Lamar, *Far Southwest*
Myers, *New Mexico Military Installations*
Rathbun & Alexander, *Military Place Names*
Twitchell, *Leading Facts*, Vol. II

Sundance Kid
See Longabaugh, Harry Alonzo

Sutton, Raymond, Sr. (1873-1930)
Union County Sheriff, U.S. Department of Treasury, Prohibition Bureau Agent

A resident of Clayton, New Mexico, Agent Sutton visited Raton to meet with other officers with whom he would search the nearby area for rumrunners. He disappeared on August 29, 1930, and was never seen again. His car was found later, with blood on the rear seat. One James Perry Caldwell was tried for the murder, but was acquitted. Most observers, then and now, believe that bootleggers killed the agent because he was much too ardent in his work.

Bullis, *New Mexico's Finest*
Chuck Hornung, "The Mystery Death of Federal Prohibition Officer Ray Sutton," *National Association & Center for Outlaw and Lawman History*, University of Wyoming, Laramie, April-June, 1991

-T-

Taber, Walter Grange (1897-1937)
New Mexico State Police Officer

Officer Taber died as a result of a motorcycle accident in Santa Fe on September 22, 1937. He was the first New Mexico State Police officer to be killed while in the line of duty.

Bullis, *New Mexico's Finest*

Taft, William Howard (1857-1930)
President of the United States (1909-1913)

On January 6, 1912, at 1:35 p.m., President Taft signed a proclamation making New Mexico the 47th State of the Union. He said upon that occasion, "Well, it is all over. I am glad to give you life. I hope you will be healthy." Taft

Officer Walter Grange Taber

became the first president of the 48 contiguous United States when Arizona was admitted to the Union in February 1912. Taft was appointed Chief Justice of the U.S. Supreme Court in 1921 and served until 1930 when he resigned a month or so before his death. No one else in U.S. History served as both president and chief justice.

Degregorio, *The Presidents*
New Mexico Blue Book, 2003-2004

Tasker, Ralph (1919-1999)
Hobbs High School Basketball Coach (1949-1998)

Tasker, a native of West Virginia, began his coaching career in Ohio. He arrived at Kirtland Base in Albuquerque as a member of the U.S. Army Air Corps during World War II. He began coaching in New Mexico at Lovington in 1946 and moved to Hobbs in 1949. Coach Tasker led his high school basketball teams to 12 state championships. In more than 50 years of coaching, his record was 1,222 wins against 291 losses (these numbers vary slightly depending on the source) for a winning record of about 80%. Of the players he coached, more than 100 went to

college on basketball scholarships, 50 were named to All-State squads, nine were selected as prep school All-Americans, and 13 were drafted by professional basketball teams. Tasker was selected for the National High School Hall of Fame in 1988. U.S. Senators Pete Domenici and Jeff Bingaman (see entries) recognized his service to Hobbs and New Mexico on the floor of the Senate upon the occasion of his retirement in 1998. Ralph Tasker Arena in Hobbs is named for him.
Newspaper accounts abundant

Teller, Edward (1908-2003)
Los Alamos Nuclear Physicist
Teller was born at Budapest, Hungary, and was educated at the Institute of Technology at Karlsruhe and the universities of Munich and Leipzig, all in Germany. In 1941 he became a part of the Manhattan Project, which developed the world's first atomic bomb at Los Alamos, New Mexico. He worked on projects at Columbia, the University of Chicago and at Los Alamos. He became professor of physics at what is now Lawrence Livermore National Laboratory in 1952. He was a leading proponent of the development of a hydrogen bomb, a program opposed by J. Robert Oppenheimer (see entry), who had directed the creation of the atomic bomb. Teller won the dispute. Teller also supported the continued testing of thermonuclear weapons while working on development of the peaceful uses for nuclear energy. He retired in 1975.
Literature abundant

Tettenborn, William Rogers aka Tethenborn, Waldemar "Russian Bill" (c.1850-1881)
Hidalgo County Horse Thief
Tettenborn is said to have been born in Russia. He went to sea at an early age, but jumped ship in San Francisco and wandered around the American West. He was injured in fights in both Denver and Fort Worth. He arrived in Shakespeare, New Mexico, in 1880. He wore two guns and high boots and is said to have made much of himself as a bad man. Then one day he stole a horse. He was soon captured by Grant County Deputy Sheriff Dan Tucker and turned over to the Shakespeare folks who promptly took him away from another officer and hanged him, along with outlaw Sandy King. Legend holds that when a citizen was asked why the two men had been hanged, the citizen pointed to King and replied, "He was a horse thief, the other one—a damned nuisance."
Alexander, *Six-Guns*
Bullis, *99 New Mexicans*
Other literature abundant

Thomas, Benjamin Morris (1843-1892)
New Mexico Indian Agent, Territorial Secretary
A native of Indiana, Thomas was educated as a dentist. He migrated to New Mexico in 1870 because of ill health and joined the U.S. Indian Service the following year. He served as agent for several New Mexico tribes, including the Apaches,

232

Navajo and Pueblos. Twitchell (see entry) called him a man of "forceful character." Thrapp says that because he was rigid and could not be intimidated, he was not as popular with his Indian charges as some other agents. He was also a staunch Presbyterian and contributed much to that church in New Mexico. President Benjamin Harrison appointed him New Mexico Territorial Secretary in 1889, a position he held until his death.

Thrapp, *Encyclopedia*
Twitchell, *Leading Facts*, Vol. II

Benjamin Morris Thomas. After Twitchell.

Thornton, William Taylor (1843-1916)
Governor (Territorial) of New Mexico (1893-1897)

A native of Henry County, Missouri, Thornton, a Democrat appointed by President Grover Cleveland, is the only governor of New Mexico to have served on the Confederate side in the Civil War. He served in the Missouri House of Representatives before he moved on to New Mexico where he was elected to the Territorial Council (Senate) in 1880. He was elected mayor of Santa Fe in 1891 and appointed governor in 1893. Thornton was generally considered a "law and order" governor. He died at Santa Fe and is interred there.

Curry, *Autobiography*
Lamar, *Far Southwest*
Twitchell, *Leading Facts*, Vol. II

Gov. William Taylor Thornton. After Twitchell.

Thorp, N. Howard "Jack" (1867-1940)
New Mexico Cowboy/Songwriter/Storyteller

Thorp was one of those Easterners—born in New York—who moved west and became a true Westerner. Early on, in 1886, he worked for a time as a cowboy in Lincoln County but discovered cowboy songs and set out to record as many as he could, and he wrote a few himself. His most famous song, "Little Joe the Wrangler," still appears frequently in western music anthologies. His research resulted in the production of *Songs of the Cowboys* in 1908, the first such book published in the United States. It was printed by the Estancia, New Mexico, *News* with a press run of 2,000 copies. Fifty pages in length and containing 23 songs, Thorp was obliged to pay for it himself ($120.00). Thorp also served for a time as a New Mexico cattle inspector. During the Great Depression of the 1930s he wrote for the Works Progress Administration. *Along the Rio Grande: Cowboy Jack Thorp's New Mexico* (1988) is a collection of his writings. It is an interesting book, but many of his recollections were not historically correct. They are important, however, because they reflect the popular view of events of the day.

Jack D. Rittenhouse, "Early Southwest Imprints," *Book Talk*, June 1974

Marc Simmons, *The New Mexican*, "Trail Dust" August 13, 2005
White & White, *Along the Rio Grande*

Tight, Dr. William George (1865-1910)
University of New Mexico President (1901-1909)

A native of Ohio, Tight was a graduate of Denison University, and held a Ph.D. from the University of Chicago, earned in 1901. Tight became the third president of the University of New Mexico at age 36. His salary was $2,000 per year. He is said to have ridden a horse around the campus at night to drive off cattle that wandered in to sup on the grass he'd planted, and coyotes that tended to interrupt social activities. Under his administration, both the Engineering School and the Associated Student Union were created. Tight made the beginnings of Pueblo architecture for buildings constructed on the Albuquerque campus during his tenure. He saw the university as a "pueblo on the mesa." That vision was not well received by many local residents. "[A] reversion to the primitive," they called it. Tight was ultimately dismissed as president for what Historian Marc Simmons (see entry) has called "architectural indiscretion." Tight died the following year, but his idea did not die with him. It was revived by UNM President James Zimmerman (see entry) and architect John Gaw Meem (see entry) in the 1930s.

Davis, *Miracle on the Mesa*
Garcia, *Albuquerque*
Ollie Reed, Jr., Albuquerque *Tribune*, September 28, 2005
Simmons, *Albuquerque*

Tijerina, Reíes López, "King Tiger" (1927-)
Rio Arriba County Land Grant Activist

Born of sharecroppers in Falls City, south of San Antonio, Texas, Tijerina founded the *Alianza Federal de Mercedes Reales*, or "The Federal Alliance of Land Grants" in 1963. It was this group that raided the Rio Arriba County, New Mexico, courthouse in the village of Tierra Amarilla on June 5, 1967 in an effort to arrest District Attorney Alfonso Sánchez (who, it turned out, was not there). During the attack, two peace officers, State Policeman Nick Saiz and jailer Eulogio Salazar were shot and wounded; Deputy Sheriff Pete Jaramillo and United Press International newsman Larry Calloway were taken hostage at gunpoint. Reaction was massive, including the mobilization of the New Mexico National Guard. Democratic elected officials Santa Fe County District Attorney Alfonso Sánchez and State Senator Edmundo Delgado blamed Republican Governor David Cargo (see entry). "I think the governor must assume full responsibility for this because he dignified that status of this organization [the Alianza]," Delgado said. "He gave the people who have been duped false hope. Those of us who have been around here for a long time and who are from old Spanish families, would have made claims on that land long ago if we had thought there was any legitimate claim." Tijerina was captured less than a week after the attack, but later acquitted of all charges. Two years later, in 1969, he was involved in burning a U.S. Forest Service sign at the Echo Amphitheater in the Santa Fe National Forest and arrested after he pointed a gun at a Forest Service officer. He was not acquitted that time. He spent 22 months in federal prison, much of it in a medical/psychological unit. He was released in 1971. In 1974, he was tried again on different charges related to the courthouse raid, convicted at sent to the New Mexico state penitentiary for six months. Governor Jerry Apodaca pardoned Tíjerina in 1978.

Albuquerque *Journal*, June 5 & 6, 1967; January 9, 1979; June 5, 1997
Busto, *King Tiger*
Hillerman, "Quixote in Rio Arriba County," *The Great Taos Bank Robbery*
Frances L. Swadesh, "The Alianza Movement: Catalyst For Social Change in New Mexico," *Spanish Speaking People in the United States*, Proceedings of the 1968 Annual Spring Meeting of the American Ethnological Society

Tingley, Carrie Ellen Wooster (1877-1961)
New Mexico First Lady/Benefactor

Carrie Wooster was born in Bowling Green, Ohio, to a wealthy farmer and oilman. After her father died in 1910 and she contracted tuberculosis, Carrie and her mother took a train west. As the story goes, their original destination was Arizona, but by the time they reached Albuquerque, Carrie was too ill to continue. Carrie recovered from her disease and married Clyde Tingley (see entry) in April 1911, in Albuquerque. One biographer said of her: "...Carrie was just friendly. She didn't care who you were. She went downtown every afternoon, shopping or to the movies, and she knew every clerk by name, every little newsboy." When a hospital for crippled children was built at Hot

Carrie and Clyde Tingley, c. 1912. Courtesy The Albuquerque Museum Photoarchives PA1976.142.004.

Springs (now Truth or Consequences) with federal and private money, Carrie donated money for medical treatment of the children. The people of Hot Springs voted to name the facility for Carrie Tingley and her name stayed with the hospital when it was relocated to Albuquerque.

Lundy, *Clyde Tingley*
Simmons, *Albuquerque*

Tingley, Clyde Kendle (1881-1960)
Chairman of Albuquerque City Commission (1916-1934), Governor (State) of New Mexico (1935-1938)

Tingley was born on a farm in Madison County, Ohio. He left the farm as a young man and became a machinist, eventually employed by Graham Motor Cars in Bowling Green, Ohio. It was there that he met Carrie Wooster (see entry), daughter of a prosperous farmer and oilman. When Carrie became ill with tuber-culosis and moved west, Clyde followed to be near her and took a job as a machinist for the Santa Fe Railroad in Albuquerque. He and Carrie were married there in April 1911. Clyde was elected to the Albuquerque City Commission in 1916, and never looked back. He was elected Governor of New Mexico in 1934 and again in 1936. He held one political office or another for about 35 years. A friend of President Franklin D. Roosevelt, Tingley was able to use New Deal federal largesse to the benefit of Albuquerque and New Mexico. A number of public works, especially in the Albuquerque area, are named for Tingley.

Lundy, *Clyde Tingley*
Simmons, *Albuquerque*
Other literature abundant

Tombaugh, Dr. Clyde W. (1906-1997)
New Mexico State University Astronomer

Dr. Clyde W. Tombaugh

Clyde Tombaugh was born at Streator, Illinois, and reared on a nearby farm. (Some recent accounts have reported that Tombaugh was born in Kansas.) At age 12 he became interested in astronomy and telescope making. In his early 20s, he was offered a job at the Lowell Observatory in Flagstaff, Arizona, which included stoking the furnace and clearing snow from the dome. His other responsibility involved operation of a photographic telescope that took long exposures of the sky. On February 18, 1930, Tombaugh discovered the planet Pluto (It was not announced until March 13, 1930). He was 24 years old at the time. Controversy surrounded the discovery from the beginning. Some astronomers argue that Pluto is too small to be a real planet; that its orbit is erratic. Others, though, assert that it is large enough, that it has an atmosphere and that it has moons. In 2006, the International Astronomical Union demoted Pluto from planet to dwarf planet. Tombaugh moved to New Mexico State University in Las Cruces in 1946 and continued his work there until he was 90 years old. Over the years he was credited with other discoveries including a globular star cluster, a supercluster of galaxies, variable stars and numerous asteroids. He also did research on artificial satellites. Fellow astronomers named an asteroid after Tombaugh in 1980.

Albuquerque *Journal*, February 19, 1980, September 15, 1991, August 25, 2006
Hsi, *Sundaggers*
Levy, *Clyde Tombaugh*

Treviño, Juan Francisco de (fl. 1675)
Governor (Spanish) of New Mexico (1675-1677)

During his first year in office, Governor Treviño mounted a campaign against "Indian idolatry" and ordered the arrest of 47 religious leaders from various New

Mexico Pueblos. Four of the Indians were hanged and one committed suicide. The remainder were released, some after they'd been flogged. A San Juan Indian named Po'pay (see entry) was one of those whipped and released. He went on to lead the Pueblo Revolt in 1680.

Sando, *Po'pay*

Simmons, *New Mexico*

Trujillo, Miguel H. (1904-1989)
Educator/Indian Rights Activist

Miguel Trujillo was born at Isleta Pueblo. His father died when he was seven years old and he was obliged to begin working to help support his mother, brother and two sisters. His mother recognized the importance of education and young Miguel was sent to the Albuquerque Indian School, and later to the Haskell Indian Institute in Kansas. He secured a teaching certificate and taught at Yuma, Arizona and Tohatchi, on the Navajo Reservation. On June 14, 1948, Trujillo tried to register to vote in Los Lunas, Valencia County, New Mexico. He was denied the right to do so by county recorder, Eloy Garley, under the provisions of the New Mexico Constitution that held that because Indians were not taxed, they could not vote. Trujillo sued in federal district court, and on August 3 of the same year, a three-judge panel in Denver ruled that Article VII, Section 1 was unconstitutional. (Today, Article VII , Section 1 only excludes "…idiots, insane persons and persons convicted of felonious or infamous crime..." from voting.) New Mexico Native Americans, about 18,000 of them at the time, thus gained the right to vote some 36 years after New Mexico became a state. Pueblo Indian Historian Joe Sando compares Miguel H. Trujillo to civil rights leaders such as Martin Luther King and Rosa Parks, and he writes that Trujillo "earned a place among the great leaders of this country."

Albuquerque *Journal*, August 4, 1948

Bronitsky, Gordon, "Isleta's Unsung Hero," *New Mexico Magazine*, August 1989.

Sando, *Pueblo Profiles*

Tunstall, John Henry (1853-1878)
Lincoln County Rancher/Merchant, Lincoln County War Figure

Tunstall was born in Middlesex, England. As a young man his family sent him to North America with capital to invest, presumably in ranching. Through a series of events, he arrived in Lincoln County, New Mexico, in the late fall of 1876. He purchased a ranch there, not far from the town of Lincoln. He and Lincoln Attorney Alexander McSween (see entry) also went into the mercantile business. With cattleman John Chisum (see entry), they established a bank in Lincoln. These activities angered Lawrence Murphy (see entry) and his minions who had previously operated similar businesses without competition. Matters came to a head in February 1878 when on the 18th, Sheriff William Brady (see entry), a supporter of Murphy and friends, dispatched a posse allegedly to serve a writ of attachment on Tunstall's cattle. Instead Brady's deputies killed the Englishman, who was then 24 years old. It was this event that sparked the Lincoln County War, which would take countless lives before it was finally ended in July 1881 with the killing of William H. Bonney (Billy the Kid, see entry).

Keleher, *Violence*
Nolan, *The Life and Death*
Utley, *High Noon*
Wilson, *Merchants*
Other literature abundant

Twitchell, Ralph Emerson (1859-1925)
New Mexico Historian

Ralph Emerson Twitchell.
After Twitchell.

Many historians over the years have relied heavily on Twitchell's extensive writings on the history of New Mexico, and there is no question that his biographical work is invaluable to basic research. Much of his work, however, must be considered in the context of his political affiliations and his professional associations. Born in Michigan, Twitchell was educated in Missouri and the University of Kansas before he graduated from the University of Michigan Law School in 1882. He found his way to Santa Fe the same year, employed as a representative of the Atchison, Topeka & Santa Fe Railroad, a position he held until he retired in 1915. He was a staunch Republican throughout his life and as such was associated with such prominent men as Thomas Catron (see entry) and Henry Waldo (a Democrat), both founding members of the Santa Fe Ring. (Note: it is a curiosity that one historian includes Stephen B. Elkins (see entry) among Twitchell's associates. Most historians agree that Elkins left New Mexico for West Virginia in 1877, and Twitchell didn't arrive until 1882.) Throughout his career in New Mexico, Twitchell served in several capacities: president of the Bar Association, Judge Advocate of the Territorial Militia (it was with this appointment that he acquired the title, "Colonel"), appointed by Governor Miguel Otero (see entry); Gubernatorial representative to Washington, D.C., appointed by Governor George Curry (see entry). It was Governor Curry, too, who appointed Twitchell an unofficial territorial historian (Curry himself would hold the position in 1946-47). Former New Mexico State Historian Robert Tórrez has written that Twitchell's books "have…become the standard by which all subsequent books of New Mexico history are measured." Some of Twitchell's books include: *History of the Military Occupation of New Mexico, 1846-1851* (1909), *Leading Facts of New Mexico History*, five volumes (1911-1917), *The Spanish Archives of New Mexico*, two volumes (1914), *Historical Sketch of Governor William Carr Lane* (1917), *Col. Juan Bautista de Anza: Diary of His Expedition to the Monquis in 1780* (1918), *Spanish Colonization in New Mexico in the Oñate and De Vargas Periods* (1919), *Dr. Josiah Gregg, Historian of the Santa Fe Trail* (1924), and *Old Santa Fe: The Story of New Mexico's Ancient Capital* (1925).

Elizabeth Rogers, "S. B. Elkins: Business in New Mexico's Early Banking Era, 1873-1875," *New Mexico Historical Review*, January 1995.
Tórrez, *UFOs*
Thrapp, *Encyclopedia*

-U-

Ufer, Walter (1876-1936)
Taos Painter

Some sources claim that Ufer was born in Germany and removed to the state of Kentucky at a young age. Others claim that he was born in the U.S. In any event, he returned to Europe as a teenager and studied at the Dresden Royal Academy and the Royal Applied Art School. He returned to the U.S. for a time, married, and returned to Europe where he and his wife painted in some of the major cities. Upon his return to the U.S. he settled in Chicago where he met Carter Harrison who sponsored an extended painting trip to Taos. Upon seeing the town for the first time, in 1914, he declared, "God's country! I expect to live and die here." And he did. He joined the Taos Society of Artists in 1915, and set about painting. John Singer Sergeant asserted that Ufer was one of America's best painters. Ufer was a nonconformist and something of a socialist. He was known for his disruptive behavior and he drank heavily. "He liked to wear bits of military uniform—a jacket, hat and puttees he could buy cheaply at a surplus store;" this in spite of the fact that he was earning upwards of $50,000 per year in the late 1920s; the best income among the Taos painters of the day. After the onset of the Great Depression in 1929, he found it necessary to take on students to earn a living. He died at 60 of peritonitis, the result of appendicitis. His ashes were scattered among the mesas of northern New Mexico.

Ina Sizer Cassidy, "Art and Artists of New Mexico," *New Mexico*, January 1933
"Walter Ufer: Passion and Talent," *American Artist*, January 1978
Other literature abundant

Ugarte y la Concha, Hernando de
Governor (Spanish) of New Mexico (1649-53)

Governor Ugarte y la Concha discovered what might have been the beginnings of a Pueblo revolt in 1650 when Indians from Jémez, Sandía and Alameda allowed Apaches to steal royal livestock during Holy Week, a time when the Spaniards were otherwise occupied. Ugarte y la Concha ordered nine of the leaders executed, and other tribal members were enslaved for ten years. Simmons (see entry) reports that from that time until 1680, there were frequent rumors of Pueblo Indian unrest.

Sálaz Márquez, *New Mexico*

Sando, *Po'pay*

Simmons, *Spanish*

Unser Family
Albuquerque Auto Racers

The Unsers have called Albuquerque home since 1936, and have brought positive attention to New Mexico. Notably, six Unsers have started, and three members of the family have enjoyed a combined nine victories at the famed Indianapolis 500 auto race, held each year over the Memorial Day weekend. Of the 14 races run from 1968 to 1981, one of the Unsers won half of them. The Unser Racing Museum opened in Los Ranchos, north of Albuquerque, in September 2005.

Jerome Henry Unser

Jerome Henry "Jerry" (1899-1967) and his brothers, Louis (1896-1979) and Joseph "Joe" (1897-1929) were among the early Pike's Peak racers and in fact were the first to take a motorcycle to the top, in September 1915. Brother Joe was killed while test-driving a racecar in Colorado in 1929. Jerry and his family moved to Albuquerque in 1936 and he opened a garage at the intersection of Central Ave. and Rio Grande Boulevard, although he later moved further west on Central.

Jerry Henry Jr. (1932-1959) raced up Pike's Peak and was a successful stock car driver, having won the USAC championship. He aspired to drive at Indianapolis and finished 31st in the 1958 race. The following year, however, he hit the wall during a practice run, and his car erupted in fire. He died 17 days later. His son, Johnny, is also a race driver and has competed at Indianapolis.

Louis Jefferson "Louie" (1932-2004) was Jerry's twin brother. A race driver, too, he was profoundly affected by his brother's death, and decided to quit racing. That only lasted a few months before he was back at it, winning races and setting records. While he was an outstanding driver, he was best known in racing circles for his ability as a mechanic and tuner. He was diagnosed with multiple sclerosis in 1964, but that didn't slow him down. He operated Louie Unser Racing Engines in California for a number of years.

Robert William "Bobby" (1936-) was born in Albuquerque and at age 15 was driving in auto races. By age 20 he'd won two modified stockcar championships, and moved on to Pike's Peak, where he won in 1956 and then won six years in a row from 1958 to 1963. Also in 1963, he made his first try at the Indianapolis 500, but didn't win. That didn't happen until 1968. He won again in 1975 and yet again

Alfred Unser, Sr. and Robert William Unser

in 1981. After he retired a couple of times, he entered and won the Pike's Peak race yet again in 1986. His uncle Louie had won it nine times before he was killed in 1929; Bobby won it a total of 10 times. In 1990 he entered the Pirelli Classic, which covered seven European countries in seven days. He set a record at the Stelvio hill climb. He finally retired in the late 1970s, and has since written a book, *Winners are Driven*, published in 1993. His sons, Bobby, Jr., and Robby, are also racecar competitors.

Alfred Sr. "Al" (1939-) is the younger brother of Bobby. He began racing at age 18 driving roadsters and sprint cars. He first entered the Indianapolis race in 1965, and finished ninth. Al won the race in 1970, making him and Bobby the first brothers ever to win. Al won again in 1971, making him only the fourth driver to win back-to-back races. He nearly made it three in a row, finishing second in 1972. He won a fourth time in 1978 at age 47 thus becoming the oldest driver to win at Indy. Another first in the car-racing world occurred in 1983 when Al raced against his own son, Al, Jr. Al, Sr. retired on May 17, 1994.

Alfred Unser, Jr.

Alfred Jr. "Little Al" or "Al Jr." (1962-) was, needless to say, born to auto racing. By his 10th birthday he was driving go-carts. He graduated to sprint cars and made his Indy debut at age 20. He also competed at Pike's Peak, winning it in 1983. He won the IROC championship in 1986. He won the Indy 500 in both 1991 and 1994, thus becoming the first second-generation driver to win there. Little Al announced his retirement in 2004. He returned to Indy in 2006, however, and crashed into the wall on the 146th lap. He finished 24th.

Cody Michelle (1987-) is the daughter of Al, Jr. At age 12, in 1999, she was stricken with transverse myelitis, a rare inflammation of the spine, which left her paralyzed from the chest down and confined to a wheelchair. Like her great-uncle Louie before her, she did not let the disorder slow her down. She created her own foundation, called the Cody Unser First Step Foundation (www.cufsf.org), to build awareness of the disease and to promote cooperation among researchers. She has received a great deal of recognition for her work, including accolades from President George W. Bush and New Mexico Governor Gary Johnson.

John Richard Arnold, "Rev it up, Los Ranchos Unveils Unser Museum," *New Mexico Magazine*, January 2006

Amber Hartley, "Cody Unser, The New Unser Legacy," *New Mexico Magazine*, February 2005

Kirby, *The Unser Legacy*

Newspaper accounts abundant

-V-

Valdez, Antonio Lino (d. 1880)
San Miguel County Deputy Sheriff, Jailer

Deputy Valdez was shot and killed by either Dave Rudabaugh (see entry) or Little Allen Llewellyn, both of whom sought the illegal release of J. J. Webb from the San Miguel County, New Mexico, jail. Valdez had refused to give up the cell keys. Llewellyn died a short time later and Rudabaugh was captured and sentenced to hang for the Valdez killing. He escaped from custody but was killed in 1886 by Mexican citizens at Parral, Chihuahua, after he killed two men in a dispute over a card game.

Bullis, *New Mexico Finest*
Other literature abundant

Vance, Vivian (1909-1979)
Actress

Born Vivian Roberta Jones in Cherryvale, Kansas, Vance took an interest in acting at an early age. Her first efforts were not successful, but after her family moved to Albuquerque she became active in the Little Theater; and was so successful that directors there arranged a special show to raise money to send her to New York for dramatic training. Progress in the Big Apple was slow, but in 1932 she won a role in "Music in the Air" and later she was understudy to Ethel Merman in "Anything Goes." Desi Arnaz saw her while she starred in "Voice of the Turtle." He was interested in casting her in a new TV show with his wife, Lucille Ball, entitled *I Love Lucy*. With some reluctance, Vance took the part. *I Love Lucy* ran for ten years, from 1951 to 1961. Vance became the first woman to win an Emmy for Best Supporting Actress, in 1954. She remained with Lucille Ball when *The Lucy Show* aired in 1962, staying until 1965. She died from cancer in Belvedere, California, near San Francisco in 1979.

Vivian Vance. Courtesy The Albuquerque Museum Photoarchives PA 1978.153.

Brooks & Marsh, *The Complete Directory to Prime Time*
García, *Three Centuries*
Internet Movie Data Base

Vargas, Diego de (1643-1704)
Governor (Spanish) of New Mexico (1691-1697 and 1703-1704)

According to historian Thomas E. Chávez (see entry), his full name and title was Diego José López de Zápata y Luján Ponce de León Cepeda Alvarez Contreras y Salinas, Marqués de Villanueva de la Nava de Braciñas. In addition to being governor twice, he held the title of captain general. Born at Madrid, Spain, he arrived in Mexico in 1672. He served as *alcalde* in several communities and in the late 1680s he requested appointment to the governorship of New Mexico, which was at the time in the hands of Pueblo Indians following the revolt of 1680. He was given the post and arrived at El Paso in the fall of 1691. He marched north in the summer of the following year and by September had succeeded with his re-conquest. Chávez writes, "[In 1692] Vargas...led an army into New Mexico and, without a violent conflict, met with various Pueblo emissaries, usually over cups of hot chocolate, to prepare the way for the subsequent return of the colonists." By 1693, though, any pretenses of peace had disappeared and the Spanish dealt harshly with the insurgents: Seventy Indians were executed and 400 women and children were sold into slavery. Another uprising occurred in 1696 during which 21 Spanish soldiers and five missionaries were killed. A new governor, Pedro Rodríguez Cubero (see entry), arrived in 1697. Based on allegations by the *cabildo* (council) at Santa Fe, Cubero charged de Vargas with a plethora of offenses, including mismanagement and embezzlement—he was even blamed for the famine of 1695-1696—and imprisoned him for three years. Officials in Mexico City ordered his release and de Vargas returned to Mexico in 1700. By 1703 he had been cleared of all the charges against him and reappointed governor of New Mexico. As he started north Cubero fled, declaring that he had business elsewhere. Then de Vargas led a campaign against Apaches in the spring of 1704, during which he became ill and died at the town of Bernalillo. The Santa Fe Fiesta was originally a celebration in honor of Diego de Vargas.

Chávez, *New Mexico*
Ellis, *New Mexico, Past and Present*
Kessell, *The Journals of don Diego*
Simmons, *Hispanic Albuquerque*
Simmons, *New Mexico*
Thrapp, *Encyclopedia*
Twitchell, *Leading Facts*, Vol. I

Velarde, Pablita (1918-2006)
Santa Clara Artist

She was born at Santa Clara Pueblo in northern New Mexico and named Tse Tan, which translates as "Golden Dawn." Her mother died when she was five, and she was sent to St. Catherine's Indian School in Santa Fe where her name became Pablita Velarde. She broke with tribal tradition and chose to do painting rather

244

than pottery. Male art students wouldn't accept her, and her father did not support her artistic endeavors. He sent her to Española to study bookkeeping and typing. Among the first female Indian painters—only Tonita Peña preceded her—Velarde's work is valued for its detail. Her murals appear at the Bandelier National Monument, and other of her works are on display at the Smithsonian and the Museum of New Mexico, but the Arizona State Museum at the University of Arizona at Tucson has the largest collection of her paintings. The French government awarded her the *Palmes Academiques* in 1954 for her contributions to art. That marked the first time a European government recognized an Indian artist. She died in Albuquerque, where she had lived for many years. Her son, Herbert Hardin II, and her daughter, Helen Hardin (d. 1984), were also artists: Herbert a sculptor and Helen a painter. Granddaughter Margarete Bagshaw-Tindell is also an artist.

Albuquerque *Tribune*, Jan. 12, 2006
Other literature abundant

Viarial, Jacobo "Jake" (1946-2004)
Pojoaque Pueblo Governor

Jake Viarial became a legend in his own time. As governor of the smallest of New Mexico Pueblos, in both population and area, Viarial was one the most progressive. It was he who convinced the tribal government to borrow money that could be used to advance economic development on the reservation. Pojoaque now operates the Cities of Gold Casino as well as the Downs at Santa Fe horse racing track, which also includes a casino. The Pueblo was the first Indian tribe to form a partnership with Hilton Hotels to construct a $250 million resort. Viarial was also at the center of several controversies. He engaged in a dispute with the Attorney General over some of the provisions of the gaming compacts between the Pueblos and the state. At one point he threatened to close U. S. Route 84-285, which crosses Pueblo land, and to collect tolls on the road to offset any revenue lost to the Pueblo should the state close the casino. Viarial had served for more than 20 years as Pueblo governor at the time of his death.

Albuquerque *Journal North*, June 28, 2004
Indian Pueblo Cultural Center

Victorio (c. 1825-1880)
Apache, Mimbreno/Warm Springs Indian Chief

Historian Dan Thrapp quotes an unidentified frontier military officer as saying that he "considered Victorio the greatest Indian general who had ever appeared on the American continent." Anyone writing about his exploits in Old Mexico, New Mexico, Arizona and Texas between 1877 and his death in 1880 must acknowledge his superior competence as a tactician and a guerilla fighter. He was also known as Lucero, Bidu-ya and Beduiat. Thrapp reports that he was killed along with nearly 80 of his people, 60 of them warriors, in the Tres Castillos Mountains

Victorio. After Twitchell.

in the Mexican state of Chihuahua, by Mexican troops under the command of Col. Joaquin Terrazas, on October 15, 1880. Historian Sherry Robinson says that Victorio died in the battle, but was not killed by Mexican soldiers. "When he could see the situation was hopeless, he fell on his own knife, as did others of his warriors, to avoid being taken captive." This about marked the end of Apache hostilities in Texas, but the war continued in New Mexico as Victorio was succeeded as leader by another Warm Springs Apache named Nana, who eventually joined Geronimo (see entry). The Victorio Mountains of southwestern New Mexico are named for him.

Robinson, *Apache Voices*
Thrapp, *Encyclopedia*
Utley, *Frontier Regulars*
Other literature abundant

Vierra, Carlos (1876-1937)
Painter, Founder of the Santa Fe Art Colony

Carlos Vierra was born of Portuguese parents at Moss Landing, California. He studied in San Francisco at the Mark Hopkins Institute and then traveled to New York to seek his fortune. After a slow start, he became a successful cartoonist and marine painter. Around the turn of the century in 1901, he developed severe respiratory problems and on the advice of his doctor, he moved to Santa Fe, New Mexico, in 1904 where he took up residence at the Sunmount Sanatorium, located on a hill above Canyon Road. He is generally considered the first member of the Santa Fe Art Colony. Historian Twitchell wrote, "...he quickly acquired the spirit of the mountains and the mesa, the sunshine and the atmosphere [of New Mexico]." A strong supporter of Santa Fe's traditional architecture, he wrote, "Nothing will push Santa Fe off the map... so quickly as ... the majestic mansion, the cute bungalow or the old adobe with a new razorback roof, if we persist in building them until they strangle our own architecture and individuality." Architect John Gaw Meem (see entry) was greatly influenced by Carlos Vierra.

Tobias & Woodhouse, *Santa Fe*
Twitchell, *Leading Facts*, Vol. V

Gov. Donaciano Vigil. After Twitchell.

Vigil, Donaciano (1802-1877)
Governor (U.S. Civil) of New Mexico (1847-1848), Secretary (1846-1851)

A native of Taos, Vigil was self-educated and a progressive thinker. He had a record of service to New Mexico under Mexican and U.S. governance. As a military man, he participated in action against the Navajo in the 1820s and 1830s. He served as military secretary under Governor and General Manuel Armijo (see entry) and was an officer under Armijo at the time of the American Occupation by Stephen Watts Kearny (see entry) and the Army of the West in August 1846. Vigil is said to have supported the American Occupation because he believed that it would lead to reform of the Catholic Church and the expansion of public education, in which he had a strong, enduring interest. Kearny appointed Vigil to the office of secretary at the same time that he appointed Charles Bent (see entry) governor, in the fall of 1846. Vigil became acting governor upon the assassination of Bent in early 1847; and he served as civil governor and secretary until 1848 while Col. Sterling Price (see entry) served as military governor. Price abolished the offices of secretary, U.S. Attorney and U.S. Marshal in February 1848, but they were re-established later the same year when Col. John M. Washington (see entry) became military governor and Vigil was reappointed secretary. Vigil subsequently served several terms in the territorial legislature, and in an 1848 address he said: "It is particularly important in a country where the right of suffrage is accorded and secured to all that all should be instructed and that every man should be able to read to inform himself of the passing events of the day and of the matters interesting to his country and government." In 1876, late in his life, he continued to be a strong supporter of public education. He died in 1877. Historian R. E. Twitchell (see entry) wrote, "There are not two opinions as to his high character, his patriotism, and his sagacity."

Lamar, *Far Southwest*
Mondragón & Stapleton, *Public Education*
Twitchell, *Leading Facts*, Vol. II

Vigil, Francisco X. "Frank" (d. 1898)
Valencia County Chief Deputy Sheriff

Frank Vigil was shot to death when he and other officers attempted to arrest train robbers "Bronco Bill" Walters and "Kid" Johnson—some believe that a third outlaw, "Red" Pipkin, was also involved—on the Alamo Navajo reservation in May of 1898. The officers were out-gunned, and according to one historian, outclassed in that Walters was a superior gun-hand. Vigil was married but had no natural children. He and his wife had adopted an Indian girl from the Albuquerque Indian School. One newspaper described Vigil as "one of the bravest officers in New Mexico." He is buried in the churchyard at Valencia.

Bullis, *New Mexico's Finest*
Bryan, *Robbers*
Tanner & Tanner, "Red Pipkin, Outlaw From the Black River Country," *Wild West Magazine*, Oct. 2003

Villa, Francisco "Pancho" (1878-1923)
Mexican Revolutionary

Villa was born Doroteo Arango near Durango, Chihuahua. A bandit of sorts as a young man, he joined the Mexican Revolution led by Francisco Madero in 1910. As the revolution succeeded and failed over the years, Villa fought on. On March 9, 1916, Villa's troops attacked the town of Columbus in southern New Mexico. When the smoke cleared, 18 Americans were dead, and so were more than 100 of Villa's troops. Reasons for the raid have been debated from that day to this, but one of the most plausible is that Villa was angry that President Woodrow Wilson had allowed Mexican regular army troops to travel inside the U.S. to reach northern Mexico, where they contributed to a defeat of revolutionary troops at Agua Prieta, Sonora, in November 1915. There is also an ongoing debate as to whether or not Villa was present during the Columbus raid. Some witnesses claim they saw Villa in Columbus; others swear he remained in the rear and never entered the town. The result of this raid was an incursion into Mexico by U.S. troops under the command of General John "Black Jack" Pershing (see entry); an effort that was unsuccessful. Villa was assassinated at Parral, Chihuahua, in 1923.

Richard H. Dillon, "Down Mexico Way, In Pursuit of Pancho Villa, *True West*, May 2005
Bullis, *99 New Mexicans*
Fugate & Fugate, *Roadside History*
Charles H. Harris III and Louis R. Sadler, "Pancho Villa and the Columbus Raid," *New Mexico Historical Review*, October 1975
Hurst, *Villista Prisoners*
Johnson, *Heroic Mexico*

Villagrá, Gaspar Pérez de (c. 1555-1620)
Spanish Soldier/Poet

Born at Puebla de Los Angeles in New Spain, Villagrá was educated in Europe, though the years he spent there are not made clear by any of his biographers. He was back in Mexico (New Spain) by 1596 when he joined Juan de Oñate (see entry) and his *entrada* of the northern Spanish New World frontier. After the party's arrival at San Juan, near the present-day Española, in 1598, several of the settlers deserted and fled south toward Mexico. Villagrá was dispatched after some of them and reportedly killed two men on the trail. He was also a part of the military action against the Acoma Pueblo people in early 1599 that resulted in the deaths of many Indian people, and the capture of many more. Later in 1599, Villagrá was sent back to Mexico to secure military reinforcements for Oñate. He remained in Mexico where he held several administrative positions. He probably returned to Spain by 1605. His famous epic poem, *Historia de la Nueva México, 1610*, an account of Oñate's *entrada*, was published at Alcalá de Henares, Spain. At the time it gained him little, as repeated petitions for an audience with King Philip III were unsuccessful. Back in New Spain, he was tried in absentia for the 1598 killings of the Spanish deserters, and convicted. His punishment was banishment from Mexico for six years, essentially meaningless since he was then living in Spain. His poem is considered the first published history of any part of the Americas. In 1619 or 1620, Villagrá was appointed *alcalde* of Zapotitlan in Guatemala. He died at sea while en route to that post.

Encinias, *Historia*
Simmons, *New Mexico*
Thrapp, *Encyclopedia*

-W-

Walker, E. S. Johnny (1911-2000)
U.S. Congressman (1965-1969)

Walker was born in Fulton, Kentucky, and began his education there. Along with his family, he moved to Albuquerque in 1926 and graduated from Albuquerque High School. He attended the University of New Mexico and George Washington University before he served in the U.S. Army during World War II, in both North Africa and Europe. As a Democrat, he held a variety of elected offices in New Mexico including House of Representatives, 1949-1952; Land Commissioner, 1953-1956 and again from 1961-1964; and of the Bureau of Revenue, 1960. He was also Director, State Oil & Gas Accounting Commission. During his service in the state legislature he sponsored the bill that allowed women to serve on juries. Elected to the U.S. Congress in 1964, he sponsored legislation that created Pecos National Monument. Walker was defeated in a re-election bid by Republican Ed Foreman (see entry). He died in Albuquerque of leukemia.
News accounts abundant

Wallace, Lewis "Lew" (1827-1905)
Mexican War & Civil War Military Officer, Governor (Territorial) of New Mexico (1878-1881), Novelist

A native of Indiana, Wallace was a law student when the Mexican War started in 1846 and he was called upon to serve as an officer in a volunteer regiment. He distinguished himself during the Civil War and attained the rank of Major General. General Ulysses S. Grant (see entry) admired him. In 1865, he served on the military court that tried those accused of the assassination of President Abraham Lincoln (see entry) and in fact drew sketches of most of the defendants. President Rutherford B. Hayes appointed him governor of New Mexico in 1878. He is most noted for attempting to deal with William H. Bonney (Billy the Kid, see entry), offering immunity and failing to deliver it. He was named minister to Turkey, a position he held from 1881 to 1885. He left New Mexico in May 1881 before Pat Garrett (see entry) killed Bonney at Fort Sumner in July. He declined to

approve payment of a $500 reward to Garrett. Wallace finished writing his epic novel, *Ben Hur: A Tale of the Christ*, while he resided in Santa Fe. He wrote two other novels: *The Fair God* (1873) and *The Prince of India* (1893). He is also noted for the following quote, taken from a letter he wrote to his wife, Susan, while he resided in Santa Fe: "Every calculation based on experience elsewhere fails in New Mexico."

Jason Emerson, "Aftermath of an Assassination," *American History*, June 2006

J. K. Shishkin, "The Wonderful Year of 1880," *La Gaceta, el Boletín del Corral de Santa Fe Westerners*, Vol. V, No. 3, 1970,

Marc Simmons, "New Mexico's Most Famous Book," *Prime Time*, September 2004

Thrapp, *Encyclopedia*

Gov. Lewis Wallace. After Twitchell.

Twitchell, *Leading Facts*, Vol. II

Other literature abundant

Walters, Mary C. (1922-2001)
Supreme Court Justice (1984-1989)

Walters served as a transport pilot for the Women's Auxiliary Service Pilots during World War II. She was appointed to the Albuquerque District Court bench by Governor Bruce King (see entry) in 1971, served as a Judge on the New Mexico Court of Appeals from 1978-1984 and as a Justice of the Supreme Court from 1984 to 1989. She died of complications from bronchitis and is interred in the National Cemetery in Santa Fe.

News sources abundant

Walton, William Bell "Billy" (1871-1939)
Silver City Lawyer/U.S. Congressman

A native of Pennsylvania, Walton moved to New Mexico in 1891. He studied law and was admitted to the bar in 1893. He established a practice in Deming but moved on to Silver City. He served in the Territorial House of Representatives in 1901 and 1902 and as Grant County Clerk, 1903 to 1906. He held a number of offices in the Democratic Party and was a delegate to the New Mexico Constitutional Convention in 1910. He served in the State Senate from 1912 to 1916 when he entered the race for U.S. Congress. He defeated B. C. Hernández (see entry) and served from 1917 to 1919. In 1918 he ran for the U.S. Senate, and was the personal choice of President Woodrow Wilson. He was defeated, however, by Holm O. Bursum (see entry). He returned to the practice of law in Silver City until he was elected District Attorney in 1926 and

Congressman William Bell Walton. After Twitchell.

served until 1932. Walton died in Silver City a few years later.
Curry, *Autobiography*

Warner, William Riddle (1884-1947)
Grant County Artist

Born in Canada, Warner served in the U.S. Army during World War I and subsequently worked for both the U.S. Indian Service and the U.S. Forest Service in the Gila National Forest. He began painting in 1930 at age 47, without any formal training. His work was displayed at the Philadelphia Academy of Art during the 1930s. Interest in Warner's work was revived with an exhibition of his work at the Silver City Museum in the fall of 2005. Warner died of a heart ailment at Fort Bayard.
Press Release, Silver City Museum, November 23, 2005

Washington, Col. John Macrea (1797-1853)
Governor (Military) of New Mexico (1848-49)

A career military man, Washington graduated from West Point in 1817. During his time as military governor, and because of hostile acts by the Navajo, he mounted an expedition into the Navajo homeland in 1849 during which an important headman named Narbona (see entry) was killed. He forced a treaty upon the Navajo that was soon repudiated by all parties, and Washington was transferred to New Hampshire. Washington Pass in the Chuska Mountains, on the Navajo Reservation, was named for him, in spite of Indian opposition.

Col. John Macrea Washington. After Twitchell.

Susan Landon, "The Hidden History of Washington Pass," Albuquerque *Journal*, December 4, 1988
Thrapp, *Encyclopedia*

Waters, Frank (1902-1995)
"Grandfather of Southwestern Literature"

Waters was born in Colorado Springs and attended Colorado College for a few years in the early 1920s. He spent a number of years traveling widely and working at a variety of jobs, including everything from oil field day laborer to propaganda analyst during World War II. He also spent time as a writer in Hollywood. All the while he was writing books. His first novel was *Fever Pitch* (1930) and his most famous novel was *The Man Who Killed the Deer* (1942). Probably his best-known non-fiction work is *Masked Gods: Navajo and Pueblo Ceremonialism* (1950). He wrote an additional 25 books, all of which reflect his deep interest in the culture and religion of the Navajo, Hopi, Pueblo and pre-Columbian people. He was nominated for the Nobel Prize several times and was awarded honorary doctorate degrees from seven universities, including the University of Albuquerque, New Mexico State University and the University of New Mexico. A permanently endowed creative writing fellowship in Waters' name was established at New Mexico

251

State University, and the Frank Waters Foundation carries on his ideas and work, besides sponsoring the Frank Waters Southwest Writing Award. He died at Arroyo Seco, New Mexico and his cremains are buried there.

L. D. Clark, Nomination essay for the Western Writers of America Hall of Fame, *Roundup Magazine*, December 2005

T. N. Luther, "Collecting Taos Authors," *Book Talk*, November 1992

Marc Simmons, "Two Writers Lost," *Trail Dust*, August 9-15, 1995

Frank Waters, "The Southwest: Visions and Revisions," *Book Talk*, April 1987

Weaver, Dennis (1924-2006)
Television Actor

Dennis Weaver

Craddock, *VideoHound*

Born in Joplin, Missouri, Weaver acted in nearly 30 films beginning in 1952. He became best known for his role on the long-running television series *Gunsmoke*, in which he played Chester Goode, Marshal Matt Dillon's side-kick, for nine years (1955-1964). Of greatest interest to New Mexicans is the television series *McCloud* in which Weaver starred as Taos, New Mexico, Marshal Sam Mc-Cloud, who was on detached assignment to the New York City Police Department. It ran from 1970 to 1977.

Associated Press, February 27, 2006
Brooks & Marsh, *Complete Directory*

Weightman, Richard Hanson (1816-1861)
Soldier/Lawyer/Congressional Representative/Newspaperman/Duelist

Richard Hanson Weightman. After Twitchell.

Weightman was born in Washington, D.C., and graduated from the University of Virginia. Legend holds that he was expelled from West Point for knife fighting. After service in the Mexican War, in which he attained the rank of Major, he made his way to Santa Fe in 1849, where he served as Indian Agent. He was New Mexico's first elected delegate to the Congress at Washington, D.C. (1851-1853). His temper was legendary. In 1849, he engaged in a duel with Judge Joab Houghton in which no blood was shed. Weightman's shot missed, and Houghton claimed he hadn't heard the command to fire, and so did not discharge his pistol. Weightman published the newspaper *El Amigo del Pais* in Albuquerque for less than a year during 1853. Back in Santa Fe in 1854, Weightman quarreled with François X. Aubry (see entry) and stabbed him to death. He was acquitted at trial upon a plea of self-defense. He left New Mexico shortly afterwards. A Colonel in the Confederate Army, he was killed at the Civil War battle of Wilson Creek, Missouri, in August 1861 and was

interred nearby.
Thrapp, *Encyclopedia*
Twitchell, *Leading Facts*, Vol. II

Westphall, Lieutenant David (d. 1968)
Vietnam Casualty, Monument Inspiration

Lieutenant David Westphall and 12 other Marines were killed by enemy machinegun fire in Vietnam on May 22, 1968. His father, Victor "Doc" (1914-2003), his mother Jeanne and his brother Walter, determined to use David's insurance money to erect a monument to his memory and to the memory of all the other U.S. military personnel who did not survive combat during the Vietnam War (1959-1975). Thus was born the Vietnam Veterans National Memorial. They chose to use land they owned on U.S. Route 64 near Angel Fire, New Mexico, and built a striking white chapel in the early 1970s. A 6,000 square foot visitor's center was added later. (The Vietnam Veterans Memorial in Washington, D.C., was not built until 1982.) In November 2005, Westphall's memorial became a part of the New Mexico state park system.

Martin Salazar, "Park to Honor Vietnam Veterans," Albuquerque *Journal*, November 10,
    2005
Vietnam Veterans Memorial

White, Alvan N. (1869-1945)
New Mexico State Superintendent of Schools

Born in Tennessee, White was educated in that state's public schools and attended Carson-Newman College, after which he began a career as a teacher. He also studied law and was admitted to the bar in Tennessee and New Mexico. He moved to Silver City, New Mexico, in 1896 and took up the practice of law. He was elected Grant County Superintendent of Schools in 1900. He was elected to the state superintendency in 1912. Even though the school systems in New Mexico were decentralized, and the superintendent's office had limited authority, White sought re-election in 1916, but the Democrats declined to re-nominate him in favor of John L. G. Swinney. White later served in the state House of Representatives from 1926 to 1937; as Speaker from 1931 to 1937. He died at Silver City.

Stern & Chávez, *New Mexico Historical Review*, Spring 2005

White, James Larkin "Jim" (1882-1946)
Carlsbad Caverns "Discoverer"

Born on a ranch in Mason County, Texas, White arrived in New Mexico as a boy in 1892 where he worked on the X-X-X Ranch. He claimed that he "discovered" the Carlsbad Caverns of southeastern New Mexico in 1901 when he observed a huge flight of bats rising from the ground. But of course Indian people and earlier ranchers knew about it before then. White was the first to enter the open maw of the cave by use of a crude ladder. He wrote, "I kept going until I found myself in the mightiest wilderness of strange formations a cowboy had ever laid eyes on." White had a difficult time making people believe what he had seen, and it was about 20 years before he was able to talk a photographer into taking pictures of the place. In 1923 he led General Land Office officials on a survey of the caverns, and they recommended that the site be designated as a national monument. White City, located at the entrance to the Carlsbad Caverns National Park, is *not* named for Jim White; but rather for Charlie White, a farmer and merchant who settled there in 1927.

Julyan, *Place Names*
Pike, *Roadside New Mexico*
Fugate & Fugate, *Roadside History*

White, Dr. James M. (d. 1849)
Santa Fe Trader

While enroute to Santa Fe, White and his party, made up of his wife and child, and two others described as a Negro and a Mexican, were attacked by a band of Jicarilla Apaches in northeastern New Mexico. White, the Negro and the Mexican were killed and his wife and child were carried off. A company of dragoons under the command of William Nicholson Grier (c. 1813-1885) and scouted by Kit Carson (see entry) was sent in pursuit of the miscreants. The soldiers located the Indian band and, in the fight that followed, six Apaches were killed, but Mrs. White and the child were murdered by their captors. Twitchell (see entry) cites Carson as reporting that "the principal chief of this band came into Santa Fe wearing a necklace made of the teeth of Dr. White…."

Simmons, *Kit Carson*
Twitchell, *Leading Facts*, Vol. II & III

Whitehill, Harvey Howard (1838-1906)
Grant County Sheriff

(Note: The dates above are as shown on Whitehill's tombstone. There is some dispute as to his correct dates of birth and death.) Born in Ohio, and educated there, he became a railroad engineer for a few years in his early life. He headed west by 1860 and enlisted in the Union Army at Fort Union in 1861. But, according to historian Bob Alexander, he missed the Battle of Glorieta in March 1862. He spent some time in Elizabethtown, New Mexico, before he reached Silver City in 1870. Whitehill became Grant County Sheriff in April 1875, by appointment, after Sheriff Charles McIntosh ran off to Mexico with an estimated $3,000 of the county's money. (Note: Thrapp reports that Whitehill was elected in 1874. Ball and Alexander agree that he was appointed in 1875.) He served in that office, off and on, until 1891. His greatest claim to fame is that he was the first lawman to arrest Henry Antrim who would become famous as William H. Bonney, or Billy the Kid (see entry). Whitehill was well regarded as a peace officer during his lifetime.

Alexander, *Whitehill*
Alexander, *Six-Guns*
Ball, *Desert Lawmen*
Thrapp, *Encyclopedia*

Whitman, Walt (1819-1892)
Poet

Famed in his own lifetime, primarily for the numerous editions of *Leaves of Grass* (1855 and later), Walt Whitman lived a poet's existence, although poverty rarely visited him. His biographers make little of Whitman's adventure into capitalism, but there is clear evidence that beginning in 1883 he came into possession of 200 shares of stock in Sierra Grande Mining Company of Lake Valley, New Mexico. He never visited Lake Valley, so far as anyone knows. The furthest he ever got from the New York City/Washington D.C. area in his lifetime was New Orleans, and that didn't last long. His friend Robert Pearsall Smith gave him the shares, and suggested that dividends in the amount of $50.00 per month could be expected. Smith closed a letter to the poet with, "And may its use prove of as much pleasure to you as it gives me to ask to place the income at your disposal." Indications are that Whitman only received nine dividend checks in the nine years until his death. This is something of a puzzle since Sierra Grande Mining owned the Bridal Chamber mine near Lake Valley, one of the top-producing silver mines in the world until 1893 when the bottom dropped out of the silver market.

William White, "Walt Whitman and the Sierra Grande Mining Company," *New Mexico Historical Review*, July 1969

Whittlesey, Charles F. (1867-1941)
Albuquerque Architect

Whittlesey designed the Alvarado Hotel in Albuquerque, constructed in 1902 at a cost of about $200,000. A Fred Harvey hotel, it was constructed in the California mission style, popular at the time, and contained 118 rooms. In 1903, Whittlesey built the imposing log house on Highland Park Circle that became the Albuquerque Press Club in 1972. He also designed buildings in Los Angeles, San Francisco and Chicago, and the El Tovar Hotel at the Grand Canyon (modeled after his log house in Albuquerque). American Architects' Biographies says of him: "He was noted for designs of hotels and railway stations and the use of reinforced concrete." He died in Los Angeles. The railroad tore down the Alvarado Hotel in 1970. As a footnote, the hotel was named for Hernando de Alvarado (see entry), an artillery commander for Francisco Vásquez de Coronado who explored New Mexico in 1540-1542.

American Architects
Garcia, *Three Centuries*
National Register of Historic Places
Special Collections Pamphlet and Travel Brochures, University of Arizona

Williams, Ben "Shotgun Ben" (1861-1935)
Doña Ana County Lawman

Williams was born in France (or Ireland, depending on the source). Details surrounding his early life are obscure. He arrived in Las Cruces about 1873, and worked for the Singer Sewing Machine Company collecting late payments and repossessing sewing machines, apparently an arduous and dangerous occupation at the time. Over the years he worked as a stock detective, Las Cruces constable, Doña Ana County chief deputy sheriff (he was a member of Sheriff Pat Garrett's [see entry] posse in the gunfight at Wildy Well in July 1898), Santa Fe Railroad special agent, and private investigator. He was shot and wounded in a gunfight with Albert Bacon Fall (see entry) and his brother-in-law, Joe Morgan, in 1895. He seems to have been generally well-regarded.

Gibson, *Life & Death*

Metz, *Pat Garrett*

Owen, *Two Alberts*

R. A. Suhler, "Ben Williams, Lawman," *Password*, El Paso County Historical Society, Spring 1982

Williamson, John Stewart "Jack" (1908-)
Science Fiction Author

Born at Pecos, Texas, Williamson moved north to Roosevelt County, New Mexico, in 1915, in a covered wagon. He graduated from high school at Richland, a community that is today completely abandoned. He began writing science fiction while still in his teens, and at age 20 sold his first story, "The Metal Man," to *Amazing Stories* magazine. In the years since, he has written and published 20 or so short stories and 60 novels including such classics as *Darker Than You Think* (1948), *The Humanoids* (1949), *Dragon's Island* (1951), *Trapped in Space* (1968), *The Black Sun* (1997), and his most recent, *The Stonehenge Gate* (2005). The Science Fiction Writers of America named Williamson a Grand Master in 1976. His autobiography *Wonder's Child: My Life in Science Fiction* (1985) won a Nebula Award for autobiography. Williamson was a Professor of English at Eastern New Mexico University from 1960 to 1977. Walter Jon Williams, a two-time Nebula Award winner, says this: "Jack doesn't belong to any one era. Whatever was happening in science fiction, Jack was a part of it." Williamson is credited with coining the terms "genetic engineering" and "terraforming." He continued to write well into his 90s. Many consider him the "Dean of Science Fiction."

Ollie Reed, Albuquerque *Tribune*, August 19, 2005

Wendell Sloan, "Jack Williamson, Science Fiction Pioneer Still Ponders Future," *New Mexico Magazine*, March 2005

Other literature abundant

Woofter, Roy (1880-1911)
Roswell Town Marshal

Roy Woofter was a native of West Virginia. He had served as a peace officer in Albia, Iowa, before he arrived in Roswell, New Mexico, in 1909 and joined the police department. He became chief later the same year. The following year, the town of Roswell enacted an ordinance that prohibited the sale of beer and liquor in the town limits, and Chief Woofer was earnest in enforcing the law. In May 1911, Marshal Woofter attempted to serve a warrant on bootlegger Jim Lynch only to be shot and killed for his trouble. Lynch was convicted of first-degree murder. A minister said this about Woofter: "[He] submerged every private interest, the comforts of

home and his own personal safety to act against the criminal element. Fearless in his duty he had gone forth and because of that duty he now lay cold in death."
Alexander, *Lawmen*
Bullis, *99 New Mexicans*

Wootton, Richens Lacy "Uncle Dick" (1816-1893)
Colfax County Mountain Man/Entrepreneur

A native of Virginia, Wootton arrived at Bent's Fort in Colorado in 1836. He and Kit Carson (see entry) were friends. Wootton participated in a number of commercial activities both before and after the American occupation of New Mexico in 1846; which included driving 9,000 sheep from New Mexico to California. He is best known for his toll-road through the Raton Pass along the Mountain Route of the Santa Fe Trail, and for controlling the access of railroads into New Mexico. Legend holds that the toll money he collected filled whiskey kegs that he hauled to the bank in Raton. An enigma, Wootton allowed Indians to pass over his toll road free of charge, and yet he was one of the few old-timers to support Col. John Chivington (see entry) and the Sand Creek massacre in southern Colorado (November 1864). In 1878 when both the Denver & Rio Grande railroad and the Atchison, Topeka & Santa Fe railroad raced for access through the Raton Pass and into New Mexico, Wootton sided with the AT&SF which allowed it to win. Wootton died near Trinidad, Colorado.
Bullis, *99 New Mexicans*
Mark Gardner, "Race for Raton Pass," *New Mexico Magazine,*" May 2005
Thrapp, *Encyclopedia*

-X-

Xenome, Diego (16th century)
Tewa Indian Leader

Diego Xenome was member of Nambé (Nampe) Pueblo who worked with Po'pay (see entry), and others, in planning the Pueblo Revolt of 1680.
Sando, *Po'pay*

-Y-

Yarberry, Milton J. "Milt" aka John Armstrong (1849-1883)
Albuquerque Lawman/Killer

Yarberry was born in Arkansas as John Armstrong. He began his career as a killer and thief at an early age in both Arkansas and Texas. Two of his associates were outlaws Dave (Mysterious Dave) Mather (see entry) and Dave Rudabaugh (see entry). It is reported that he'd killed five or six men before he arrived in Albuquerque and became town marshal in 1881. He was soon in trouble for killing one Harry Brown, a rival for the affections of Miss Sadie Preston. Yarberry got off on a plea of self-defense even though Brown was not armed when Yarberry shot him. That was in March 1881. In June of the same year, Yarberry shot and killed Charles Campbell for no crime other than walking down the street at the wrong time. The self-defense plea didn't work that time. The marshal was tried, convicted and sentenced to death. He was hanged in Albuquerque on February 9, 1883.

Bryan, *Albuquerque*
Metz, *Encyclopedia*
Simmons, *Albuquerque*
Other literature abundant

Young, Code aka Cole Estes, Bob Harris (c.1871-1896)
Valencia County Train Robber

Young was a member of the High Fives Gang that roamed widely in New Mexico and Arizona in the 1890s. He was shot and killed by deputy U.S. Marshal Will Loomis during a train robbery at Rio Puerco, about 34 miles southwest of Albuquerque.

Tanner, *Musgrave*
Donald Cline, "Cole Young, Train Robber," *Old West*, Summer 1985

-Z-

Zimmerman, James Fulton (1887-1944)
University of New Mexico President (1927-1944)

Zimmerman was born in Missouri and educated, first at Vanderbilt University and then Columbia University where he earned a Ph.D. in 1925. He was offered positions teaching history at both Ohio State University and the University of New Mexico, and he chose the later. He was named UNM President only a year and a half later and he faced a daunting task: five of his predecessors had been "hounded out of office." He succeeded where others had failed, according to William E. Davis—who served as UNM President from 1975 to 1982—because, "He was gracious without being ingratiating, proud, but with a true humility, and aggressive but not arrogant. Best of all, he could lead; but he could also listen." In spite of political attacks and other barbs and criticism, Zimmerman remained in the president's chair for 17 years. Although there had been considerable opposition when UNM President William Tight (see entry) tried to establish Pueblo architecture as a standard for UNM buildings early in the 20th century, Zimmerman was succeeded in doing so. He hired John Gaw Meem (see entry) as campus architect in 1933. Davis continued, "James F. Zimmerman left a rich, enduring legacy. It is fitting that the most majestic building on the campus, Zimmerman Library, was named in honor of this dynamic and revered president. [He] rose from the ranks of the faculty. He knew them, he had their respect, and he listened to them. A teacher and scholar as well as an able executive, he made wise and strategic appointments... He had a feeling for the Southwest—its languages, its Hispanic and Indian cultures..." Dr. Zimmerman died unexpectedly of a coronary thrombosis while having dinner with friends.

Albuquerque *Journal*, October 21, 1944
Davis, *Miracle on the Mesa*
Horn, *University in Turmoil*
Simmons, *Albuquerque*

Zollinger, Norman (1922-2000)
Albuquerque Novelist

Norman Zollinger was born in Chicago, and educated at Downers Grove, Illinois, and at Cornell College in Mount Vernon, Iowa. He served in the 15th Air Force during World War II, stationed at Roswell Army Air Field, and thus became acquainted with New Mexico. After the war, and after 25 years in the manufacturing business in the Chicago area, he moved to Albuquerque in 1971 and opened the Little Professor Book Store in the Fair Plaza Shopping Center near the State Fairgrounds. His first novel, *Riders to Cibola*, after 14 rejections, was published by the Museum of New Mexico Press in 1978. It became a best seller. His second novel was *Corey Lane*, published in 1981. Among his other books are *Passage to Quivira*, *Lautrec, Not of War Only* and *Meridian: A Novel of Kid Carson's West*, all of which were published in the late 1980s or early 1990s. Zollinger won the 1978 Western Writers of America Spur Award for *Riders to Cibola*.

Jo Ann Baldinger, "Norm Zollinger's love affair with hard, empty Tularosa," *Pasatiempo*,
    March 22-28, 1991
Tony Hillerman, "Remembering Norman Zollinger," *Book Talk*, April 2000
Literature abundant

Zuñi, Juan (fl. 1629)
Hopi Impersonator/Philanderer, Santa Fe Thief

Historian Sálaz Márquez tells the story: "Zuñi, a 27-year-old Hopi [was] charged with the sacrilegious impersonation of Fray Alonso de Posada by inviting Awatovi villagers to church where he mimicked Posada saying mass and performing other rites. He [was] also charged with cohabiting with 'fourteen Indian women' of the Pueblo. He [was] found guilty and ordered to render personal service in the convent in Santa Fe where he [could] receive instruction in the Faith." He apparently did not learn his lesson. In 1659 he was charged with stealing from the convent storeroom. Tried for that offense, he was sentenced to receive 200 lashes and to serve in forced labor for ten years.

Sálaz Márquez, *New Mexico*

Bibliography

Alberts, Don E. *The Battle of Glorieta: Union Victory in The West*, Texas A. & M. University Press, 1998.

_____. *Rebels on the Rio Grande*, Merit Press, 1993.

Alexander, Bob. *Dangerous Dan Tucker: New Mexico's Deadly Lawman*, High-Lonesome Books, 2001.

_____. *Fearless Dave Allison: Border Lawman*, High-Lonesome Books, 2003.

_____. *Lawmen, Outlaws, and S. O. Bs.*, High-Lonesome Books, 2004.

_____. *Lynch Ropes & Long Shots: The Story of an Old West Train Robbery*, High-Lonesome Books, 2006.

_____. *Six-Guns and Single-Jacks: A History of Silver City and Southwestern New Mexico*, Gila Books, 2005.

_____. *Sheriff Harvey Whitehill, Silver City Stalwart*, High-Lonesome Books, 2005.

Ayer, Mrs. Edward E., Translator. *The Memorial of Fray Alonso Benevides, 1630*, Horn & Wallace, 1965.

Bachrach, Arthur J. D. H. Lawrence in New Mexico "The Time is Different There," University of New Mexico Press, 2006.

Baker, Richard Allan. *Conservation Politics: The Senate Career of Clinton P. Anderson*, University of New Mexico Press, 1985.

Ball, Larry D. *Desert Lawmen: The High Sheriffs of New Mexico and Arizona 1846-1912*, University of New Mexico Press, 1992.

_____. *The United States Marshals of New Mexico & Arizona Territories 1846-1912*, University of New Mexico Press, 1978.

Barnett, John. *Carlsbad Caverns National Park: Silent Chambers, Timeless Beauty*, Natural History Association, 1981.

Betenson, Lula Parker (as told to Dora Flack). *Butch Cassidy, My Brother*, Penguin Books, 1976. (Originally published by Brigham Young University Press, 1975.)

Bethune, Martha Fall. *Race With The Wind: The Personal Life of Albert B. Fall*, A Novio Book (El Paso, Texas), 1989.

Bickerstaff, Laura M. *Pioneer Artists of Taos*, Old West Publishing, 1983.

Boyd, E. *Portfolio of Spanish Colonial Design*, LPD Press, 2001.

Brooks, Tim & Earle Marsh. *The Complete Directory to Prime Time Network and Cable TV Shows, 1946—Present*, Ballantine Books, 2003.

Bryan, Howard. *Albuquerque Remembered*, University of New Mexico Press, 2006.

_____. *Robbers, Rogues, and Ruffians: True Tales of The Wild West*, Clear Light Publishers, 1991.

_____. *Wildest of the Wild West, True Tales of A Frontier Town on The Santa Fe Trail*, Clear Light Publishers, 1988.

Bullis, Don. *New Mexico's Finest: Peace Officers Killed in The Line of Duty, 1847-1999*, New Mexico Department of Public Safety, 2000.

_____. *99 New Mexicans...and a few other folks*, Science & Humanities Press, 2005.

Burns, Walter Noble. *The Saga of Billy the Kid*, University of New Mexico Center for The American West & the University of New Mexico Press, (Introduction by Richard W. Etulain), 1999. (Originally published by Doubleday in 1925.)

Busto, Rudy V. *King Tiger, The Religious Vision of Reis López Tijerina*, University of New Mexico Press, 2005.

Cabeza de Vaca, Álvar Núñez. *Cabeza de Vaca's Adventures in the Unknown Interior of America* (Translation by Cyclone Covey), Collier Books, New York, 1961.

Campbell, Glen. *Rhinestone Cowboy*, Villard, 1994.

Chávez, Fray Angélico. *But Time and Chance: The Story of Padre Martínez of Taos, 1793-1867*, Sunstone Press, 1981.

Chávez, Thomas E. *An Illustrated History of New Mexico*, University of New Mexico Press, 1992.

_____. *Spain and the Independence of the United States*, University of New Mexico Press, 2002.

Chávez, Fray Angélico and Thomas E. Chávez. *Wake for a Fat Vicar: Father Julian Felipe Ortiz, Archbishop Lamy, and the New Mexican Catholic Church in the Middle of the Nineteenth Century*, LPD Press, 2004.

Church, Peggy Pond. *The House at Otowi Bridge; the Story of Edith Warner of Los Alamos*, University of New Mexico Press 1960.

_____. *When Los Alamos was a Ranch School; Historical Profile of Fermor and Peggy Pond Church*, Los Alamos Historical Society, 1974.

Clary, David A. *Rocket Man: Robert H. Goddard and the Birth of The Space Age*, Theia, an imprint of Hyperion, 2003.

Cleaveland, Agnes Morley. *No Life for a Lady*, Houghton Mifflin, 1941.

Cline, Donald. *Alias Billy the Kid: The Man Behind the Legend*, Sunstone Press, 1986.

Cobos, Rubén. *A Dictionary of New Mexico & Southern Colorado Spanish*, Museum of New Mexico Press, 2003

Coke, Van Deren. *Taos and Santa Fe: The Artist's Environment, 1882-1942* University of New Mexico Press, 1963.

Córdova, Kathryn M. *¡Concha! Concha Ortiz y Pino, Matriarch of a 300-Year-Old New Mexico Legacy*, A La Herencia Publication, 2004.

Coulter, Lane & Dixon, Maurice Jr. *New Mexico Tinwork 1840-1940*, University of New Mexico Press, 1990.

Covey, Cyclone, Translator, *Cabeza de Vaca's Adventures in the Unknown Interior of America*, Collier Books, New York, 1961.

Craddock, Jim, Ed. *VideoHound's Golden Movie Retriever*, Thompson Gale, 2004.

Crutchfield, James A. *It Happened in New Mexico*, Falcon Publishing, 1995.

_____. *Tragedy at Taos: The Revolt of 1847*, Republic of Texas Press, 1995.

Cuba, Stanley L. *Olive Rush: A Hoosier Artist in New Mexico*, Minnetrista Cultural Foundation, 1992.

Curry, George, with Hening, H. B., Ed. *George Curry, 1861-1947: An Autobiography*, University of New Mexico Press, 1958.

Dary, David. *Red Blood and Black Ink: Journalism in the Old West*, University Press of Kansas, 1998.

Davis, Ellis Arthur, Ed. *The Historical Encyclopedia of New Mexico*, New Mexico Historical Association, 1945.

Davis, William E. *Miracle on the Mesa, A History of the University of New Mexico 1889-2003*, University of New Mexico Press, 2006.

DeArment, Robert K. *George Scarborough: The Life and Death of a Lawman on the Closing Frontier*, University of Oklahoma Press, 1992.

Degregorio, William A. *The Complete Book of U.S. Presidents*, Barricade Books, 2005.

Drumm, Stella M, ed. *Down the Santa Fe Trail and into Mexico: The Diary of Susan Shelby Magoffin, 1846-1847*, Yale Western Americana, 1962.

Duffus, R. L. *The Santa Fe Trail*, University of New Mexico Press, 1930.

Dunlay, Tom. *Kit Carson & The Indians*, University of Nebraska Press, 2001.

Eisler, Benita. *O'Keeffe and Stieglitz: An American Romance*, Doubleday, 1991.

Ellis, Richard N. *New Mexico, Past and Present: A Historical Reader*, University of New Mexico Press, 1971.

Espinosa, Gilberto Espinosa & Tibo J. Chávez (Carter Waid, Ed.). *El Rio Abajo*, privately published.

Esquibel, Jose Antonio, and Charles Carrillo, *A Tapestry of Kinship: The Web of Influence Among Escultores and Carpinteros in the Parish of Santa Fe, 1790-1860*, LPD Press, 2004.

Etulain, Richard W., *Beyond the Missouri: The Story of the American West*, University of New Mexico Press, 2006.

_____. Ed. *New Mexico Lives: Profiles and Historical Stories*, University of New Mexico Press, 2002.

_____. *Western Lives: A Biographical History of the American West*, University of New Mexico Press, 2004.

Evans, Max. *Madam Millie: Bordellos from Silver City to Ketchikan*, University of New Mexico Press, 2002.

Fergusson, Erna. *New Mexico: A Pageant of Three Peoples*, Alfred A. Knopf, 1951.

Fitzpatrick, George, ed. *This is New Mexico*, Horn & Wallace, Albuquerque, 1948.

Fleming, Elvis E. *J. B. 'Billy' Mathews, Biography of a Lincoln County Deputy*, Yucca Tree Press, Las Cruces, 1999.

_____. *Captain Joseph C. Lea: From Confederate Guerrilla to New Mexico Patriarch*, Yucca Tree Press (In cooperation with the Historical Society for Southeast New Mexico), 2002.

_____. *Treasures of History IV: Historical Events of Chaves County, New Mexico*, iUniverse, Inc, 2003.

Flint, Richard & Flint, Shirley Cushing, Eds. *The Coronado Expedition: From the Distance of 460 Years*, University of New Mexico Press, 2003.

Fugate, Francis L. and Roberta B. Fugate. *Roadside History of New Mexico*, Mountain Press Publishing, 1989.

García, Nasario (with Richard McCord). *Albuquerque ¡Feliz Cumpleaños! Three Centuries to Remember*, La Herencia, 2005.

Gardner, Mark L. *Bent's Old Fort*, Southwest Parks and Monuments Association, 1998.

Gavin, Robin Farwell. *Traditional Arts of Spanish New Mexico*, Museum of New Mexico Press, 1994.

Gibson, A. M. *The Life and Death of Colonel Albert Jennings Fountain*, University of Oklahoma Press, 1965.

Gilbreath, West. *Death on the Gallows: The Story of Legal Hangings in New Mexico, 1847-1923*, High Lonesome Books, 2002.

Gonzales, Edward, and David L. Witt. *Spirit Ascendant: The Art and Life of Patrocino Barela*, Red Crane Books, 1996.

Gregg, Josiah. *Commerce of the Prairies: Life on the Great Plains in the 1830's and 1840's*, The Narrative Press, 2001.

Gutiérrez, Ramón. *When Jesus Came, the Corn Mothers Went Away*, Stanford University Press, 1991.

Hammett, Kingsley. *Santa Fe: A Walk Through Time*, Gibbs Smith, Publisher, 2004.

Harkey, Dee. *Mean as Hell*, University of New Mexico Press, 1948, reissued by Ancient City Press, 1989.

Harrison, Fred. *Hell Holes and Hangings, An Informal History of Western Territorial Prisons*, Clarendon Press, 1968.

Heaphy, Mary Lou. *A Cliffie Experience, Tales of New Mexico 1902-1940*, Diamond Press, 2005.

Hignett, Sean. *Brett: From Bloomsbury to New Mexico*, Hodder & Stoughton, 1984.

Hill, Janaloo. *The Hill Family of Shakespeare: How a Cowboy and a Schoolmarm Got Married and saved a Historic Ghost Town*, privately published, 2001.

Hillerman, Tony, Ed. *The Great Taos Bank Robbery and Other Indian Country Affairs*, University of New Mexico Press, 1973.

_____. *Seldom Disappointed*, Perennial, 2001.

_____. Ed. *The Spell of New Mexico*, University of New Mexico Press, 1976.

266

Hilliard, George. *Adios Hachita: Stories of a New Mexico Town*, High-Lonesome Books, 1988.

Hilton, Conrad. *Be My Guest*, Prentice Hall, 1957.

Horgan, Paul. *Great River: The Rio Grande in North American History*, Texas Monthly Press, 1984 (originally published by Rinehart, in 1954).

_____. *Peter Herd: A Portrait Sketch from Life*, University of Texas Press, 1964.

_____. *Lamy of Santa Fe*, Wesleyan University Press, 1975.

Horn, Calvin. *The University in Turmoil and Transition: Crisis Decades at the University of New Mexico*, Rocky Mountain Publishing, 1981.

Hornung, Chuck. *Fullerton's Rangers: The History of the New Mexico Territorial Mounted Police*, McFarland & Company, 2005.

_____. *The Thin Gray Line: The New Mexico Mounted Police*, Western Heritage Press, Fort Worth, 1971.

Hornung, Chuck and Roberts, Gary, eds. *True Tales and Amazing Legends of the Old West*, True West Magazine, 2005.

Hsi, David, and Janda Panitz, eds. *From Sundaggers to Space Exploration: Significant Scientific Contributions to Science and Technology in New Mexico*, New Mexico Journal of Science, Vol. 26, No. 1, February 1986.

Hughes, Debra. *Albuquerque in Our Time: 30 Voices, 300 years*, Museum of New Mexico Press, 2006.

Hurst, James W. *The Villista Prisoners of 1916-1917*, Yucca Tree Press, 2000.

Jenkinson, Michael. *Ghost Towns of New Mexico: Playthings of the Wind*, University of New Mexico Press, 1967.

Johnson, Byron A. *Old Town, Albuquerque, New Mexico: A Guide to Its History and Architecture*, City of Albuquerque, 1980.

Johnson, David R. *Conrad Richter: A Writer's Life*, Penn State University Press, 2001.

Johnson, William Weber. *Heroic Mexico, The Narrative History of a Twentieth Century Revolution*, Harcourt Brace Jovanovich, 1984.

Julyan, Robert. *The Place Names of New Mexico*, University of New Mexico Press, 1996.

Katz, Ephraim. *The Film Encyclopedia*, Harper Perennial, 1994.

Katz, William Loren. The *Black West: A Documentary and Pictorial History*, Anchor Books, 1971.

Keleher, William A. *The Fabulous Frontier: Twelve New Mexico Items*, University of New Mexico Press, 1962.

_____. *The Maxwell Land Grant*, University of New Mexico Press, 1942.

_____. *Violence in Lincoln County, 1869-1881: A New Mexico Item*, University of New Mexico Press, 1957.

Kelly, Charles. *The Outlaw Trail: A History of Butch Cassidy and His Wild Bunch*, Bonanza Books, 1959.

Kessell, John L., et al. *The Journals of don Diego de Vargas: New Mexico, 1691-1704.* 6 Vols. University of New Mexico Press, 1989-2002.

King, Bruce. *Cowboy in The Roundhouse: A Political Life*, Sunstone Press, 1998.

Kirby, Gordon. *The Unser Legacy: Four Generations of Speed*, Motorbooks, 2005.

Klasner, Lily (Eve Ball, Ed.). *My Girlhood Among Outlaws*, University of Arizona Press, 1972.

Knappman, Edward W., Ed. *Great American Trials: 201 Compelling Courtroom Dramas from Salem Witchcraft to O. J. Simpson*, Barnes & Noble Books, 1994.

Lamar, Howard R. *Charlie Siringo's West: An Interpretive Biography*, University of New Mexico Press, 2005.

_____. *The Far Southwest, 1846-1912: A Territorial History*, University of New Mexico Press, 2000.

Larson, Carole. *Forgotten Frontier: The Story of Southeastern New Mexico*, University of New Mexico Press (in cooperation with the Historical Society of New Mexico), 1993.

Lavish, Donald R. *Sheriff William Brady: Tragic Hero of The Lincoln County War*, Sunstone Press, Santa Fe, 1986.

Luther, T. N. *Collecting Santa Fe Authors*, Ancient City Press, 2003.

Maltin, Leonard. *Movie Encyclopedia*, Dutton, 1994.

Martin, Craig. *Valle Grande: A History of The Baca Location No.1*, All Seasons Publishing, 2003.

McLoughlin, Denis. *Wild and Woolly: An Encyclopedia of the Old West*, Barnes & Noble Books, 1975.

Mauldin, Bill & Ambrose, Stephen E., *Up Front*, W. W. Norton, 2000.

Meketa, Jacqueline Dorgan. *From Martyrs to Murderers: The Old Southwest's Saints, Sinners & Scalawags*, Yucca Tree Press, 1993.

_____. *Legacy of Honor: The Life of Rafael Chacón, A Nineteenth-Century New Mexican*, Yucca Tree Press, 2000.

Melzer, Richard. *Ernie Pyle in the American Southwest*, Sunstone Press, 1996.

Metz, Leon Claire. *The Encyclopedia of Lawmen, Outlaws, and Gunfighters*, Checkmark Books, 2003.

_____. *Pat Garrett, The Story of a Lawman on the Western Frontier*, University of Oklahoma Press, 1973.

_____. *The Shooters*, Mangan Books, 1976.

Metzger, Robert. *My Land is the Southwest: Peter Hurd Letters and Journals*, Texas A&M University Press, 1983.

Miller, Kristie. *Ruth Hanna McCormick: A Life in Politics, 1880-1944*, University of New Mexico Press, 1992.

Mondragón, John B. Mondragón & Ernest S. Stapleton. *Public Education in New Mexico*, University of New Mexico Press, 2005.

Montaño, Mary. *Tradiciones Nuevomexicanas: Hispano Arts and Culture of New Mexico*, University of New Mexico Press, 2001.

Myers, Lee. *New Mexico Military Installations*, Southwest Monuments Association (Limited Edition, 500 copies), 1966.

Myrick, David F. *New Mexico Railroads, An Historical Survey*, Colorado Railroad Museum, 1970.

Nelson, Mary Carroll. *Legendary Artists of Taos*, Watson-Guptill, 1980.

Nolan, Frederick. *Bad Blood: The Life and Times of the Horrell Brothers*, Barbed Wire Press (Stillwater, Oklahoma), 1994.

Nunn, Tey Marianna. *Sin Nombre: Hispana & Hispano Artists of the New Deal Era*, University of New Mexico Press, 2001.

O'Neal, Bill. *Encyclopedia of Western Gunfighters*, University of Oklahoma Press, 1979.

Otero, Miguel Antonio. *My Life on the Frontier, 1864-1882*, University of New Mexico Press, 1987.

_____. *My Nine Years as Governor of the Territory of New Mexico*, Albuquerque, 1940.

Ousby, Ian, Ed. *The Cambridge Guide to Literature in English*, Cambridge University Press, 1993.

Owen, Gordon R. *Las Cruces, New Mexico 1849-1999: Multicultural Crossroads*, Red Sky Publishing, Las Cruces, New Mexico, 1999.

_____. (with Forward by Leon Metz), *The Two Alberts: Fountain and Fall*, Yucca Tree Press, 1996.

Pappas, Mike J. *Raton: History, Mystery and More*, Coda Publications, Raton, 2003.

Parsons, Chuck. *Clay Allison, Portrait of a Shootist*, Pioneer Book Publishers, Seagraves, Texas 1983.

Patterson, Barbara Corn. *The Rock House Ranch: My Lazy-A-Bar Days*, Barbed Wire Publishing (Las Cruces, New Mexico), 2002.

Patterson, Paul E. *Hardhat and Stetson: Robert O. Anderson, Oilman and Cattleman*, Sunstone Press, 1999.

Peña, Abe (Foreword by Marc Simmons). *Memories of Cíbola: Stories from New Mexico Villages*, University of New Mexico Press, 1997.

Pike, David. *Roadside New Mexico: A Guide to Historic Markers*, University of New Mexico Press, 2004.

Rakocy, Bill. *Ghosts of Kingston/Hillsboro, N. Mex.*, Bravo Press, El Paso, 1983.

Randles, Slim. *Ol' Max Evans: The First Thousand Years, A Biography*, University of New Mexico Press, 2004.

Rathbun, Daniel C. B. & David V. Alexander. *New Mexico Frontier Military Place Names*, Yucca Tree Press, 2003.

Raynor, Ted. *The Gold Lettered Egg & Other New Mexico Tales*, Privately Published, 1962.

Remley, David, ed. *Adios Nuevo Mexico: The Santa Fe Journal of John Watts in 1859*, Yucca Tree Press, 1999.

Rhodes, Richard. *The Making of the Atomic Bomb*, Simon & Schuster, 1986.

Rickards, Colin. *Sheriff Pat Garrett's Last Days*. Sunstone Press, 1986.

Riley, Glenda & Etulain, Richard W., eds. *Wild Women of the Old West*, Fulcrum Publishing, 2003

Roberts, Susan A., and Calvin A. Roberts. *New Mexico*, University of New Mexico Press, 1988.

Robertson, Edna & Nestor, Sarah. *Artists of the Canyons and Caminos, Santa Fe, the Early Years*, Peregrine Smith, 1976.

Robinson, Sherry. *Apache Voices: Their Stories of Survival as Told to Eve Ball*, University of New Mexico Press, 2000.

Rudnick, Lois Palken. *Mabel Dodge Luhan: New Woman, New Worlds*, University of New Mexico Press, 1984.

Sálaz Márquez, Rubén. *New Mexico: A Brief Multi-History*, Cosmic House, 1999.

Salmon, Pamela. *Sandia Peak: A History of the Sandia Peak Tramway and Ski Area*. Albuquerque, Sandia Peak Ski & Tramway, 1998.

Samuels, Peggy & Harold. *The Illustrated Biographical Encyclopedia of Artists of the American West*, Doubleday, 1976.

Sando, Joe S. *Pueblo Profiles: Cultural Identity through Centuries of Change*, Clear Light Publishers, 1998.

Sando, Joe, and Herman Agoyo, eds. *Po'pay: Leader of the First American Revolution*, Clear Light Publishing, 2005.

Schimmel, Julie & White, Robert R. *Bert Geer Phillips and the Taos Art Colony*, University of New Mexico Press, 1994.

Serna, Louis F. *Tessie Maxwell of the Maxwell Land Grant Family of Cimarron, New Mexico*, Privately Published.

Sherman, James E. & Barbara Sherman. *Ghost Towns and Mining Camps of New Mexico*, University of Oklahoma Press, 1975.

Simmons, Marc. *Albuquerque, A Narrative History*, University of New Mexico Press, 1982.

_____. *Hispanic Albuquerque*, 1706-1846, University of New Mexico Press, 2003.

_____. *Kit Carson & His Three Wives*, University of New Mexico Press, 2003.

_____. *Murder on the Santa Fe Trail, An International Incident*, Texas Western Press, 1987.

_____. *New Mexico: An Interpretive History*, University of New Mexico Press, 1988.

_____. *Ranchers, Ramblers & Renegades, True Tales of Territorial New Mexico*, Ancient City Press, 1984.

_____. *When Six-Guns Ruled: Outlaw Tales of the Southwest*, Ancient City Press, 1990.

_____. Ed. *On the Santa Fe Trail*, University Press of Kansas, 1986.

_____. *Spanish Pathways: Readings in the History of Hispanic New Mexico*, University of New Mexico Press, 2001.

Sinclair, John L. *Cowboy Writer in New Mexico: The Memoirs of John L. Sinclair*, University of New Mexico Press.

Smith, Pamela S. & Polese, Richard. *Passions in Print: Private Press Artistry in New Mexico, 1834-Present*, Museum of New Mexico Press, 2006.

Snow, David H. *New Mexico's First Colonists: The 1597-1600 Enlistments for New Mexico under Juan de Oñate, Adelante & Gobernador*, Hispanic Genealogical Research Center of New Mexico, 1996.

Steele, Thomas J. Steele, S.J., Ed. *Archbishop Lamy: In His Own Words*, LPD Press, 2000.

_____, Ed. *Historical Sketch of the Catholic Church in New Mexico by the late Very Reverend James H. Defouri*, Yucca Tree Press, 2003.

_____, Ed., *Historical Sketch of the Catholic Church in New Mexico*, Yucca Tree Press, 2003.

_____, with Paul Rhetts & Barbe Awalt, Eds. *Seeds of Struggle/Harvest of Faith, The Papers of the Archdiocese of Santa Fe Catholic Cuarto Centennial Conference of the History of the Catholic Church in New Mexico*, LPD Press, 1998.

Szasz, Ferenc M. *Larger Than Life, New Mexico in the Twentieth Century*, University of New Mexico Press, 2006.

Tanner, Karen Holliday. *Doc Holliday: a Family Portrait*, University of Oklahoma Press, 1998.

Tanner, Karen Holliday & John D. Tanner, Jr. *Last of the Old-Time Outlaws: The George Musgrave Story*, University of Oklahoma Press, 2002.

Tatum, Stephen. *Inventing Billy the Kid: Visions of the Outlaw in America, 1881-1981*, University of New Mexico Press, 1982.

Taylor, Anne. *Southwestern Ornamentation & Design: The Architecture of John Gaw Meem*, Sunstone Press, 1989.

Thompson, Jerry. *Confederate General of the West: Henry Hopkins Sibley*, Texas A&M University Press, 1996.

Thrapp, Dan L. *Encyclopedia of Frontier Biography* (Three Volumes), University of Nebraska Press, 1988.

Tobias, Henry J. & Woodhouse, Charles E. *Santa Fe: A Modern History 1880-1990*, University of New Mexico Press, 2001.

Tórrez, Robert J. *UFOs Over Galisteo and Other Stories of New Mexico's History*, University of New Mexico Press, 2004.

Tuska, Jon. *Billy the Kid: His Life and Legend*, University of New Mexico Press, 1994.

Twitchell, Ralph Emerson, Esq. *The Leading Facts of New Mexican History*, Vol. II & V, The Torch Press (Cedar Rapids, Iowa), 1912.

Utley, Robert M. *Frontier Regulars: The United States Army and the Indian, 1866-1891*, University of Nebraska Press, 1873.

_____. *High Noon in Lincoln: Violence on the Western Frontier*, University of New Mexico Press, 1987.

Weigle, Marta, and Peter White. *The Lore of New Mexico*, University of New Mexico Press, 2003.

White, Peter & Mary Ann White, Eds. *Along the Rio Grande: Cowboy Jack Thorp's New Mexico*, Ancient City Press, 1988.

Wilson, John P. *Merchants, Guns & Money, The Story of Lincoln County and Its Wars*, Museum of New Mexico Press, 1987.

Witt, David L. *The Taos Artists: A Historical Narrative and Biographical Dictionary*, Ewell Fine Arts Publications, 1984.

Specialized Indices

ARCHITECTS
Meem, John Gaw
Whittlesey, Charles F.

ATHLETES/COACHES/COMPETITORS
Baker, John
Bowyer, Ralph S.
Foster, Robert "Bob"
Franklin, Jimmy Marshall
Giddens, Frank
Henson, Lou
Johnson, Charlie
McDonald, Thomas F.
Perkins, Don
Tasker, Ralph
Unser Family

BUSINESS PEOPLE (INCLUDING LAWYERS)
Abruzzo, Ben
Anderson, Maxie
Anderson, Robert O.
Austin, John Van "Tex"
Becknell, William
Bibo, Nathan
Bibo, Solomon
Blake, Ernie
Boellner, Louis B.
Butterfield, John
Chávez, Antonio J.
Cooper, David

Cusey, Mildred Clark
Daniels, Bill
Dodson, J. L.
Doheny, Edward L.
Dunigan, James P. "Pat"
Eddy, Charles B.
Fogleson, E. E. "Buddy"
Hagerman, James J.
Hammer, Armand
Haut, Walter
Hernández, Benigno Cárdenas
Hilton, Conrad
Horn, Calvin
Huning, Franz
Jackson, Sherwood Young, "S.Y."
Jaffa, Nathan
LaLande, Jean Baptiste
Lea, Joseph L.
Lopez, Lucy "Mama Lucy"
Luna, Solomon
McMullan, John J.
Magoffin, James Wiley
Madina, Mariano
Murphy, Lawrence G.
Myers, Dwight
Noggle, Anne
Nordhaus, Robert
Orchard, Sadie Jane
Ralston, William C.
Rodey, Bernard S.
Schaefer, R. J.
Seligman, Milton

Sierra, Mateo
Simms, Albert G.
Smith, Jedediah
Smith, Van Ness Cummings
St. Vrain, Ceran
Staab, Abraham
White, James Larkin
White, James D.
Wootton, Richens L.

CONSERVATIONISTS
Barker, Elliot S.
Leopold, Rand Aldo

EDUCATORS
Cháves, J. Francisco
Chávez, Amado
Cobos, Rubén
Hammer, Armand
Harwood, Thomas
Leach, John
Lusk, Georgia
Martínez, Padre Antonio José
Milne, John
Milton, Hugh M.
Ortiz, Alfonso
Patrón, Juan Batista
Rhee, Lawrence
Saavedra, Louis E.
Simms, Ruth Hanna McCormick
Tight, William G.
White, Alvan N.

ENTERTAINERS/MUSICIANS/ ACTORS
Campbell, Glen
Edmister, Grace T.
Edwards, Ralph
Fountain, Albert Jennings
Garrett, Elizabeth
Garson, Greer
Sanchez, Albert (Al Hurricane)
Vance, Vivian
Weaver, Dennis

GAMBLERS
Barceló, Gertrudes (La Tules)
Earp, Wyatt
Holliday, John Henry
Smith, Van Ness Cummings

GOVERNORS, AMERICAN OCCUPATION
Bent, Charles
Price, Sterling
Vigil, Donaciano
Washington, John Macrea

GOVERNORS, MEXICAN
Armijo, Manuel
Gonzáles, José Ángel (Insurection)
Pérez, Albino

GOVERNORS, SPANISH
Chacón, Jose Medina Salazar y
    Villaseñor
Cubero, Pedro Rodríguez
Cuervo y Valdés, Don Francisco
Melgares, Facundo
Mendizábal, Bernarod López de
Peñalosa, Diego Dionisio de
Peralta, Pedro de
Rosas, Luis de
Treviño, Juan Francisco de
Ugarte y la Concha, Hernando de
Vargas, Diego de

GOVERNORS, STATE OF NEW MEXICO
C de Baca, Ezequiel
Campbell, John M. "Jack"
Cargo, David F.
King, Bruce
Larrazolo, Octaviano A.
Mechem, Edwin
Miles, John E.
Seligman, Arthur

Simms, John F. Jr.
Tingley, Clyde

GOVERNORS, TERRITORIAL
Axtell, Samuel B.
Calhoun James
Connelly, Henry
Curry, George
Giddings, Marsh
Hagerman, Herbert J.
Lane, William Carr
Meriwether, David
Mills, William J.
Mitchell, Robert B.
Ortiz, Miguel Antonio II
Pile, William A.
Prince, LeBarron Bradford
Rencher, Abraham
Ross, Edmund G.
Sheldon, Lionel A.
Thornton, William T.
Wallace, Lew

HEROES
Baca, Don Domingo
Baker, John
Botts, Charles Milton
Braden, John
C de Baca, Mackie
Romero, Doña Antonia
Rooke, Sarah "Sally"
Westfall, David

HISTORIANS
Alberts, Don E.
Bourke, John G.
Chávez, Fray Angélico
Chávez, Thomas E.
Curry, George
Fulton, Maurice G.
Horgan, Paul
Horn, Calvin
Jenkins, Myra Ellen
Keleher, William A.

Liebert Martha
Lumis, Charles F.
Nolan, Frederick
Read, Benjamin M.
Rittenhouse, Jack D.
Ruxton, George F.
Sanchez, Jane Calvin
Sando, Joe
Simmons, Marc
Steele, Thomas J.
Twitchell, Ralph E.

JUDGES
Beaubien, Charles H.
Benedict, Kirby
Bratton, Sam G.
Campos, Santiago
Chávez, Tibo
Easley, Mack
Johnson, Hezekiah S.
Neill, Hyman G.
Palen, Joseph G.
Patrón, Juan Batista
Simms, John Sr.
Slough, John P.
Walters, Mary C.

LAND BARONS
Beaubien, Charles H.
Catron, Thomas B.
Maxwell, Lucien B.

LAWMEN
Baca, Efego, Socorro Co.
Baca, Santos, Bernalillo Co.
Ballard, Charles Littlepage, Chaves Co.
Carson, Joe, Las Vegas
Clever, Charles, U. S. Marshal
Gonzáles, José María, Santa Rosa
    Marshal
Gray, Clifford, Southern NM
Harkey, Daniel "Dee", Southeastern
    NM
Heard, J. H. U. S. Customs Inspector

Kilburn, William H., Silver City
    Marshal
Love, Henry, Colfax Co. Posseman
McGuire, Robert, Albuquerque
    Marshal
Martínez, Juan, Lincoln Constable
Masterson, James P., Colfax Co. Militia
Olinger, Robert A., Lincoln Co.
Ortiz, Filimon J., NM Dept. of
    Corrections
Rowe, Truett E., FBI
Sutton, Raymond, Prohibition Bureau
Woofter, Roy, Roswell Town Marshal
Yarberry, Milton J., Albuquerque
    Marshal

LINCOLN COUNTY WAR FIGURES
Bonney, William H.
Boyle, Andrew
Brady, William
Brewer, Dick
Chisum, John S.
Dudley, Nathan A. M.
Dummy, The
Garrett, Patrick F.
Hindman, George
Kinney, John
McSween, Alexander
Mathews, J. B.
Murphy, Lawrence G.
O'Folliard, Tom
Olinger, Robert A.
Patrón, Juan Batista
Roberts, Andrew "Buckshot"
Tunstall, John

MILITARY FIGURES
Archuleta, Diego
Beale, Edward F. Camel Corps
    Commander
Bourke, John G.
Bullis, John L.
Butler, Edmund
Canby, Edward R. S.
Cannon, James D.

Carleton, James H.
Carson, Christopher "Kit"
Chacón, Rafael
Chivington, John M.
Cooke, Philip St. George
Doniphan, Alexander W.
Dudley, Nathan A. M.
Flipper, Henry O.
Hatch, Edward
Haut, Walter
Hinójos, Blas
Kearny, Stephen Watts
Mackenzie, Ranald S.
Milton, Hugh M.
O'Leary Dennis
Pershing, John Joseph
Pike, Zebulon
Price, Sterling
Sibley, Henry Hopkins
St, Vrain, Ceran
Sumner, Edwin Vose
Washington, John Macrea

NATIVE AMERICANS
Abeita, Pablo, Isleta
Begay, Harrison, Navajo
Dodge, Henry Chee, Navajo
Geronimo, Apache
Gorman, R. C., Navajo
Jonva, Nicolas de la Cruz, Tewa
Martínez, Esther, Tewa
Martínez, Julián "Paddy", Navajo
Martínez, Maria Antonia Montoya,
    San Ildefonso
Maxwell, Deluvina, Navajo
Nakai, Raymond, Navajo
Naranjo, Domingo, Tewa
Nabona, Navajo
Ollito, Francisco El, Tewa
Ortiz, Alvonso, San Juan Peublo
Po'pay, Ohkay Owingeh
Velarde, Pablita, Santa Clara
Victorio, Apache
Xenome, Diego, Tewa
Zuñi, Juan, Hopi

NEWPAPER PEOPLE

Acuff, Mark D. NM *Independent*
Acuff, Mary Beth, NM *Independent*
Conklin, A. M., Socorro *Sun*
Cutting, Bronson, *Santa Fe New Mexican*
Johnson, Hezekiah S., *Rio Abajo Press*
Kendall, George W. of Texas
Kusz, Charles L., *Gringo & Greaser*
Looney, Ralph, Albuquerque *Tribune*
McCarty Gallegos, Frankie, Albuquerque *Journal*
Maestas, Frank, Albuquerque *Journal*
Magee, Carleton D., Alabuquerque *Journal* & *Tribune*
Montoya, Nestor, *La Voz del Pueblo* & *La Bandera Americana*
Pyle, Ernest Taylor, World War II Correspondent
Smith, Guthrie, Santa Fe Weekly *Record*
Weightman, Richard H., *El Amigo del Pais*

OLD TIMERS

Blount, Helen
Hill, Janaloo

OUTLAWS

Adamson, Carl
Allison, Robert "Clay"
Angel, Paula
Bonney William Henry
Bowdre, Charles
Brazel, Jesse Wayne
Christian, Robert
Christian, William
Crockett, David
Fall, Albert Bacon
Fowler, Joel A.
Horrell Family
Johnson, Thomas
Joy, Christopher "Kit"
Ketchum, Samuel W.
Ketchum, Thomas E.
Kinney, John

Kirker, James
Longabaugh, Harry Alonzo
Mather, David
Mentzer, Gus
Miller, James B.
Nelson, David Cooper
Nelson, Martin
O'Folliard, Tom
Olinger, Robert A.
Parker, Robert Leroy
Perry, Charles C.
Pipkin, Daniel
Rogers, Dick
Rudabaugh, Dave
Selman, John Henry
Shaw, James Madison
Silva, Vicente
Stanton, Edward "Perchmouth"
Stockton, Ike
Stockton, Port
Tettenborn, William Rogers
Yarberry, Milton J.
Young, Code

PAINTERS/POTTERS/SCULPTORS

Barela, Patrocinio
Begay, Harrison
Crumbo, Woodrow Wilson
DeLavy, Edmund
Gorman, R. C.
Hurd, Peter
Martínez, Maria Antonia Montoya
Miera y Pacheco, Bernardo
O'Keeffe, Georgia
Rush, Olive
Sánchez, Juan Amadeo
Sharp, Joseph
Ufer, Walter
Velarde, Pablita
Warner, William Riddle
Miera y Pacheco, Bernardo de

POLICE OFFICERS

Allison, Wayne, NM State Police
Armino, Richard, Albuquerque PD

Arviso, John B. Gallup PD
C de Baca, Mackie, NM State Police
Chacón, Philip H., Albuquerque PD
Chávez, Victoria, Farmington PD
Davis, Oscar, Ratón PD
Fornoff, Fred, NM Mounted Police
Galusha, J. R. "Chief" Albuquerque PD
Garcia, Nash Phillip, NM State Police
Higgins, Frederick, NM Mounted
Police
Knapp, Lewis A. "Alex", Albuquerque
PD
McClure, J. A., Railroad Police
Mickey, Lewis, Railroad Police
Miller, K. K., NM State Police
O'Grady, Patrick F., Albuquerque PD
Peña, Lee Vicente, Taos PD
Ramsey, John C., NM State Police
Rosenbloom, Robert, NM State Police
Rusk, J. B., NM Mounted Police
Shaver, Paul A., Albuquerque PD
Speight, William T., NM State Police
Taber, Walter G., NM State Police

POLITICIANS
Alvarez, Manuel, American Consul
Ancheta, Joseph A., Territorial
Legislator
Anderson, Clinton P., U. S. Senator
Bingaman, Jesse F., Jr. "Jeff", U. S.
Senator
Bratton, Sam G., U. S. Senator
Breen, Victor, Quay Co. District
Attorney
Bursum, Holm, U. S. Senator
Catron, Thomas B., U. S. Senator
Cháves, J. Francisco, Territorial
Legislator
Chávez, Dennis, U. S. Senator
Chávez, Tibo, Lt. Gov., State Senator
Cutting, Bronson M., U. S. Senator
Dempsey, John J., Governor, U. S.
Congressman
Domenici, Pete V., U. S. Senator

Easley, Mack, Governor, Lt. Gov., State
House of Representatives.
Elkins, Stephen B., Delegate to U.
S.Congress
Fall, Albert Bacon, U. S. Senator
Fergusson, Harvey Butler, U. S.
Congressman
Fernández, Antonio Manuel, U. S.
Congressman
Foreman, Edgar F. "Ed", U. S.
Congressman
Fountain, Albert Jennings, Legislator
Hernández, Benigno Cárdenas, U. S.
Congressman
Hurley, Patrick J., Candidate
Irick, John B., State Senator
Jaffa, Nathan, Mayor of Roswell
Jones, Andrieus A., U.S. Senator
King, Bruce, Governor
Larrazolo, Octaviano A., U. S. Senator
Lea, Joseph C., Mayor of Roswell
Lusk, Gene, Gubernatorial Candidate
Lusk, Georgia, U.S. Congresswoman
McMullan, John J., NM House of
Representatives
Marron, Owen N., Mayor of
Albuquerque
Martínez, Donaldo, San Miguel Co.
District Attorney
Mechem, Edwin, Governor, U. S.
Senator
Miles, John E., U. S. Congressman
Montoya, Joseph M. U. S. Senator, et al
Montoya, Nestor, U. S. Congressman
Morris, Thomas G., U. S. Congressman
Morrow, John, U. S. Congressman
Muñoz, Edward, Mayor of Gallup
Ortiz, Filimon J., Delegate to U. S.
Congress
Ortiz, Miguel Antonio I, Delegate to U.
S. Congress
Rhodes, Virgil, Candidate for Lt. Gov.
Rynerson, William L., Territorial
Legislator

278

Saavedra, Louis, Mayor of
    Albuquerque
Sandoval, Alejandro, Constitutional
    Conventions
Schiff, Steven H., U. S. Congressman
Schmitt, Harrison, U. S. Senator
Simms, Albert F., U. S. Congressman
Simms, Ruth Hanna McCormick,
    Republican Women
Tingley, Clyde, Albuquerque City
    Commission, Governor
Walker, E. S. Johnny, U. S.
    Congressman
Walton, William Bell, U. S.
    Congressman
Weightman, Richard H., Delegate to U.
    S. Congress

PRESIDENTS OF THE
UNITED STATES
Coolidge, Calvin
Grant, U. S.
Harding, Warren G.
Hoover, Herbert
Lincoln, Abraham
Polk, James Knox
Taft, William Howard

RANCHERS & FARMERS,
Austin, John Van "Tex"
Belcheff, George
Bond, Franklin
Brewer, Dick
Bursum, Holm
Casey, Robert
Chisum, John S.
Cleaveland, Norman
Córdoba, Doña Ana María de
Corn, Martin Van Buren
Cox, W. W.
Crockett, David
Dietz, Robert E.
Eddy, Charles B.
Fogleson, E. E. "Buddy"

Fowler, Joel A.
Gutierrez, Juan
Lee, Oliver Milton
Luna, Solomon
Lusk, Georgia
McSween, Susan Barber
Maxwell, Peter M.
Perea, José Leandro
Romero, Juan
Tunstall, John H.

RECORD SETTERS
Abruzzo, Ben, Balloonist
Anderson, Maxie
Aubry, François X.

RELIGIOUS FIGURES
Agreda, María de Jesús de
Benavides, Fray Alonso de
Chávez, Fray Angélica
Lamy, Bishop Jean Baptiste
Lee, John D., Mormon Elder
Martínez, Padre Antonio José
Mingues, Fray Juan
O'Keefe, Sister Vincent
Pío, Fray Juan
Segale, Sister Blandina

SCIENTISTS
Ashworth, Frederick "Dick"
Bandelier, Adolphe
Cushing, Frank H.
Garcia, Fabian
Goddard, Robert H.
Gutierrez, Sidney McNeill
Hibben, Frank C.
Hyde, Benjamin T. B.
Leach, John
Lovelace, William Randolph
Lovelace, William Randolph II
McJunkin, George
Nayakama, Roy
Oppenheimer, J. Robert
Schmitt, Harrison H.

Schroeder, Albert H.
Stapp, John Paul
Teller, Edward
Tombaugh, Clyde W.

SHERIFFS & DEPUTIES
Batton, George Washington, Eddy Co.
Bedford, Thomas C. Jr., Lincoln Co.
Bell, James W., Lincoln Co.
Brady, William, Lincoln Co.
Burgen, William A., Colfax Co.
Candelaria, Emilio, Bernalillo Co.
Carlyle, James B., Lincoln Co.
Carmichael, Mack, McKinley Co.
Clifton, J. M., Lea County
Copeland, John N., Lincoln Co.
Corn, Jasper, Lincoln Co.
Dow, James L. "Les", Eddy Co.
Dunnahoo, Rufus J., Chaves Co.
Garrett, Patrick F., Lincoln & Doña
    Ana Cos.
Gurule, Leopoldo C., Santa Fe Co.
Gylam, Lewis J., Lincoln Co.
Hall, Thomas, Grant Co.
Hall, Thomas H., Luna Co.
Hernández, Benigno Cárdenas, Rio
    Arriba Co.
Higgins, Frederick, Chaves Co.
Hindman, George, Lincoln Co.
Hurley, John, Lincoln Co.
Jerrell, W. L., Doña Ana Co.
Jones, Thomas W., Lincoln Co.
Kearney, Kent, Doña Ana Co.
Kemp, David L., Eddy Co.
Kent, James I., Union County
Lee, Stephen L., Taos Co.
McKinney, Thomas, Lincoln Co.
Mason, Barney, Lincoln Co.
Mills, Alexander Hamilton, Lincoln
    Co.
Olinger, Robert A., Lincoln Co.
Peppin, George W. "Dad", Lincoln Co.
Perry, Charles C., Chaves Co.
Pipkin, Daniel, McKinley Co.
Poe, John W., Lincoln Co.

Rainbolt, William, Chaves Co.
Rutherford, William L., Otero Co.
Smithers, A. L., Luna Co.
Stephens, Dwight B., Luna Co.
Sutton, Raymond, Sr., Union Co.
Valdez, Antonio Lino, San Miguel Co.
Vigil, Francisco X., Valencia Co.
Whitehill, Harvey H., Grant Co.
Williams, Ben, Doña Ana County

SPANISH EXPLORERS
Alvarado, Hernando de
Bustamente, Pedro de
Cabeza de Vaca
Castañada, Pedro Francisco de
Dorantes de Carranza, Andrés
Estevánico
Niza, Fray Marcos
Oñate, Juan de

U.S. GOVERNMENT OFFICIALS
Angel, Frank W.
Arney, William F. M.
Blair, Francis P.
Bland, Richard D.
Bushnell, Samuel B.
Clever, Charles P.
Colfax, Schuyler
Colyer, Vincent
Dodge, Henry L.
Fisher, Walter Lowrie
Gadsden, James
Marcy, William L.
Quay, Matthew S.
Thomas, Benjamin M.

VICTIMS (MURDER)
Arquette, Kaitlyn
Brady, William
Breen, Victor
Casey, Robert
Dow, James Leslie
Fountain, Albert Jennings
Garrett, Partick F.
Heard, J. H.

Hindman, George
McSween, Alexander
Patrón, Juan Batista
Valdez, Antonio Lino

WRITERS/POETS
Austin, Mary
Barker, Elliot
Barker, Squire Omar
Bunche, Ralph
Bynner, Harold Witter
Cather, Willa
Chávez, Fray Angélico
Chávez, Tibo
Church, Peggy Pond
Clark, Walter Van Tilburg
Eastlake, William D.
Evans, Max
Fergusson, Erna
Fergusson, Harvey
Henderson, Alice Corbin
Horgan, Paul
LaFarge, Oliver

Lawrence, D. H.
Luhan, Mable Dodge
Magoffin, Susan Shelby
Martínez, Esther
Morrell, David
Pattie, James
Rhodes, Eugene Manlove
Richter, Conrad M.
Schaefer, Jack W.
Scott, Winfield Townley
Silko, Leslie Marmon
Sinclair, John L.
Siringo, Charles
Steele, S.J., Thomas J.
Stern, Richard Martin
Thorp, Jack
Villagrá, Gaspar Pérez de
Wallace, Lew
Waters, Frank
Whitman, Walt
Williamson, Jack
Zollinger, Norman

Index

293

other titles from
rio grande books & lpd press

*A Tapestry of Kinship: The Web of Influence among Escultores
and Carpinteros in the Parish of Santa Fe, 1790-1860*
by José Antonio Esquibel and Charles M. Carrillo

Archbishop Lamy: In His Own Words
edited and translated by Thomas J. Steele, S.J., Afterword by
Archbishop Michael Sheehan

Charlie Carrillo: Tradition & Soul/Tradición y Alma
by Barbe Awalt & Paul Rhetts

Dejad a los Niños: The History of the Guadalupe Parish
by John M. Taylor

Faces of Faith/Rostros de Fe
photos by Barbe Awalt; Foreword by Thomas J. Steele, S.J.

Frank Applegate of Santa Fe: Artist & Preservationist
by Daria Labinsky and Stan Hieronymus; Foreword by
William Wroth

Holy Faith of Santa Fe: 1863-2000
by Stanford Lehmberg

Memories of Cibola
by Abe Peña; Foreword by Marc Simmons

*Navajo and Pueblo Earrings 1850 - 1945
Collected by Robert V. Gallegos*
by Robert Bauver

New Mexico: A Biographical Dictionary
by Don Bullis

*New Mexico in 1876-1877: A Newspaperman's View,
The Travels and Reports of William D. Dawson*
by Robert J. Tórrez

Nicholas Herrera: Visiones de mi Corazón
by Barbe Awalt & Paul Rhetts; Foreword by Cathy L. Wright

Our Saints Among Us: 400 Years of New Mexican Devotional Art
by Barbe Awalt & Paul Rhetts

Portfolio of Spanish Colonial Design in New Mexico
  by E. Boyd Hall; Introduction by Barbe Awalt & Paul Rhetts

Religious Architecture of Hispano New Mexico
  by Thomas L. Lucero and Thomas J. Steele, S.J.

Saints of the Pueblos
  by Charles M. Carrillo; Foreword by Ron Solimon

Santos: Sacred Art of Colorado
  edited by Thomas J. Steele, S.J., Barbe Awalt & Paul Rhetts

Seeds of Struggle Harvest of Faith: History of the Catholic Church in New Mexico
  edited by Thomas J. Steele, S.J., Barbe Awalt & Paul Rhetts; Introduction by Archbishop Michael Sheehan

The Complete Sermons of Jean Baptiste Lamy: Fifty Years of Sermons (1837-1886)
  edited and translated by Thomas J. Steele, S.J.

The Regis Santos: Thirty Years of Collecting 1966-1996
  by Thomas J. Steele, S.J., Barbe Awalt & Paul Rhetts

Villages & Villagers
  by Abe Peña; Foreword by Marc Simmons

Wake for a Fat Vicar: Father Juan Felipe Ortiz, Archbishop Lamy, and the New Mexican Catholic Church in the Middle of the Nineteenth Century
  by Fray Angélico Chávez and Thomas E. Chávez; Foreword by Bernard L. Fontana

Tradición Revista — Magazine featuring at the art, history and tradition of the Southwest

RIO GRANDE BOOKS
925 SALAMANCA NW
LOS RANCHOS DE ALBUQUERQUE, NEW MEXICO 87107-5647
PHONE 505-344-9382/FAX 505-345-5129/EMAIL INFO@NMSANTOS.COM

ABOUT THE AUTHOR

Don Bullis is the author of three non-fiction books and two novels, including *The Old West Trivia Book* (1993), *New Mexico's Finest: Peace Officers Killed in the Line of Duty, 1847-1999* (1999), *Bloodville* (2002) *99 New Mexicans … and a few other folks* (2005), and *Bull's Eye* (2006). The editor and publisher of the *New Mexico Historical Notebook*, he is a member of the Westerners International, Western Writers of America, Western History Association, National Association of Outlaw & Lawman History, Albuquerque Historical Society, Sandoval County Historical Society, and Southwest Writers.

New Mexico: A Biographical Dictionary
Vol. I

SUGGESTION SUBMISION FORM

All suggestions will be appreciated and considered for inclusion in future volumes of the Biographical Dictionary. No guarantee is made, however, that submissions will be used. Please keep in mind that my interest is in folks who have made an impression on New Mexico, or New Mexicans (the fact that my aunt won a blue ribbon for her cookie recipe at the state fair in 1939 would not earn her a place in the Biographical Dictionary). Please use this form to suggest any amendments to entries in Volume I that you might think appropriate.

Thank you for your help.

Name of Suggested Entry (Please be as complete as possible, and include alternate spellings if appropriate) _____

Contribution to New Mexico's history _____

Date and Place of Birth _____

Date and Place of Death _____

Place of New Mexico Residence _____

Education, if known, and dates of completion _____

Profession _____

Sources of information on the subject (news items, books, magazine articles, scholarly work, etc. Be sure to include dates of publication).

_____

Photos you have or photo sources for this individual _____

Please use additional pages, or separate attachments, to explain why your suggestion is appropriate for inclusion in the Biographical Dictionary. Such attachments cannot be returned. Please mail this completed form to:

Don Bullis
Rio Grande Books
925 Salamanca NW, Los Ranchos, NM 87107-5647

Submitted by: _____

Contact Address, Phone Number and/or E –Mail _____

Printed in the United States
76497LV00004B/139-234